T0407618

# A New Development Model and China's Future

The need for China to find a new, environmentally sustainable development path is widely accepted among Chinese scholars and policy makers. This book makes available for the first time to an English-speaking audience Deng Yingtao's ground-breaking book *A New Development Model and China's Future* (新發展方式與中國的未來). Published in 1991, the book was far ahead of its time. Deng subjects the development model of the high-income countries to rigorous analysis and explores the environmental implications of China following this model. His clear conclusion is that the carrying capacity of the physical environment and nature is limited, that economic and social development should not exceed the carrying capacity of resources, and that China should not adopt the Western development path. Based on insights from economics, engineering and human psychology, the book analyses the environmental impact of the current Western development model, demonstrates the catastrophic impact this would have in terms of China's own development and in terms of China's relationship with the world, and argues that China's rich intellectual and scientific tradition will allow Chinese people to play a central role in finding the solution to the profound environmental and development challenges the world currently faces.

**Deng Yingtao** was Director of the Economics and Cultural Research Centre of the Chinese Academy of Social Sciences.

**Nicky Harman** is the translator of the text. Ms Harman used to lecture at Imperial College London, UK, and now works full-time as a literary translator.

**Peter Nolan**, Director of the Centre of Development Studies, University of Cambridge, UK, wrote the Foreword.

**Phil Hand** is the translator of the Afterword. He studied Chinese and linguistics at Cambridge University, interpreting at Shanghai International Studies University and translation at Birmingham University. He specializes in translating social science research.

# Routledge studies on the Chinese economy

**Series Editor:**
Peter Nolan
Sinyi Professor, Judge Business School,
Chair, Development Studies, University of Cambridge

**Founding Series Editors**
Peter Nolan, University of Cambridge and
Dong Fureng, Beijing University

The aim of this series is to publish original, high-quality, research-level work by both new and established scholars in the West and the East, on all aspects of the Chinese economy, including studies of business and economic history.

1 **The Growth of Market Relations in Post-reform Rural China**
A micro-analysis of peasants, migrants and peasant entrepreneurs
*Hiroshi Sato*

2 **The Chinese Coal Industry: An Economic History**
*Elspeth Thomson*

3 **Sustaining China's Economic Growth in the Twenty-First Century**
*Edited by Shujie Yao and Xiaming Liu*

4 **China's Poor Regions**
Rural-urban migration, poverty, economic reform and urbanisation
*Mei Zhang*

5 **China's Large Enterprises and the Challenge of Late Industrialization**
*Dylan Sutherland*

6 **China's Economic Growth**
*Yanrui Wu*

7 **The Employment Impact of China's World Trade Organisation Accession**
*A.S. Bhalla and S. Qiu*

8 **Catch-Up and Competitiveness in China**
The case of large firms in the oil industry
*Jin Zhang*

9 **Corporate Governance in China**
*Jian Chen*

10 **The Theory of the Firm and Chinese Enterprise Reform**
The case of China International Trust and Investment Corporation
*Qin Xiao*

11 **Globalisation, Transition and Development in China**
The case of the coal industry
*Huaichuan Rui*

12 **China Along the Yellow River**
Reflections on rural society
*Cao Jinqing, translated by Nicky Harman and Huang Ruhua*

13 **Economic Growth, Income Distribution and Poverty Reduction in Contemporary China**
*Shujie Yao*

14 **China's Economic Relations with the West and Japan, 1949–79**
Grain, trade and diplomacy
*Chad J. Mitcham*

15 **China's Industrial Policy and the Global Business Revolution**
The case of the domestic appliance industry
*Ling Liu*

16 **Managers and Mandarins in Contemporary China**
The building of an international business alliance
*Jie Tang*

17 **The Chinese Model of Modern Development**
*Edited by Tian Yu Cao*

18 **Chinese Citizenship**
Views from the margins
*Edited by Vanessa L. Fong and Rachel Murphy*

19 **Unemployment, Inequality and Poverty in Urban China**
*Edited by Shi Li and Hiroshi Sato*

20 **Globalisation, Competition and Growth in China**
*Edited by Jian Chen and Shujie Yao*

21 **The Chinese Communist Party in Reform**
*Edited by Kjeld Erik Brodsgaard and Zheng Yongnian*

22 **Poverty and Inequality among Chinese Minorities**
*A.S. Bhalla and Shufang Qiu*

23 **Economic and Social Transformation in China**
Challenges and opportunities
*Angang Hu*

24 **Global Big Business and the Chinese Brewing Industry**
*Yuantao Guo*

25 **Peasants and Revolution in Rural China**
Rural political change in the North China Plain and the Yangzi Delta, 1850–1949
*Chang Liu*

26 **The Chinese Banking Industry**
Lessons from history for today's challenges
*Yuanyuan Peng*

27 **Informal Institutions and Rural Development in China**
*Biliang Hu*

28 **The Political Future of Hong Kong**
Democracy within Communist China
*Kit Poon*

29 **China's Post-Reform Economy –
Achieving Harmony, Sustaining
Growth**
*Edited by Richard Sanders and
Chen Yang*

30 **Eliminating Poverty Through
Development in China**
*China Development Research
Foundation*

31 **Good Governance in China – A
Way Towards Social Harmony**
Case studies by China's rising
leaders
*Edited by Wang Mengkui*

32 **China in the Wake of Asia's
Financial Crisis**
*Edited by Wang Mengkui*

33 **Multinationals, Globalisation
and Indigenous Firms in China**
*Chunhang Liu*

34 **Economic Convergence in
Greater China**
Mainland China, Hong Kong,
Macau and Taiwan
*Chun Kwok Lei and Shujie Yao*

35 **Financial Sector Reform and
the International Integration
of China**
*Zhongmin Wu*

36 **China in the World Economy**
*Zhongmin Wu*

37 **China's Three Decades of
Economic Reforms**
*Edited by Xiaohui Liu and Wei
Zhang*

38 **China's Development
Challenges**
Economic vulnerability and public sector reform
*Richard Schiere*

39 **China's Rural Financial
System**
Households' demand for credit
and recent reforms
*Yuepeng Zhao*

40 **Sustainable Reform and
Development in Post-Olympic
China**
*Edited by Shujie Yao, Bin Wu,
Stephen Morgan and Dylan
Sutherland*

41 **Constructing a Developmental
Social Welfare System for All**
*China Development Research
Foundation*

42 **China's Road to Peaceful
Rise**
Observations on its cause, basis,
connotation and prospect
*Zheng Bijian*

43 **China as the Workshop of the
World**
An analysis at the national
and industry level of China
in the international division of
labor
*Yuning Gao*

44 **China's Role in Global
Economic Recovery**
*Xiaolan Fu*

45 **The Political Economy of the
Chinese Coal Industry**
Black gold and blood-stained coal
*Tim Wright*

46 **Rising China in the Changing
World Economy**
*Edited by Liming Wang*

47 **Thirty Years of China's
Reform**
*Edited by Wang Mengkui*

**48 China and the Global Financial Crisis**
A comparison with Europe
*Edited by Jean-Pierre Cabestan, Jean-François Di Meglio and Xavier Richet*

**49 China's New Urbanization Strategy**
*China Development Research Foundation*

**50 China's Development and Harmonisation**
Towards a balance with nature, society and the international community
*Bin Wu, Shujie Yao and Jian Chen*

**51 Chinese Firms, Global Firms**
Industrial policy in the age of globalization
*Peter Nolan*

**52 The East Asian Computer Chip War**
*Ming-chin Monique Chu*

**53 China's Economic Dynamics**
A Beijing consensus in the making?
*Edited by Jun Li and Liming Wang*

**54 A New Development Model and China's Future**
*Deng Yingtao. Translated by Nicky Harman, with a foreword by Peter Nolan and an Afterword translated by Phil Hand*

# Routledge studies on the Chinese economy – Chinese economists on economic reform

**1 Chinese Economists on Economic Reform – Collected Works of Xue Muqiao**
*Xue Muqiao, edited by China Development Research Foundation*

**2 Chinese Economists on Economic Reform – Collected Works of Guo Shuqing**
*Guo Shuqing, edited by China Development Research Foundation*

**3 Chinese Economists on Economic Reform – Collected Works of Chen Xiwen**
*Chen Xiwen, edited by China Development Research Foundation*

**4 Chinese Economists on Economic Reform – Collected Works of Du Runsheng**
*Du Runsheng, edited by China Development Research Foundation*

**5** **Chinese Economists on Economic Reform – Collected Works of Lou Jiwei**
*Lou Jiwei, edited by China Development Research Foundation*

**6** **Chinese Economists on Economic Reform – Collected Works of Ma Hong**
*Ma Hong, edited by China Development Research Foundation*

**7** **Chinese Economists on Economic Reform – Collected Works of Wang Mengkui**
*Wang Mengkui, edited by China Development Research Foundation*

**8** **Chinese Economists on Economic Reform – Collected Works of Yu Guangyuan**
*Yu Guangyuan, edited by China Development Research Foundation*

# A New Development Model and China's Future

**Deng Yingtao**

*Nicky Harman* is the translator
*Peter Nolan* wrote the Foreword
*Phil Hand* is the translator of the Afterword

LONDON AND NEW YORK

First edition published in Chinese in 1991 by CITIC Press under the title
新發展方式與中國的未來.

This English translation published 2014
by Routledge
2 Park Square, Milton Park, Abingdon, Oxon, OX14 4RN

and by Routledge
711 Third Avenue, New York, NY 10017

*Routledge is an imprint of the Taylor & Francis Group, an informa business*

© 2014 Deng Yingtao

The right of Deng Yingtao to be identified as author of this work has
been asserted by him in accordance with the Copyright, Designs and
Patent Act 1988.

Publication of this book was made possible thanks to a grant from the
Cambridge Malaysian Education and Development Trust and the
Cambridge China Development Trust.

All rights reserved. No part of this book may be reprinted or reproduced
or utilised in any form or by any electronic, mechanical, or other means,
now known or hereafter invented, including photocopying and recording,
or in any information storage or retrieval system, without permission in
writing from the publishers.

*Trademark notice:* Product or corporate names may be trademarks or
registered trademarks, and are used only for identification and explanation
without intent to infringe.

*British Library Cataloguing in Publication Data*
A catalogue record for this book is available from the British Library

*Library of Congress Cataloging in Publication Data*
Deng, Yingtao.
[Xin fa zhan fang shi yu Zhongguo di wei lai. English]
    A new development model and China's future / Deng Yingtao.
        pages cm. – (Routledge studies on the Chinese economy ; 54)
"First edition published in Chinese in 1991 under the title Xin fa zhan
fang shi yu Zhongguo di wei lai."
    Includes bibliographical references and index.
    1. China.–Economic policy–1976–2000. 2. Economic development–
Environmental aspects–China. 3. Sustainable development–China.
I. Title.
HC427.92.T452813 2014
338.951–dc23                                                2013039687

ISBN: 978-0-415-61092-6 (hbk)
ISBN: 978-1-315-81916-7 (ebk)

Typeset in Times New Roman
by Sunrise Setting Ltd, Paignton, UK

Printed and bound in the United States of America by Publishers Graphics,
LLC on sustainably sourced paper.

# Contents

| | |
|---|---|
| *List of figures* | xii |
| *List of tables* | xiii |
| *Foreword by Peter Nolan* | xiv |
| *Translator's preface by Nicky Harman* | xxxii |

| | |
|---|---|
| **Introduction** | 1 |
| *The 'three-body' problem  1* | |
| *An arduous exploration  4* | |
| *Overview of this book  8* | |

| | | |
|---|---|---|
| **1** | **Making a choice under pressure** | 11 |
| | *The flea and the elephant  12* | |
| | *There is only one China  16* | |
| | *Comparisons and pressures  19* | |

| | | |
|---|---|---|
| **2** | **Detrimental effects of redundancy** | 27 |
| | *Pause for thought  27* | |
| | *Excessive nutrition  27* | |
| | *The rights and wrongs of the matter  32* | |
| | *The facts come to light  36* | |

| | | |
|---|---|---|
| **3** | **Breakdown of natural resources** | 39 |
| | *Renewability  40* | |
| | *Exclusivity  45* | |
| | *Externality  48* | |

| | | |
|---|---|---|
| **4** | **The economy of waste** | 53 |
| | *Private-ownership and collective-ownership disasters  53* | |
| | *Killing the goose that lays the golden eggs  56* | |
| | *Eating the seed grain  59* | |

x   *Contents*

*Hard-pressed 62*
*The unvarnished truth 66*
*Wastage and growth 70*

**5   Humans and entropy**                                        77
*More storms 77*
*The principle of entropy growth 81*
*A plethora of ambiguities 89*
*A multitude of barriers 93*
*Which way forward? 97*

**6   Making a fresh start**                                     100
*Grossly over-rated 100*
*Time flies and waits for no one 103*
*The phoenix rises from the ashes 107*

**7   Engel's Law**                                              110
*Micro-foundations 110*
*An elementary extension 114*
*Social intervention 118*

**8   The principle of equivalence**                             120
*Specious arguments 120*
*An analysis of need 124*
*A paradox 126*
*A new way 131*

**9   Overcoming barriers**                                      135
*The safety rule 135*
*The minimum rule 140*
*The equivalence rule 146*
*The priority rule 150*

**10   A blueprint for reconstruction**                          155
*The truth in all its clarity 155*
*Blazing new trails 160*
*Some thought-provoking general comparisons 169*

**11   Desperate measures are called for**                       177
*Making a U-turn 177*
*The means to achieve this end 181*
*China at the crossroads 183*

**Appendix: differential pricing, Pareto efficiency, property rights**      188

*Differential pricing  188*
*Pareto efficiency  188*
*Property rights  189*

**Afterword – interviews with Deng Yingtao in hospital in the last year of his life, translated by Phil Hand**      191

*Modernization for the many  191*
*Key technologies for water in western China  197*
*The environment: from protecting to building  206*
*Progress through changing the development model  211*
*Markets, bureaucracies, reciprocity  213*
*Is communism so unrealistic?  222*
*Modernization for the many: making it happen  226*
*The political revolution  236*

*References*      257
*Index*      265

# Figures

| | | |
|---|---|---|
| 1.1 | The three-body problem | 2 |
| 3.1 | Three relationships | 42 |
| 3.2 | Congestion | 44 |
| 4.1 | Human beings and the environment | 63 |
| 4.2 | Accumulated external diseconomy | 64 |
| 4.3 | Flow chart of accumulated externality | 65 |
| 5.1 | Isolated system | 82 |
| 5.2 | Sealed system | 83 |
| 5.3 | The Earth approximates to a sealed system | 83 |
| 5.4 | The city is an open system | 84 |
| 5.5 | Gasses of different temperatures mix | 86 |
| 5.6 | Distribution of molecules | 87 |
| 7.1 | Engel's curve | 111 |
| 7.2 | S-curve | 113 |
| 7.3 | How constraints function | 117 |
| 8.1 | Changes in the structure of human activities | 128 |
| 8.2 | Equivalence principle | 132 |
| 9.1 | Two models of use | 136 |
| 9.2 | Countermeasures to uncertainty | 139 |

# Tables

| | | |
|---|---|---:|
| F1 | IEA's Reference Scenario for energy-related $CO_2$ emissions, 2005–30 (million metric tons) | xxvi |
| A1 | Transformation of the livelihood of China's urban and rural population | xxix |
| A2 | Changes in China's energy-related $CO_2$ emissions in comparative perspective: the IEA's Reference Scenario, 2005–30 | xxx |
| 1.1 | Comparison between per capita levels of China's main resources and average levels worldwide (%) | 17 |
| 1.2 | Comparison between China's per capita 1980 consumption levels and average world levels in 1960 and 1970 | 20 |
| 1.3 | Indices for the FDR, Soviet Union and Japan at the time when they reached GNP or GDP of approximately US$800 | 25 |
| 2.1 | Number of years during which global mineral resources can be exploited | 37 |
| 5.1 | The theoretical basis of evolution | 90 |
| 9.1 | Benefits to the environment of recycling in USA (%) | 142 |
| 9.2 | Energy intensity of various transportation modes in the USA | 145 |
| 9.3 | Total costs of energy (free energy) needed to produce a car | 147 |
| 9.4 | Methods of car recycling, and service life | 147 |

# Foreword

This foreword is being written in January 2013. Beijing is shrouded in freezing smog, with concentrations of micro-particulates far above internationally accepted safe levels. The intensity of pollution in China's capital city has provoked deep public debate about the country's development path. Deng Yingtao's book, *New Development Pattern and China's Future* was published in 1991. Its re-publication in Chinese in 2012, and the publication of Nicky Harman's English language translation, will stimulate reflection both inside and outside China about the development path that the country has pursued since the book's first publication in 1991. The book holds up a mirror to the history of China over the past two decades.

Deng Yingtao was a scholar in the Chinese Academy of Social Sciences. Unlike many of his contemporaries, he did not seek government office or business wealth. He died on 13 March 2012. His academic life was devoted mainly to the study of China's energy and environment, with a wide array of publications in books and journals in Chinese. Although he was widely read and respected within China, he is hardly known outside the country. The publication of this translation of this book provides an opportunity for non-Chinese readers to become better acquainted with one of China's most original scholars writing in an area of critical importance for China and the world.

I first met Deng Yingtao on 10 October 1991, when he visited Cambridge together with Zhang Baomin, both of whom were scholars from the Rural Development Research Institute, Chinese Academy of Social Sciences. We all had dinner together in Jesus College. Towards the end of his life, even in the depths of his illness, Deng Yingtao's face retained its bright-eyed, mischievous character. He remained indomitably optimistic. On 6 December 1991, I visited the Rural Development Research Institute in Beijing and Deng Yingtao gave me a copy of his newly-published book, *New Development Pattern and China's Future*. The overall conception of the book made a deep impression on me, with its far-seeing analysis of the importance of energy and the natural environment in development. Two decades later, the transformation of China's development model has today become an issue in the country's political economy and its international relations. It is only now, with the benefit of hindsight and in the light of China's subsequent pattern of development, that the full significance of this book can be appreciated.

Like many of the most profound Asian thinkers, Deng Yingtao has a rigorous, open-minded scientific approach, drawing freely upon works from different cultures and languages, combined with deep roots in Asian philosophical traditions. The book conveys a profound sense of the fragile physical reality of the conditions of life for the whole human species. He reminds his readers that our existence is entirely dependent on the natural world that surrounds us: water, the atmosphere, the earth and all the other living things on the planet. Without food human beings can live for only five weeks, without water, for only five days and without air, for only five minutes.

Deng Yingtao contrasts the old 'classical' development pattern of today's developed countries with the 'new development pattern', which he considers to be necessary for the long-run sustainable development of the whole human species. In the classical pattern, which was pursued over a long period in today's high-income countries, short-run economic efficiency took priority over the long-term sustainability of the natural environment. This model came into being in a small number of today's high-income countries, which have only around one-sixth of the world's population. They were able to regard the supply of natural resources as limitless. People blindly sought for a limitless increase in their material consumption and accepted the enormous waste that resulted. Growth was founded upon the large-scale consumption of non-renewable resources, and the heavy depletion of stocks of renewable resources. This model is unsustainable for the world's population as a whole, which will reach 8–9 billion in the coming century.

Deng Yingtao argues that a new definition of progress is required, which satisfies people's basic needs and allows them to develop their potential, but does not over-exploit renewable resources and/or deplete the stock of renewable resources. He warns that developing countries should not attempt to reach the level of material abundance seen in the USA. His analysis is strongly influenced by the concept of 'entropy'.[1] This approach, which is followed by many Western scholars, places the world's energy resources, which ultimately come from the sun, at the centre of the analysis of the unsustainable nature of the classical path of development. Deng Yingtao argues that if developing countries follow the Western development path, this will 'lead the whole planet to disaster': 'The exponential growth of technological society is a one-way ticket to disaster.' Instead, he argues that developing countries should seek a new development path that replaces high-energy technologies with low energy, appropriate technologies. The only way forward is to 'transform the way we live, cutting out excessive waste, so that improvements in our standard of living are sustainable within the limits of available resources and the environment'. Deng Yingtao's book anticipates the recent proliferation of research interest in 'sustainable consumption' (e.g. OECD 1997; Jackson 2009) and 'sustainable energy' in the West (e.g. Smil 2003; McKay 2009).

In 1991, China's reform and opening up was in its early stage. Deng Yingtao argued that even at this early point in its modernization, China should reflect deeply on the pattern of development being followed. Although China could benefit greatly from the 'advantages of the latecomer', advanced science and technology are double-edged swords, with both helpful and harmful impacts. According

xvi *Foreword*

to Deng Yingtao China would face insurmountable difficulties if it followed the classical approach to development. It should not continue blindly down the existing development path until it reaches maturity and only then try to resolve the problems created along the way. It cannot expect to face the same advantageous natural resource conditions that today's developed countries faced in the past.

Deng Yingtao argued that China had a dramatic example to learn from right in front of its eyes in the shape of the USA, which has only a small percentage of the world's population but accounts for a large fraction of its natural resource consumption. It is self-evident that China cannot follow the American path of development. It has a huge population, so it would inevitably face a sharp contradiction between its own demand for energy and the limited extent of global energy supply if it followed the classical development approach: 'When we see the United States, which accounts for six per cent of the world's population, consuming fifty per cent of the world's resources, why on earth would we follow that model to resolve our own problems?' Deng Yingtao urged China to 'reject the way in which the developed world has modernized' and 'do it now'! China should absorb only those parts of the West's development experience that are rational and discard others, no matter how attractive they may appear superficially. He emphasizes that in order to establish a new development path, it is necessary to 'take the entire population with us, convincing them of the need to balance the books in a rational way'.

Deng Yingtao advocated a new pattern of development for China in which a clean and healthy environment would be the top priority, followed by the satisfaction of basic needs for the whole population, with the short-run pursuit of economic efficiency only in third place. Renewable resources should form the foundation of the new development pattern, with a large expansion of the production and use of renewable sources of primary energy, especially solar and wind power, and new types of renewable materials to substitute for non-renewable ones. Throughout his life as a scholar, Deng Yingtao maintained a passionate interest in renewable energy sources, regarding them as a necessity not only for China, but also for the whole of humanity.

Under the new development model people would not blindly seek for increased material consumption. Instead, there should be a rational restraint on consumption and lifestyle, including strict control on population growth. The new pattern of development places cooperation in first place, emphasising common interests and mutual responsibilities in respect to the environment. Theoretically, everyone is free to join in the 'free competition'. A minority of the population consider themselves to be the 'winners' in this competition, while the majority of the population, who are the principle victims of environmental damage, live in poverty with inadequate resources. However, Deng Yingtao pointed that the world is becoming ever more crowded and the distance between people is ever shrinking. As environmental damage becomes more widespread, for example, through the destruction of tropical rainforests, no one will be able to escape the ecological crisis: 'When the nest is overturned, all the eggs are broken [*fuchao wu wanluan*]' (i.e. in a great disaster no-one escapes). The original 'winners' will not be winners in the end. Those who harm others in order to benefit themselves only harm themselves in the end. Faced with this prospect, the only logical path is cooperation, common understanding and benefiting ourselves by benefiting others. In his ardent advocacy of the importance of trust and cooperation in order to achieve a sustainable future for the human species, Deng Yingtao follows in a long tradition from Kropotkin (1955), to Rachel Carson (1962) and to Edward Wilson today (2012).

Deng Yingtao argued that the best way to approach China's pattern of development is to start from the desired endpoint of the country's development, and work back from there to the production system in the immediate future, in order to close the loop between the final destination and the starting point of China's modernization. He argued that China could choose to organize the economy in ways that involve relatively low levels of material consumption without reducing the quality of life. His approach anticipates the recent interest in 'happiness' studies (e.g. Layard 2005). He emphasizes that beyond a certain level of material consumption, human well-being is increased mainly by non-material consumption, which includes not only intellectual activity and the company of other people, but also enjoyment of 'fresh air, unspoiled natural landscapes, limpidly clear lakes and rivers, blue seas, towering forested mountains, green fields, beautiful flowers and bird song'. A great advantage of non-material consumption is that it generally requires only limited amounts of resources.

Education of the entire population occupies a central place in the development pattern advocated by Deng Yingtao. Education itself is a cost-effective form of social investment, requiring limited physical resources. Human beings' interaction with the natural environment, including both ethical and scientific aspects, would become an important part of public education:

> We must educate people in ecology and the environmental sciences...[O]ur moral view of the world [should be] founded on co-existence with nature... This moral view is rooted...in harmonious relations between humans and the ecosystems of which their environment is made up.

His view of the moral significance of the relationship between the human species and the natural world echoes that of Rachel Carson (1962). She warned that the 'control of nature' is a phrase 'conceived in arrogance, born of the Neanderthal age of biology and philosophy, when it was supposed that nature exists for the convenience of man'. She questioned 'whether any civilization can wage relentless war on life without destroying itself, and without losing the right to be called civilised'. This also echoes China's own long tradition of reflecting on the moral significance of human beings' relationship with the natural world around them.[2]

Deng Yingtao identified numerous ways in which a new pattern of clothing, food, housing, transport and health could transform the three main areas of the economy (primary, secondary and tertiary) in order to put into place a new pattern of long-run sustainable development in China.

In the agricultural sector, the objective in food production would be to achieve a balance between animals and plants, avoiding heavy emphasis on meat in people's diet. This would include increasing the contribution of soybeans in order to

xviii  *Foreword*

improve the quantity and quality of protein supply. Deng Yingtao is optimistic about the contribution that modern biotechnology can make to improve Chinese crop yields and people's diet. In addition to taking advantage of technical progress, he argues that in order to reduce pressure on cotton production, people should avoid having large wardrobes, use their clothing for longer and recycle clothing fabrics. In order to minimize environmental damage and economize on a non-renewable resources, China should avoid a petroleum-based agriculture. Trees have an important place in Deng Yingtao's new development path. China has a large amount of land capable of growing trees, which is not currently used for this purpose. A large-scale expansion of tree-planting would not only have great amenity value for the whole population, but would also increase the supply of chemicals from a renewable source to substitute for chemicals from petroleum. Deng Yingtao calculates that each individual only needs the produce of five trees in their whole lifetime in order to meet their clothing needs. He is confident that technological progress in the use of forest resources will have a revolutionary impact on farming, with forests assuming 'a central position in the air-water-organisms-soil biosphere'. He believes that the world stands on the edge of an eco-industrial revolution. Since this book was first published, progress in the sciences surrounding farming, forestry and biomass, has vindicated his optimistic vision.

Deng Yingtao stresses that the industrial sector is the most important one for establishing a new pattern of development across the whole economy. In his view, China has the opportunity to establish itself at the forefront of a revolution in ecological production based upon innovation in the industrial sector. China should develop high technology, energy-efficient materials, such as new types of high-strength and heat-resistant ceramics, which can be used in gas turbines and automobile engines to reduce energy consumption and increase work efficiency. However, he emphasizes that not all energy-saving technologies need to be high technology. They can include simple techniques for reducing the energy needed for storing eggs and new techniques used to store vegetables in the home and preserve them in good condition.

Deng Yingtao emphasized the wide implications of the revolution in information technology for China's sustainable development. He argued that China should take full advantage of the revolution in communication technologies using fibre optic cables in order to make a leap forward in telecommunications, which could provide a mass communication system much more cheaply than a traditional copper wire-based system, and permit a great saving in an exhaustible resource – copper. This would then enable the telecommunication and computer systems to be linked together, giving a great stimulus to China's modernization. Deng Yingtao emphasized that the key to the new development model lay in the machine-building sector. He argued that China should develop new types of energy-efficient machines, maximising the application of advances in information technology to reduce waste of non-renewable resources and introduce renewable materials to replace non-renewable ones. Since the book was written, the application of information technology has produced a revolution in the nature of machinery. 'Intelligent', energy-saving machinery is now widely employed in the modern sector of the global economy, from chemical and steel plants to automobiles and elevators.

*Foreword* xix

In the transport system, the new pattern of development would give priority to bicycles, taxis and public transport, including small public buses. China should tightly control the development of privately-owned cars for personal transport:

> The old way of looking at the car might lead people to ask: How can we improve the engine and make it more successful? What we really ought to be asking are quite different questions: Can we really not live without a car? Has the car really improved our lives and our health and made us more civilised? Have today's cars expropriated the energy necessary for the next generation to sustain life? If something was not worth having in the first place, then its success or failure is not worth discussing. If a car is not worth having, then it is irrelevant whether it does 20 or 50 miles to the gallon.

Bicycles would be the main form of personal transport within urban areas. The main form of housing would be four- or five-storey buildings, with stairs rather than elevators, as in the USSR. A large proportion of the energy supply for heating and household electrical appliances would come from solar power on the roofs. Such a pattern of living would help to avoid the loneliness inherent in the classical pattern of development based on private transport and dispersed housing. Deng Yingtao's arguments about the role of the automobile in the new pattern of development echo those of Jane Jacobs in her visionary study *The Death and Life of Great American Cities*:

> Traffic arteries…are powerful and insistent instruments of city destruction.…Landmarks are crumbled or are so sundered from their contexts in city life as to become irrelevant trivialities. City character is blurred until every place becomes like every other place, all adding up to Noplace.
>
> (Jacobs 1991: 440)

Deng Yingtao argued that in the transport of goods, China should give priority to rail and water transport in relation to trucks and road transport. This would permit large reductions in the consumption of steel, aluminium and plastics used in vehicle construction, energy used to power vehicles and energy-intensive materials (including cement, tarmac and steel) used to build and repair highways. This would in turn economize on the use of electricity to produce these products. In this way, the new pattern of development would conserve non-renewable resources and help to control the growth of pollution. It would also have large implications for physical and mental health, for interpersonal relations and for the pattern of urban development.

Under the new development model, urban development would focus on medium and small cities, with trees planted throughout and around the town. The energy for towns would be supplied by renewable sources, with solar and wind power playing a central role. Recycling would be highly developed. China has huge amounts of waste from discarded materials, mostly in the industrial sector. Deng Yingtao argued that China should establish extensive systems of waste collection

xx  *Foreword*

and facilities for recycling in order to reduce waste and economize on energy use and lower resource consumption, as well as reduce environmental pollution.

Deng Yingtao's study is remarkable for setting out so clearly, and at such an early date, the key environmental challenges that China faces and for linking these to the challenges faced by the whole of humanity. Like most of China's deepest thinkers, Deng Yingtao does not think simply in terms of China's own development. He is acutely sensitive to the role that China's new pattern of development might play in the construction of a sustainable future for the whole of humanity. His study is remarkable for identifying concrete and detailed measures that China might adopt if it wished to set in motion a long-term pattern for environmentally sustainable development. It is remarkable also for being linked to a comprehensive philosophy of development and social relationships. Deng Yingtao argues that abandoning the classic development path depends 'as much upon our collective will and judgement as it does on scientific and technological breakthroughs'. He believes that the classical  development model is especially unsuited to China's conditions of modernization because of the fact that the relative abundance of resources enjoyed by Western countries when they industrialized, is not available to China.

In recent years, more and more Chinese writers have begun to address the themes in Deng Yingtao's book. Since he wrote it the issue of identifying a new, sustainable development path has moved to the centre of political discourse in both China and the world at large. At the time that he wrote the book, the Soviet Union was disintegrating and China was digesting the implications of 4 June 1989. In that context it is all the more remarkable that Deng Yingtao should have concentrated his attention on such a profound issue in China's long-term development, far removed from the political-economic drama of that period. His book concludes by arguing that the new development model provides an historic opportunity for China and other developing countries: 'Will China be able to seize this opportunity? We not only can, we must. There is no other way!'

At the outset of the book, Deng Yingtao identifies three interconnecting aspects of China's modernization: its external environment, its internal structure and its pattern of development. In his view, the way in which these three analytical spaces interact will determine whether China's modernization succeeds or fails. What has happened to these three interconnecting elements in the twenty-odd years since Deng Yingtao's book was published?

## International environment

The international environment and China's relationship with it has changed profoundly since 1991. Since the policies of 'reform and opening up' began in the late 1970s, China has become ever more deeply integrated into the international economy. In 1995, China was the world's tenth largest exporter, with smaller exports than Belgium. Today, China's economic growth is closely linked to the global economy. China is the world's largest exporter and a huge number of its workers are reliant on exports. Energy imports have become critically important. China has just 1.5 per cent of the world's natural gas reserves and a mere 1.1 per cent of its oil reserves. The growth of China's oil and gas consumption has increasingly outpaced its growth of domestic production (BP 2011). By 2010, net oil imports amounted to 59 per cent of China's total consumption, and the prospect is for this to keep rising. Energy security has become ever more important in China's international relations.[3]

Since the early 1990s the global business system has gone through comprehensive restructuring. In almost every sector a small group of giant companies with leading technologies and brands has emerged. Between them they command 50 per cent or more of the global market in their respective sectors. Pressure from the 'cascade effect' exerted by 'system integrator' firms has stimulated comprehensive restructuring of the value chain surrounding core companies and intense industrial concentration has taken place far down into the supply chain (Nolan 2012). The companies that have established themselves at the core of the global business system almost all have their headquarters in the high-income countries. Global brands and global technical progress are concentrated among a small number of firms, from high-income countries, that stand at the apex of the global business system. One hundred giant firms, all from high-income countries, account for over three-fifths of the total R&D expenditure among the world's top 1,400 companies (BERR 2008). They are the foundation of the world's technical progress in the era of capitalist globalization. Leading firms with their headquarters in high-income countries have 'gone out' into the rest of the world to establish global business systems. The outward stock of FDI rose from US$2.1 trillion in 1990 to US$19.0 trillion in 2009 (UNCTAD 2010).

Among late-industrialising countries, China has been uniquely open to foreign direct investment (FDI). The stock of FDI in China stands at over US$500 billion. Multinational firms account for around 28 per cent of the country's industrial value-added and for two-thirds of the value-added in high technology industries. They account for 55 per cent of China's total exports, and for 90 per cent of exports of high technology products (Nolan 2012). The numbers of people working in China within the value chain of foreign firms is extremely large and beyond easy calculation. Global firms in a wide range of sectors, including automobiles, information technology, consumer electronics, beverages, quick-service restaurants, media and marketing, luxury goods and branded footwear and clothing, exercise a deep influence on the pattern of Chinese development, including the direction of technical progress and the attitudes of Chinese consumers towards the country's development pattern. As China has become ever more deeply integrated into the global economy, the population's consumption desires and the pattern of consumption expenditure, especially among the urban middle class, has increasingly come to resemble that of consumers in high-income countries. Who could have imagined in 1991 that by 2012, China would have world's largest and fastest-growing car market, that automobile sales would account for one-quarter of total retail spending and that the country would be poised to produce more than 20 million cars in 2013?

## Internal structure

In the early 1990s, few people outside the country anticipated the structural transformation that China would experience in the following decades. At this time, the consensus among Western scholars and diplomats, and the international xxii *Foreword*

media, was that rule by the Chinese Communist Party could not long outlast that of the Soviet Communist Party and that the former was incapable of putting into place reforms that would permit the growth of a thriving market economy.[4] In fact, between 1990 and 2009, China's GDP (gross domestic product) growth rate was almost 11 per cent per annum compared with less than 3 per cent per annum in high-income countries. In 1995, China's GDP (at market prices) was the eighth largest in the world, less than one-tenth of that of the USA. By 2009, measured in PPP (purchasing-power parity) dollars, China was the world's second largest economy, 65 per cent of that of the USA (WB 2011). In just a decade, between 1998 and 2009, China's share of world manufacturing output tripled, from 5.9 per cent to 18.6 per cent (WB 2011).

Spending on family planning is five times more effective at cutting carbon dioxide emissions than conventional low-carbon technologies. China's 'one-child' policy has radically slowed the growth of the country's enormous population. Between 1980 and 2015, it is predicted that China's population will have expanded by 42 per cent, increasing from 977 million to 1,383 million. In the same period, India's population will grow from 673 million to a predicted 1,233 million, an increase of 83 per cent. India's efforts to control population growth have failed. China's one-child policy has been a striking success. If China had followed India's path, it would have an extra 405 million people by 2015 compared with the actual population. These 'missing millions' are an enormous, if unintended, contribution towards controlling global warming.

The structure of residence and employment in China has shifted radically since the early 1990s. Between 1990 and 2009, China's official urban population rose by 321 million people and the share rose from 26.4 per cent to 46.6 per cent (SSB 2010), and if the numbers of unofficial rural–urban migrants are included, the transformation in the structure of residence would be even more dramatic. In this period the numbers employed in urban areas increased from 170 million to 311 million, rising from 26 per cent to 40 per cent of total employment.

The living standards of both urban and rural populations were transformed between 1990 and 2009 (see Table A1). Life expectancy rose from 68 years to 73 years, a remarkably high level for a developing country. The improvement was made possible by major advances in health provision, such as the attendance of skilled staff at births. Infant mortality and maternal mortality rates fell sharply between 1990 and 2009. The amount of housing space expanded greatly. A major contribution was also made by improvements in nutrition. Between 1990 and 2011, in China's urban areas, the average per capita consumption of eggs increased from 7.3 to 10.1 kg, milk and milk products increased from 4.6 kg to 13.7 kg, meat increased from 25.2 kg to 35.2 kg, aquatic products increased from 7.7 kg to 14.6 kg and fruit increased from 41.1 kg to 52.1 kg (State Statistical Bureau 2012: 350). The spread of domestic and commercial refrigeration, as well as other improvements to the food distribution and processing system, meant that there was less wastage of food on its journey to the final customer.

In the cities, the average housing space per capita rose from $14 \, m^2$ in 1990 to $27 \, m^2$ in 2009, and in the countryside the amount increased from $18 \, m^2$ to $34 \, m^2$.

This constituted a large improvement in the quality of life. Tremendous progress occurred in the ownership of consumer durables in both urban and rural areas. The widespread diffusion of washing machines, refrigerators, air conditioners, water heaters, microwave ovens and colour TVs, made an enormous impact upon the quality of daily life for the vast majority of the urban population and a large fraction of the rural population. The revolution in information technology had a profound impact on the whole population. By 2009 there was near universal use of mobile phones and ownership of computers was spreading rapidly. By 2009, 30 per cent of the population used the internet (WB 2011).

## Pattern of development

China's pattern of development since the early 1990s has relied on exceptionally high rates of investment. Its gross domestic investment has risen from the already high level of around 32 per cent of GDP in the early 1980s, to the remarkable level of around 43 per cent today (SSB 2009: 54). Once an economy is locked into an unbalanced growth pattern, it is difficult to move off the path. Heavy industrial output is itself intensive in the use of other heavy industrial products, including transport systems, as well as using large amounts of electricity per unit of output. It has proved difficult to shift the Chinese economy away from this 'unbalanced growth path', despite the leadership's frequently stated intention to do so.

No country in history has experienced such explosive growth of the urban population as China since the 1980s. The pattern of urban development has been radically different from that advocated in Deng Yingtao's new development path. Instead, it has been based mainly on high-rise buildings in mega-cities. By 2011, China had no less than 127 cities with more than one million residents, of which fourteen cities had more than four million residents and thirty-one had between two and four million residents (SSB 2012: 385). China's urban areas have become 'concrete forests', replicating Hong Kong's development pattern across the whole country. The total floor space completed for all types of building across the whole country rose from 196 million $m^2$ in 1990 to 2.2 billion $m^2$ in 2008 (SSB 2009: 592). Building construction projects on the scale undertaken in China requires vast amounts of steel, cement and glass, all of which are highly energy intensive. The energy efficiency of Chinese buildings has progressed due to government regulation. However, the most urgent need for China's urban population has been to provide 'a roof over the heads' of as many people as possible as quickly as possible, in order to meet the immediate welfare needs of the vast army of new urban dwellers and avoid social disorder. The energy efficiency standard of China's urban buildings is still 'low and varied' (IEA 2007). It is anticipated that China's urban building codes will not reach the level of today's OECD member countries until 2030 (IEA 2007: 383). By that point, China's massive urban residential construction boom will be almost complete. In other words, China's vast urban housing stock, consisting mainly of high-rise dwellings, will have been built mainly with levels of insulation and ventilation systems that are far below the standards of OECD member countries. Re-engineering the xxiv *Foreword*

vast stock of high-rise buildings in order to substantially increase their energy efficiency would be a mammoth task.

A large fraction of China's residential buildings is supplied with rooftop solar heaters. However, these are small devices, able only to heat water for showers. They are not able to supply heating and cooling for giant high-rise apartment blocks. Few of China's residential tower blocks are being built with centrally provided heating and cooling systems, which have a high installation cost but are much more energy-efficient. Instead, the vast bulk of residential blocks use air conditioners attached to the outside of the building, which is a far more energy-intensive way to heat and cool buildings. The stock of household appliances has increased rapidly alongside the growth of urban incomes. Due mainly to government regulation, the energy efficiency of each type of appliance is increasing. However, the energy efficiency of Chinese household appliances is still considerably less than the average in OECD countries.

China's pattern of transport development has been fundamentally different from that advocated by Deng Yingtao in 1991. Between 1990 and 2009, there was a dramatic shift towards highways and trucks in the carriage of freight. In this period the length of railways increased by 38 per cent, while the length of highways increased almost fourfold (SSB 2010). In the same period, the number of trucks increased from 3.7 million to 13.7 million. In 1990, China's railways carried more than three times the amount of freight as China's highways (in terms of ton-km), but by 2008 China's highways carried one-third more freight than the railways (SSB 2010). In other words, China is moving down the same path of truck-based freight as that which has been followed in high-income countries. China's stock of passenger vehicles increased from 1.6 million in 1990 to over 48 million in 2009 (SSB 2010). In 2009, China became the world's biggest car market. Around 80 per cent of car sales are from multinational assemblers, which mainly sell locally produced vehicles. It seems likely that China will follow the high-income countries, with rapidly rising passenger car ownership for the middle class alongside increasing provision of public transport for the lower income deciles of the population.

China's structure of electricity generation has been radically different from that envisaged in Deng Yingtao's new development path. The country's electricity output has grown at around 10 per cent per annum since 1990 (SSB 2009: 540–3). China has been extraordinarily successful at virtually eliminating 'energy poverty'. Electricity output per person rose from 157 kWh in 1990 to 2,790 kWh in 2009 (SSB 2010). By 2005, thanks to rising incomes and a policy of making modern energy services available to the whole population, 99 per cent of the population had access to electricity, compared with only 62 per cent in India (IEA 2007: 281). However, due to the low base from which China began, and the huge population, China's output of electricity per person is still relatively small. In 2005, China's electricity output per person was just 18 per cent of that of the OECD countries and a mere 13 per cent of that of the USA (WB 2008: 304–6). Although China's energy efficiency is likely to continue its improvement of recent years, continued rapid growth would require enormous increases in electricity supply. The IEA projects that China's total electricity output (i.e. 8,500 Twh in 2030) will be comparable to the total electricity production of OECD countries of Europe and North America combined (IEA 2007: 344).

China's electricity generation remains almost entirely reliant on non-renewable sources of fuel. China has a relative abundance of domestic coal and this will continue to form the foundation of the expansion of China's electricity generation capacity. The technologies for large-scale commercial use of solar power are still many years away. The share of coal in China's electricity generation industry rose from 71 per cent in 1990 to 79 per cent in 2009, while the share of the main renewable source of energy, hydropower, fell from 20 per cent to 17 per cent in the same period (SSB 2010). Coal has a low ratio of value to weight, and is very intensive in its demands upon the country's transport system, both rail and road. Coal accounts for 44 per cent of total freight traffic on China's trains. Consequently, there are high indirect energy costs involved in using coal as the dominant primary energy source for China's power stations. China already has a huge stock of coal-fired power stations put into place in recent years. Most of these will continue in operation for several decades, embodying technologies that are increasingly outdated, but which still operate effectively from the perspective of market profitability.

Deng Yingtao warned that under the classical development model, China's voracious demand for non-renewable resources from across the world would produce tensions in its international relations. China's unbalanced growth path under the policies of reform and opening up was accompanied by rapid growth of heavy industrial output. This growth path has been extraordinarily intensive in the use of heavy industrial products. In 2006, China accounted for 20 per cent of the world's population. Nevertheless, in terms of key economic indicators it had still far from 'caught up' with the world's high-income countries. In terms of global consumption of heavy industrial products, China had not only 'caught up' with the high-income countries, but had surpassed them. Its share of a wide range of heavy industrial products was now much greater than its share of world population. In 2006 it accounted for 22 per cent of global copper consumption, 23 per cent of aluminium consumption, 28 per cent of iron ore and zinc consumption, 30 per cent of ammonia output, 34 per cent of steel output, 38 per cent of coal consumption and 46 per cent of cement output (IEA 2007: 142, 294–6).

China's continued reliance mainly on coal-fired power stations presents a huge policy challenge in terms of $CO_2$ production. Although China is at the forefront of global efforts to develop carbon capture and sequestration technologies, these are only in the very earliest stages of development. Moreover, even if rapid progress is made in techniques of carbon capture, sequestration also presents enormous technical challenges not only in China but in the OECD countries also. A large proportion of the captured carbon will need to be transported long distances to a suitable site for sequestration. This will entail a massive and extremely expensive process of building pipelines or other forms of transport. It will involve high energy costs in capturing and transforming the carbon into a form that can be transported. It involves unresolved issues of storage capacity and safety at the storage sites.

xxvi  *Foreword*

The IEA's 'Reference Scenario' for the period 2005–30 is based on the assumption that China's rate of economic growth rate slows down as the economy matures, the availability of rural surplus labour dries up, the population levels off and the dependency ratio increases as the population begins to age seriously. The IEA assumes that the GDP growth rate for this period slows to around 6 per cent per annum. The IEA also assumes that all the energy-saving measures included in the eleventh Five Year Plan are successfully put into place, leading to a fall of 2.6 per cent per annum in energy intensity between 2005 and 2030 (IEA 2007: 286). However, China's energy consumption per person in 2005 was still only 24 per cent of that of the high-income countries and 17 per cent of that of the USA (WB 2008: 154–6). Even with the IEA's cautious assumption concerning China's GDP growth, and relatively optimistic assumptions concerning energy-efficiency, China's demand for energy is projected to more than double, from 1,742 Mtoe in 2005 to 3,819 Mtoe in 2030, growing at 3.2 per cent per annum over the whole period (IEA 2007: 287). The IEA projects that the share of coal in total energy consumption will remain unchanged at 63 per cent of the total.

Under these relatively cautious assumptions, the IEA projects that China's energy-related $CO_2$ emissions will increase from 5.1 billion tonnes in 2005 to 11.5 billion tonnes in 2030, an annual increase of 3.3 per cent (see Table F1). The share of total emissions from coal is projected to fall only slightly, from 82 per cent in 2005 to 78 per cent in 2030 (IEA 2007: 315).

In analysing the implications for China's international relations, it is necessary to consider the prospects not only for China, but the prospects for change in energy use and climate change for the whole world. Under the IEA's Reference Scenario, China's share of total global energy-related $CO_2$ emissions increases from 19 per cent in 2005 to over 27 per cent in 2030 (see Table F1). China alone accounts for over two-fifths of the total global increase in $CO_2$ output between 2005 and 2030. By 2030, China's $CO_2$ output is projected to be 65 per cent greater than that of the USA and almost three times as large as that of the EU. The $CO_2$ output of the EU and the USA combined will be almost identical to that of China, i.e. around 11 billion tonnes. In this sense, it appears that China will have almost 'caught up' with the high-income countries.

*Table F1* IEA's Reference Scenario for energy-related $CO_2$ emissions, 2005–30 (million metric tons)

|  | *2005* | *2030* | *Average annual increase (%)* |
|---|---|---|---|
| Power generation | 2,500 | 6,202 | 3.7 |
| Industry | 1,430 | 2,373 | 2.0 |
| Transport | 337 | 1,255 | 5.4 |
| Residential and services | 468 | 715 | 1.7 |
| Other | 365 | 903 | 3.7 |
| Total | 5,101 | 11,488 | 3.3 |

Source: IEA (2007: 314).

*Foreword* xxvii

China's population is around 30 per cent larger than all the high-income countries combined. In 2005, China's $CO_2$ emissions per person were only 2.2 tonnes, compared with an average of 11.0 tonnes in the OECD countries as a whole; 8.0 tonnes in the EU, and 19.7 tonnes in the USA (Table A2). Despite the huge growth of China's total emissions, even in 2030, under the Reference Scenario, China's $CO_2$ emissions per person will be only 7.9 tonnes; compared with 8.4 tonnes in the EU; 11.6 tonnes across the whole of the OECD, and 19.0 tonnes in the USA.

Deng Yingtao's warning of the implications for international relations if China followed the classical pattern of development was loud and clear. His warning has been proved correct. The high-income countries are deeply alarmed at the large increases in prospect for developing countries, especially China, and the impact that these will have upon global ecology: 'A level of per capita income in China and India comparable with that industrialised countries would, on today's model, require a level of energy use beyond the world's energy resource endowment and the absorptive capacity of the planet's ecosystem' (IEA 2007: 215). The IEA expresses the hope that 'all countries – China, India, the industrialised countries and the rest of the global community – cooperate on moving quickly towards a genuinely sustainable lifestyle' (IEA 2007: 215).

However, China and other developing countries fear that development will be restrained by binding international agreements when their $CO_2$ emissions per person are still far behind those of high-income countries. $CO_2$ emission per person in developing countries today is only one-fifth of that of the OECD countries, and only around one-tenth of that of the USA (see Table A2). Moreover, OECD countries have been emitting large amounts of $CO_2$ since the Industrial Revolution. It seems only just that China and other developing countries should be permitted to increase their $CO_2$ emissions per person alongside a reduction in emissions per person in the OECD countries, until developing countries are level with the OECD countries.

The population of the developing countries is likely to expand from around seven billion today to around 9–10 billion towards the end of the century. Increased energy efficiency will help to contain the rate of growth of $CO_2$ emissions globally. However, it is hard to imagine that technical progress will be sufficiently rapid or that the pattern of consumer demand will alter sufficiently to enable developing countries to follow a completely new path of 'clean and sustainable' economic development. It is hard to imagine that developing countries will agree to bind themselves to targets for $CO_2$ emissions that prevent their populations enjoying the advances in income that already developed countries have achieved. Under these circumstances, there is a high chance that $CO_2$ emissions will exceed the upper 'safe' concentration level of 450 ppm (parts per million) and global average temperatures will rise far above 2°C. If global energy-related $CO_2$ emissions follow the path of the IEA's Reference Scenario, it is likely that world $CO_2$ emissions will not stabilize until the final decades of the twenty-first century, reaching a level of around 660–790 ppm, which would mean an increase in global average temperature of around 4.9–6.1°C compared with pre-industrial levels (IEA 2007: 206). In the view of most analysts, this would be disastrous for the human species.

## Conclusion

In the two decades since Deng Yingtao's book was published, China's pursuit of the policy of 'reform and opening up' has produced widespread and undeniable benefits, not least making use of the 'advantages of the latecomer' through access to global technical progress. China's development path has greatly improved the welfare of the mass of the Chinese population. The conditions of life for the mass of the Chinese population are far beyond those in India, which is the most relevant country against which to compare China. However, China's pattern of development has been radically different from the 'new development path' advocated in this book.

The final section of Deng Yingtao's book is entitled 'China at the Crossroads.' Two decades after the book's publication, China has moved far beyond the 'crossroads' in its development and far away from the path that he advocated. Instead of a 'new pattern of development', China has essentially pursued the classical, energy-intensive development path that was followed by the high-income countries themselves. China's urban population mainly lives in vast mega-cities, where the urban skyline has been transformed from mainly Soviet-style, low-rise apartment blocks into a forest of high-rise apartment buildings festooned with air conditioning units on the outside and packed with consumer appliances inside. China is the most important market for global car manufacturers, including the producers of luxury vehicles. Bicycles have almost disappeared from urban China. Far from restraining consumption and buying simple, utilitarian products, China's consumers avidly seek to acquire fashionable global luxury goods or their cheap imitations.

This pattern of development has had deeply problematic consequences for China's own environment as well as for its international relations. After two decades following the 'classical' development path, China is now attempting belatedly to alter course and follow a 'new development path'. However, the forces of path dependence are great. There is little prospect that China will put into place the development model advocated in Deng Yingtao's book. In 1962, Rachel Carson warned:

> We now stand where two roads diverge....The road we have long been travelling is deceptively easy, a smooth superhighway on which we progress with great speed, but at its end lies disaster. The other fork of the road – the one 'less travelled by' – offers our last, our only chance, to reach a destination that assures the preservation of our earth. The choice, after all, is ours to make.

Deng Yingtao's book serves as a poignant reminder of the 'road less travelled by' that China might have chosen, but did not take.

Peter Nolan.
Centre of Development Studies,
University of Cambridge.

# Statistical Appendix

*Table A1* Transformation of the livelihood of China's urban and rural population

|  | 1990 | 2009 |
|---|---|---|
| *Whole population* | | |
| Life expectancy at birth (years) | 68 | 73 |
| Births attended by skilled staff (%) | 50 | 99 |
| Infant mortality rate (no/000) | 37 | 17 |
| Maternal mortality rate (no/000) | 110 | 38 |
| Access to improved water (%) | 67 | 89 |
| Access to improved sanitation (%) | 41 | 55 |
| Promotion rates (%) | | |
| primary to junior secondary | 75 | 99 |
| junior secondary to senior secondary | 41 | 86 |
| senior secondary to higher education | 27 | 78 |
| Population living on less than US$1.25 per day (million)* | 683 | 208 (2005) |
| Population living on less than US$2 per day (million)* | 961 | 474 (2005) |
| *Urban population* | | |
| Engel coefficient | 54.2 | 36.5 |
| Average pc housing space (m$^2$) | 13.7 | 27.1 (2006) |
| Ownership of consumer durables | | |
| washing machines | 78 | 96 |
| refrigerators | 42 | 95 |
| colour TVs | 59 | 136 |
| air conditioners | negligible | 107 |
| water heaters | 30 | 83 |
| microwave ovens | negligible | 66 |
| computers | negligible | 57 |
| mobile phones | 0 | 181 |
| *Rural population* | | |
| Engel coefficient | 58.8 | 41.0 |
| Average pc housing space (m$^2$) | 17.8 | 33.6 |
| Ownership of consumer durables | | |
| washing machines | 9.1 | 53.1 |
| refrigerators | 1.2 | 37.1 |
| air conditioners | negligible | 12.2 |
| motor cycles | 1.0 | 57 |
| mobile phones | negligible | 115 |
| colour TVs | 5 | 109 |
| computers | 0 | 7 |

Source: SSB (2010).

Note
*data from WB (2011).

xxx  *Foreword*

*Table A2*  Changes in China's energy-related $CO_2$ emissions in comparative perspective: The IEA's Reference Scenario, 2005–30

| | Total $CO_2$ emissions | | | | $CO_2$ emissions pc | | | |
|---|---|---|---|---|---|---|---|---|
| | 2005 | | 2030 | | 2005 | | 2030 | |
| | b tonnes | Share of global emissions (%) | b tonnes | Share of global emissions (%) | pc | % of world average (%) | pc | % of world average (%) |
| World | 26.6 | 100 | 41.9 | 100 | 4.1 | 100 | 5.1 | 100 |
| OECD | 12.8 | 48.1 | 15.1 | 36.0 | 11.0 | 268 | 11.6 | 227 |
| USA | 5.8 | 21.8 | 6.9 | 16.5 | 19.5 | 476 | 19.0 | 373 |
| EU | 3.9 | 14.7 | 4.2 | 10.0 | 8.0 | 195 | 8.4 | 165 |
| Developing countries | 10.7 | 40.2 | 22.9 | 54.7 | 2.2 | 54 | 3.5 | 69 |
| China | 5.1 | 19.2 | 11.4 | 27.2 | 3.9 | 95 | 7.9 | 155 |
| India | 1.1 | 4.1 | 3.3 | 7.9 | 1.0 | 24 | 2.3 | 45 |

Source: IEA (2007: 199).

## Notes

1   The concept of entropy was first formulated by Rudolf Clausius, the German theoretical physicist, in a paper published in 1865. He adopted the term 'entropy' in order to measure the degree of disorder in a closed system. Vaclav Smil explains the term 'entropy' in the following fashion:

> Entropy is always one-way street, a flow of any kind of energy from a more ordered state that could be transformed into useful action to a more disordered state from which no useful benefit can be derived. For example, a lump of coal (highly ordered chemical energy with low entropy) can be transformed into heat and motion, but once these conversions run their course they end as dissipated heat, a high entropy form of energy that cannot be used for anything useful. No energy has been lost when the heat from burning coal rises through the atmosphere or when the rotation of wheels creates friction, and again heat, on contact with rails or ground, but the opportunity to use the final result of those various energy conversions to do something useful has been lost forever: the arrow of entropy travels irreversibly, leaving behind just low-temperature dissipated heat. So simply: rise of entropy is the loss of the potential to do useful work/action.
>
> (personal communication from Vaclav Smil, February 2013)

The concept of entropy is central to the second law of thermodynamics, which was also formulated by Clausius: 'The second law of thermodynamics, the universal tendency towards heat death and disorder, became perhaps the grandest of all cosmic generalisations' (Smil 2006: 6). Despite its central position in the life of the earth, 'energy is not a single, easily definable entity, but rather an abstract and elusive concept' (Smil 2006: 9).

2   Elvin (2004) provides a detailed account of the pressures that China's growing population density placed upon the country's natural environment over the long sweep of its history.

Foreword   xxxi

3   The impact of the recent 'shale oil' and 'tight gas' revolution upon China's energy security remains to be seen.
4   For criticism of this view see Nolan (1995).

## References

BERR (Department for Business Enterprise and Regulatory Reform) (2008) *The 2008 R&D Scoreboard*, London: BERR.

BP (2011) *Statistical Review of World Energy*, London: British Petroleum.

Carson, R. (1962) *Silent Spring*, New York: Houghton Mifflin.

Elvin, M. (2004) *The Retreat of the Elephants: An Environmental History of China*, New Haven: Yale University Press.

International Energy Association (IEA) (2007) *World Energy Outlook*, Paris: OECD.

Jacobs, J. (1993) *The Death and Life of Great American Cities*, New York: Random House (originally published in 1961).

Jackson, T. (2009) *Prosperity without Growth: Economics for a Finite Planet*, London: Earthscan.

Kropotkin, P. (1955) *Mutual Aid: A Factor in Evolution*, London: Penguin Books (originally published in 1902).

Layard, R. (2005) *Happiness: Lessons from a New Science*, London: Penguin Books.

McKay, D. (2009) *Sustainable Energy – without the Hot Air*, Cambridge: UIT.

Nolan, P. (1995) *China's Rise, Russia's Fall*, London: Macmillan.

Nolan, P. (2012) *Is China Buying the World?* Cambridge: Polity Press.

OECD (Organisation for Economic Cooperation and Development) (1997) *Sustainable Consumption and Production*, Paris: OECD.

Smil, V. (2003) *Energy at the Crossroads*, Cambridge, MA: MIT Press.

Smil, V. (2006) *Energy*, Oxford: Oneworld.

State Statistical Bureau (SSB) (2009) *Chinese Statistical Yearbook*, Beijing: State Statistical Bureau.

State Statistical Bureau (SSB) (2010) *China Statistical Yearbook*, Beijing: State Statistical Bureau.

State Statistical Bureau (SSB) (2012) *China Statistical Yearbook*, Beijing: State Statistical Bureau.

UNCTAD (United Nations Conference on Trade and development) (2010) *World Investment Report*, Geneva: UNCTAD.

Wilson, E.O. (2012) *The Social Conquest of Earth*, New York: W.W. Norton & Company.

World Bank (2008) *World Development Indicators*, Washington, DC: World Bank.

World Bank (2011) *World Development Indicators*, Washington, DC: World Bank.

# Translator's preface

Professor Peter Nolan warned me that this was a challenging book, but I had no misgivings. After all, from my initial reading, I could see how clearly Deng Yingtao expresses himself. I am an experienced translator of non-fiction, so I know all about finding the correct technical terminology. How difficult could this translation be? I soon found out. Deng Yingtao's book posed particular problems for two reasons.

First, as Professor Nolan says in his introduction, 'Deng Yingtao has a rigorous, open-minded scientific approach, drawing freely upon works from different cultures and languages.' Specifically, Deng is not just an economist but draws from different disciplines. This was borne in on me when I looked for economists willing to check specific terms for me. One said: 'My impression is that you need someone with substantial physics rather than an economics background to help you.' So we're talking physics as well as economics? At this point, my heart sank just a little.

Second, there was an additional difficulty associated with terminology.

Some terms that occur in the book are so innovative that they exist in at least two different forms in each language. An example is: 外在不经济性, also written as 外部不经济性. In English, this is referred to as non-economic externality, external diseconomy or negative externality. My experience as a translator tells me to choose the standard, validated term. But what if there is not one standard term? After extensive discussion and some research, I went for external diseconomy. Interestingly, this is an example of how quickly technical language changes. Since I first tackled this term, negative externality appears to have become standard, although external diseconomy runs it a close second.

Deng Yingtao took over my life for a year. But, even as I struggled over yet another complex concept, I still found the labour immensely satisfying. I was never in doubt about the force and cogency of Deng's arguments. They say the translator is the author's best reader. Leaving aside the highly technical aspects of this work, much of what Deng says is applicable to everyday life. Some of his references to life in the West may sound to our ears quaintly old-fashioned – his praise in Chapter 10 of 'the British [who make] each outfit [of clothing] last 8–10 years', for instance. But his arguments against the throwaway society and in favour of making do and mending are not just appealing, they are more relevant than ever today. In fact, 'Deng Yingtao would approve' (or not) has become a bit of a watchword in our household, as we try and fix the dishwasher/kettle/radio in spite of the manufacturers' best efforts to make us buy a new model!

My sincere thanks go to three people whose careful reading of this translation has made all the difference: Brian Heatley, Sharon Liang (梁曉) and Dr Zhang Jin. They did it, I believe, not just because I badgered them but because they were convinced, as I am, that it is important to get Deng's work out there to the English-speaking world.

Any remaining errors are, of course, my own responsibility.

A final note on references:

1 Where a Chinese book is referred to, I have transliterated author and publisher, and translated book title. The Chinese original book name comes first, the transliteration (of the publisher) and translation (of the title) is in brackets.

2 Where a non-Chinese book is referred to, and the original is identifiable, I have given that book name and any other available data first, and the Chinese afterwards in brackets, with name of publishers and date transliterated.

3 Where a non-Chinese book is referred to, and the original is not identifiable, I have followed 1, above.

Nicky Harman[1]
February 2013

## Note

1 Nicky Harman used to lecture at Imperial College London and now works full-time as a literary translator. She has also translated *China Along the Yellow River: Reflections on Rural Society* by Cao Jinqing (Routledge 2005).

# Introduction

Whether China can successfully implement the Four Modernizations[1] and, if so, when and how, are questions that should concern every Chinese citizen.

## The 'three-body' problem[2]

The reality is that the answer to that question is intimately connected to the way China is currently implementing economic reforms; it cannot be answered in isolation. In addition, there are two other basic questions with a significant bearing on the answer. The first is: Which long-term model of development should China choose? This is the subject of this book. The second is: What role should China play economically, politically and strategically on the world stage? To what extent should China be influenced by what is happening in the world, and how should it handle international relations, ensuring that these evolve in a favourable direction towards itself?

What I have called the 'three-body problem' – the combination of the external environment, China's internal structure, and its goals and the direction in which it evolves – directly determines the way in which China modernizes, and the degree of success it achieves. These 'three bodies' are both interconnected and yet have independent content (see Figure 1.1)

For example, even where the appropriate system is in place, it is doubtful whether China can modernize successfully if the appropriate long-term development model is not found. And even if the correct choices are made, significant strategic errors in international relations will make it difficult for China to modernize successfully.

Experience and education have taught us the importance of China's internal structure. However, we are a long way from making the correct choices here and, furthermore, too little attention has been paid to the other 'two bodies'. Of course, it is difficult to evaluate the importance of these other 'two bodies' and the disastrous consequences of strategic mistakes made in relation to them, by looking simply at China's experience. Hence the importance of learning as much as we can from the ways in which other countries have developed historically.

After World War II, many non-Western developing countries adopted what we call the 'classic' development model, used by the Western developed world, in

## 2  Introduction

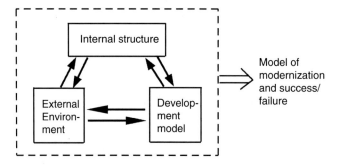

*Figure 1.1* The three-body problem.
Source: Author's own construct.

order to modernize; they adopted a series of development policies such as opening up to the West, attracting international capital, importing Western science and technology and prioritizing economic growth. Led by the United Nations, many Western countries donated significant amounts of aid to non-Western developing countries in the form of technology, capital and resources. Between 1960 and 1970, these recipient countries experienced enormous growth in their economies or, to be precise, in their gross national product (GNP). This rose, on average, 5.2 per cent per year. The figure for developed countries for the same period was 4.9 per cent.[3]

However, one fact is clear: although GNP has grown, there are still structural problems in the economies both of China and globally. This can be seen chiefly in the following areas:

- Even though the gap between a few developing countries and the developed countries has narrowed, it has increased between the vast majority of poor countries and the developed world, both in terms of nominal and of actual income.
- Trade conditions have deteriorated, even for manufactured exports.
- Multinationals originating in the developed world have infiltrated practically every sector of developing economies, and have gained a stranglehold.
- Fluctuations and recessions in developed economies are easily passed on (through international trade and the activities of multinationals) to developing economies where they wreak havoc.
- The debt burden of developing countries continues to grow heavier.[4]

In sum, the course of development of almost all non-Western developing countries in the last 30 years is proof that the 'classic' development model does not work for them. Moreover, it has led to a world economy dominated by the developed West and based on an inequitable international division of labour, which has actually proved a major obstacle to modernization in the developing world.

*Introduction* 3

We can draw several important conclusions in the light of these historical experiences. First, those developing countries that have adopted the 'classic' development model have had poor rates of success. This is true overall, in spite of the fact that they have differing ideologies and economic and political systems, and that many of them have market-driven economies. Thus we can see that the choice of development model has an importance which is independent of, and does not arise naturally from, that country's political or economic system.

Second, we cannot count on developed countries offering genuine, generous aid. Leaving aside ideological, political and economic factors, there exists a tacit agreement between the developed countries to maintain, and indeed to reinforce, the historically unfair international setup which is, crucially, at the core of their shared interests. This is the best way for them to protect their dominant position. No matter how fierce the conflict between them, they will always be unanimous on the need to unite to make war on the developing world. It is totally naïve to believe that the developed countries (with the exception of a tiny number of their politicians) will ever help the developing ones to become stronger. On this crucial question, the vast majority of politicians and industrialists in the developed world have never wavered. Their guiding philosophy is crystal clear – the law of the jungle rules.

Nature provides us with a vivid illustration of how this works, in the example of the hunter and the hunted (for instance, a fox and a rabbit). Thus if developing countries want to make rapid progress towards development, they need to find a way to transform the unfavourable position (that of the hunted) in which they find themselves in the global economy. In the 40 or so years since World War II, the majority of developing countries have had little success in this respect. Even if, to varying degrees, they have opened up their economies (and many have opened up very thoroughly), their position vis-à-vis the global economy has actually grown weaker. There is a profound historical lesson here, which it behoves us to heed: different ways of opening up can have different, indeed completely opposite results. So we cannot simply ask the question whether or not countries have opened up to the outside. The key thing is *how* they opened up; how these developing countries have chosen to deal with global political, economic and strategic relations. Increasing demands for a new global economic order, including what is known as 'South–South Cooperation', show that the developing world is becoming aware of the need to modify the way in which each country opens up to the outside world, to strengthen cooperation, and to break up existing, unfair, global economic relations, which have become bogged down in inertia.

Third, according to the Western theory of modernization, Western and non-Western countries alike pass through the stages of tradition and modernization, the only difference being the time when this happens and how long each stage takes. Dependency theory, however, states that, although Western and non-Western countries both experienced an earlier period when they were 'undeveloped', their paths diverged after the former expanded colonial rule and brought

4 *Introduction*

the latter within their sphere of influence: the West moved from the 'undeveloped' stage to the 'developed' stage and non-Western countries evolved from 'undeveloped' to 'developing'.[5]

This idea can, to a certain degree, can be illustrated by means of bifurcation theory: non-linear systems are very sensitive to initial conditions. That is to say, early-developing countries were subject to particular initial conditions as they underwent the 'classic' form of modernization. However, this very process eliminated the initial conditions of development. That is, after World War II, the initial conditions confronting most developing countries were quite different from those of 100–200 years previously. An important component of the conditions facing the developing countries now is the dominance, in the global economic context, of the developed countries. It can be conjectured that the setbacks suffered by most developing countries during the process of post-war modernization is linked to this dominance.

It follows naturally that, faced with current inequitable global economic relations, developing countries should modify not only the way they open up to the outside world, but also their development model, these two being inextricably linked together.

In brief, developing countries, especially China, face the need to transform themselves in all aspects of the 'three-body' problem – a gigantic task. If we fully absorb the lessons of post-war development and cease to repeat the mistakes of the past, then this will give an enormous boost to the construction of a socialist, modernized China.

## An arduous exploration

The first Chinese studies of development models date to the end of 1984. It was clear at that time that China could not, and should not, go the same way as the developed world and adopt the 'classic' development model. There was also a growing awareness that the development model then current in China, which had as its chief aim the satisfaction of people's basic needs, had drawbacks. It was these basic questions that I felt impelled to research. The reality is, in China's case, that modernization does not mean simply making the choice of goals for development, observing and discarding where necessary, and of the means necessary to achieve them. In order to clarify these issues, we need to reflect on the arduous process of choosing a development model experienced by developing countries in the four decades following World War II.

Put simply, the so-called 'classic' development model is based on the large-scale consumption of non-renewable resources ('stocks resources') and carried out by means of large-scale 'stocks technology'. Its overriding aim is to increase GNP, as a route to achieving national prosperity. This model is regarded as universally appropriate.

Consciously or not, this was the model adopted by most developing countries in the 1960s. Their hope was to industrialize as quickly as possible by raising GNP, because countries that had successfully industrialized earlier had all taken

*Introduction* 5

this route. Very few people were willing to confront the potential risks of this development model.

However, their illusions were soon shattered. The painful result of their endeavours has been that the gulf between developed and developing countries and between rich and poor within the developing countries continues to deepen. A huge disparity in GNP between rich and poor countries already existed in 1960: GNP in the former had reached $2,408 while in the latter it was only $207, only 8.6 per cent of that of the developed world. By 1969, the expected turn for the better had not only failed to happen, the situation had got worse. GNP in the developed world was $3,528, and in the developing world, $275, or 7.8 per cent of the former. This greatly dismayed the developing countries and was also a wake-up call, raising doubts about the suitability of the 'classic' development model.

It is obvious that the reasons why poor countries developed so slowly in the 1960s, and why the gap between rich and poor countries continued to increase, was that the conditions they faced were hugely different and, at the same time, the basic economic and social internal structures of underdeveloped countries were ill-suited to the 'classic' development model.

I have said above that underdeveloped countries made the choice to follow the 'classic' development model after World War II, but that only a few of them achieved notable success and for most countries the attempt ended in failure. As a result, at the beginning of the 1970s, they abandoned this model and switched to a model that had as its main aim the satisfaction of the needs of the majority of their populations. This model, rather than concentrating efforts on raising GNP, focussed on indices such as calorific intake, life expectancy and literacy rates. This focus on satisfying basic needs, rather than competing to overtake other countries in the development stakes, was aimed at leading developing countries back onto a more workable path to development. Success or failure was measured by development indicators, such as the ASHA[6] index.

This index consisted of rates of employment ($A$), literacy ($B$), average life expectancy ($C$), annual increase in GNP ($D$), birth rate ($E$) and infant mortality rate ($F$) and was used to determine how a country should develop and clarify how far it needs to go to satisfy those basic needs. The ASHA index is calculated as follows:

$$\text{ASHA} = \frac{A \cdot B \cdot C \cdot D}{E \cdot F} \tag{1}$$

These six parameters were given specific numerical values, for example: if average annual growth in GNP was 3.5 per cent, employment was 85 per cent, literacy rate was 85 per cent, the birth rate was 2.5 per cent, the infant mortality rate was 5 per cent and average life expectancy was 70 years, then the ASHA index worked out at 1,416. It was suggested that all developing countries should improve their employment, education and health programmes so that they could achieve an ASHA index of 1,416 by the year 2000.

## 6  Introduction

It was pointed out that if developing countries pursued overall development (that is, reforming the social system, achieving social justice, promoting education and sanitation and health care programmes, while at the same time setting appropriate GNP growth targets) instead of focusing exclusively on raising GNP, then a country could achieve an ASHA index of 1,416 with a per capita GNP of only $800. However, if they pursued economic growth to the exclusion of other goals, a per capita GNP of $2,000 was necessary.

In the mid 1970s, international aid organizations, Third World governments and the International Labour Organization (ILO) continually promoted the basic needs agenda, citing impressive levels of average life expectancy, literacy and nutritional status in countries such as Cuba, Sri Lanka and China, to support their case.

However, although investment in health, nutrition, education and housing is vital to the welfare of the poor, developing countries also needed to create the economic basis to fund this investment. Thus, by the beginning of the 1980s, economists had begun to shift the emphasis to economic growth and investment in a variety of areas such as irrigation works and health facilities. This shift in emphasis by no means implied abandoning the 1970s goals of achieving equitable development but reflects growing awareness that it was impossible for poor countries to rely exclusively on the redistribution of wealth to provide rapidly increasing populations with a decent standard of living. In the early 1980s, this realization led the World Bank to turn to growth-orientated models, and the basic needs agenda gradually began to take a back seat.[7]

We can see now that countries that adopted the satisfaction of basic needs development model achieved only a modest degree of success. In general, developing countries have failed successfully to resolve a number of basic problems, especially that of generalized poverty, by following this model. As a result, this development model has gradually lost favour, while an emphasis on economic growth has attracted lively support. Although the latter development model has not achieved the predicted results, I believe that the basic thinking which underpinned it was both positive and rational; it offered, for the first time, an alternative development model that can serve as the precursor to the new development model to be discussed in this book.

Since the 1980s, the emphasis on economic growth has taken centre stage. Both in theory and in practise, it is now fashionable to become a newly-industrialized country. I will subject this to particular analysis further on, and will limit myself here to looking at the results of taking this route.

It was a feature of the world economy in the 1980s that economic conditions in the South continued to deteriorate, and the North–South wealth–poverty divide increased visibly. During this decade, economic growth in developing countries in South Asia, the Middle East, Black Africa and Latin America was slower than in the 1970s; only East and South-east Asia bucked the trend. In many developing countries, current per capita income levels are now lower than in the 1980s, because their population has grown faster than the economy. For example, in Latin America, per capita national income reached $2,010 in 1980, but had

*Introduction*  7

dipped to $1,800 by 1988. In Africa, per capita national income has fallen by over 20 per cent since 1980. By contrast with developing countries, the economies of the North, the developed world, grew for seven successive years after emerging from the recession in 1982. Their national per capita incomes grew by 40 per cent, from $10,650 in 1980 to $14,580 in 1987. During the same period, national per capita incomes in developing countries grew by only 6 per cent, from $680 to $720. If Asia is excluded, then it can be seen that incomes in the remaining countries actually fell. Within the countries of the South, the reasons for economic setbacks can be found in errors in economic development strategies and policies. For example, Latin American countries borrowed recklessly, and although they attempted to deal with this problem in the 1980s by means of a variety of measures, for instance by increasing trade protectionism, these reforms have so far met with limited success due to extremely unfavourable external economic conditions.[8]

After shaking off the energy crisis at the beginning of the 1980s, the industrialized North hardened its attitude to the countries of the South. At the Uruguay Round trade negotiations (1986–94), the developed countries took a tougher line on those areas involving developing countries, such as agricultural and textile products and technology transfer, with the result that North–South trade discussions reached deadlock. In addition, during this decade, developed countries used their more favourable position with respect to international finance, the market, technology, production materials and food to exert pressure on and split the developing countries, forcing the South to increase its dependence on the North.[9]

To sum up, the situation of post-war developing countries proves the accuracy and the importance of the conclusions reached above on the subject of the 'three-body problem'; that is to say, the choice of development model is vital, and a completely separate question from the other two aspects of the problem. If developing countries cannot find an appropriate development model, their future prospects are bleak.

China's situation is somewhat unusual. Its development strategy has undergone repeated changes since 1949. However, there has been a continued emphasis on the satisfaction of basic needs. As in most socialist countries, the planned economy has had notable success in eliminating overall poverty, while at the same time finding itself unable to spread prosperity and to modernize to a high level. Many people have concluded that the crux of this problem lies in the planned economy system. But as we have seen in the preceding analysis, the answer is rather more complex than it appears.

At the present time, over 90 per cent of Chinese people can feed and clothe themselves. For this reason, an economic model which focuses on the satisfaction of basic needs no longer has a role to play, although fundamental thinking on issues raised by this model, such as overall development and appropriate growth, is still very relevant. On the other hand, the sorry outcomes for post-war developing countries that adopted the 'classic' development model should sound a warning to us to avoid recklessly importing the modernization model of Western

8 *Introduction*

developed countries. Thus, we now face a new and important decision: which development model to adopt, in order to achieve a high level of modernization. Are we about to repeat the mistakes of other developing countries? Or can we, exceptionally, achieve modernization through the 'classic' development model? If we cannot, then what is the alternative? It is the chief purpose of this book to analyse these questions and deliver a verdict.

## Overview of this book

This book consists of 11 chapters. Chapter 1 analyses long-term material constraints on the Chinese economy, and the influence of the Western lifestyle, and shows, by means of international comparative research, the impossibility of replying on the 'classic' development model in order to modernize China. In this chapter, I have highlighted basic problems facing China as it chooses a new long-term development model while coping with the twin pressures of material constraints and consumerism.

Chapter 2 considers the characteristics and consequences of the 'classic' development model. Obviously, this step must necessarily precede any comprehensive investigation into a new development model. As this chapter explains, the fundamental flaw of the 'classic' development model lies in its wastefulness, and the squandering of resources to which economic growth gives rise.

Chapter 3 consists of a discussion of categories of natural resources and their technical and social nature and introduces analytical concepts necessary to Chapter 4, because the 'classic' development model is based on the particular initial and boundary conditions that obtained when the first few countries industrialized, that is, on the location and availability of natural resources.

Chapter 4 analyses in some depth the genesis of the 'classic' development model, its systemic structure, its operating and adjustment mechanisms, its long-term effects and theoretical underpinnings. It also reveals how the vectors for this development model (the classic combination of the market and private ownership) are flawed with regard to allocation and use of resources. That is to say that the vast discrepancy in order of magnitude between the human timescale and the geological timescale in which stocks resources are formed, and the grave consequences which follow from this. (The current system for the distribution of resources basically has no mechanism for showing this discrepancy.)

Chapter 5 explores the meaning of entropy, and uses it as a basis to discuss the relationship between the 'classic' development model and the natural environment. This analysis demonstrates how industrialized societies characterized by excessive growth in man-made material wealth have damaged the water and biological cycles of the natural world; they cannot avoid the constraints of the second law of thermodynamics and stagnation.

Chapter 6 provides a detailed explanation of the 'classic' development model, which has GNP as its core national accounting unit, and points out that much so-called 'progress' is actually achieved by means of deficit spending. It criticizes some of the more contemptible cultural aspects of the Western development

*Introduction* 9

model. This chapter also looks at the basis for a new development model in terms of resources and technology, and its interrelationship with ancient civilizations.

Chapter 7 analyses in detail the micro-foundations of Engel's Law, drawing from it some useful analytical concepts and conclusions that prepare the ground for discussion in the following chapter.

Chapter 8 provides the philosophical background and theoretical basis for a new development model and makes two key deductions: a generalized Engel's Law and a principle of equivalence. We can draw from these the compelling conclusion that a developing country like China, now that it has satisfied the basic needs of its people, can actively choose satisfactory ways of keeping material consumption relatively low without affecting the levels or quality of development for the country and its people.

Chapter 9, having drawn conclusions at the practical level in connection with the new development model, attempts to measure what is happening on the ground in China against four rules, and to offer principles, directions and standards applicable to China. This chapter derives a general energy-matching rule and, additionally, analyses and assesses the problem of making a match between our goals and the means of achieving them.

Chapter 10 proposes a strategy for implementing a new development model in China at the practical levels of food and clothing, housing, transport, consumer products, medicine, agriculture, industry and the service sector, and provides a detailed comparison with China as it is today, on the basis of ten indicators of modernization. This is followed by an analysis of the two weakest links – the service sector and urbanization – and of how urbanization will happen in the future. The chapter concludes that it is essential that we put our faith in facts and science, and sustain long-term efforts in the social, political, economic and cultural domains.

Chapter 11 summarizes the basic structure and characteristics of the new development model under seven headings, and proposes some methods and principles that China should adopt in the future. Finally, this chapter briefly discusses the most important means by which we may realize our ultimate goals and some common attitudes that may impede our progress.

## Notes

1 Defined by Zhou Enlai in 1963: *Agriculture, Industry, National Defense and Science and Technology. Trans.*
2 A term from mechanics: in its traditional sense the three-body problem is the problem of taking an initial set of data that specifies the positions, masses and velocities of three bodies for some particular point in time and then using that set of data to determine the motions of the three bodies. *Trans.*
3 嚴立賢:〈依附理論述評〉,《國外社會科學》 1988 年第 4 期, 第 13 頁。 (YAN Lixian, 'On dependency theory', in *Foreign Social Sciences*, 1988 issue 4 page13).
4 Ibid., page 18.
5 Ibid., page 13.
6 Possibly referring to an index adopted by the World Health Organization and proposed by the American Social Health Association (ASHA). *Trans.*

10    *Introduction*

7  約翰·斯塔茲、卡爾·艾切爾: 〈農業發展觀的歷史考察〉, 《經濟學譯叢》1987 年第　11 期, 第 42 頁。 (Staats, John and Eicher, Carl, 'A historical investigation into agricultural development', in *Translations of Economics Documents*, 1987, issue 11, page 42).

8  劉昕: 〈南北貧富差距擴大的十年〉, 《人民日報》1990 年 2 月 2 日。 (LIU Xin, 'Ten years of the widening gap between rich and poor', *Renminribao* newspaper, 2 February 1990).

9  Ibid.

# 1  Making a choice under pressure

In the decade between 1978 and 1988, the Chinese economy grew at an astonishing rate, with an increase in GNP of around 10 per cent per annum (around 9 per cent per capita), the highest in the world.[1] These figures mean that China's 1988 actual GNP was double that of 1980, that is, it had doubled two years before originally planned: a truly remarkable achievement. The Chinese economy was able to satisfy the basic needs of its people by about 1984 and thereupon entered a new stage in which consumer demands began to diversify. At that point, China faced a series of key choices, which involved putting short-term issues to one side and giving careful consideration to far-reaching, long-term problems. The most prominent of these, and directly relevant to the choice of a long-term development model, was the need to focus on the form that new consumer needs were taking and the means with which to satisfy them.

At this new stage, in which consumer demand is being formed, two factors are crucial although they have hitherto been given insufficient importance: (1) once a developing country can satisfy the basic needs of its people, it comes under increasing pressure from lifestyle trends in the developed world; and (2) material constraints, which are less noticeable at the low-income stage of a developing country's economic growth, become ever more obvious as that economy expands in size and living standards rise. To cope with this dual pressure, Chinese people will need all the intelligence and energy they can muster in order to develop a unified and far-sighted national consciousness. Whether or not this happens is a matter of great concern to China's long-term development.

There are several reasons why we need to investigate very thoroughly the long-term development model adopted in China: in order to prevent our economy from being dominated by short-sighted thinking, to prevent the limited surplus generated by economic growth being improperly distributed so that there is nothing left to provide a firm basis for future development, and to prevent any negative consequences arising from reforms in the country's economic structure, which could cause China to lag behind and fail to achieve substantive progress in the socialist economy.

## 12 *Making a choice under pressure*

### The flea and the elephant

In order to answer the question of whether China, exceptionally, can achieve a high level of modernization by following the 'classic' development model, I shall use a metaphor:

> It is an experimental fact that muscle force is approximately proportional to $l^2$ where l is the linear dimension of the muscle. The energy produced by a muscle is 'force × segment' and thus proportional to $l^2 \times l = l^3$. Consider a flea. . . A leaping flea can reach a height nearly 200 times its own height. The energy required to do this can be expressed by the formula 'weight x height of leap'. Imagine a giant flea geometrically similar in shape but ten times larger in its linear dimension. The energy required to jump 200 times as high as its own height would be $10^3 \times 10 = 10^4$ times greater than for the ordinary flea. This, however, cannot be done by the giant flea because its muscle strength has increased by a factor of $10^3$ only. Thus it could reach a height of only 20 times its own height. By the same token, a 'supergiant' flea 100 times larger in its linear dimension than an ordinary flea could leap to a height that is only twice its own height despite a tremendous leaping muscle.'[2]

Similarly, a creature with 1,000 times normal linear dimensions will still only be able to jump to a height which is 0.2 per cent of its body height. A cursory look at the numbers involved shows us that the length, width and height of a flea are measured in millimetres, while the dimensions of an elephant are measured in metres. The linear dimensions of the latter are about 1,000 times those of the former; the absolute jumping ability of the elephant is equivalent to the absolute jumping ability of the flea, but the former's jumping ability relative to its body height is only one-thousandth of the latter.

Let us imagine that there are people who do not understand this rule of biology; they might criticize the elephant for having such poor jumping ability by comparison with that of the flea, and urge it to try really hard to overtake the flea since it has much more massive musculature. But the elephant, however hard it tries, will never achieve success and will be reduced to despair at its own inadequacy.

This metaphor is by no means as obvious and laughable as it seems at first sight. In real life, people repeatedly commit this kind of mistake; to put it in everyday language, they add two and two and make five. That is to say, they extrapolate from individual achievements and apply their conclusions indiscriminately to the whole entity. In the Chinese economy, the most obvious example in the last couple of years has been the proposal that China should promote an export-orientated strategy, on the grounds, largely, that the economies of the Asian Tiger countries (Taiwan, South Korea, Singapore and Hong Kong) have boomed as a result of the same strategy.

There is practically no difference between this erroneous analogy and the mistake contained in the elephant–flea metaphor; it even takes the same form. The

*Making a choice under pressure* 13

most obvious problem is this: if we take population as the most basic measure, then the 'Asian Tiger' countries' combined population is lower than China's by a factor of ten. If we take a step back in time, post-war Japan also achieved miraculously speedy economic growth by means of an export-orientated strategy, but Japan's population was smaller than China's by a factor of ten. Thus, proposing that China follow in the footsteps of these countries is equivalent to saying to the elephant: 'if you put all your energies into learning from the flea, you'll be able to jump 100 metres high', and then blaming the beast for failing to perform as well as a flea!

In effect, by the beginning of the 1980s, a number of economists could not see a way forward for the basic needs model, and recommended that under-developed countries adopt a variant of the 'classic' development model, as the newly-industrialized nations had done. From the end of the 1970s to the end of the 1980s, a simple, universal prescription was recommended to under-developed countries globally: imitate the newly-industrialized nations in developing your economies by means of exports. The chief basis for this advice was that from the late 1960s and during the 1970s, Cuba, Hong Kong, Mexico, Singapore, South Korea and Taiwan had all broken into the world market and, by 1978, together with India, provided 70 per cent of all exports of manufactured goods from the developing world. Just as with their exports growth, the growth in their GNP was unparalleled in any other countries worldwide.

It seemed reasonable, therefore, to call on other under-developed countries to follow the same route as the 'Asian Tigers'. Indeed, the World Bank held them up as an example to the second level of developing nations in the late 1970s. Scores of countries made the attempt. But what successes had they achieved ten years later? In 1988, a paper by Robin Broad and John Cavanaugh-O'Keefe called 'No more NICs', which appeared in the American journal *Foreign Policy*, issue 72, analysed this very question.

Broad and Cavanaugh-O'Keefe pointed out that, in spite of the numbers of countries which had adopted this model, the only ones to have achieved some success were Malaysia and Thailand. For the remainder, the model was a dead-end, which was why there would be no more newly-industrialized countries. The reason was that the global economy had undergone profound changes: from the shift in the export market from primary products to synthetic products, through to the intolerable burden of foreign debt, everything led to a global marketplace so saturated that newcomers could make no inroads. By 1988, after eight years of slowing growth in global trade, it was clear that this route to industrialization had failed. According to Broad and Cavanaugh-O'Keefe, World Bank economists had predicted as early as February 1979 that the competition was growing ever fiercer, making it even more difficult for latecomers. In other words, the few countries that would succeed would not leave any opportunities open for other countries.

It was Broad and Cavanaugh-O'Keefe's belief that the World Bank was pitting developing countries against each other as they struggled to enter the ranks of the newly-industrialized nations. This led to fierce competition in two

## 14 *Making a choice under pressure*

areas: (1) developing countries vied to attract the assembly lines of multinational companies away from their competitors by offering lower wages, a more docile workforce and more favourable economic incentives; and (2) there was a struggle for the few remaining export markets, which meant that multinationals found themselves in a favourable bargaining position when seeking the most attractive investments and sub-contracts, thus encouraging increased exploitation of the local workforce.

Still more disappointing was the fact that, according to a detailed analysis of sub-contracting in the electronic industry, the long-term outlook, in 'net appreciation' figures, for industrial production in developing countries was bleak. For example, from 1977, the value added to electrical appliance prices increasingly went into the pockets of foreign companies. According to one confidential report, in the Philippines, only 25 cents of every US dollar earned by non-traditional exports remained in the country; the remainder was offset against the cost of paying for imported raw materials. A low level of 'net appreciation' was the harsh reality facing the Philippines in the new international division of labour.

Broad and Cavanaugh-O'Keefe point out that it is vital that worldwide trade, in the light industrial products that drive the growth in newly-industrialized countries' economies, must increase year-on-year. Yet between the end of the 1970s and the beginning of the 1980s, when the developing countries were being encouraged to develop non-traditional exports, those necessary conditions had already ceased to exist. Between 1963 and 1973, global commodity export figures grew on average by 8.5 per cent annually. But starting in 1973, economic development slowed; in that year, the rate of increase dropped to 4 per cent. By 1980, export figures were only 1 per cent up on the preceding year and in 1981, there was hardly any increase at all. More countries were by now fighting over an export market in recession, causing prices on the international market to plummet. The situation deteriorated steadily and by 1986 was very serious indeed. The relative value of developing countries' exports over imports had declined by 30 per cent, while developed countries had profited to the tune of $94 billion. Another problem facing under-developed countries, was the fact that exports were now subject to tight quotas, and this affected 50 per cent of world trade overall. In 1979, one World Bank economist calculated that these protectionist measures aimed to mitigate the effects of economic recession within the country concerned; the so-called 'new trade protectionism' hit clothing, textiles and shoe-making industries hardest. These were precisely the export sectors, together with wooden furniture, electrical appliances and other light industrial goods, which the World Bank imagined would drive economic growth in the newly-industrialized countries. As a result, for the whole of the 1970s, out of 30 of those countries, only one achieved an annual increase in exports of more than 12 per cent. In the first five years (1980–5) of the World Bank's Programmatic Structural Adjustment Loans (PSALs), only nine countries' exports grew by more than 4 per cent and another nine countries, the Philippines among them, experienced negative growth.

It appeared, at this point, that the success of a few newly-industrialized countries was a one-off. The reason was that something completely new had happened

*Making a choice under pressure* 15

to the world economy: in the concluding part of Broad and Cavanaugh-O'Keefe's article, they point out that the debt crisis arose from an export-orientated development strategy and that this strategy, because it relied on large-scale borrowing to finance the creation of social infrastructure, gave rise to corruption and a drain on capital. For example, in 1982, the net inflow of funds into developing countries was $18.2 billion, but by 1984 this trend was in reverse, and the net outflow of funds had reached $43 billion by 1988. In addition, developing countries' debts grew from $831 billion at the time of the 1982 debt crisis to $1,165 trillion.[3] Second, technical breakthroughs in the substituted products that took the place of Third World raw materials proved a setback to the growth of developing economies. Technical successes in plastics, synthetic fibres, food chemistry and biotechnology were bringing about corresponding, far-reaching changes in the market for raw materials and commodities. These substitute products gradually pushed millions of Third World workers to the margins of the market, thereby further putting the brakes on global demand. Third, new technology was also changing the economies of developed countries; the electronic revolution, the biggest breakthrough for 20 years, was totally different from previous technological breakthroughs, and gave a huge boost to the developed countries' economies. However, this kind of labour-saving technology also pushed up unemployment rates in Western Europe to a 17-year high. The result of these three major changes was that the goods produced by global industry were beyond the purchasing power of consumers. This new kind of saturation in the global economy co-existed with a situation where billions of people had great needs but insufficient purchasing power.

Broad and Cavanaugh-O'Keefe conclude that, with current changes in the world economy, there is an urgent need to re-consider the steps necessary to achieve growth and development. The newly-industrialized countries are a product of a global economy, which was very different then from today's. The scale of those changes is shown by the fact that in the 1980s, it was not possible to replicate their success. Developing countries, rather than being dependent on an unfavourable global environment, would be better off making efforts to reduce that dependency by diversifying their trading partners and products. To do this means cautiously re-adjusting trade relations to bring them in line with internal economic development. If the national economy cannot advance by means of external growth, then it is necessary to strengthen purchasing power within the country. This is a great challenge, which will effectively give a decisive role to social demand. Fulfilling this demand depends, first, on the products produced and the labour available internally; second, on the regional market; only lastly does it depend on the wider global market. In 1987, a United Nations research report provided data on the developing countries that had grown quickest between 1980 and 1985. During these five years, 14 countries' gross domestic product (GDP) exceeded 2.5 per cent annually, and the economic strategies of eight of them focused on the domestic, rather than the external, market.

The reason for quoting so extensively from the above article and its conclusions is that it underscores a fact mentioned above: the sensitivity of non-linear

16  *Making a choice under pressure*

economic systems to initial conditions. That is to say, the internal logic of the 'classic' development model and its variant (as adopted by the newly-industrialized countries) can never be imitated by the vast majority of developing countries because the failure of the great majority is a prerequisite for the success of the few. In the 'classic' development model, the few and the many are mutually inter-dependent elements. A similar phenomenon occurs in the dynamics of animal communities; for example, in the animal world, according to the 'one-to-ten rule', the number of herbivores that predators like tigers (who are at the top of the food chain) can each control is of an order of magnitude of one or two. Imagine the result if rabbits could turn into predators! To put it bluntly, the 'classic' devel-opment model can only accommodate a select few countries; no sooner have a minority of countries taken that route to development than it becomes impossible for the majority to follow them. The route is too narrow and its capacity is lim-ited. Even if, by some lucky fluke, a few later rise to join the ranks, this success cannot be significantly scaled up to include the majority of countries.

The disappearance of the initial conditions that can ensure successful development through the 'classic' model or its variants is by no means the only difficulty facing China. An equally grave problem lies in its huge size. China is 20 times bigger than most great powers, which have populations in the tens of millions, and it is ten times bigger than the few great powers with populations of 100 million or so. This fact alone ensures that China will never be among the lucky few. Let us take this argument further: if China really moves fast and arrives in the first rank of industrialized countries within two or three hundred years, it will mean that America, Europe and Japan no longer exist in their present form. There is only one China on the earth, and, in the world of today, it appears destined to go its own way.

## There is only one China

Any country's economic activity operates within the constraints of its natural resources. Progress in technological advances can alter the extent and form of those constraints, but cannot do away with them altogether. To a certain extent, those resources shape the type of economic activity carried out in the country, ultimately imposing restrictions on what it produces and consumes. In this respect, China faces the harsh test of negotiating between humans and nature.

Table 1.1 compares per capita levels of China's main resources and average levels worldwide. The figures are calculated on the basis of a population in China of one billion, and in the world of 4.5 billion, and date from about 1982.

From Table 1.1, it can be seen that, with the exception of tungsten and rare earths, which are abundant, China has smaller quantities of other resources than the world average. Levels per capita of many resources account for less than one-third of the world average. In respect of resources that can significantly limit long-term economic development, such as fresh water, arable land, sources of energy, iron ore and so on, the per capita figure for China is less than one-half the world per capita figure.

*Table 1.1* Comparison between per capita levels of China's main resources and average levels worldwide (%)

| Resources | China's per capita resources as a percentage of world levels |
| --- | --- |
| Land | 32 |
| Arable land | 32 |
| Forests | 13 |
| Grassland | 33 |
| Land fit for farming, forestry or grazing (including uncleared waste-land) | 31 |
| Forest reserves | 13 |
| Fresh water | 24 |
| Coal (geological reserves) | 47 |
| Exploitable reserves of same | 40 |
| Petroleum (geological reserves) | 32–64 |
| Hydroelectric power (overall reserves) | 61 |
| Exploitable hydroelectric power | 81 |
| Iron ore (proven reserves) | 48 |
| Copper (proven reserves) | 29 |
| Aluminium (industrial reserves) | 33 |
| Tungsten (industrial reserves) | 225 |
| Tin (proven reserves) | 70 |
| Rare earths (industrial reserves) | 338 |
| Titanium (proven reserves) | 100 |
| Nickel (proven reserves) | 25 |
| Lead (proven reserves) | 54 |
| Zinc (proven reserves) | 100 |
| Sulphur (proven reserves) | 85 |
| Phosphorus (proven reserves) | 52 |

Source: 「2000年研究」小組著:《2000年的中國》, 科學技術文獻出版社　1984　年; 國務院技術經濟研究中心《2000　年的中國》研究報告之一: 〈2000　年中國的自然資源〉, 1984 年。(The year 2000 Research Group, *China in the year 2000*, published by Kexuejishuwenxian Chubanshe Publishers, 1984; State Council Technology and Economics Research Centre, China, Year 2000, Research Report 1: 'China's natural resources in the year 2000', 1984).

A line drawn from Heilongjiang province to Yunnan province roughly bisects China, but 90 per cent of the population is concentrated in the half of the country to the east of the line, while most of China's energy resources, especially mineral resources, are distributed west of that line. The latter area consists largely of mountains and valleys, plateaux and deserts so that, although it is rich in subterranean resources, conditions on the surface are harsh. The mismatch between areas of dense population and resources make it extremely difficult to organize production and coordinate economic development, and the problem cannot entirely be solved through large-scale migration.

The per capita availability of fresh water in China is less than a quarter of the figure for the rest of the world; moreover, those resources are very unevenly distributed in terms of where and when they are plentiful and the form they take.

## 18   *Making a choice under pressure*

Geographically, water is plentiful in the southeast, and peters out gradually towards the north-west, where it is scarce. Seasonally, 60 per cent of annual rainfall falls in three to four months in summer and autumn, as rainstorms. As far as the form those water resources take, about 70 per cent of groundwater occurs in the south, which is already rich in watercourses, while in north China there is a serious shortage of groundwater.

When we look at energy and water resources in combination, it is clear that they are unevenly matched. The south, which has abundant fresh water, lacks energy resources and this has held back the development of its economy; while the north is short of fresh water, which means it cannot effectively exploit its abundance of energy. In short, the distribution of water, land, energy, minerals, processing capacity and human resources (both qualitative and quantitative) is both very uneven and very unfavourably matched in China.

Once we have also factored into the equation the continuing degradation of the environment, we can see the physical constraints that China's long-term economic development operates under. While the population is between 600 million and one billion it may still be possible to provide for people's basic needs, while at the same time establishing a basis for industrialization and taking the first steps towards modernization. However, these constraints will seriously limit the ability of a population of 1.2 billion to achieve its aim of $1,000 annual per capita income. Given these circumstances, an exclusive emphasis on short- and medium-term growth in China will inevitably be at the expense of its long-term development. Even if moderate prosperity is achieved, the prospects for China after the year 2000 will be grim, because of wastage of resources – our 'capital'. This is not scaremongering; it is an objective, fact-based assessment.

China has achieved remarkable success hitherto, with economic growth over the last decade topping 10 per cent on average annually. But it has paid an immense price for this growth. In my calculations, in the ten years between 1979 and 1988, taking 1979 as the basis, the cumulative growth of GNP (calculated at the base price) came to approximately RMB 3 trillion. Of this, roughly half, or RMB 1.5 trillion was made up of three components: overseas deficits, i.e. outstanding external debt; borrowing from inherited funds (partial depreciation of state-owned assets converted into consumer funds); and borrowing from our descendants – the environmental deficit. For reasons that will be explored in Chapter 4, net figures for growth during that decade only amounted to about one-half of these gross figures, i.e. the real annual growth in GNP was only 5 per cent. By the end of the twentieth century, if GNP has doubled again and is driven forward by a similar development model to that employed during those ten years, then the deficit will account for approximately RMB 3 trillion. This means that wastage of the 'capital' will also have doubled. China, with its per capita resource poverty and its huge population, cannot support this kind of large-scale deficit spending in the long term.

Thus, when we analyse the important issues in China's long-term development, we must not lose sight of the fact that China and its problems are unique in the world.

## Comparisons and pressures

China is already under pressure from the influence of consumerism in the developed world. The pressure arises from the gulf separating China and the developed countries socially and economically. Since China's Opening-up Policy took effect, this gulf has become apparent to more and more people. When we make a medium- to long- term assessment, we should be fully aware that the consumer pressure inherited with China's economic development model will continue to exist long-term and indeed will become more pronounced.

According to World Bank reckoning, average per capita GNP in China in 1980 was $300 (at the 1980 dollar value). Suppose that China's population in the year 2000 is 1.2 billion, and that GNP then quadruples. Thus, a per capita GNP in China in the year 2000 of $1,000 (at the 1980 dollar value) is approximately $500 if calculated at the 1970 dollar value. This is lower than global per capita GNP in 1960, and is only equal to Japan's per capita GNP at the end of the 1950s. And this assessment may be on the low side.

I have used Zheng Zhuyuan's data[4] to adjust World Bank calculations and estimate per capita GNP in China in 1980 to be $410 (at 1980 rates), or approximately $205 if calculated at the 1970 dollar value. If the above supposition remains unchanged, then by the end of the twentieth century, per capita GNP will be $700, equivalent to world per capita levels of the mid 1960s or Japan's GNP at the beginning of the 1960s. This assessment is accurate, or may err on the conservative side.

According to the above calculations, if we take world per capita GNP in 1960 and 1970 as the base line and top line respectively of China's average per capita GNP in the year 2000, then global consumption at this level will be an intolerable burden on China at the end of the twentieth century (see Table 1.2).

According to Table 1.2, by the end of the twentieth century, and by comparison with world levels of 1960 or 1970, the most serious problems for China will be the shortage of primary energy, electricity, iron and steel, cars, synthetic fibres, sulphuric acid, refrigerators, milk, fish stocks and timber.

As regards primary energy production, if calculations are made on the basis of energy of equal value, China by the end of the twentieth century will still need to have tripled its energy production, even if the benchmark is world energy levels in 1960. Doubling it will not be enough. If the benchmark is world energy levels in 1970, then energy production needs to have at least quadrupled; the same goes for electricity. On the basis of the last few years, it appears that it will be difficult to fulfil this requirement:

- Iron and steel: even if the benchmark is world 1960 levels, China's steel output will still need to be 137.4 million tons by the end of the twentieth century; similarly, car production figures must increase to 5.45 million, yet both these targets seem unattainable.
- Fertilizers: taking 1970 world levels as the benchmark, China's production of nitrogen fertilizer will need to quadruple by the end of the twentieth

*Table 1.2* Comparison between China's per capita 1980 consumption levels and average world levels in 1960 and 1970

| Item of consumption | Unit | World | | China |
|---|---|---|---|---|
| | | *1960* | *1970* | *1980* |
| Gross domestic product | US$ | 610–630 | 889[a] | 210 |
| Per capita expenditure on consumption | US$ | — | 576[a] | — |
| Proportion of urban population | % | — | 36.52[a] | — |
| Daily calorie consumption | Kcal | — | 2.4[a] | 2.465[c] |
| Daily protein consumption | grams | — | 66[a] | 64.4[c] |
| Daily fat consumption | grams | — | 62.2[c] | 29.9[c] |
| *Primary energy production (per capita)* | | | | |
| Solid fuel | Tons standard fuel | 0.6726 | 0.6243 | 0.4480 |
| Liquid fuel | Tons standard fuel | 0.5246 | 0.9456 | 0.1536 |
| Gas fuel | Tons standard fuel | 0.1972 | 0.3624 | 0.0194 |
| Electricity | Tons standard fuel | 0.0314 | 0.0428 | 0.0245 |
| Total | Tons standard fuel | 1.4258 | 1.9751 | 0.6456 |
| *Industry (per capita)* | | | | |
| Capacity of electrical energy generating equipment | watts | 175 | 310 | 60 |
| Electrical energy | kilowatt/hour | 760 | 1368 | 304.56 |
| Steel | kg | 114.5 | 164 | 37.6 |
| Pig iron | kg | 79.8[b] | 118[b] | 38.5 |
| Cars | 10,000 items/100 million people | 54.5 | 80.9 | 2.25 |
| Other: goods vehicles | 10,000 items/100 million people | 12.19 | 18.4 | — |
| Tractors | 10,000 items/100 million people | 3.34 | 4.289 | 3.215 (incl. walking tractors) |
| Sulphuric acid | $H_2SO_4$kg | 15.92 | 23.8 | 7.74 (unconverted) |

*Table 1.2* Continued

| Item of consumption | Unit | World | | China |
|---|---|---|---|---|
| | | *1960* | *1970* | *1980* |
| Caustic soda | NaOHkg | 33.31 | 6.2 | 1.948 (unconverted) |
| Sodium bicarbonate | $Na_2CO_3$kg | 33.79 | 4.59 | 1.634 (unconverted) |
| Nitrogen fertilizer | Nkg | 3.568 | 9.00 | 10.124 (unconverted) |
| Phosphate fertilizer | $P_2O_5$kg | 3.336 | 5.74 | 2.338 (unconverted) |
| Potassium fertilizer | $K_2O$kg | 2.874 | 4.937 | 0.02 (unconverted) |
| Synthetic fibres | kg | 1.094 | 2.24 | 0.456 |
| Cement | kg | 104.7 | 156.9 | 81.91 |
| Confectionary | kg | 18.16 | 20.49 | 2.603 |
| Newspapers | kg | 4.61 | 5.96 | — |
| Radios | 10,000 items/100 million people | 171.06 | 297.87 | 304.34 |
| Televisions | 10,000 items/100 million people | 65.47 | 126.57 | 25.248 |
| Bicycles | 10,000 items/100 million people | 66.23 | 97.64 | 131.95 |
| Sewing machines | 10,000 items/100 million people | 32.16 | 40.38 | 77.8 |
| Cameras | 10,000 items/100 million people | 59.435 | — | 3.78 |
| Washing machines | 10,000 items/100 million people | 39.72 | 68.32 | 2.48 |
| Refrigerators | 10,000 items/100 million people | 40.64 | 78.92 | 5.19 (1984 figures) |
| Watches | 10,000 items/100 million people | 185.05 | 477.69 | 224.47 |
| *Agricultural production (per capita)* | | | | |
| Grain | kg | 318 | 335 | 287 |
| Roots and tubers | kg | — | 126.5 | 29.64 |
| Soybean | kg | 9.02 | 12.85 | 8.07 |
| Other protein products | kg | — | 24.97[a] | 7.79 |
| Meat (pork, beef, lamb) | kg | 20.38 | 23.32 | 12.21 |

(*Continued*)

Table 1.2 Continued

| Item of consumption | Unit | World | | China |
| --- | --- | --- | --- | --- |
| | | 1960 | 1970 | 1980 |
| Milk | kg | 103.93 | 101.2 | 1.86 |
| Eggs | kg | 4.36 | 5.9 | — |
| Fish | kg | 13.05 | 14.48 | 4.56 |
| Cotton (ginned) | kg | 3.6 | 3.24 | 2.74 |
| Wool | kg | 0.835 | 0.765 | — |
| Felled timber | kg | 0.593[b] | 0.653[b] | 0.0546 |

Source: Except where referenced below, the source of these figures is not recorded. I have taken them from 《世界经济统计简编 (1982)》, 叁联书店, 1983年。 (*Concise World Economic Statistics*, Sanlianshudian Publishers, 1983); and 《光辉的 35 年》, 中国统计出版社, 1984年。 (*A Glorious 35 Years*, Zhongguotongji Chubanshe Publishers, 1984).

Notes
a 《世界经济的未来》, 商务出版社, 1982 年。 (*Future of the world economy*, Shangwu Chubanshe Publishers, 1982).
b 《日本一百年》, 时事出版社, 1984 年。 (*Japan: One Hundred Years*, Shishi Chubanshe, Publishers, 1984).
c 《2000年研究》小组: 《公元2000年的中国》, 科学技术文献出版社, 1984 年。 (The year 2000 Research Group, *China in the year 2000*, Kexuejishuwenxian Chubanshe Publishers, 1984.)

century; phosphates must grow more than tenfold, and potassium more than a hundredfold. With respect to synthetic fibres, production must more than quadruple.

- Refrigerators: taking world levels in1970 as the benchmark, China must increase its production fourteen-fold, starting from 1984.
- Agricultural production: China must increase milk production 49 times, fish catches 2.5 times, and timber ten times, compared with world 1970 levels.

The above simple comparisons make it clear that these problems are directly or indirectly connected to the availability of China's national resources. Quantities of energy resources, such as primary energy, chemical fertilizers, synthetic fibres and so on, are linked to the fact that China's petroleum is too small a proportion of its total energy reserves; numbers of refrigerators are linked to the development of electrical power; iron and steel and cars are linked to the distribution and exploitation of iron ore; and agricultural production is linked to the fact that China's per capita figures for arable land, pasture and woodland are low. There is no doubt that the growth of consumerism must exert very considerable pressure on China's physical resource base.

Since the 1970s, world per capita GNP has again risen. We may predict that within the next 10 to 20 years, this rise will proceed at a similar speed to the past. It is therefore clear that pressures on China will be even greater than described above. It should also be pointed out that consumer-focused pressures do not normally come from comparisons with global levels of consumption but rather from comparisons with typical developed countries, with the result that lifestyle discrepancies appear even greater.

If China's per capita GNP reaches $800 by the year 2000, and assuming that after 2000 it doubles every 20 years, and that the population stabilizes at 1.5 billion, then by 2060, per capita GNP will have reached $5,120 (at the 1970 dollar value). That figure is $10,240 when converted to the 1980 dollar value, or a little higher than America's per capita GDP in 1970. Provided that this figure really can be attained, then we can say that China will truly have achieved a high level of modernization.

What is the significance of these hypothesized figures? We need to make comparisons in order to clarify their importance. America and Japan have been chosen for the purpose of comparison, and the basic benchmark is an approximate per capita GNP (or GDP) of $5,000. America reached a per capita GDP of $4,794 in 1970, and Japanese reached a per capita GDP of $4,436 in 1980.

If China achieves a high level of modernization following the American model, then in 2060, Chinese per capita energy consumption will be 10.87 billion tons of fuel, making a total energy consumption of 14.131 billion tons of standard fuel if we calculate the population to be between 1.2 and 1.3 billion. That is equivalent to 2.17 times total world energy consumption in 1970. With regard to raw materials, China's consumption will exceed total world consumption in 1980 by the following amounts: aluminium, 2.5 times; copper, 2 times; iron, 1.7 times; lead,

## 24  *Making a choice under pressure*

1.5 times; tin, 1.5 times; zinc, 1.6 times; chromium, 1.2 times; gold, 1.6 times; nickel, 2.3 times; mercury, 1.5 times; molybdenum, 2.4 times; platinum, 1.8 times; silver, 1.6 times; and tungsten, 1.3 times.[5]

If China follows the Japanese model, then in 2060, Chinese per capita energy consumption will be 4 tons, making a total energy consumption of 5.2 billion tons, equivalent to 80 per cent of total world energy consumption in 1970. If calculated according to energy units of equal value, then it could be higher. With respect to raw materials, China needs more than half, at least, the 1970 total of global consumption.

The above comparisons are with world average levels. The use of such wide-ranging average values sometimes obscures significant structural problems. I have therefore chosen some representative countries and made some comparisons with them at the point at which they achieved per capita GNP (or GDP) of $800. I have chosen those indices on the basis of important problems facing China, which emerge from the above comparisons, and I have used as benchmark countries, Japan, German Democratic Republic (FDR) and the Soviet Union (see Table 1.3).

If we make a further comparison between typical countries in their major aspects, Table 1.3 shows that we come to the same basic conclusions as in Table 1.2 with respect to the most notable indices, such as per capita energy use for the year, per capita volume of electrical equipment, cars and iron output per capita.

Taking Tables 1.2 and 1.3 together, we may conclude that, even to achieve modest levels of prosperity, China cannot continue with the current development model. There are underlying problems that will persist in manifesting themselves as we continue to develop, putting ever more severe constraints on China in the long term.

It is obviously unthinkable that China should follow the American model in achieving a high level of modernization. Even going the Japanese way will be enormously problematic. In terms of energy resources, if we rely exclusively on Chinese petroleum, our geological reserves will be insufficient to last ten years; if we use international resources, the result will be intense competition. If we also bear in mind that the majority of developing countries are following the same model, then it will be clear that this will impose an intolerable burden on the global environment.

Up until now, countries which have achieved a high level of modernization, whether in the East or the West, whether capitalist (like America and Japan) or socialist (like the Soviet Union), and irrespective of their social systems, are very similar in the way in which they consume large amounts of non-renewable resources in order to speed up economic growth. If it is impossible for China to follow this route in the future, then what model can we put in its place?

Currently China, squeezed as it is between the dual pressures of limited natural resources and consumer demand, faces a fundamental choice. There are three scenarios for modernization: (1) to forever teeter at the threshold of success; (2) to adopt short-sighted and passive strategies (this means following in the

*Making a choice under pressure* 25

*Table 1.3* Indices for the FDR, Soviet Union and Japan at the time when they reached GNP or GDP of approximately US$800

| Year in which per capita GNP of $800 was attained<br>Per capita consumption of primary resources | | GDR<br>1950 | USSR<br>1955 | Japan<br>1962 |
|---|---|---|---|---|
| Solid fuel | Tons standard fuel | 2.49 | 1.71 | 0.75 |
| Liquid fuel | Tons standard fuel | — | 0.46 | 0.69 |
| Gas fuel | Tons standard fuel | 0.11 | 0.06 | 0.02 |
| Electricity | Tons standard fuel | — | 0.01 | 0.11 |
| Total | Tons standard fuel | 2.60 | 2.25 | 1.57 |
| *Industrial/agricultural productivity per capita* | | | | |
| Capacity of electrical energy generating equipment | watts | 245 | 200 | 251 (1960) |
| Electrical energy | kilowatt/hour | 930 | 867 | 1277 (1960) |
| Steel | kg | 253 | 230 | 235 (1960) |
| Pig iron | kg | 198 | 169 | 131 (1960) |
| Cars | 10,000 items/ 100 million people | 63 | 22.7 | 51.2 (1960) |
| Of which: goods vehicles | 10,000 items/ 100 million people | 18.6 | 20.4 | 33.6 (1960) |
| Consumption of fertilizer (100% discount) | kg | 29.8 | 12 | 19.5 (1960) |
| Synthetic fibres | kg | 3.38 | 0.54 | 5.87 (1960) |
| Refrigerators | 10,000 items/ 100 million people | — | 24.7 (1960) | 96 (1960) |
| Confectionary | kg | 21.3 | 18 | 1.59 (1960) |
| Production of raw timber | Cubic metres | 0.54 | 1.7 | 0.74 (1960) |

Source of data: Apart from figures on Japan's energy, taken from 《日本一百年》, 时事出版社, 1984 (*Japan: One Hundred Years*, Shishi Chubanshe, Publishers, 1984) other figures have been taken from 《國際經濟統計資料(1950-1981)》中國統計出版社, 1982 年12月。 (The National Statistical Bureau, *International Economic Statistical Data*, Zhongguotongji Chubanshe Publishers, December 1982).

footsteps of developed countries – and will inevitably require China to perform a volte-face in the not-too-distant future, for which the country will pay a heavy price); and (3) to be prepared henceforth to make gradual, far-sighted adjustments in the development model it adopts.

Is China capable of implementing the third choice successfully?

## Notes

1 喻權域、李曉崗: 〈析人均國民生產總值三百美元〉,《人民日報》 1990 年 1 月 22 日。 (YU Quanyu and LI Xiaogang, 'An analysis of $300 per capita GNP', *Renminribao* newspaper, 22 January 1990).

## 26 *Making a choice under pressure*

2 楊紀坷等:《生物數學概論》, 科學出版社 1982 年 9 月, 第 70 頁, (YANG Jihe *et al.*, *The Mathematics of Biology*, Kexue Chubanshe Publishers, 1982: 70, translated from Batschelet, Edward, *Introduction to Mathematics for life scientists*, 1979: 96).

3 劉昕: 南北貧富差距擴大的十年〉,《人民日報》1990 年 2 月 2 日。 (LIU Xin, 'Ten years of the widening gap between rich and poor', *Renminribao* newspaper, 2 February 1990).

4 鄭竹園:《臺灣海峽兩岸的經濟發展》, 臺北市聯經出版事業公司 1983 年, 第 181 頁。 (ZHENG Zhuyuan, *Economic Development on Both Sides of the Taiwan Straits*, Taibeishilianchuban Shiyegongsi Publishers, 1983, page 181.) This book uses American CIA figures, which state that American GNP in 1980 (at the 1980 dollar rate) was $538. I believe this figure may be on the high side, so I have taken the mid–point between this and World Bank calculations, giving a figure of $410 (Author's note).

5 *The Limits of Growth* Donella H. Meadows, Dennis L. Meadows, Jørgen Randers, and William W. Behrens III, published by the Club of Rome, 1972. (米多斯等:《增長的極限》, 商務印書館 1984 年 [Shangwuyinshuguan Publishers, 1984]).

# 2 Detrimental effects of redundancy

Before investigating a model for China's long-term economic and social development, it is worthwhile giving serious consideration to the 'classic' development model adopted by the developed countries; many Chinese have fastened on to this model, convinced that is the only way forward.

## Pause for thought

Hitherto, all countries achieving a high level of modernization, whether in the East or the West, whether they are capitalist or socialist, no matter what their social system, their culture, their natural reserves or their historical starting-point and patterns of consumption, are similar in two respects: they squander non-renewable resources and their materials economy grows at an ever-increasing rate. The governments and people of almost all developing countries have put their faith in this model of development. This is their Holy Grail, the means by which, they believe, they will overtake the developed world.

Yet there are increasing numbers of doubters, who are challenging this model as a result of previously unforeseen outcomes and pressing problems that have arisen. This is illustrated in a mass of evidence from Western analysts who have studied developed countries.

## Excessive nutrition

Less than 20 per cent of the entire amount of energy expended on food in America goes into grain production. The remaining 80 per cent is expended on the multiple links in the food chain – processing, packaging and distribution.

Jeremy Rifkin in his book, *Entropy: A New World View*, vividly illustrates this by analysing the entire 'life cycle' of what Americans call the 'English muffin', from production to consumption. Each muffin undergoes 17 industrial processes and yet each serving of muffin only contains 130 calories.[1] The entire procedure not only consumes countless calories of energy, it also produces a food product that may seriously damage people's health because it is loaded with chemical additives and lacks cellulose. At the same time, the energy introduced in its manufacture is negligible compared to the energy wasted at each stage of the production process.

## 28  Detrimental effects of redundancy

Every year, American food is supplemented with $500 million's worth of chemical compounds in the form of food additives – 2,500 different kinds of them. In 1979, every American consumed on average 7 lb in weight of food additives, double the figure for 1970. Currently, four million pounds of food dye is added to food annually, 16 times the figure for 1940. This year, Americans will eat more synthetic and artificial foods than what Rifkin calls 'the real thing'.[2] And the working time (the human energy) directed to ensuring that prices for specially manufactured products continue to rise, will exceed that saved in the kitchen.

In contemporary society, the majority of work is done sitting down and our calorific intake is rarely needed to maintain the body's temperature, because houses and factories are heated. However although most people would, in theory, like to consume fewer calories, they find high-calorie foods irresistible and maintaining a calorie balance very difficult. It is clear that the biggest culprits in this respect are the large amounts of highly-processed, high-fat (and/or sugar) foods and alcoholic drinks, as well as certain basic foodstuffs like meat and cheese, which they eat.[3]

Fat and sugar are not only high in calories, but have a nutritional content that bears no comparison to their calorie content. For example, chips contain more calories than plain potatoes but their nutritional content is quite low. There are now even special terms that apply to this feature of highly-processed foods: 'useless calories' and 'junk food'. Obviously, eating such food in large quantities provides an excess of calories and insufficient nutrients. However, statistics show that the proportion of highly-processed food consumed by Americans is on the increase. In addition, although meat and cheese products are rich in protein and other nutrients, they also contain large amounts of fat (and this includes lean meat). Thus, eating a lot of meat and cheese can lead to a calorie imbalance.[4]

The ill effects of obesity and other nutritional problems, such as dietary imbalance, are a general matter for concern in America. A report of the US Senate Select Committee on Nutrition and Human Needs expressed serious concern, pointing out that food available in America was generally high in fat, sugar and salt and that this was linked to high blood pressure, heart disease, stroke, certain cancers and diabetes. The report urges the public to eat more cereals, fruit and vegetables per day and to cut down on fat, sugar and salt.[5]

An equally persuasive reason to eat more fruit and vegetables and less meat is that the environmental price paid for meat production is very high. In America and other wealthy countries, livestock is reared largely on cultivated products, such as maize and soy beans. In America, over 90 per cent of grain production goes into feeding cattle, pigs and poultry. In other words, America's annual meat consumption requires more than 200 million tons of cereals per year, equivalent to one ton per person. In the process of turning cereals into meat, approximately 90 per cent of what is effectively food, is wasted. As far as sustaining human life goes, there is absolutely no need to waste 90 per cent of what could be eaten. It is similarly unnecessary to expend resources on this kind of supplementary production, which has such a damaging effect on the environment. If individuals make the choice to reduce their consumption of meat products, on the other hand, this is both effective in countering global warming and beneficial to their health. To sum up, the diet of third-level consumers, those who eat herbivores, is an enormously wasteful luxury. With an ever-increasing world population and ever-decreasing resources, it is doubtful whether we can afford such a luxury in the long-term.[6]

### 'Car erosion'

American consumers spend one-quarter of their income on cars, which is more than they spend on food. American transport industries swallow up 41 per cent of the nation's entire energy consumption. The car industry consumes around 20 per cent of America's steel, 12 per cent of its aluminium, 10 per cent of its copper, 51 per cent of its lead, 95 per cent of its nickel, 35 per cent of its zinc and 60 per cent of its rubber.

It has been said that, although cars reduce the time it takes to get from A to B, most people do not use cars to save time going to and from the office or when shopping, but to enable them to live ever further away, so that their journey time does not change. In short, they save no time at all.[7] One does not know whether to laugh or cry.

Second, the death toll and damage caused by cars is truly frightful. Traffic accidents claim 55,000 lives annually, and five million people suffer long-term injury. The American National Safety Committee estimates that the number of people who have died under the wheels of a car exceeds the total number of war deaths for the past 200 years. From an economic point of view, the loss of life due to road accidents costs ten times as much as other forms of violent crime. In 1975, expenditure on social damage including cars reached $37 billion. Cars also cause serious damage to the environment. Massive road development schemes have taken over 30 per cent of the land in 53 urban centres in the USA. In the commercial districts of Los Angeles, around two-thirds of the land has been designated as parking lots or driving areas. Planners looking at wastage in urban transport systems have coined a new term: 'car erosion'.

Finally, pollution must not be ignored. America's 150 million cars emit energy in the form of a combination of $CO_2$, nitrogen oxide and hydrocarbons. Today, 60 per cent of air pollution in American cities is caused by vehicle emissions. It has been estimated that in 1971, damage to buildings and property caused by air pollution totalled $10 billion. There is a recognized link between the rise in the numbers of deaths from heart disease and cancers, and air pollution caused by vehicle emissions.

Today, it is high-energy transport systems that are chiefly responsible for the fragmentation of society and the exhaustion of energy reserves. If we do not want to see societies destroyed and our countries' very existence threatened, then we cannot continue to tolerate this reckless destruction.

### Urban expansion

Cities today have expanded well beyond the production capacity of energy resources in their locality. This means that, once the limits of the energy base

## 30  Detrimental effects of redundancy

both within a country and internationally have been reached, they may very well collapse. This is quite clear as far as urban food needs are concerned. A typical city of a million inhabitants requires four million pounds of food daily. For this, it is obliged to rely on agricultural systems based on fossil fuels, yet those very fuels are in decline and becoming more expensive. Thus modern cities – dependent as they are on petroleum-based agricultural systems – are under threat.

In America, the building and maintenance of buildings (mainly in big cities) demands 75 per cent of national electrical power, with a quarter going on lighting alone. Without access to energy, cities will decline, their inhabitants will lose their jobs and urban life will become intolerable.

However, bringing the necessary energy into cities causes enormous environmental change; the average annual temperature of a large city is 3–4°C higher than the surrounding countryside, as a result of thermal pollution and sunlight reflected off highways and buildings. Air pollution in cities is more than ten times higher than in the countryside. High-level energy consumption in cities, and the waste it produces, has a serious effect on city dwellers' health. Compared with populations living in low-energy-consuming environments, city dwellers also display much more anti-social behaviour.

### *The paradox of medical treatment*

Nowadays, health is the third biggest industry in America, taking up 9 per cent of its GNP. A large part of the $150 billion invested in medicine goes to purchase ever more complex and sophisticated technical equipment. Modern hospitals and clinics are stuffed with diagnostic equipment and patients find costs of their health care soaring. Between 1950 and 1976, per capita medical expenses grew from $76 to $552 ($230 if calculated at the 1950 dollar value, but this still represents a doubling of the cost).[8] Yet, as we will see below, life expectancy during this period scarcely changed. The growth in costs of personal medical care can be attributed in large part to the increasing cost of maintenance of medical institutions.

In fact, a temporary remission of the disease after a medical procedure often brings in its wake long-term medical problems. Part of the reason is that 75–80 per cent of those who consult a doctor have an illness that will either heal itself, or cannot be treated. Yet doctors still operate and prescribe drugs, which can cause the patient more suffering than before they started treatment.

Every 24 (or 36) hours, between 50 and 80 per cent of Americans will take a dose of a medically prescribed drug. These drugs may relieve the immediate symptoms, but in the long run, they will inevitably cause major side effects. Antibiotics are the most obvious example of this. They kill all germs, but in the process they destroy many organisms within the body that are crucial to the maintenance of health. Vaginitis, digestive tract infections, vitamin deficiency and other disorders can all be blamed on the continuous use of antibiotics. Over-use of these drugs has also led to an increase in drug-resistant strains of bacteria.

Antibiotics are only one part of the problem. An exhaustive report by a US Senate Committee in 1962 revealed that of 4,000 drugs sold legally in the previous 24 years, almost half were not medically proven remedies. According to some researchers, deaths from 'secondary disorders' brought on by medicinal drugs exceeded those from breast cancer. Some researchers believe that the side effects from medicinal drugs constitute one of the ten main causes for hospital admissions and are responsible for 50 million admissions annually.

Life expectancy statistics are often drawn on to prove the great achievements of modern medicine. In fact, the latter has proved markedly ineffective in eradicating the main killer diseases. Researchers have shown that in the past 150 years, the main factors that have helped to extend longevity are improved sanitation and hygiene and improvements in diet. The main reason for the fall in America's mortality rate since 1900 has been the eradication of 11 main contagious diseases. And apart from influenza, whooping cough and polio, the others were all in decline long before the intervention of modern medical treatments.

Average life expectancy in the USA continued to rise until 1950, after which it stabilized. Today, at least among men, it is reckoned to have fallen. The interesting thing is that this reversal is occurring precisely at the time when high-tech medical care has really taken off. In a highly industrialized environment, the main reason for disease lies in environmental pollution caused by non-renewable energy sources and fossil fuels.

### Depletion of mineral reserves

In 1974, every American consumed on average 10 tons of mineral resources, of which 1,340 lb were metal and 18,900 lb were non-metallic minerals. Every American consumes, on average, 700 tons of mineral products in his/her lifetime, of which 50 tons are metals. If fossil fuels and timber are factored in, average per capita consumption doubles to 1,400 tons, and this does not include water and food requirements.

It is clear that the world cannot bear the burden of another America, and can scarcely even support one America. Generally speaking, the global average per capita calorie consumption is 2,000 Kcal daily. However, per capita daily consumption in America (including not just food but also cars and electricity) has actually reached 200,000 Kcal, or 100 times the amount required. Even when America only had a population of 225 million, its population consumed the energy needs equivalent to that necessary to sustain a population of 22 billion.[9]

A redundancy rate of 100 times may not be detrimental, indeed may have many advantages, assuming that we ignore the possible side effects (disease caused by over-eating, environmental pollution and so on), in a situation where mined resources are limitless. However, the question of whether natural resources are in fact infinite has frequently aroused fierce controversy. On one side of the argument are the 'limits to growth' theorists and on the other are advocates of 'abundance theory'. An analysis of each point of view follows.

## 32 *Detrimental effects of redundancy*

## The rights and wrongs of the matter

'Limits to growth' theorists point out that the Earth has physical limits, and we cannot continue to exploit it endlessly, otherwise, sooner or later, its natural resources will be used up. Advocates of 'abundance theory' acknowledge the logic of this argument but point out that the Earth is enormous and contains such large amounts of minerals that they cannot be used up. Who is right? Nebel has carried out a detailed analysis of this question in his book *Environmental Science: The Way the World Works*. Let us look at what he says.

### *Total quantities of natural resources and their usability*

It is important to realize that the different elements which make up the Earth are not all equally abundant. Analysis shows that 90 per cent of the Earth's crust is made up of only eight elements – oxygen 46.6 per cent, silicon 27.2 per cent, aluminium 8.3 per cent, iron 5.8 per cent, calcium 3.6 per cent, sodium 3 per cent, potassium 2.6 per cent and magnesium 2.1 per cent. These percentages are known as the 'average abundance of the Earth's crust' (AAEC). It should be noted that iron and aluminium are over 1 per cent, but mercury, gold and silver constitute under 0.1 ppm (parts per million). However, the Earth's crust is enormous and even where individual elements make up only a tiny percentage of the AAEC, they can be present in substantial amounts. For instance, gold makes up only 0.0035 ppm of the AAEC, but that represents 47 billion tons of gold, or around 10 tons per capita globally. Looked at from this point of view, even the scarcest element that exists in the smallest amount should suffice at least for the foreseeable future.

However, there is a huge difference between calculations of abundance and the usability of those resources. It is important to acknowledge that the AAEC is just that – an average. For example, 70 per cent of iron reserves are made up of hematite, of which there are huge deposits in the western part of Lake Superior. Minerals in other places contain very little iron or none at all. A similar situation exists for other elements, especially rare elements. It is vital to underline this point: there is an abundance of deposits in certain areas, but they are by no means evenly distributed throughout the Earth.

It is a fact that, as the quality of ore declines, the costs of extracting and smelting it rises; when the costs have reached a point where they exceed the value of the ore extracted, then profits and losses are reversed and the ore is no longer of any value for the economy. Thus, in general, the quantities of any economically exploitable elements are far, far smaller than the overall quantity of that element as calculated in the AAEC. On the other hand, where products are in short supply, prices will rise commensurately, and technology can reduce the costs of extraction and processing. In this way, the lowest grade of ore, or the deepest and most remote mineral deposits, can become economically viable so that former losses can be turned to a profit. For example, in 1900, the lowest viable copper-containing ore was 3 per cent copper, whereas now, copper can be extracted from 0.35 per cent ore. Thus, the ability to mine low-grade ore can significantly expand this resource base. 'Abundance theorists' argue this in order to rebut the 'limits to growth' theorists' prediction that natural resources are finite; that is, they insist that even though exploitation continues to increase, usable resources will always increase rather than decrease because of economic factors and technological advances.

In contrast, the 'limits to growth' theorists believe that the resources base cannot be extended ad infinitum. Their reasoning is as follows: first, it is too glib to say that that as the quality of the ore declines so the quantity of the ore will necessarily increase. They cite copper as one of several examples: when reserves of 1 per cent copper ore are exhausted, we should turn to 0.3 per cent copper ore, but there is only one-quarter the quantity of this ore, containing only one-fifteenth the amount of copper. As a result, when we begin to exploit 0.3 per cent copper reserves, it will only increase copper deposits by less than 10 per cent. Furthermore, if it becomes economically viable to mine 0.2 per cent copper ore, this will only increase copper deposits by less than 1 per cent.

There is therefore a huge discrepancy between viable low-grade ore and the 'limitless' deposits promised in the AAEC. If we take other important elements into consideration, then this discrepancy is even more apparent. For example, the AAEC figure for gold is 0.0035 ppm, but economically viable grades of gold amounted (1975 figures) to 0.0035 parts per thousand. That means that the ratio of viable grade ore to AAEC is 1:1,000 or, in other words, ore containing less than 0.0035 parts per thousand is economically valueless. It is only with the most ordinary elements, such as iron and aluminium, that we can continue to enjoy 'infinite' supplies by dint of continually increasing the amount of low-grade ore we exploit. These infinite supplies exist in the AAEC. Where this kind of geological transformation is absent, it is hard to see how economic trends or technical progress can bridge the gap between exploiting low-grade ore and infinite quantities of ordinary rock, which only contains trace quantities of the abundance of the Earth's crust.

Second, even if we discount economic factors, it is not viable to obtain the necessary quantities of these elements by means of extracting vast quantities of trace-containing ordinary rock. That is to say, in the process of extraction, huge amounts of energy and/or materials will be necessary, and the sums must add up: what is produced must exceed what is consumed, that is, there must be a net gain. For example, the extraction of petroleum requires large amounts of energy in the drilling of wells and other steps; at the point when this energy equals the energy obtained, the petroleum can only be considered as exhausted, irrespective of how much oil the oilfield contains. This is because no matter what the price and the costs are, they have no meaning when the energy expended is greater than the energy obtained. Another example: the mining of tungsten ore requires tungsten to be consumed (wear and tear and damage to the tools uses up some tungsten). If the tungsten ore obtained is of a reasonably high grade, then there will be a net gain. But if the ore is only present in trace quantities or in quantities near to the AAEC figure, then the extraction will produce a net loss, that is to say, the tungsten used up will exceed that extracted. In this case, the tungsten reserves

34  *Detrimental effects of redundancy*

are not viable. An infinite supply of cheap energy could prevent natural resources drying up in this way. However, it is very clear that future energy reserves are not inexhaustible, nor are they cheap, and these two factors will limit the production of many resources.

Third, waste disposal is a particularly important factor. As the grade of the ore declines, the amount of waste produced increases many times over. Long before the exploitation of non-renewable resources reaches its limits, its harmful effects on soil, air and water may well have reached intolerable levels. This situation has forced people to choose between increasing this exploitation and protecting the environment. Thus, effects on the environment effectively limit the use of the lowest-grade ore reserves.

In conclusion, it appears most probable that long before natural resources are actually exhausted, a number of factors, singly or in combination, will have put a stop to the extraction of those resources.

### Discovery, substitution and re-use

The unfavourable forecast above has had little impact on the 'abundance' theorists. For a start, they hope (indeed insist) that new, high-grade ore deposits will be found. Unfortunately, however, this looks increasingly unlikely, for the following reasons: if we were to take a piece of paper and draw a series of black dots of varying sizes on it to represent the size of ore deposits, and if we were to roll a dice onto this piece of paper, we would probably hit the biggest dots first. In terms of natural resources, this means that even though we may come across randomly scattered ore deposits, we would have a far greater chance of lighting on those main deposits discovered a long time ago. In fact, the latter is far more likely both because the ore is not randomly distributed and because, unlike when we throw a dice, our search is not random. There is a great deal of knowledge of the Earth's chemical processes that can lead us to rich mineral deposits, so that we know where to start exploration first. As a result, the probability of discovering major new deposits continually diminishes. In fact, in the last 30 to 40 years, the growth in our natural resources base has been achieved through low-grade deposits. Almost no new rich deposits have been found.

The seabed is an exception to this rule, because it has not yet been exhaustively explored. Recently, it has been discovered that a huge area of the seabed is covered with manganese nodules, rich in manganese, copper, nickel and other metals. However, exploiting these reserves will have to operate within the constraints of the energy supply and/or pollution produced during the process of transporting the ore from the mining site.

However, the main reason for refuting the argument that the discovery of new reserves will have a major part to play in development is the following: even if new reserves are discovered, they will be unlikely to change the basic situation. For example, as the *Limits to Growth* authors point out, even if new discoveries amount to twice (or ten times) the amount of known reserves, they will only last for ten (or 40) years, assuming an annual growth rate in the consumption of resources by the economy of 7 per cent. No matter what the quantity of new natural resources, the exponential growth in development will, in a very short space of time, reduce us from a situation of plenty to one of disastrous shortages.

'Abundance theorists' have rebutted this by saying that in the event that a natural resource is exhausted, then substitution may be possible, i.e. people can switch to the use of a more plentiful resource. This has actually happened in the past with, for example, synthetic fibres, manufactured from then-cheap and abundant petroleum-based resources, taking the place of natural cotton fibre.

However, it is unreasonable to assume that every time a natural resource is exhausted, it will be possible to substitute another cheap and plentiful resource. This assumption presupposes that people always start by using the scarcest resource and progress towards use of the most plentiful resource (even though history contradicts this). What is much more likely is that future substitute products will become ever scarcer and more expensive, and will be subject to strict legal controls. For example, now that petroleum reserves are being used up, timber is being considered as an energy substitute and also as a substitute for plastic and synthetic fibres. Even leaving aside other problems if forests, which have been established on the basis that they will produce over a very long period, are used as a substitute for petroleum, they will only be able to satisfy a small proportion of today's needs.

In addition, many other resources will run out, including nitrates, tungsten and mercury. Each of these has peculiar properties for which there are no substitutes. Thus when reserves have been exhausted, it will be more and more difficult to find substitutes for the uses to which they have been put. Silicon, iron and aluminium are so plentiful that they have always been regarded as inexhaustible, yet there are limits to the uses to which these elements can be put. In fact, iron and aluminium are nowadays mixed into alloys, that is, other elements are combined with them to give the properties needed by humans. For example, 10–20 per cent of chromium is added to iron to produce stainless steel. This means that, even if iron and aluminium supplies are inexhaustible, there will be shortages of other metals used in manufactured alloys.

Finally, substituting one material for another does not normally reduce the amount of energy needed during its production. Indeed, energy needs may actually increase rather than reduce. For example, aluminium can easily be used as a substitute for any other building materials, but smelting aluminium is the most energy-intensive of all industrial processes. In the near future, when people are forced to turn to the only resource still plentiful – low-grade ore – the energy needed to smelt aluminium will obviously increase. Thus, with any substitute product, the viability of natural resources may well be dramatically reduced because we lack sufficient energy resources. At the same time, the use of substitutes will result in unacceptable environmental damage, such as the chopping down of all forests for timber.

Supporters of abundance theories often cite recycled and/or renewable resources as a final possibility. Recycling has many advantages: it saves on land and energy, reduces pollution and saves on resources too. Moreover, society

## 36 *Detrimental effects of redundancy*

ultimately will increasingly rely on the re-use of industrial and agricultural products. However, no matter how good recycling is in theory, it does not give us a continually growing quantity of resources. In fact, effective recycling can only double the resource base. For example, if the consumption of resources grows by 3.5 per cent per year, recycling of the same class of resources can only extend the time at which they will be exhausted from 20 years to 40 years hence.

The reason is the following: during the recycling, supplies are sourced from discarded materials, and that source cannot supply more than what has already been used. Thus, unless further natural minerals are exploited, the supplies for recycling cannot grow. If the materials consumed during economic development doubles in 20 years, (that is, there is a 3.5 per cent annual increase in the consumption of natural resources), then only half the increase can come from recycled materials. The other half must be freshly sourced. In other words, recycling can only double the period of use of non-recycled resources and once all usable resources are within the cycle of use, further growth will be brought to a halt.

The argument for recycling also presupposes that it is 100 per cent effective, but actually this is impossible. The reason is the following: a component of the resources used will become products in permanent, or, at least, in long-term use. Thus that component cannot be recycled. Second, even where recycling is attempted, some loss of the resource is inevitable. For example, the mercury in mercury batteries cannot be recovered because collecting such disparate objects together is so difficult that recycling them would not result in a real net yield. Depending on the element and the uses to which it is put, the maximum effectiveness of recycling can be expected to fall within the range of 60–80 per cent. Finally, we should not ignore the fact that the exploitation of all natural resources, whether recycled or not, depends on energy and fossil fuel (currently around 95 per cent of energy is derived from fossil fuel) can never be recycled.

### The facts come to light

The above analysis makes the following very clear: natural resources are not only limited (indeed substantially limited), but, in addition, a continual increase in the use of natural resources cannot be maintained in the long term. Both theoretical analysis and empirical evidence lead to the same conclusion (see Table 2.1).

As Table 2.1 shows, if ten billion people were to consume resources annually between now and 2030 at the rate of current levels of consumption in the USA, most important mineral deposits (calculated according to total reserves) would not last another 50 years; that is, they will exhausted well before the end of the twenty-first century. It is clear that for most of the Earth's inhabitants, the American-style 'classic' model of development is a luxury they cannot afford.

If we also take into consideration the numerous other side effects of this 'classic' development model, such as diseases caused by environmental pollution and over-eating, then America's hundred-fold over-consumption of energy cited above is doubly damaging: it not only consumes large amounts of limited natural resources, which worsens the long-term prospects for humanity, but the side

*Table 2.1* Number of years during which global mineral resources can be exploited

| | Calculations according to current rate of consumption | | Annual consumption of 10 billion people by 2030 at current US levels | |
| --- | --- | --- | --- | --- |
| | Mineable reserves using current technology (mineable years) | Total reserves (mineable years) | Mineable reserves using current technology (mineable years) | Total reserves (mineable years) |
| Aluminum | 256 | 805 | 124 | 407 |
| Copper | 41 | 277 | 4 | 26 |
| Cobalt | 109 | 429 | 10 | 40 |
| Molybdenum | 67 | 256 | 8 | 33 |
| Nickel | 66 | 163 | 7 | 16 |
| Platinum | 225 | 413 | 21 | 39 |
| Coal | 206 | 3326 | 29 | 459 |
| Oil | 35 | 83 | 3 | 7 |

Source: *Scientific American*, quoting from the (British) *Economist* magazine, issue 1, 16 September 1989 (《科學美國人》轉引自英國《經濟學家》, 1989年9月16日第1期。).

effects are also harmful. Obviously, to the extent that we reduce this over-consumption, we will benefit commensurately.

The above analysis has been carried out taking the USA as the model and shows that 80 per cent of American families spend over 70 per cent of their household income on energy, food, housing and medical care. It is very clear from the evidence that there are overall problems inherent in the 'classic' development model, widely respected though it is. Economic demand greatly exceeds reasonable material needs. This demand conceals within it an enormous amount of 'economic' waste – the spendthrift factors in economic growth. The so-called benefits of this kind of waste are greatly outweighed by the harm caused. The reality is that it is possible, by taking appropriate measures, to rationalize and thus vastly to reduce material waste, with all its attendant ill effects, all without lowering people's standards and quality of life.

Why do we have this waste of natural resources, which leads to such inappropriate lifestyles and modes of production? How and why have developed countries taken this route to development? The answer is simple: the 'classic' development model stems from a time when the relative abundance of natural resources concealed the cumulative contradictions arising from spendthrift growth.

## Notes

1 Jeremy Rifkin and Ted Howard, *Entropy: A New World View*, The Viking Press, New York, 1980. (杰里米 里夫金等《熵: 一種新的世界觀》 1987 年, 第 227 頁, 上海译文出版社 [Shanghaiyiwen Chubanshe Publishers, 1987 page 227]).

2 Ibid.

38 *Detrimental effects of redundancy*

3 Nebel, B. J. and Wright, R. T., *Environmental Science: The Way the World Works*, (B. J. 內貝爾:《環境科學: 世界存在與發展的途徑》 1987 年, 第 110–111 頁, 科學出版社 [Kexue Chubanshe Publishers, 1987, page 110–11]).
4 Ibid.
5 Ibid.
6 Ibid.
7 Ibid.
8 《世界經濟統計簡編 (1982)》三聯書店 1983 年, 第 240 頁。(*A Digest of World Economic Statistics for 1982*, Sanlianshudian Publishers, 1983, page 240).
9 Jeremy Rifkin and Ted Howard, *Entropy: A New World View*, The Viking Press, New York, 1980. (杰里米 里夫金等《熵: 一種新的世界觀》 1987 年, 上海译文出版社 [Shanghaiyiwen Chubanshe Publishers, 1987]).

# 3 Breakdown of natural resources

The formation of the 'classic' development model presupposes a unique set of initial and boundary conditions – in terms of resources and their distribution – which obtained during the development of the small number of countries that industrialized first. A thorough appraisal of different categories of natural resources is necessary in order to analyse to what extent this 'classic' development model is dependent on these conditions, what the consequences of this dependence are and the confusion that surrounds these issues.

Resources can broadly be classified into four categories: natural resources, scientific and technical knowledge, human resources (qualitative and quantitative) and capital resources (equipment, machinery and factories). Even though the last two categories comprise, in part, the physical manifestation of scientific and technical knowledge, they still have to be considered independently because, at given productivity levels, part of scientific and technical knowledge exists in stored form, and has not yet entered and taken physical form within human and capital resources.

In order to exist and reproduce, human beings need certain basic things from the natural and biological environment with which they are associated: air, sunlight, water and food, clothing and shelter. And in order to obtain these things, human beings have to carry out certain productive activities; this requires a combination of the four categories of resources listed above. Basically, however, all material things that humans want to obtain and use are produced by means of human labour, which, in turn, exploits, processes or manufactures natural resources. In this chapter, I shall focus primarily on natural resources and discuss the questions that arise.

Human beings need to fully understand technology and the economy (or society) in order to make the best use of natural resources. The three attributes most closely linked to the topic of this book are: renewability, separability and exclusivity. The first of these is an attribute of technology and the last two are attributes of the economy (or society). The combination of attributes that is found in a certain resource depends on the unique nature of the resource: physical, chemical, biological and so on, which in turn determines the specific mechanism by means of which it is put to use.

## 40 *Breakdown of natural resources*

## Renewability

At the technological level, natural resources can be divided into three main types: (1) renewable resources, (2) recyclable non-renewables and (3) non-recyclable non-renewables. According to the law of conservation of matter, any natural resource is composed of matter, and all matter necessarily comes from somewhere and goes somewhere. The only way to sustain material resources indefinitely is to recycle or re-use them in some way.

The term, 'renewable resources' means that the resources can be replenished by means of a relatively swift natural cycle. For example, replenishing the oxygen in air through photosynthesis and replenishing biological products (food, fibres, timber) through the natural cycles of growth and reproduction. In general, the timescale for renewal of these resources is fairly close to a human timescale. In this text, I have called these 'flow' resources.

Recyclable, non-renewable resources include all those non-energy mineral resources deposited within the Earth's crust, for example metal deposits such as copper and aluminium. The mineral content of the Earth's crust is not evenly distributed. It is formed from chemical changes in the Earth, which have taken place over billions of years, producing specific elements and minerals in abundance, and depositing them in certain places. If these minerals are exploited, they cannot be recovered, at least not quickly enough to satisfy the demands of human existence. Thus, looked at from the perspective of a human timescale, they are non-renewable. But, at least in theory, once people have used these materials, they can recover and re-use them.

Non-recyclable, non-renewable resources are energy resources of a mineral nature, that is, fossil fuel (oil and natural gas). The latter currently provide us with upwards of 90 per cent of our energy resources. Fossil fuel is formed of organic matter laid down in a biological and geological process that has lasted billions of years. This is a geological timescale – from the perspective of a human timescale, this fuel is clearly non-renewable. Besides, the formation of certain types of minerals is determined by specific conditions and time periods. Conditions today cannot lead to the deposit of organic matter and its evolution into oilfields and coalfields; thus it is clear that these reserves are limited. At the same time, the second law of thermodynamics shows us that they cannot be recycled either. So if we use fossil fuel for energy, then that energy will be lost forever. Non-renewable reserves are also referred to below as 'stocks' resources.

These three categories of resources are not totally unrelated. For example, in the production of today's farm products (which are renewable), petroleum-based agriculture requires the large-scale consumption of fertilizers, such as phosphates, and these are a non-renewable resource; machinery manufactured from iron and steel, copper and other metals, is used in the production and transport of farm products; energy is extensively used to produce machinery and make it run, in the production of fertilizer and pesticides and the processing of food products. Farm and factory workers, and everyone else, need food and water to survive. When we link all this together, it is clear that when one link in the process is

*Breakdown of natural resources* 41

out-of-kilter, then that can affect the entire system. For example, serious oil shortages will make it impossible for petroleum-based agriculture to properly produce renewable resources.

In theory, renewable resources are infinitely sustainable. But this does not mean that renewable resources will really last forever. The truth is that they are currently in grave danger of running out. This is because the renewing of all such resources is obviously constrained by natural systems. For example, underground water is swiftly renewed by water continuously percolating down into the ground. But in many areas, underground water has dried up because the extraction rate is faster than the recovery rate.

Crucially, renewable resources may be destroyed. For example, good-quality land needs to be protected against erosion by application of appropriate quantities of organic material, to ensure that the soil remains a renewable resource. Denuded, eroded land is not only non-renewable; it continues to deteriorate. Nowadays, because of the large-scale use of non-renewable resources, there is an increasing danger that renewable resources will turn into non-renewables.

Finally, apart from the damage inflicted on renewable resources through direct over-use, they can also be adversely affected, or even completely destroyed, by other elements. For example, air and water can deteriorate as a result of pollution and be rendered unusable. In summary, we can only sustain our use of resources by using the system itself to recycle them. This being so, we need to ensure that we protect the environment by minimizing the inevitable pollution and environmental damage to the best of our ability. This is the only way in which resources can be renewed and made available for our use.

### *Separability*

If we look at resources from the point of view of economic and social use, we can distinguish and study two aspects: separability and exclusivity. These two important concepts formulated by Alan Randall in his book *Resource Economics*,[1] form the basis for each section of this chapter. To put it simply, separability means the following: to the extent that a certain quantity of resources (or goods) are used (or consumed) by certain people, it is inevitable that other people will be able to use less of them. For example if two people have four buns, then each person has two buns. But if one person eats three, then the other person can only eat one. Again, if we take a certain quantity (or quality) of land – a renewable resource: if certain people use more of it, then others will have less to use. When quantities are fixed, the separability of resources means that there is a competitive relationship, i.e. more for you means less for me, and vice versa.

By contrast non-separable goods means that using a certain quantity of goods or resources does not lead to this kind of competition. A non-competitive relationship means that you and I both have plenty. In other words, what certain people consume does not reduce the quantity that remains for others. For example, when you have grasped a certain kind of knowledge and gained a certain degree of satisfaction from it, the fact that others have gained a degree of satisfaction

## 42  Breakdown of natural resources

from the same knowledge will not reduce the satisfaction you have gained. Again, if there is a given quality of air, everyone can breathe it freely and the amount of air available to others is not thereby reduced. When a group of people enjoy a beautiful view in each other's company, the same rule applies. Indeed, being together may heighten the degree of satisfaction felt by each individual.

Figure 3.1 expresses this idea in diagrammatic form. The line $A_1$ shows that 'you get more means I get less', while $A_2$ shows 'when you and I both have plenty' and $A_3$ shows a complementary relationship, 'when you have more, I can have more too'. $A_1$ shows how separable resources are used, and $A_2$ and $A_3$ show how non-separable resources are used.

We can generalize further about non-separability: horizontal non-separability means that when everyone consumes this resource (or these goods) at the same time, there is no rivalry between them; for example, air of a given quality. Vertical non-separability means that different generations can use a certain quantity of resources and there is no rivalry between the generations. For example, when the resources of land and fresh water are sustained within renewable limits, and the older generation uses a lot of water, this does not mean that the younger generation has less water to use. Obviously, horizontal non-separability does not apply to land, while air of a given quality, and sunshine, are both horizontally and vertically non-separable.

In the three categories of resources mentioned above, the concept of vertical non-separability applies to all renewables providing that they are maintained within the limits of renewability. By contrast, only some renewables possess both horizontal and vertical non-separability. Non-recyclable, non-renewable resources are a classic case of separability. As far as recyclable non-renewables go, the concept of vertical non-separability only applies to those resources which can be 100 per cent recycled. Strictly speaking, since this is an impossibility,

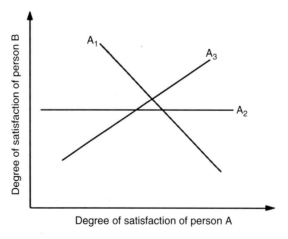

*Figure 3.1*  Three relationships.

Source: Author's own construct.

these must be regarded as separable resources although within a limited time frame they possess weak vertical non-separability (assuming a very high rate of recycling, such as 90–95 per cent).

We can draw the following conclusions about non-separable resources or goods: there is no pricing system that treats everyone the same (see Appendix), which can make the private sector's production of non-separable goods achieve Pareto efficiency. In the non-separable goods economy, the conditions for Pareto efficiency can only be satisfied when perfect price discrimination is enforced for non-separable goods. Generally speaking, it has proved impossible to enforce Pareto efficiency and perfect price discrimination for non-separable goods (see Appendix for an explanation of these concepts).

### *Congestion*

There are certain categories of resources (or goods) where competition between the different users will not appear when the number of users increases from zero to a very large number. Here, 'you have plenty and I have plenty too' still prevails. Thus, in this situation, all resources are non-separable, without distinction. But as the number of users constantly increases until it nears the capacity restrictions for these resources, the phenomenon of congestion makes its appearance. At this moment, if there is a further increase in the number of users, the share of each user in the quantity of resources and the level of satisfaction thus obtained will be reduced. Let us look at a given level of congestible resources: before congestion begins, the marginal cost of adding additional users is always zero (that is, the supplementary cost required to enable the addition of an additional user is always zero). But when the ever-increasing number of users exceeds a certain level, the marginal costs of adding additional users begin to escalate. Finally when the absolute limits of capacity have been reached, the marginal costs of adding additional users become infinitely great (see Figure 3.2(a)). Any resource or good which is provided for the use of many people but then reaches the limits of capacity, can be described as congestible where, before those limits are reached, the fixed costs of supply far exceed the marginal costs of adding additional users.

Figure 3.2(b) shows how, within the limits of capacity, congestible resources are characterized by, 'you have plenty, I have plenty too' (unrelatedness) or even, 'you have more means I have more too' (complementarity). But once the limits of capacity are exceeded, the situation where 'you have more means I have less' may arise (competition or substitution). Congestible goods or facilities include roads, bridges, ports and airports and almost any services within an enclosed space supplied to the general public, such as restaurants, musical entertainments and so on. Many natural or environmental enjoyments are characterized by congestibility, such as bathing places, scenic spots, architectural remains, and lake-fishing, hunting and skiing areas.

Readers will easily see from the above analysis that non-separable and congestible resources are distinguished by whether or not they have limits of

## 44  Breakdown of natural resources

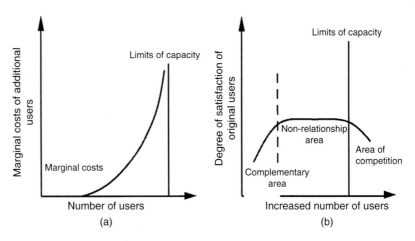

*Figure 3.2* Congestion.

Source: Author's own construct.

capacity. Within their limits of capacity, non-separable and congestible resources are extremely similar. Therefore, congestible resources are very similar to separable resources once their limits of renewability have been exceeded.

As regards renewable resources, so long as they are sustained with the limits of renewability, even if the limits of capacity have already been reached – with the result that horizontal non-separability ceases – vertical non-separability is sustained. For example, scenic areas can still be appreciated at certain periods, so long as they have not been destroyed by congestion, even if, at times, they are extremely congested to the point where many visitors feel they have become unattractive. However, if congestion leads to overstepping the limits of capacity, so that the resource is no longer renewable, then at that point vertical non-separability is lost.

A resource's limit of capacity mirrors the degree of scarcity of that resource. Once certain resources reach a given level of scarcity, there will inevitably be limits to capacity. For instance, air of a given quality does not have congestibility, even if the users increase from billions to billions of billions, because it exists in large quantities and biological limitations mean that each person can only breathe in very limited amounts of it. In other words, non-separable resources represent the extreme limits of congestible resources when the limits of capacity tend towards the infinite. The following formula shows relationships between the two:

$$\text{Congestible resources} \longrightarrow \text{non-separable resources} \quad (3.1)$$
$$\text{Limits of capacity} \longrightarrow \infty$$

Those congestible resources, where the limits of capacity are infinite, are what Western economists term 'non-scarce resources', hence they also have no price. This phenomenon has hardly ever been made the object of economic research.

*Breakdown of natural resources* 45

However, with the recent industrial boom, the category of resources previously recognized as inexhaustible, such as air and fresh water, have demonstrated capacity limits thanks to the increasingly damaging effects of environmental pollution. It goes without saying that the limits of capacity of fresh water are daily more evident, with the exponential growth of the human population. Air, on the other hand, has not reduced in quantity, but the effects of ever-increasing pollution have caused a gradual reduction in air quality; thus air becomes less usable and less of it is usable, so that its capacity limits cannot be ignored. We may say that non-separable resources used by human beings, which are often fundamental to human existence, are reducing in quantity at precisely the moment when human beings are becoming aware of their value. However, the greatest advantage of these resources, the fact that they are inexhaustible and do not cost money, is gradually being eroded by congestibility because the resources have been damaged. Western mainstream economics has been short-sighted in this regard, and has ignored the negative side of the above relationships:

$$\text{non-separable resources} \longrightarrow \text{congestible resources} \tag{3.2}$$
$$\text{damage factors cause capacity to reach limits}$$

These negative relationships have brought about a situation where non-scarce resources have turned into scarce resources – a situation that Western mainstream economists have found very hard to cope with.

## Exclusivity

Exclusivity means that the benefit or damage resulting from an action is directly assumed by the people who have the right to choose that action (i.e. its owners). Non-exclusivity is the attenuation of property rights (see Appendix) and there is a sense in which it will lead to a degree of inefficiency. If no one has exclusive rights to certain resources or goods, then no one can levy a charge on the use or consumption of those resources. In this situation, prices cannot be the means by which these resources or goods are distributed between different users. Nor can they act as an incentive to produce those goods or to protect or maintain resources.

A whole range of diverse resources, goods, services and pleasant environments provided by nature are non-exclusive. In this situation, resources or other goods are typically allocated such that, relative to optimal efficiency supply levels, there is an insufficient supply of goods and pleasurable experiences, or there are too many instances of harmful goods and disagreeable experiences; relative to optimal efficiency levels of exploitation, resources are over-exploited or there is insufficient investment in environmental protection or the maintenance of their production capacity.

In places where exclusive and non-attenuated property rights can be established over certain resources, it is possible to take independent action entirely for individual gain, in order to guarantee that optimal efficiency will be achieved (the limitations on achieving that result will be examined below). Many societies

## 46  *Breakdown of natural resources*

have imposed exclusivity on what, in the past, were non-exclusive resources. For example, over-grazing by livestock, which arose from a shortage of exclusive usage rights, was curbed by the establishment of land property rights.

However, some resources and goods continue to be non-exclusive up until the present day, even in countries and societies where private ownership is predominant. There two main reasons why this occurs: the first is for cultural and political reasons. In reality, every society marks off a few categories of resources, goods, services and pleasurable experiences and exempts them from the realm of commercial exchange. Even in America, it is generally recognized that the natural environment, waterways and historical monuments should not be treated as part of the marketplace.

The second main reason has nothing to do with social spheres such as culture, tradition and politics but derives from the intrinsic nature of the resources themselves. For instance, eels hatch in an area of deep ocean, which stretches from east of the South Asia Archipelago to Luzon Island; after this, they follow the Kuroshio ('black tide') to the coastal waters of Japan and disperse into fresh water areas. But when mature they follow the Kuroshio in the reverse direction, back to the waters where they hatched. It is impossible to demarcate the various seawaters, estuaries and coastal rivers that the eels frequent, and to impose property rights on them. As a result, exclusive property rights cannot be established over the eels. In this respect, eels are unlike domestic livestock animals, which belong to a certain person from birth to death. Ownership over the eels is only established by fisherfolk once the eels have been caught. We can extend this example to many different kinds of resources and goods over which it would be inappropriate to establish exclusive property rights, because of their intrinsic nature. The benefits, if one attempted to do so, would be far outweighed by the costs.

Any attempt to achieve optimal efficiency by establishing property rights over such non-exclusive resources and goods is doomed to failure. Many natural resources, which are crucial to human existence and development, as well as pleasurable experiences provided by the environment, fall into this category. They include sunlight, air, fresh and salt water; migratory wild beasts and wildlife, which as yet have no commercial value; non-farmed fish, which are too numerous for any private person to own; much of the oil, natural gas and groundwater resources, which lie beneath land that humans are using, and so on. In addition there are other, disagreeable 'resources', which can never be exclusive and which have a negative value, such as pests, hard-to-eradicate germs, and pollutants found in non-exclusive waterway systems.

The establishment of exclusive property rights, in places where this is possible, is a political decision. In places where exclusive, non-attenuated property rights cannot be established, this severely limits the political choices that can be made. Simply from the standpoint of economic efficiency, a complete lack of exclusivity or individual ownership has serious shortcomings. Societies can, however, establish systems of common ownership and can issue laws defining who is allowed to use what resources and goods under what conditions. For example, hunters can be required to obtain permits, and be subject to quotas and limitations on the hunting season, and on the uses of their catch. Regulations on the use of such resources do not have the optimal efficiency of non-attenuated property rights but they are a feasible alternative in areas where exclusive property rights cannot be enforced. When property is collectively owned, laws on use of that property can be subject to a number of different provisions.

Here, it is worth considering both the relative efficiency that results from different laws, and some general principles that relate to them. For instance, where resources have been over-exploited, the straightforward imposition of limits on exploitation – for example, quotas for over-fished species – is more effective than imposing limits on investment in the exploitation process. Where it is necessary to impose such restrictions, optimal efficiency is achievable if the rights provided under these regulations are transferable.

Alan Randall states that regulating even optimal efficiency common ownership systems cannot lead to Pareto efficiency.[2] But I believe that, in any case, Pareto efficiency is not an appropriate standard of measurement. It is quite clear that altering restrictions (which may or may not involve imposing exclusivity) often has the effect of changing the optimal solution; indeed, it makes no sense to argue which is the optimal solution when comparisons involve differing constraints. The only meaningful comparisons to be made are those between differing solutions subject to the same constraints.

Thus, in areas where it is not possible to implement exclusive rights, meticulously planned regulation of the use of resources can still result in a production capacity that is feasible and sustainable in the long-term; this inhibits wasteful investment and can ensure that enterprises in the industry concerned can achieve optimal efficiency and safeguard their turnover.

According to the theories of separability and exclusivity, resources and goods can be divided into four categories: separable, exclusive resources (or goods), separable, non-exclusive resources (or goods), non-separable, exclusive resources (or goods), and non-separable, non-exclusive resources (or goods). Each of these four categories is differentiated according to whether it is supplied by the market, the public sector or private enterprise and whether or not this supply has Pareto efficiency.

Separable, exclusive resources – such as rice, bread and some mineral products – can be supplied by the market. If we assume that this is a perfect market, that is, that prices have been established relative to non-attenuated property rights and optimal efficiency, then Pareto efficiency can be achieved when the resources are delivered.

Separable, non-exclusive resources, on the other hand, cannot be supplied by private enterprise or market mechanisms because there is no reward in supplying them. They can be supplied by privately-run charities (though normally in less than optimal quantities) or by the public sector. When the public sector supplies these goods, it receives financial subsidies. If it were realistic and economically possible to introduce exclusive rights to the market for these resources, the public sector could levy a fee for the use and consumption of these resources at the same time as it supplies them. If it was possible to set up and implement exclusive, non-attenuated property rights (that is, in a scenario where non-exclusivity does

48  *Breakdown of natural resources*

not arise from something intrinsic in the resource itself) then private companies could also supply these goods and, moreover, achieve Pareto efficiency.

Non-separable, exclusive resources can be supplied by the public sector, which can levy a fee for the use and consumption of these resources. Additionally, these resources can be supplied by the private sector but, as perfect price discrimination is impossible, the non-separability of these resources makes it impossible to achieve Pareto efficiency. Only less than perfect results can be achieved.

Non-separable, non-exclusive resources have to be supplied by privately-run charities (though normally in less than optimal quantities) or by the public sector (which may receive financial subsidies). If the exclusive ownership of these goods is a realistic and an economic possibility, and it is acceptable politically, then exclusive rights may be established. In this way, these resources can be supplied through the market or the public sector on the basis of fees paid by the consumer. If that situation obtains, then optimal efficiency according to other standards may be achieved, even if Pareto efficiency itself is unattainable.

## Externality

In analysing the consumption and use of resources and goods, there is one very important concept, called externality (also known as 'external effects'). Put simply, externality is a spillover effect from costs and benefits. For example, pollution can be termed a kind of externality.

In a system of non-attenuated rights, because exclusivity prevails, the rewards and punishments from any activity (or costs and benefits) accrue to the individual or group who carried out this act. But in the real world, it often happens that many actions are chosen not because the benefits outweigh the costs, but because the individual or group who choose the action have done so because they have discovered that some or all of the costs incurred can be transferred to other people. In these cases, this action may be carried out when the portion of the total costs, which the individual or group has to assume, is outweighed by the total benefits that accrue. In other words, in the case of attenuated property rights, there is an obvious imparity between costs and benefits because exclusivity cannot be guaranteed. This point is illustrated in the formulae that follow:

1   The total costs of an action = that part of the costs assumed by the person or people who undertake the action + the cost assumed by other people who are not party to the action.
2   The total benefits of an action = the real benefits that accrue to the person or people who undertake the action + the benefits accruing to the person or people who are not party to the action.

Let,

$C$ = the total social costs of an action,
$C_1$ = that part of the costs assumed by the person or people who undertake the action, and
$C_2$ = the external costs.

Similarly, let

$B =$ the social benefits of an action,
$B_1 =$ the individual (or private) benefits and
$B_2 =$ the external benefits.

Now let us suppose that for a certain action, $C$ is greater than $B$. In that case, we can assume that a rational person or group of people will not undertake this action, or at least will not undertake it very often once the consequences are understood. However, when this type of action occurs, as it does regularly, the only explanation (assuming that the consequences are clear) is the following (for the sake of convenience, we will say that $B_2 = 0$ and $B = B_1$): $C > B$ but, yet even though this is the case, $C_1 < B_1 = B$; while $C_2 > B_2 = 0$. This type of behaviour is termed by most ordinary people 'personal gain made at the expense of others'.

Pollution happens not because the overall benefits of $B$ of dumping harmful pollutants into the environment is greater than the overall costs of $C$, but because the benefits of dealing with waste in this way outweigh that part of the costs borne by the polluters. The concept of externality is therefore used to illustrate how, when the costs and benefits of an action are not taken into consideration by the decision-makers who decided to carry out this action, the result is what is generally known as low efficiency. (Strictly speaking, this should be called social inefficiency, since in a certain sense the efficiency of the action is optimal – the greater the proportion of costs that can be transferred, the higher the efficiency.) In other words, certain benefits are conferred, or certain costs forced, on people who did not decide to implement this action. Within society, many conflicts of interest between individuals or groups bring in their wake persistent, detrimental consequences to society as a whole; in addition, persistent, huge discrepancies between the collective and the individual can also be explained in terms of externality.

In the following, more stringent formulation, it can be seen how, when the situation below occurs, externality can be said to have occurred: $U_j = U_j (X_{1j}, X_{2j}, . . X_{nj}, X_{mk})$, in $j \neq k$, where $X_{ij}$ ($i = 1, . . ., n, m$) represent economic activities (or other activities), and $j$ and $k$ indicate individuals or groups.

According to this formula, externality is said to exist when the welfare or interests of one person or group, $U_j$, is affected not only by the economic activities that they control themselves ($X_{ij}, i = 1, . . .n$), but also by the economic activity, $X_{mk}$, controlled by at least one other person or group, $k$. This formula shows that externality means that the interests of a person or group are a function of a combination of the activities, which they control and which others control. A simple observation of the people and activities that surround us will show that almost any economic activity has externality.

When the affected part, $j$, wants to make the actor, $k$, change his/her activity, then relative externality exists; conversely, when the affected party is indifferent to externality, this is known as non-mutual externality. The latter generally occurs in the following two situations: (1) when the party is not aware of the detrimental effects of externality on him/herself; or (2) when s/he benefits from this externality. The latter is known as economic, or positive, externality; for example, when the people with whom one shares accommodation regularly clean

## 50  *Breakdown of natural resources*

it and, although one is indifferent to this activity, one receives tangible benefits from it.

When one party, $j$, is adversely affected by an activity, $X_{mk}$, of another party, $k$, and seeks to persuade $k$ to reduce the level of that activity or change it altogether, this is known as external diseconomy, or negative externality. If there is the possibility of reducing an activity, $X_{mk}$, in such a way that one party benefits without the other party suffering detrimental effects, then this external diseconomy is Pareto-relative. (Obviously there must exist the potential for improvements to Pareto efficiency, that is, this phenomenon illustrates how this economic activity is inefficient in Pareto terms.) As an example of external diseconomy, new industrial methods may enable the polluter, $k$, to reduce the amount of its pollutants, while maintaining its overall profits. That is, the polluting party does not suffer losses while, at the same time, the party that suffers the pollution, $j$, benefits.

When Pareto-related, external diseconomy exists in production, the price of the products tends to be low and output is high. This is a general conclusion. The reasoning is very simple: if we take pollution as an example, the producers have externalized the costs associated with pollution, thus reducing the share of costs borne by them, pushing down the price of their product and increasing their competitiveness. This has the effect of increasing both sales and output.

The low efficiency of Pareto-related, external diseconomy shows this phenomenon to be a manifestation of attenuated property rights. For example, air can be polluted by anyone. Air is a kind of 'property' that belongs to no one person or group and, indeed, individual property rights over the air cannot be effectively regulated or implemented. And just because air is the property of no one, anyone can disperse waste into it and thus avoid the need to assume the direct costs of dealing with waste. Indeed no one can benefit directly from limiting their own polluting activities. This is the reason why there are too many harmful or disagreeable things like pollution and insufficient control over them.

A basic principle in overcoming this type of externality is the strengthening of the exclusive nature of property rights (and the abolition of controls over the highest prices), a principle known as internalization. This is done by making the external costs, $C_2$, equal zero (when $C = C_1 + C_2 = C_1$) or as close to zero as possible, for example by levying a tax on effluent discharge. To put it simply, the polluters bear the consequences of their actions, and it is made impossible for them to pass on their costs to others. This forces the polluters to limit their harmful activities or switch to other methods.

The above is the classic expression of externality. Several points need to be stressed: (1) imposing internality, or the strengthening of the exclusive nature of property rights, is by no means the same as privatization. The latter is only one means of imposing internality; indeed it has its own ultimate capacity. Types of externality and the sphere in which they operate, are very varied, and are also closely related to the concepts of separability and exclusivity of resources and goods covered earlier in this chapter. This means that using privatization as a way of imposing internality and combatting externality will entail almost insuperable problems. However, there are many options open when choosing an effective system of non-private property rights; (2) when Pareto-related, external diseconomy exists (that is, when there exists no possibility of strengthening the degree of exclusivity of the system of property rights), attempting to make all economic activities more efficient by strengthening market mechanisms is simply perverse and doomed to failure; each individual activity can be made more efficient but the whole structure will become more inefficient.

To take pollution as an example, it is clear that it is those enterprises and companies who emit most pollution that are the most competitive. In this situation, not only is it not the case that the best companies are the most profitable in optimal efficiency relative price systems (that is, market mechanisms which are not subject to any interference or control), but the reverse is true: the worst companies (in terms of pollution emissions) will always make the most profits. Given this kind of market aberration, the 'adverse selection' mechanism will always ensure that enterprises that survive and develop are those who do the polluting because they are the most successful at externalizing the costs, which they should assume themselves. Thus, self-interest thrives and, as a corollary, the less self-interested will be mercilessly eliminated by the adverse selection mechanism. This analysis can be used to understand all kinds of harmful phenomena, which have pervaded the Chinese economy in the last ten years; (3) the concept of Pareto-related, external diseconomy is too limited and this reduces its usefulness as an analytical tool. I have thus broadened its definition to enable it to be applied to broader situations.

First, 'correlation' is normally taken to mean the horizontal relation between people of the same generation (within one generation we can ignore the time-lag process which operates in external diseconomy) because the people of one generation cannot require the previous generation who are already dead to change their activities; still less can future generations still unborn make that demand. However, between the generations, the transmission of external diseconomy, especially the subsequent cumulative effects, poses a serious problem for the continuance and progress of the human race. Thus, we should broaden the definition of 'correlation' while putting increased emphasis on the cumulative, vertical, non-economic external consequences. It is in this sense that cumulative, external diseconomy (or cumulative externality, for short) will be used below.

Second, I believe that Pareto limits should be relaxed. The reasons are clear: let us imagine that the pollution produced by the productive activities of an enterprise cause the social costs to be $C > B$ ($B$ being the social benefits); let us further suppose that, with current technology, it is impossible to ensure that social benefits are accrued without enterprises suffering losses, as a result of which the company has to be closed down (the quantity of benefits being $|B - C|$). Obviously, in this situation there is no room for Pareto improvement although in principle, closing the company down is an action worth taking because the net benefits to society are greater than zero.

This means that in many circumstances, it is not necessarily appropriate to use Pareto criteria to measure the efficiency of an entire economy. Of course, when we use other criteria (such as that of $B \geq C$) we will come up against technical

## 52 *Breakdown of natural resources*

questions, such as comparisons between different costs and benefits, or even sums to compensate the party who suffers losses, all of which makes the clarity and reliability of these other criteria appear problematic. But as social practice, theoretical studies and analytical techniques are developed; these problems should not prove insoluble. In the analysis that follows I have given no special emphasis to Pareto criteria and I have recognized more wide-ranging standards, such as $B \geq C$.

## Notes

1 Randall, Alan, *Resource Economics: An Economic Approach to Natural Resource and Environmental Policy*, 1981. (阿蘭·蘭德爾: 《資源經濟學: 從經濟角度對自然資源和環境政策的探討》, 1989 年, 商務印書館, 第193頁。 [Shangwuyinshuguan Publishers, 1989, page 193]).
2 Ibid.

# 4 The economy of waste

In Chapter 3, we saw how only under conditions of strict separability and exclusivity of goods and resources could we rely on a combination of the perfect market[1] and privately-run businesses to supply those goods and resources at Pareto-efficiency levels. It is normally only with such 'final products' as bread and rice that strict separability and exclusivity obtains. However, in any economic system, other resources will need to be used if such goods are to be produced. Thus, generally speaking, it is impossible to achieve conditions of strict separability and exclusivity throughout an entire economic system. In these circumstances, the long-term results for the economy may be contrary to those desired: the striving for efficiency of each part often results in waste for the whole. Contrary to popular belief, there is no invisible hand bringing private profit-seeking activity automatically into line with the interests of society as a whole.

In the following analysis, we will see just how complex the actual situation has become, both from the technical aspect (renewability and recyclability of resources) and the social aspect (separability, exclusivity and externality). This is not only because there are multiple categories of goods and resources (defined according to separability and exclusivity), but also because even specific goods (for example, timber) can have multiple social properties. Let us begin by looking at private-ownership and collective-ownership disasters.

## Private-ownership and collective-ownership disasters

The concept of collective-ownership disasters, also known as disasters of collective resources, can be exemplified as follows: formerly, in England, the government gave free grazing rights to all graziers on public land. The thinking behind this may have been rooted in considerations of social benefits, but these rights actually benefited those peasants who grazed most livestock most. If one peasant did not make use of this common land, then another would. The result was that competition between peasants led to them grazing too many animals on common land, and to a deterioration of that land from over-grazing. A natural disaster resulted because, even though everyone knew that the guiding principle should be to make that resource last as long as possible in order to preserve the long-term productivity of the resource (land), competition (the 'adverse selection'

## 54  *The economy of waste*

mechanism) between two or more individuals or groups brought disaster in its wake.

This case is often used as a basis on which to criticize the low efficiency of common systems in general and to argue the case for privatization as the solution. However, it is clear from the examination of exclusivity in the previous chapter, that both this criticism and this recommendation are groundless. In actual fact, the concept of collective-ownership disaster is by no means clear-cut. Strictly speaking, it only means disaster caused by the misuse of common resources within certain legal systems or, put more accurately, disaster caused by the open-access use of resources. Under a different legal or regulatory framework, if the common ownership of resources must be preserved, the sale of (bequeathable) grazing permits or the renting out of pasture can eliminate this kind of disaster. I use the term 'collective-ownership disaster' to mean disaster caused by the open-access use of resources. Additionally, this kind of disaster can be aggravated if the market for livestock products is unregulated: the inevitable result will be ever more acute over-grazing and degradation of resources. By contrast, if the market for livestock products is subject to tight regulation, (for example, if a state monopoly buys these goods at a low price) this may mitigate against collective-ownership disaster. (I am not making a recommendation here, but simply illustrating possible different outcomes.)

What is hard to understand is why the concept of private-ownership disaster is never discussed. We will examine it here: let us suppose that a company (with a single owner or with limited liability) had the total capacity to manage and utilize all whale resources (let us limit it to one species – the Southern Blue Whale). Given that past whaling activities have reduced the total number of whales to 75,000, we may as well suppose that the maximum sustainable yield (MSY) is around 2,000 whales per year. That is to say, if the yearly catch is greater than 2,000, the whale will become extinct. Let us imagine that the market value for one Blue Whale is $10,000, a price that, if the MSY principle is adhered to, will give an annual income of $20 million. But that company may decide to ignore the need for sustainability, and to catch all remaining 75,000 animals. Let us further suppose that this is actually possible and let us ignore for the moment the effect on prices of flooding the market with millions of tons of whale oil: the result would be that the company earns $750 million from the catch. If this money is invested in other industries at 5 per cent annual interest, then $750 million will earn an annual interest of $37.5 million (and if the rate of interest were 10 per cent, the interest earned would be $75 million, or nearly four times $20 million). These crude figures show how a policy of exterminating the Blue Whale is far more profitable than a policy of sustainability (MSY). The reality is that the owners of all resource populations tend to think of those populations as assets, and this is equally true of renewables and non-renewables. Thus owners hope that their assets will net them big dividends at regular rates of interest, otherwise they will have to liquidate their assets. This is recognized as the most basic law of resource economics, established in 1931 by Harold Hotelling, and known as Hotelling's Rule.[2]

The economy of waste 55

In the above case, property rights are non-attenuated (because this is a privately-owned company), there is no interference with prices (meaning there is optimal efficiency), resources are separable and exclusive and we can conclude that Pareto efficiency has been achieved. However, the real result is that a species has been driven to extinction. Hotelling's Rule is generally effective with low-grade assets, the term applied when the profitability of the MSY of a resource is lower than market interest rates. Hotelling's Rule, with respect to low-grade assets, can therefore be summed up as follows: when prices are not regulated, and assets are separable, exclusive and in private ownership (that is, a system of non-attenuated property rights pertains), making this a perfect market, then the optimal method in Pareto-efficiency terms is the method whereby the owners make these resources extinct. Private owners of resources thus have no incentive to protect natural resources. This theory can therefore also be termed 'Hotelling's Rule of private-ownership disaster'. It describes the disastrous consequences of private ownership of natural resources: a system that combines such private ownership with a perfect market leads to over-exploitation and destruction of those resources. Moreover, the lower the level of the assets (i.e. the greater the discrepancy between the profitability of MSY and market interest rates), the greater the degree of over-exploitation and destruction of the resources.

At this point, we will abandon the example of a privately-owned company with complete control over the whaling business because it is clear from our analysis of exclusivity that whales, as a resource, are by their very nature unsuited to exclusive ownership. A more realistic supposition would formulate that any country or company can freely, and at no cost, enter this business. This formulation is not constrained in any way and leads to the other (extreme) relative to private-ownership disaster: completely non-exclusive resources, which belong to no one. Readers will see at a glance that this leads to collective disaster, with all its foreseeable consequences.

Let us imagine that the market for whale products is subject to absolutely no controls or interference, with resulting efficient pricing, but that property rights are no longer non-attenuated. Now whales become an open-access (or common) resource, subject to no controls. The economic theory of open-access resources was formulated by H. S. Gordon in 1954. Gordon's Rule addresses the diminution of profits with open-access resources, and is recognized as the second basic rule in resource economics, supplementing Hotelling's Rule on the private ownership of resource populations. Because, in the case of many ecological resources, it is impossible to establish ownership, Gordon's Rule may be even more important than Hotelling's Rule. Gordon's Rule has many important consequences, such as the fact that open-access exploitation is more widespread than maximized profits management, and is more likely to entail unfavourable biological consequences, including extinction. Growth in demand can drive up exploitation of open-access resources and, once the MSY threshold is crossed, productivity levels will gradually drop. Technical progress can make exploitation more efficient; however, it can also lead to the opposite of the intended effect – the lowering of productivity.[3]

## 56  *The economy of waste*

In the abstract, the open-access exploitation system may be taken as the extreme point of optimum private management when the discount rate tends to infinity. That is, when the discount rate tends to infinity, Hotelling's Rule and Gordon's Rule are equal. Intuitively speaking, this is obvious, because in freely entered into, open-access exploitation, intense competition generated by excessive numbers entering the field dampens enthusiasm for measures that protect these resources for the future. (Put more clearly, limiting concern to the present means high discount rates – when the short term tends to zero, the discount rate tends to infinity.) Thus, if high discount rates have been adopted, many unfavourable conditions produced by open-access exploitation may also make their appearance in private ownership. With regard to whaling and forestry, when the annual discount rates (or the market annual interest rates) reach 10 per cent, this is enough to have a severe impact on the protection of resources, or even result in destruction of those resources. The non-reversibility of this impact (once a species is extinct, it cannot be revived) shows that over-exploitation should be avoided. Thus it is normally recognized that high interest rates are harmful to the protection of resources. However, in practice, an overall zero rate of interest is also impossible. This means that, whatever the ownership systems, it is necessary to impose regulations that protect natural resources (protection standards, for short) which, in combination with short-term efficiency criteria (connected to interest rates), enable horizontal and vertical fairness and efficiency to be achieved.

Hotelling's Rule and Gordon's Rule lead us to the following conclusions: (1) unregulated market systems do not necessarily lead to optimum efficiency in the use of resources; (2) systems that combine the free market and private enterprise are no panacea in effective resource allocation; (3) systems that combine the free market and open-access resource exploitation are open to widespread abuse; and (4) (probably the most important conclusion) the special characteristics of resources in the mid-space between Hotelling's Rule at one extreme and Gordon's Rule at the other, mean that differing limits must be imposed on completely private and completely open-access systems, so that a broadly diverse property ownership system can take shape. It is only in this way that protection and exploitation (for example, the fishing and sales quotas of Hotelling's Rule) can both operate effectively.

## Killing the goose that lays the golden eggs

It has been shown that three-quarters of the value of forests lies in environmental protection and other natural benefits, while only one-quarter of their value lies in forestry products. For example, in 1972, the annual economic benefits of Japan's forests in terms of water conservation, preventing soil erosion and landslips, the provision of oxygen, the protection of bird life and promotion of human health, amounted to 12.82 trillion Japanese yen, equivalent to Japan's total annual budget for that year. And this does not include the various ways in which forests afford environmental protection, by regulating air temperature, cleansing the air and

*The economy of waste* 57

reducing noise.[4] At an exchange rate of 1:300, this converts to approximately $43 billion (at the 1972 dollar value). Calculated on the basis of Japan's 60 per cent forest coverage, the environmental benefits per hectare amount to approximately $2,000 (or $4,000 at the 1980 dollar value). The value of Japanese forestry products was approximately $1,333 per hectare at the 1980 dollar value.

In spite of the benefits they bring, forests continue to diminish: in 1958, forests covered approximately one-quarter of the Earth's surface; by 1978, that figure had dropped to one-fifth,[5] representing a loss over 20 years of 600 million hectares, or 30 million hectares per year. This represents a loss to the economy in the region of $25.2 trillion (at the 1980 dollar value), or $1.26 trillion annually – an enormous figure. This phenomenon can be explained from a number of different perspectives. First, let us suppose that forests only serve to provide forestry products; in this case Hotelling's Rule tells us that reduction in forests will continue to happen because many varieties of forest trees are low-grade assets.

Second, however, in terms of the economic benefits they provide to the environment, forests are by no means low-grade assets. Calculated on the basis that their natural growth rate is 5 per cent, if we include the environmental benefits they bring, then the broad profitability of forests is as high as 20 per cent, or twice the normal market interest rates. Forests represent a visible resource – timber – and can be treated as a separable, exclusive resource, but in terms of their environmental benefits they are obviously a non-separable, non-exclusive resource. Thus it is clear that forests as a resource, or a good, are simultaneously two very different things: a separable, exclusive resource and a non-separable, non-exclusive resource. An attempt to deal with annual losses worth $1.26 trillion through a combination of private ownership and the free market is doomed to failure. Hotelling's Rule tells us that this will only lead to the faster extinction of forests. For private enterprise, the only aspects of forests that are separable and exclusive, are the low-grade assets forests provide: the tangible resource of timber.

It is therefore clear that the environmental benefits enjoyed by a private forest owner, relative to other non-owners, are negligible; that is, the ill effects caused to the owner by destruction of these benefits are so small as to be minimal. Conversely, since these benefits or services are strictly non-separable and non-exclusive, it is impossible to charge a fee to others to enjoy these benefits or services. So the owner's only choice is to continue to fell trees; the owner has no incentive to preserve this resource even though s/he may recognize how important its benefits are for humanity. Total privatization is not the way to resolve this problem because, due to the nature of this kind of resource, it cannot be totally privatized. A more effective method is to restrict felling and impose quotas on sales. Inevitably, this gives rise to a different kind of ownership system; for example, imposing these restrictions on a basis of complete private ownership means restricting private ownership itself.

I will now proceed to an analysis of arable resources. Arable land is a horizontal, separable and exclusive resource; at the same time, it is also a renewable resource, forming, together with forests, two of the main support systems that sustain life

## 58   *The economy of waste*

on Earth. What, then, is the situation of arable land and the soil? Let us take the USA as an example: up until the beginning of the 1980s, American farmers and the United States Department of Agriculture (USDA), spent upwards of $1 billion annually on controlling the erosion of arable land, paying roughly half each. Be that as it may, a 1982 study showed that America was losing 3.1 tons/acre per year of top soil to wind erosion, well exceeding the acceptable level of 2 tons; it also showed that 6 tons of top soil were lost to American farmers for every ton of grain produced.[6] Loss of top soil had doubled compared with the 1.53 tons/acre per year lost in 1977–8.[7]

Arable land in the USA is basically all privately-owned, so that establishing the exclusivity of arable resources, in the form of exclusive property rights, has not been a problem. The market for agricultural products has been almost unregulated, which ought to mean that the system runs at optimal efficiency. How, then, should we explain the erosion problem mentioned above?

During the boom in world wheat prices in the mid 1970s, the amount of land left fallow in the USA dropped from 17 million hectares in 1969 to 13 million hectares in 1974. The head of the US Soil Conservation Service, Kenneth Grant, warned farmers that putting increasing amounts of land under cultivation could lead to serious wind erosion and dust storms. He exhorted farmers not be seduced by the unprecedented rise in wheat prices, because short-term gains would come at the price of diminishing productivity of the land in the long term. A 1977 national survey of natural resources showed that in wheat-growing states like Texas and Colorado, wind erosion far exceeded permissible levels.[8]

The key problem appears to be that the land's long-term productivity cannot be made exclusive and that arable land is non-separable – vertically speaking. Even though wheat and maize produced on that land is a separable, exclusive resource, the exclusivity and separability of a complex land system (and its products) is greatly attenuated. It is therefore not surprising that private farmers react primarily to signals relevant to the separable, exclusive part. Additionally, the net current value of the long-term productivity of the land is very low (because it normally takes nature several hundreds of years to form an inch of top soil), which means that top soil is a low-grade asset and, when the price of products of the land shoots up, over-exploitation of the land, with loss of productivity in the long term, may result. This is a description of a situation when the discount rate tends to infinity, and Hotelling's Rule and Gordon's Rule are equivalent. When this happens to top soil many harmful circumstances, which are the consequence of open-ended exploitation, make their appearance. In other words, unless soil preservation measures take effect very rapidly, anyone who adopts such measures in a highly competitive marketplace where returns are low may face bankruptcy.

By about 1984, the soil loss for farmland globally was 23 billion tons, and had exceeded the new land being formed.[9] This is only one aspect of the problem; in the struggle over farm use and non-agricultural use for arable land, the former is in a weak position because arable use of land is a low-grade asset. It has been calculated[10] that the global expansion of arable land slowed in the 1950s to an average increase of less than 1 per cent, then dropped to less than 0.3 per cent in the 1970s and 0.2 per cent in the 1980s. If we bear in mind that cities often occupy good quality land, that land newly brought under cultivation is often of poor quality and that the loss of top soil causes arable land to deteriorate, then if the current area of arable land is re-calculated according to a given quality index, it may even be that the arable hectarage had already begun to fall by the 1980s.

## Eating the seed grain

The above analysis has focused chiefly on renewable resources. I will now turn to non-renewables. In actual fact, these non-renewables can continue to grow on a geological time-scale; however, their Maximum Sustainable Yield (MSY) is equal to zero on a human time-scale. Non-renewables, therefore, are renewables with an MSY that tends towards zero. The relationship between these two can be summarized as follows:

$$\text{renewables} \xrightarrow[\text{MSY} \to \infty]{} \text{non-renewables} \tag{4.1}$$

Thus we have arrived at the following deduction from Hotelling's Rule: if we suppose that prices of non-renewables are not managed, that the assets have separability and that complete private ownership is in operation, then, providing perfect market conditions, the higher the market interest rates, the greater the degree of over-exploitation, because the MSY of these assets is near to zero. Generally speaking, market interest rates are greater than zero so that, in the long term, it is difficult for private owners to avoid over-exploitation of non-renewables since they lack the motivation to protect those resources for the rest of society and for subsequent generations.

In fact, this deduction is not limited to private ownership; it can be extended to include any exclusive enterprise (such as a collective) or incorporated enterprise (such as a joint-stock company) where a resource is wholly owned. It applies in any circumstances where the aims of that enterprise are at variance with the aims of society, for example where the former aims to maximize profits and the latter to preserve resources for the use of subsequent generations. It should be pointed out that this deduction and its extension do not include monopoly ownership situations.

With respect to Gordon's Rule, if we regard non-renewables as the extreme limit of renewables (that is, where the MSY tends towards zero), certain of Gordon's conclusions can be extended to non-renewables in the same way. For example, in oil fields with common reserves, unfettered (open-access) exploitation can lead to serious economic damage. A few years ago, in Chinese mines with common seams, the policy of encouraging coal-mining activities wherever possible and by whatever means, led to a similar destruction of resources.

Mineral deposits are, to all intents and purposes, non-renewables, so will serve as an example in the following analysis. Generally speaking, if other conditions remain the same, when the discount rate (or market interest rate) is low, the rate of exploitation of mineral resources will fall. Put more vividly, when market interest rates are high, mine-owners will exploit their resources, sell them more

## 60  *The economy of waste*

quickly and turn them into cash, then turn them into high-yielding financial assets. Conversely, when market rates are low, owners tend to keep their assets in solid form (minerals) and leave them in the ground. This explanation is very similar to the core of Hotelling's Rule. A more rigorous deduction follows. Consider the following competitive model:

Let the costs of extraction be $C(q)$, where
the rate of extraction $= q$
time $= t$
the price of minerals $= p$
the tax or subsidy $= \tau$
the discount rate $= \delta$
and $C$ and $r$ are the parameters in the cost function $Cq + rq^2$,
then the mine owner's objective can be calculated as follows:

$$Ja\{q\} = \int_0^\infty e^{-\delta t}[(p - \tau)q - C(q)]dt \tag{4.2}$$

The question now is how to maximize the above objective throughout the exploitation process through adjusting the extraction rate $q(t)$. When $\tau < 0$ in the formula, it shows the allowance rate paid when wastage is reduced (in order to encourage mine-owners to make better use of the tailings). When $\tau > 0$ in the formula, it shows the exploitation tax levied on each unit of ore extracted in order to control the extraction rate. Bearing in mind that the exploitation costs function takes the form of $C(q) = Cq + rq^2$ ($q$, the extraction rate, becomes $q^2$ because the later the stage of mine extraction, the more the costs rise incrementally). Given this premise, we can express the extraction rate in the following equation:

$$q(t) = \frac{p - \tau - C}{2r}(1 - e^{\delta(t-T)}) \tag{4.3}$$

Now let us imagine that the discount rate is reduced to $\dot{\delta}$, that is, that $\delta > \dot{\delta}$. Then the extraction rate is $\dot{q}(t)$. In this formula, the only change is that $\dot{\delta}$ has replaced $\delta$ while other elements remain the same, and the two formulae are mutually reduced:

$$q(t) - \dot{q}(t) = \frac{p - T - C}{2r}(e^{\dot{\delta}(t-T)} - e^{\delta(t-T)}) \tag{4.4}$$

Suppose that $p - \tau - C > 0$; since $t < T$ ($T$ being the time when exploitation at the mine has finished), then $e^{\dot{\delta}(t-T)} = 1/e^{\dot{\delta}(T-t)}$. Another element between brackets works the same way: since $e^{\dot{\delta}(T-t)} < e^{\delta(T-t)}$ (because $\delta > \dot{\delta}$), then $1/e^{\dot{\delta}(T-t)} - 1/e^{\delta(T-vt)} > 0$ therefore $q(t) - \dot{q}(t) > 0$. In other words, this shows the rate of exploitation at times when the high discount rate, $\delta$, is higher than the lower discount rate, $\dot{\delta}$. Readers will easily prove by similar methods that when $\tau > 0$, when exploitation taxes are rather high, extraction rates will be rather low.

This shows that when discount rates are high, then extraction rates will also be high and vice versa. We now have to establish the difference between the viewpoint

The economy of waste   61

of society as a whole and that of the mine-owner (individual or collective). It is accepted that social discount rates are normally lower than market interest rates, that is, an individual owner normally focuses on immediate profits (i.e. the individual owner's discount rate is higher), while market interest rates reflect the discount rate of these individual investors. The reason is that mined products, excluding oil fields with common deposits, generally have good separability and exclusivity. Now let us suppose that private exclusive ownership rights have been established over the mines. The timescale within which private individuals invest is rather short; for example, equipment in mines and factories normally has a service life of between 20 and 40 years, i.e. no more than one human generation. Society, on the other hand, must consider humanity's continuing existence and progress and so cannot avoid being concerned as to whether many succeeding generations can continue to make use of a certain non-renewable resource or, at the very least, whether in due course technological advances can replace that resource with new non-renewable resources or renewable or recyclable resources; for example, whether solar power can replace petroleum. This means that society emphasizes long-term interests – at least the interests of two to three successive generations. That is, society's discount rate is lower than that of the private individual. A social discount rate of 4–6 per cent will not have much effect on two or three, or even more, future generations. It is reasonable to be concerned, therefore, that in the extraction of non-renewables, the discount rate decided by the market (generally 8–10 per cent) will be very much higher than the long-term social discount rate, with the former rate as much as double that of the latter.

Short-term, optimum-efficiency extraction of resources (horizontal efficiency) drives market interest rates, $r$, to become the determining factor. At the same time unregulated market interest rates are self-sustaining because if owners do not act according to short-term optimum-efficiency criteria, they may be eliminated by the market with the result that only those who do act according to short-term criteria remain in the market. In this situation, when one generation establishes criteria for 'saving' some non-renewable resources for their children and grandchildren's generations, they make arbitrary choices. The widely-held belief that short-term optimum efficiency can be used to determine equitable long-term optimum efficiency between the generations (vertical efficiency) is, in fact, groundless.

Where social discount rates are too far below market interest rates, there may be insufficient development of resources, with too little emphasis on the interests of the current generation. However 'errors' of this type can easily be adjusted, while the consequences of over-exploitation are hard to reverse, even over a period of decades or centuries. For example, the damage caused in terms of soil erosion, desertification, and insufficient absorption of carbon dioxide by over-exploitation of forests, is almost impossible to rectify in the short term, yet the irreversibility of these effects is still ignored. To correct over-extraction, extraction taxes could be imposed, thus bringing private individuals' discount rate into line with the social discount rate. To promote the extraction of resources, an allowance rate for wastage (that is, where $\tau < 0$) could be made – readers should refer back to the formulae on p. 94.

## 62 *The economy of waste*

Where owners of re-usable, non-renewable resources, such as metallic mineral deposits, are faced with market interest rates, $r$, higher than the social discount rate and the external diseconomy connected with the extraction process is greater than the interrelated external diseconomy connected to the recycling of the resource, then the socially optimum recycling rate will be greater than the recycling rate determined by the private market. In these circumstances, imposing taxes on newly extracted resources and levying a pollution tax on the external diseconomy created during the extraction process will have the effect of bringing the recycling rate on the private market closer to the socially optimal recycling rate.[12]

This general conclusion can be proved as follows: when the first condition is satisfied, the price of the products of newly-extracted resources will be lower than the socially optimal price because, relatively speaking, the rise in the discount rate is balanced by the fall in prices. This effect can be seen in the formulae on p. 94: in order to keep $q(t)$ unchanged, the rise in $\delta$ is equivalent to a fall in $p$, which makes the cost of extraction of new resources higher than the prices businesses can charge. In other words, society dictates that fewer newly-extracted resources should be used, because the socially optimal price is high, but business dictates that more newly-extracted resources should be used, because the prices that entrepreneurs can charge are low. When the second condition is satisfied, the extraction costs for private enterprise will become progressively less than the social costs, because the external costs that private enterprise can pass on are ever higher, meaning that the latter will tend to use newly-extracted resources.

## Hard-pressed

Ecosystems made up of soil, fresh water, seawater, air, sunlight and life forms can bear a degree of external pressure, and can balance themselves by means of a self-regulating mechanism. How well this self-regulating mechanism works depends on capacity. When external pressure exceeds a certain limit, the ecosystem's ability to self-regulate is reduced or may disappear, damaging the ecological balance or even causing the entire system to break down. The point at which this happens is called the ecological threshold. For example, in forest ecosystems, there is a critical annual felling limit, beyond which the system's ability to renew itself will be damaged. Capacity refers to the amount of a certain substance, which an ecosystem can accommodate and still maintain its ability to balance itself by means of self-cleansing. This capacity is determined by the nature and toxicity of the substance or pollutant, as well as the ability of the ecosystem to cleanse itself of toxins.

Within the capacity of an ecosystem, human reproduction is largely autonomous, and the damaging effects of human beings on the environment (humans → environment) can be ignored as the environment absorbs the effects and cleanses itself (analogous to elastic deformation). At this point, it is the environment that acts on humans (environment → humans), the chief factor for humans being the suitability of the environment. In these circumstances, human evolution can be divided into two parts: autonomous and affected by the environment. The interrelated, autonomous parts of the environment are independent of, and unaffected by, human activity. This can be seen in Figure 4.1, which follows.

Once humans have developed autonomously (as manifested in the exponential growth of the human population) to the point where they have outgrown the capacity of the ecosystem, then the ability of the environment to cleanse itself is destroyed; at this point, humanity's impact on the environment can no longer be ignored. The way in which human development and the environment interrelate has become crucially important. For example, we have almost reached a key moment when human activity, for the first time, is possibly changing the climate. At this point, option (a) in Figure 4.1, becomes (b) and there are now three factors at play: human autonomous development, development resulting from the inter-relationship of humans and the environment and environmental autonomous development.

Now the cumulative damaging effects of external diseconomy gradually become evident, as shown in Figure 4.2. The above analysis shows how, even if the annual increase of the damaging effects of external diseconomy is only small, their impact cannot be ignored (this is analogous to plastic, or permanent, deformation). For example, the greenhouse effect produced by the reduction of forests, and the rise in carbon dioxide emissions, has only to raise the earth's surface temperature by 4–5°C for the effect to be unimaginable. However, ordinary people are unlikely to feel the detrimental effects of cumulative external diseconomy within a single or even several generations. This is such a gradual, incremental process that each generation only feels the effects to a slight degree. As a result, they lack the motivation to take measures to curb these effects.

Moreover, if the present generation attempts to control the cumulative effects bequeathed to us by former generations for the benefit of those to come, the costs may well greatly exceed the benefits that accrue to the present generation. Added

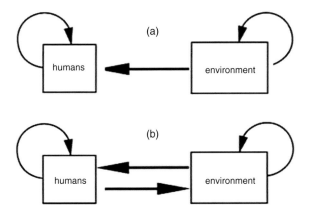

*Figure 4.1* Human beings and the environment.

Source: Author's own construct.

64  *The economy of waste*

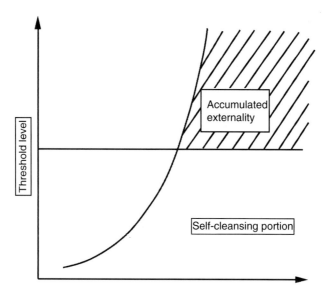

*Figure 4.2* Accumulated external diseconomy.

Source: Wade, Charles G, *Contemporary Chemistry: Science, Energy, and Environmental Change*, Macmillan, New York, 1976. (G.韋德：《能源與環境變化》科學出版社, 1983, 第 255 頁。[Kexue Chubanshe Publishers, 1983, page 255]).

to this, the benefits to individuals within the same generation are so small, and the risks involved in an ethical approach so great, that the majority of people focus on present and immediate gratification, and choose to make a living that yields a high net present value (NPV). It is commonly believed that our forebears got by, so we'll get by too, won't we? And so will our descendents, so there's no need to worry. Thus, it is only when the negative NPV of the cumulative external diseconomy is increased to the point where the NPV of environmental management reaches the highest value of all activities, that it becomes possible for the people of that generation to manage the environment. In other words, it is only possible for people to take action when the costs of this management is less than, or equal to, the benefits. However, at that point, we may face the '29th day' scenario – and it will all be too late. This process is illustrated in Figure 4.3.

The following figures show how this works: 10,000 years ago, forests covered around 7.6 billion hectares of the earth's surface. By 1862, when the steam engine had become the chief means of locomotion, the forest cover was reduced to 5.5 billion hectares – a loss of 2.1 billion hectares, or 200 thousand hectares annually. In the century from 1862–1958, there was a further decline to about 3 billion hectares, a loss of 2.5 billion hectares, or 25 million hectares annually. Between 1958 and 1978 – the golden age of post-World War II capitalism – forest cover

*The economy of waste* 65

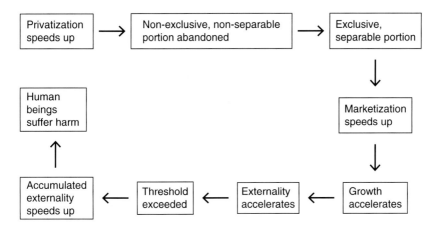

*Figure 4.3* Flow chart of accumulated externality.
Source: Author's own construct.

dropped to 2.3 billion hectares, a loss of 700 million, or 35 million hectares annually.[13] The period between 1862 and the mid-twentieth century was precisely when capitalism was developing and large-scale private ownership was established, with the latter enjoying a golden age between 1958 and 1978. This entire period saw a corresponding acceleration of deforestation.

There is a growing awareness that the non-separable, non-exclusive element of forests, such as environmental benefits and air quality, are precious assets, essential to the survival and progress of humankind. For instance, Sandra Postel[14] points out that in 1973, the state of Montana (USA) passed a law permitting government bodies to own water rights. Currently, much of this state's water resources are not utilized. This law states that substantial amounts of its water must be preserved in order to protect the ecology of its rivers. Because the state enjoys the right to protect its water resources, the bulk of the water from the Yellowstone River will be protected in perpetuity. Even though this principle of 'public trust' is rarely used, it is one of the best ways to protect water resourcesAs long ago as ancient Rome, it was recognized that the government had water rights and could take action to ensure that these rights were not eroded by private interests.[15] This is clearly an infringement of private property rights.

Throughout this chapter, I have analysed how humans make use of biological resources, forests and the Earth, as well as non-renewable resources; and the tendency to over-exploitation is quite clear. The pollution of obviously non-separable, non-exclusive resources, such as air and fresh water, in the course of over-exploitation of non-renewable resources is equally startling and happens by means of exactly the same mechanisms. Damage to the ozone layer caused by air pollution even means that the last plentiful resource we have – the sun – is being

## 66  *The economy of waste*

adversely affected. The existing resource allocation mechanisms (including property rights) appear to have many, very real flaws.

## The unvarnished truth

It is now time to link this analysis of mechanisms for allocating different categories of natural resources (including systems of property rights, price mechanisms and so on) and their consequences, to the 'classic' development model, and to draw general conclusions.

Generally speaking, the crux of the problem with the 'classic' development model is over-exploitation: on the one hand, this model is characterized by the large-scale consumption of non-renewable natural resources; on the other hand, it inflicts great damage on renewable resources. The mechanism by which the former is carried out is a combination of private enterprise and the market, the 'classic' mechanism, in short.

Fundamentally, this maximizes the 'classic' model's potential by discarding, as far as possible, all non-separable and non-exclusive elements of complex resource systems, in order better to separate off the separable, exclusive portion. This, no doubt, is the secret formula that has allowed the 'classic' development model to emerge with such rapidity over the last two or three centuries and to establish such a dominant global position. However this is just one aspect of the question. Another aspect is that the 'classic' development model is firmly rooted because, for most of the last two or three centuries, the non-separable, non-exclusive resources most essential to human survival and development – air, forests, water, land, sun and plants – really were available in almost limitless abundance, especially to those countries that were the first to develop. There was, until now, no such scarcity and thus no real constraint on the 'classic' development system (which would of course be unable to cope if these resources became seriously scarce). Those resources that are scarce happen to have a high level of separability and exclusivity – this is the greatest strength of the 'classic' development model – whereas non-separable, non-exclusive resources are virtually inexhaustible. Moreover, all external diseconomy can be discarded into the ecosystem, which must then cleanse itself. Given this ingenious match, it is no wonder that this has been the grand stratagem for the 'classic' development model.

However, in terms of the few hundred thousand years during which humans have existed, these two or three centuries are just the blink of an eye. The good times of the 'classic' development model have not lasted long. Recently, essential and plentifully available resources have begun to reach crisis point, as the cumulative external diseconomy has exceeded the capacity of the environment to deal with it. One after another, these have turned into congested and scarce resources, and the 'classic' system, the vehicle for the 'classic' development model, has proved unable to cope. In addition, separable and exclusive resources – largely non-renewable resources – have been over-exploited. This has acutely embarrassed proponents of this model. They are now faced with the dilemma that

*The economy of waste* 67

numerous resources (chiefly renewables), which could once be left unmanaged, now need managing and many resources, mainly non-renewables, which were once easy to manage, are increasingly drying up. A shortage of these managed resources has pulled the rug from under their feet.

The fact that the 'classic' development model has brought such problems on itself and destroyed the basis of its own existence is a double tragedy. Humankind may be said to face ten major environmental problems: desertification, deforestation, the crisis in water resources, species going extinct, pollution by acid rain, the greenhouse effect, damage to the ozone layer, soil erosion, pollution by toxic chemicals and a waste disposal crisis. Without exception, all these problems have been gifted to humankind by the 'classic' development model. This really is a final settling of accounts by Mother Nature.

Research carried out by the International Institute for Applied Systems Analysis predicts changes to Europe's natural environment between now and 2040. According to their report, the chief problems include increasing acidification of the soil, progressive decline in water and air quality, toxic chemical emissions at danger levels and the harmful effects brought about by global warming on agriculture, fresh water systems and the seasons. In Central Europe, the concentration of sulphuric acid deposits already exceeds safety standards by more than tenfold. The report warns that unless every European government takes immediate action, a 'chemical time-bomb', caused by sulphuric acid and other toxic chemicals that have accumulated in the soil and in wetlands – which are then deposited in river beds and estuaries – will go off, bringing even greater disasters in its wake.[16]

However it should be emphasized here that even though the above problems are largely produced by developed countries following the 'classic' development model (for example, America has 5 per cent of the world's population but releases 25 per cent of the world's carbon dioxide emissions into the atmosphere), nevertheless, the same problem also exists in socialist countries. That is to say, they combine the 'classic' development model and the open-access resource exploitation model. Theoretically, socialist countries where public ownership prevails should be able to manage non-separable, non-exclusive resources better than capitalist countries, where private property ownership predominates. However, because public ownership systems have historically lacked specific, effective legislation and a public ownership system created from such legislation, the result has been a combination of open-access resource exploitation and stress on growth. If we say that Hotelling's Rule summarizes the 'classic' development model and its foundation (the 'classic' system), then the corollary is that Gordon's Rule can be said to describe the development model of socialist countries today.

It is especially worrying if the market mechanism is added to open-access resource exploitation in socialist countries, and the 'classic' development model continues to be implemented. The combination of these three elements is especially unfavourable, because not only is the best feature of the market (easy management of separable and exclusive resources) inhibited but, in an imperfect

## 68  *The economy of waste*

ownership system, its greatest shortcomings (the mechanisms of adverse selection and over-exploitation) may be exacerbated. This is related to the three-body problem's internal structure, and cannot be investigated further in this book. I will limit myself below to a brief description of the shortcomings of market mechanisms.

There is a vast difference in order of magnitude between the human timescale and the geological timescale necessary for non-renewable resources to form, but this differential mechanism is not displayed in the way human beings allocate resources. This has had huge consequences. Take, for example, the relationship between prices and supplies: if there is a reduction in supplies, then prices will rise. In other words, if prices rise, then profits may increase in the short term, and the desire further to exploit resources that have already been over-exploited, will also increase. As a result, that exploitation will reach levels irrecoverable at least in human lifetimes.

The most difficult problem is that supply and demand relationships are unable to take long-term factors into consideration. Prices fixed according to supply and demand are based on immediate availability and cannot predict or prevent future shortages. In reality, even if individual producers attempt to raise prices on the basis of shortages that will occur in future years, they will find themselves up against competitors only concerned with short-term benefits (selling their products cheap) or courts accusing them of hiking up prices. For this reason, prices cannot rise until shortages suddenly occur, at which point it is too late to encourage recycling or to find substitutes within the time available.

The danger is that an exponential growth in the use of resources may speedily exhaust those resources, to the point where the interval between an awareness that a certain resource is running low and the moment when it becomes scarce is so short that there is no time to adopt remedies such as searching out substitute products, or recycling existing ones. Current resource allocation systems are incapable of resolving this fundamental problem effectively.

These systems, a basic prerequisite of 'classic' economic theory, have not considered the needs of future generations. There is a conviction that an unseen hand will put everything to rights, bolstered by the feeling: why should I care if disaster strikes after I die? So the reality is that, in terms of natural resources, the birthright of future generations is very much poorer than that of our own.

Thus, a resource allocation system like market pricing is essentially unable to harmonize itself with the geological timescale necessary for the formation of natural resources, because it operates on a human timescale. Some scholars believe that current problems with resources are not caused by failings in the market itself but by the fact that many resources (such as air) have not yet been properly privatized, and that, therefore, total privatization (really just internalization under a fancier name) is necessary.[17] In reality, the history of privately-owned resources over the centuries has shown that this is simply nonsense (not to speak of the fact that internalization of many resources is extremely expensive). Private ownership and market mechanisms are far from being the panacea for all the ills that humankind faces.

We can now draw the following conclusions about the 'classic' development model. First, the earliest countries to develop can be seen, in terms of a human time-scale, to have been in possession of almost limitless, global natural resources. They succeeded because they were a small minority of countries, that stripped the world of its resources by economic and non-economic means. The unique nature of these resources, and the pattern of their expropriation, was a basic precondition of the 'classic' development model, which decreed that this model would work for only a minority of countries. It was to prove impossible for the majority of countries to follow and would prove disastrous for the whole of humankind. For example, suppose that by the year 2000 there are seven billion people with a GNP as high as that of the Americans now; in that case, environmental pollution will be ten times the current level.[18]

Developing countries should not be deluded into thinking that they can reach America's standard of living within decades. Americans, who make up less than 6 per cent of the world's population, consume between one-third and one-half of mineral resources produced annually. Thus, even if there was a complete redistribution of global resources, the 'classic' development model could not, objectively speaking, be universally applied. The reason is simple: the resources that are a prerequisite for this model simply do not exist for the great majority of developing countries. It is extremely doubtful whether these conditions are sustainable, even for small numbers of developing countries. Once non-renewable resources are exhausted, the situation cannot be reversed, and the long-term problems engendered by recklessly wasteful growth will be plain for all to see.

Second, current systems of resource allocation, including market allocation mechanisms and private ownership, vastly underrate the value of resources formed on a geological timescale. The truth is that market mechanisms, which regulate supply and demand, free of interference, have greatly increased levels of scarcity of resources in the long term, leading to an entrenchment and acceleration of the many problems which the 'classic' development model has brought with it and which we see today. In the very long term, the 'invisible hand' is not only of very little use to humankind, its effects may actually be damaging, and it is only when matters reach crisis point that this damage suddenly becomes apparent. This will eventually have an irreversible adverse effect on the future of humankind, obliging us to pay a heavy price to counteract it.

In recent years, West Germany, Japan and the UK have all pushed through measures to make new cars more fuel-efficient. When the price of oil rose in 1979, West German car producers agreed to make their new cars 10–20 per cent more fuel-efficient. In the same year, Japan passed legislation requiring new cars to average at least 32 miles per gallon (mpg). These controls were direct interference enforced through the law courts, the aim being nothing less than further to distort prices already distorted by the market. This is supremely ironic, when we consider the unquestioning belief that any interference distorts prices, thus reducing the efficacy of resource allocation. Yet these examples show how humanity's future model and level of development are determined by how much it knows about its own future.

70  *The economy of waste*

## Wastage and growth

As an increasing number of people realize the limits of non-renewable resources and the way in which these resources are being squandered, they are led to question the meaning of everyday concepts such as 'progress' and 'productivity'.

However, every proposal intended to reduce the growing wastage of resources is invariably shouted down by such arguments as: 'You can't get in the way of progress.' At the same time, layers of confusion surround the consequences of our wastage of non-renewables and destruction of renewable resources, to the point where we cannot tell the difference between progress and extravagance. Ultimately, humanity needs to arrive at a true definition of progress, based on fundamental questions such as the meaning of life and the direction in which humanity is heading. We cannot stray from these questions and, if we do, inevitable difficulties and setbacks will cause them to rear their heads once again.

The philosophical and cultural basis of the 'classic' development model states that the basic aim of human existence is to satisfy all possible material needs, irrespective of how significant these needs are. In just the same way, wasteful growth arises from a failure to consider the direction and quality of that growth.

The chief task that faces us now, is to comprehensively reassess what we are doing. We should look to see whether, as resources diminish, we are still improving people's lives or simply pursuing short-term profit, depleting resources and causing economic collapse. I will examine below whether we need to adopt new lifestyles that benefit human society and civilization, rather than landing us in greater difficulties, and I will further explain the major choices that lie before us.

In the West, beef producers would have us believe that the rise in beef consumption in recent years represents progress. But there is increasing evidence to show that consuming large quantities of beef with the accompanying large quantities of saturated fats is an important contributory factor in heart disease, obesity and other related conditions. In addition, more beef production requires more feed grain, which in turn leads to an increase in soil erosion, silting up of waterways, and farm-based pollution. Obviously, none of this is beneficial to individuals or society. By contrast, if development proceeds on the basis of the volume of food required by human beings, and its nutritional content is balanced, this benefits health and reduces damage to the environment.

Then there is supersonic flight, another much-welcomed marker of 'progress', whose opponents are condemned as stick-in-the-muds. But do the costs for such travel add up? Each supersonic aircraft consumes five times as much fuel per passenger mile as a Boeing 747, with a commensurate increase in pollution, and noise levels are four times higher on take-off. This 'progress' only allows a limited number of passengers to save 30 per cent of their time in crossing the Atlantic. On the other hand, high-speed rail links to and from the airport can save on energy and reduce pollution, and cut total journey time for all air travellers by upwards of 30 per cent.[19] Should supersonic air travel be regarded, therefore, as wasteful growth or as progress? A large proportion of everything thus far labelled 'progress' looks, today, more like wasteful growth. Real progress, however, would allow people to reduce the resources used to accomplish the same function with the same efficacy.

Growth which reduces resource consumption certainly does not mean abandoning science and technology and reverting to primitive ways of living. The opposite is true: it is wasteful growth and the depletion of natural resources, which are most likely to propel society back to the primitive state. The only way for human civilization to progress is by recognizing the need to limit the consumption of natural resources and modifying our lives so that we consume only an appropriate amount of those resources.

### An economy constantly in the red

We can put precise figures on the amount that is wasted in the process of modern economic growth. The World Resources Institute published a 1989 report, *Wasting Assets: Natural Resources in the National Income Accounts*,[20] which challenged the use of GNP as a way of measuring nations' economic growth, precisely because GNP does not take into account the consumption of natural resources.

The report, written by Robert Repetto and others, looks at the case of Indonesia and makes the point that using the traditional indicator of economic growth (GNP) has the effect of over-stating true growth figures. For example, between 1970 and 1984, GNP averaged 7 per cent growth, but when consumption of resources such as forests, topsoil and fossil fuels is quantified and deducted, real economic growth drops to 4 per cent. Repetto (World Resources Institute 1989) explains that '. . .the methods by which we currently measure economic growth are misleading. . .these methods do not treat natural resources in the same way as other kinds of capital or assets.'

The report continues:

> People treat manufactured capital such as buildings and equipment as fixed capital and take into consideration their rate of depreciation. But they do not regard natural resources in the same way. Generally speaking, national income and output (equivalent to GNP minus fixed asset depreciation) do not take the wear and tear of these assets into account.
>
> (ibid.)

According to traditional methods of calculation, for every $3.5 invested in Indonesia, there is an economic benefit of $1. From 1970 to 1984, however, if consumption of natural resources is taken into account, it is necessary to invest $10 to produce an economic benefit of $1. Repetto says: 'There is not one company which can pay its workers' wages by selling off its fixed assets in the long term. But by employing misleading statistics, many countries do something very similar' (ibid.).

The World Resources Institute report warns policy-makers in countries who use natural resources to fund construction, that ignoring depletion of natural

## 72   *The economy of waste*

resources and exaggerating growth figures may cause development plans to eventually fail. Repetto believes that: 'This way of using the environmental deficit superficially increases income while actually reduces wealth' (ibid.).

Anyone who spent their inheritance on simply living would certainly be regarded as a spendthrift. Yet when a people do the same, they are universally praised, in fact the faster they do it, the better. How are we to explain such lack of logic?

In the case of Indonesia above, it is clear where the crux of the problem lies: the formula which says that GNP minus fixed asset depreciation = national income = expenditure + investment, means that only national income can be used for consumption and net investment in new growth, because it is only when depreciation funds are sufficient that it is possible to ensure that already-formed, fixed capital is maintained in good condition. Thus, depreciation cannot be used on expenditure and further investment. (This basic condition is necessary to simple reproduction.) The same principle applies to natural resources: depreciation of these resources should be deducted from the national income, i.e. a portion of the national income should be used to compensate for the depletion of natural resources and to restore them to their original state. When people, in using up natural resources, treat this depreciation as 'profit', they are effectively creating an environmental deficit. Once this vertical external diseconomy begins to accumulate, the consequences will inevitably be appalling. In the case of Indonesia, the deficit portion takes up half its real growth. In other words, the 'profit' arising from resource depreciation is cancelled out, meaning that half of the so-called growth is wastage. If the 'economic miracles' of the last two or three centuries are re-evaluated using the same yardstick, it will be seen that they have succeeded in producing a continuous acceleration of the deficit. Our forebears and our descendants would be ashamed of us.

This deficit has been caused by sheer ignorance and errors of calculation. Even more importantly, it reveals a popular, underlying assumption that there is an unlimited supply of natural resources. If this were really true, then providing the deficit is fixed within certain limits and human existence is also limited to, say, a few billion years, then we could continue to incur a deficit to our heart's content. It would be like an inheritance, bequeathed by billions of forebears, being squandered by a single spendthrift, without giving any cause for anxiety. But the prospects are by no means as rosy as we like to imagine. What is actually happening is that a large number of spendthrifts are busy squandering a single inheritance. We have already seen above how vast quantities of renewables are in the process of being turned into non-renewables, while almost all non-renewables are destined to run out in a very short time. Yet the reaction of most people is likely to be a dismissive shrug of the shoulders, 'It's not my problem. Let future generations sort that one out!'

The parlous state of the national income calculation model based on mainstream Western economic theory is reflected in the fact that it encourages waste: one of its basic tenets is to teach people that economizing is not a virtue, and to promote ever more effective wastage. In 1776, when Adam Smith published his classic work, over-felling of England's woodlands was already a problem, yet he still advocated a combination of market mechanisms and the pursuit of personal gain as a way of protecting woodlands. How would he feel now if he could see the unprecedented speed with which forests have been depleted, starting half a century after his death and continuing today? Life is fragile, someone said, and it needs to be sustained with the utmost care. We could add that nature is not only precious – it is even more fragile than life itself.

### Re-visiting the problems

The national income calculation system, based, as it is on erroneous concepts and theories, necessarily distorts the true meaning of progress. The following analysis appears to belie common sense.

It is generally recognized that with the aid of sophisticated new technology, highly efficient non-human forms of energy can replace relatively inefficient human energy, thus creating more wealth and making life a great deal easier for humankind. That is what progress is generally understood to mean. The premise on which all this is based is: the greater the energy circulation in the unit of time, the more efficient society will become, the faster civilization will progress and the more ordered our world will be.

By contrast, if the definition of efficiency is to reduce the amount of human work required, then the greater the amount of energy that is required to keep each individual alive, the lower the efficiency. This is the precise opposite of popularly held beliefs. What we call 'work', when it comes down to it, is a waste of efficient energy. The energy that is necessary for every member of today's industrialized society to expend in order to sustain life is more than a hundred times greater than it was a million years ago. We humans are prone to self-deception, but even we cannot maintain that the use of labour-saving devices reduces the amount of work we do.

To date, the rate of production has always been defined according to the speed required for each unit of production. In recent years, studies have looked at how much energy is required to produce one car and have shown that the energy consumed in the production of a car is many times greater than necessary. This is because it is necessary to get cars off the production line as fast as possible. Much of the energy expended by modern industry is aimed at speeding up production.

If we only measure the rate of production according to the speed with which a unit is produced, then the process of transforming resources into economic effectiveness will be needlessly wasteful. However, providing there is sufficient production of fossil fuel and metals necessary to sustain industrialized manufacturing methods, then it is logical to use speed as a measure of the rate of production. But now, energy sources are beginning to dry up and entropy from past economic activities is accumulating at a rate faster than the present system

74  *The economy of waste*

is able to absorb it. As a result, in order to adapt to the thermodynamic needs of the economic process of production and consumption, economists need to transform the concept of productivity.

The old way of looking at a car might lead people to ask: How can we improve the engine and make it more successful? What we really ought to be asking are quite different questions: Can we really not live without a car? Has the car really improved our lives and our health and made us more civilized? Have today's cars expropriated the energy necessary for the next generation to sustain life? If something was not worth doing in the first place, then its success or failure is not worth discussing. If a car is not worth having, then it is irrelevant whether it does 20 or 50 miles to the gallon.[21]

The book I have quoted from above: *Entropy: A New World View*, may be biased in places, but it nonetheless represents an extremely thorough investigation by two Western economists into the 'classic' development model.

In actual fact, the economies developed on the 'classic' model during the years when resources were relatively plentiful, have been consuming more and more resources to produce less; and those industries in most serious decline now are those, which, in the past, were most wasteful. Once depletion of natural resources becomes irreversible, this technology, development model and way of thinking will surely need to change. We should question which appears most efficient and economical: the expenditure of 10 calories, or of 1 calorie of fossil fuel energy to produce the same 1 calorie of food energy. The choice is really no choice at all – the answer is obvious.

It seems that we need a new definition of progress: to satisfy basic needs and such needs as allow humans to develop, while (1) not over-exploiting renewable resources and (2) using fewer non-renewable resources than the past; (3) we should also aim to achieve the same levels of use of renewable resources as in the past. Only when we make these changes will we have real progress. This should be the fundamental principle on which a new development model, replacing the 'classic' one, rests.

In summary, there are still many questions around a new development model that remain unclear or are controversial, and these will be discussed in subsequent chapters of this book. Even so, we can by now be in no doubt that the destruction of renewable resources, and the rapid depletion of non-renewables, is bringing about a sea change in commonly-accepted ideas and fundamental thinking formed during the age of industrialization. (I am referring to the relations between economic and non-economic, between optimal and low efficiency and so on.) It is equally clear that all of us (especially people who, like the Chinese, live in a large, developing country) ought to – indeed cannot avoid – re-examining and re-evaluating the significance of each and every change in global development that has already happened, or is currently happening.

## Notes

1  Defined here as an optimal efficiency relative pricing system where there is no administrative interference and where non-attenuated property rights are in place. *Author's note.*

The economy of waste    75

2  Clark, C.W., *Mathematical Bioeconomics: The Optimal Management of Renewable Resources*. J. Wiley & Sons, New York, 1976. (C. W. 克拉克:《數學生物經濟學: 更新資源的最優管理》农业出版社, 1984第 4 頁 [Nongye Chubanshe Publishers, 1984, page 4]).

3  Ibid., page 7.

4  夏伟生:《人类生态学初探》甘肃人民出版社, 1984, 124–125 頁.  (XIA Weisheng, *An Exploration of Human Ecology*, Gansu Renmin Chubanshe Publishers, 1984 pages 124–5).

5  Ibid.

6  Lester R. Brown, *et al.*, editors, *State of the World 1988: A Worldwatch Institute Report on Progress Toward a Sustainable Society*, published by W. W. Norton, New York, 1988 (莱斯特· R. 布朗等: 《經濟社會科技 — 1988 年世界形勢述評》, 科技文獻出版社 1989 年, 第 248 頁。 [Kejiwenxian Chubanshe Publishers, 1989, page 248]).

7  莱斯特· R. 布朗等:《縱觀世界全局》, 中國對外翻譯出版公司  1985 年, 第 95 頁 [Zhongguoduiwaifanyi Chubangongsi Publishers, 1985, page 95.] Lester R. Brown, *et al.*, editors, *Comprehensive Survey of the World* (Original not identifiable). *Trans.*

8  Ibid., pages 91, 97.

9  莱斯特·  R. 布朗等:《縱觀世界全局》, 中國對外翻譯出版公司 1985 年, 第 91, 97頁. [Zhongguoduiwaifanyichubangongsi Publishers, 1985, page 91, 97.] Lester R. Brown, et al., editors, *Comprehensive Survey of the World* (Original not identifiable). *Trans.*

10  Lester R. Brown, *et al.*, *State of the World 1985: A Worldwatch Institute Report on Progress Toward a Sustainable Society*, published by W. W. Norton, New York, 1985 (莱斯特·R.布朗等:《經濟社會科技—1985    年世界形勢述評》, 科技文獻出版社 1986 年, 第  28 [Kejiwenxian Chubanshe Publishers, 1986, page 28]).

11  Clark, C.W., *Mathematical Bioeconomics: The Optimal Management of Renewable Resources*, J. Wiley & Sons, New York, 1976. (C. W. 克拉克:《數學生物經濟學: 更新資源的最優管理》农业出版社, 1984 第  161 頁 [Nongye Chubanshe Publishers, 1984, page 161]).

12  Alan Randall, *Resource Economics: An Economic Approach to Natural Resource and Environmental Policy*, 1981 (阿蘭·蘭德爾:《資源經濟學: 從經濟角度對自然資源和環境政策的探討》, 1989年, 商務印書館, 第 224頁。 [Shangwuyinshuguan Publishers, 1989, page 224]).

13  夏偉生:《人類生態學初探》甘肅人民出版社1984 年版, 第125頁. (XIA Weisheng, *An Exploration of Human Ecology*, Gansu Renmin Chubanshe Publishers, 1984, page 125).

14  Lester R. Brown, *et al.*, *State of the World 1985: A Worldwatch Institute Report on Progress Toward a Sustainable Society*, pub. W. W. Norton, New York, 1985 (莱斯特·R. 布朗等:《經濟社會科技—1985年世界形勢述評》科技文獻出版社 1986 年, 第 88 [Kejiwenxian Chubanshe Publishers, 1986, page 88]).

15  Ibid.

16  《中國科學報》1989年 4 月18日。 (*China Science* newspaper, 18 April 1989).

17  亨利:  勒帕日 《美國新自由主義經濟學》, 北京大學出版社  1985 年, 第  217 頁 [Beijingdaxue Chubanshe Publishers, 1985, page 217]. Henri Lepage, *American Neo–liberal Economics*. Possibly Henri Lepage, *Demain le liberalisme*, pub. Librairie Generale Francaise, 1980. *Trans.*

18  *The Limits of Growth* Donella H. Meadows, Dennis L. Meadows, Jørgen Randers, and William W. Behrens III, published by the Club of Rome, 1972. (米多斯等:《增長的極限》, 商務印書館 1984 年, 第 61 頁 [Shangwuyinshuguan Publishers, 1984, page 61]).

19  Nebel, B. J. and Wright, R. T., *Environmental Science: The Way the World Works*. (B. J. 內貝爾:《環境科學: 世界存在與發展的途徑》1987 年, 第 359 頁, 科學出版社 [Kexue Chubanshe Publishers, 1987, page 359]).

## 76 *The economy of waste*

20 Repetto, Robert, Magrath, William, Wells, Michael, Beer, Christine, and Rossini, Fabrizio, 1989, *Wasting Assets: Natural Resources in the National Income Accounts*, World Resources Institute, Washington, DC. Quotes have been back-translated. *Trans*. (《科技日報》1989 年 5 月 24 [*Science and Technology Daily* newspaper, 24 May, 1989.])

21 Jeremy Rifkin and Ted Howard, *Entropy: A New World View*, The Viking Press, New York, 1980. (杰里米 里夫金等《熵: 一種新的世界觀》1987 年, 第 227 頁, 上海译文出版社 [Shanghaiyiwen Chubanshe Publishers, 1987, page 227]).

# 5 Humans and entropy

At the beginning of the 1970s, the Club of Rome published its first report, 'The Limits to Growth', which revealed general doubt about the 'classic' development model focused on GNP growth. The publication of this report aroused widespread, intense controversy. Then in 1980, *Entropy: A New World View* was published in the USA. The authors, Jeremy Rifkin and Ted Howard, use the law of entropy to conduct a bold and comprehensive evaluation of the process of development of human economy and society, examining consequences and predicting future trends. Their conclusions are astonishing and raise many questions of profound significance, which it is impossible to cover fully here. I will therefore limit myself to the following: (1) a summary of the most important areas the book covers, as well as of its deficiencies; (2) an explanation, in as much detail as possible, of the concept and significance of entropy, and how it relates to the development of human society and economies; (3) an analysis of the influence of human activities on entropy.

## More storms

Almost all aspects of the issues discussed in *Entropy* have been analysed in the last 20 or 30 years by various scholars. *Entropy*, however, is unique in that it uses the second law of thermodynamics to carry out an integrated analysis of the key questions of human progress, thus prompting a new and fundamental discussion. *Entropy* elaborates the second law of thermodynamics in great depth, to a degree that has rarely been seen. Let us look at the main points that the authors of *Entropy* make.

The main premise of Entropy is: the Earth is a closed system which receives energy from the sun and disperses it into space, but which, for a number of reasons, exchanges very little matter with the rest of the solar system. On the basis of this primary supposition, the authors of this book attempt to extend the second law of thermodynamics to the whole of the Earth and to every aspect of human society, such as the development of the economy, of thinking, and so on.

In thermodynamics, entropy is the measure of the sum of all the energy that cannot be re-converted back into work. Thus, when energy is converted from one state to another state, we suffer certain penalties. In other words, we lose a certain

## 78 *Humans and entropy*

amount of energy that could do work in the future. Entropy shows us that matter and energy can only be converted in one direction, that is, from useable to non-useable, from effective to ineffective and from order to disorder. An increase in entropy means a reduction in effective energy. Energy, which becomes ineffective, constitutes pollution. Pollution is just another word for entropy. Accordingly, we should abandon the traditional mechanistic worldview, which says that the more material wealth we accumulate, the more orderly and progressive the world will necessarily become.

The authors of *Entropy* believe that the law of entropy has an objective existence, which human society cannot circumvent. It exists in every aspect of our lives, and is the basis of all human activities. Human history is also a reflection of the second law of thermodynamics; it is the dissipation of our energy resources rather than the accumulation of wealth, which is the reason for change in human history. The law of entropy has shattered the traditional concept that history is progressive and assumes that history is in fact a continual process of retrogression and decline. It also assumes that the development of human thought is not necessarily a progressive process, but is becoming increasingly complex, abstract and wasteful.

The basis of all life derives from the sun's energy. Thus, life itself cannot escape the law of entropy. Organisms evolve through absorbing negative entropy and order from the environment. The law of entropy therefore demonstrates the following truth: evolution, in the sense of building an island of increasing order, must necessarily lead to the ocean of entropy that surrounds it being rocked by ever more turbulent waves.

The law of entropy has also put paid to the idea that we should rely on science and technology to establish a more orderly world. According to the law of entropy, technology is only a device for transforming energy; increased product input due to technological changes have hastened the process of entropy and confusion in the surrounding world; and the more modernized the world becomes, the greater the degree of confusion. The exponential growth of technological society is a one-way ticket leading to the destruction of life and the Earth.

Economic and political organizations are also converters of energy; their function is to promote the circulation of energy in society. The continual acceleration of the energy flow always speeds up the process of entropy, leads to the accumulation of confusion and to greater complexity in those organizations. Growth does not mean the world benefits from greater value or increased order – quite the opposite. The law of entropy shows that the faster economic growth, the nearer we approach to doomsday. The law of entropy is the guiding principle behind all economic activities. Current economic theory cannot solve the increasingly serious crisis facing the world economy. If we do not recognize this principle, and do not adjust our economic policies accordingly, then the earth will speedily suffer economic and ecological catastrophe.

The law of entropy will eventually determine whether political systems rise or fall, whether a country enjoys freedom or slavery, whether commerce and industry will flourish, the origins of poverty and affluence and whether human beings meet with good fortune or disaster. The final conclusion of *Entropy: A New Worldview* is that it is only when we recognize the limits of our world and consciously respect the limits of the earth's resources that we can truly comprehend how precious the Earth is, and make the significant adjustments necessary for human survival. Our survival, and that of all other forms of life, depends on our reconciliation with nature, and our determination to peacefully co-exist with the ecosystem. If we human beings stubbornly continue to go our own way, destroying everything on the earth, we will sooner or later reach a dead end. At that point we will face catastrophe. Whether we like it or not, we must move towards a low-energy society. A low-entropy society must employ appropriate technology, the scale of industrial production and the service sector must be significantly reduced, and the hegemony of the multinationals must be ended. We have come to a parting of the ways: we can consciously move into a low-entropy (or low-energy consumption) society; or we can cling to the current mechanistic worldview, and be forced painfully into a low-energy consumption society.

Our current worldview and traditions are currently enmeshed in a trap of our own devising. Wherever we look, entropy has increased alarmingly, indeed, is reaching critical levels. Faced with a situation of complex confusion, we struggle to protect ourselves. We cannot avoid making urgent, major reforms to our system, to its aims and objectives and the way it functions.

In addition, the authors warn Third World countries that they should not aspire to reach the levels of material abundance that the United States has enjoyed in recent decades. Other areas of the world cannot develop in the same way as the United States. If poor countries embark on the path of industrialization taken by the US economy, entropy will accelerate to a critical level, and misguided economic policies in those countries will lead the entire planet to disaster. Third World countries should seek a model of development that is different from Western industrialized countries. High-energy and highly-centralized technology should give way to appropriate technologies. It is only after a comprehensive re-adjustment of economic priorities, that the Third World will achieve successful development.

Such are the conclusions reached in *Entropy: A New World View*. This work is the result of a concise, thorough and systematic discussion of all the major issues, supported by a massive amount of data and statistics. Its authors assert that the mechanistic worldview of which Newton's theories are representative is about to become defunct, and that the development of human science and technology is producing more harmful junk and more pollution than 'wealth'. It is only by applying the law of entropy to an examination of all aspects of society, they say, that we will succeed in slowing the growth of entropy and the approach of 'heat death'. Rifkin and Howard also adopt the law of entropy as the basis for exploring major issues such as philosophy, economics, politics, culture, education and religion, in past, present and future.

*Entropy: A New Worldview* is an extraordinary work of scholarship and a thought-provoking read. Different people will take different things from its conclusions, but I believe that its chief merits lie in the way in which it confronts us

## 80 *Humans and entropy*

with the changes undergone by human society to date and the price that we are paying for them.

When people see the implications of the price society has paid, they will have to admit that this so-called progress, far from being brilliant, casts an ominous shadow over us. This will be demonstrated in the figures below.

In 1987, the global population reached five billion. Let us suppose that at the end of the twenty-first century, this figure remains unchanged (which is certainly an under-estimate), and that global per capita GNP is equivalent to Japan's 1980 levels, that is, $4,800 (at the 1970 dollar value). By this reckoning, by the end of the twenty-first century, the total GNP of these five billion people will be equivalent to 50 Japans (whose population then was 110 million). Japan's consumption levels were the lowest of all developed countries, at about half of America's. By the end of the twenty-first century, therefore, global consumption will be equivalent to that of 12 United States (at 1970 levels). Let us further suppose that, starting from the end of the twenty-first century, there is an annual 1 per cent growth in consumption globally, so that 500 years hence (by the end of the twenty-sixth century), levels of consumption will be 128 times that of the twenty-first century, equivalent to the consumption level of 1,536 Americas in the 1970s. In 1970, the United States consumed a third of the world's natural resources, so that by the end of the twenty-sixth century, the consumption of the world's natural resources will be 500 times that of 1970.

In geological terms, 500 or 600 years is an impossibly short time for the formation of a significant quantity of natural resources. Thus, in terms of human development, zero growth in material consumption is not a sensationalist and pessimistic concept, but is, rather, overly optimistic. It seems that, after a certain point, an annual *decrease* in material consumption (at least for a period of time) is a more realistic strategy. In this sense, the aim of *Entropy*, to make a comprehensive critique of a 'classic' development model based on overwhelmingly on stocks technology, is perfectly sound.

I also regard the authors' critique of the idea that we should use new technology to keep the 'classic' model of development going, as sound. Technology has merely changed the means by which we obtain energy (for example, by using microwaves, nuclear energy, hydrogen energy and bio-technology). As long as the model of development remains unchanged, there will be no fundamental change in the way we make use of energy – cars, highways, skyscrapers, air-conditioning and so on. Thus, even if we no longer obtain energy from petroleum and coal (non-renewable, non-recyclable resources), the process of consuming energy will swallow up large amounts of non-renewable resources, which are hard to recycle satisfactorily (non-energy minerals, such as copper, iron, zinc, nickel, aluminium etc.). Continuing on the old road to development, even with the use of new technology, is not feasible in the long term. This is clear from the above calculations. In short, the demise of this strategy, which relies on rapid growth of material wealth, is imminent.

However, I am not in total agreement with the authors' view that all human progress is the process of entropy growth; some of their analyses and conclusions contain dangerous ambiguities and considerable flaws. I believe that one of the main problems with this book is that the authors take the view that the natural world proceeds increasingly from an ordered state to a disordered one. As we will see below, there is insufficient basis for this conclusion.

It is necessary to clarify and define as far as possible the specific meaning of entropy in thermodynamics, and ways in which this has been extended in popular discourse, in order to evaluate its effectiveness in different areas.

## The principle of entropy growth

Entropy is a concept in thermodynamics, a measure of the degree of disorder of molecular motion. Recently, this concept has appeared frequently in social science literature. However, its meaning varies in different situations. We must first, therefore, explain what entropy means, in order to evaluate the effectiveness of ways in which this concept is popularly used.

The law of conservation of energy constitutes the first law of thermodynamics, and states that mechanical work must be obtained by the transformation of energy. This makes it impossible for what we call perpetual motion of the first kind to create mechanical work. However, this law does not place any restrictions on the transformation of heat into mechanical work. In other words, the law of conservation of energy does not rule out the possibility of perpetual motion of the second kind, for example, a pool of water the same temperature as the outside environment, working on its own.

In 1848, William Thomson, first Baron Kelvin (1824–1907), formulated the absolute temperature scale on the basis of Carnot's 1824 theorem, pointing out the impossibility of completely changing the thermal energy of a single source of heat into mechanical work without any side effects (the so-called perpetual motion machine of the second kind). In 1850, Rudolf Clausius (1822–88) established the second law of thermodynamics on the basis of the same theorem. These two laws make up a complete system of thermodynamics.

Later, Boltzmann (1844–1906) made systematic use of statistical concepts and methods as a theoretical basis on which to introduce the concept of micro-states in a system and the probability distribution of a given micro-state. He took the macro-average state of the system as the average of its microscopic state, which enabled a statistical understanding of the second law of thermodynamics.

In other words, to convert energy to work, there must be a difference in energy concentration (that is, temperature difference) between the different parts of a system. When energy is converted from a higher concentration to a lower (or higher temperature to a lower temperature), we can say it has made work. Even more important is that each time energy is converted from one level to another level, it means that the next time less energy can be converted to make work. An example is a river flowing over a dam into a lake; when the water falls, it can be used to drive a turbine to generate electricity or for other forms of work. However, once the water drops to the foot of the dam, it is no longer in a state to make work. When the water surface is level, there is no potential energy of water to move

## 82  Humans and entropy

even the smallest wheels. These two different energy states are known respectively as 'effective' or 'free' energy (there is a fall of water), and 'ineffective' or 'closed' energy (there is no fall of water).

The increase in entropy means a reduction of effective energy. According to the first law of thermodynamics, energy can neither be produced nor disappear and, according to the second law of thermodynamics, energy can only be converted in one direction, that in which it dissipates. Entropy is therefore, a measure of a given unit and of ineffective energy in a given system. We will analyse this more precisely below.

### *Open systems and dissipative structures*

It can be said that any system can be differentiated according to whether it is isolated, closed or open. Isolated systems have no exchange of matter with the outside world, nor do they have systems of energy (and information) exchange (see Figure 5.1). Strictly speaking, no truly isolated systems exist in the world, only systems which approximate to an isolated system.

Closed systems exchange energy (and information) with the outside world, but there is no system for exchange of matter (see Figure 5.2). If we ignore falling meteors and cosmic dust, the Earth can be seen as a closed system. The Earth receives radiation from the sun and other celestial bodies, while also sending out radiation to interstellar radiation cool zones (see Figure 5.3). Naturally, if we regard human beings living on the Earth and the Earth itself as one complex system, then the whole can be regarded as approximating to a closed, or sealed, system.

An open system is one that freely exchanges matter and energy (and information) with the outside world. For example, the city is a typical open system (see Figure 5.4). Obviously, it is a centre, which imports food, fuel, building materials, all kinds of information and so on, but it also sends out manufactured products and waste materials. Any modern enterprise is an open system.

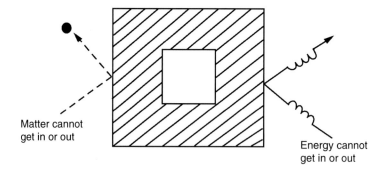

*Figure 5.1* Isolated system.

Source: Author's own construct.

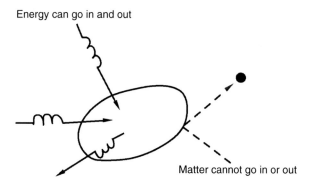

*Figure 5.2* Sealed system.

Source: Author's own construct.

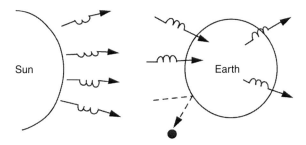

*Figure 5.3* The Earth approximates to a sealed system.

Source: Author's own construct.

Recent years have seen the rise of a new discipline – dissipative structure theory – whose main object of study is the open system. A variety of systems in the universe – whether living or inanimate, natural or social – in essence, are open systems, which are interdependent and interact with the surrounding environment.

The concept of dissipative structure stands in opposition to the concept of an equilibrium structure. Its strict, original meaning comes from physics (that is, non-equilibrium thermodynamics). Over the years, physicists have focused their research on the stability of the ordered structure of equilibrium systems, such as the equilibrium structure of the crystal. In conditions of relatively low temperature, the molecules that make up such a system are arranged in an orderly fashion, and maintain a stable structure. At this point, the thermal motion within the system only causes vibration of the molecules near the equilibrium position, and does not undermine the overall ordered state of the system. Only when the temperature increases and reaches a certain critical point is the original stable and orderly state destroyed, resulting in phase transitions (that is, changes in the structure). For example, the crystal (solid phase) can change into a liquid (liquid phase), and then

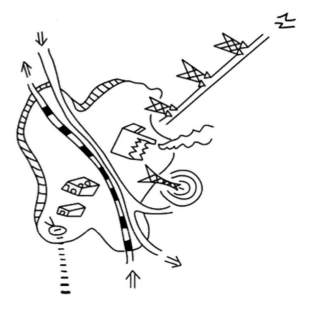

*Figure 5.4* The city is an open system.

Source: Author's own construct.

into a gas (vapour phase); the entire system can be transformed from a stable and orderly equilibrium state into a relatively disordered chaotic state, or into an equilibrium state with a low level of stability and order. These are all physical manifestations of the change from order to disorder. Questions of the mechanism of their movement and stability are usually dealt with in equilibrium thermodynamics (and its extensions). However, to deal with questions of non-equilibrium and disorder-to-order mechanisms, it is necessary to resort to new methods.

In the popular imagination, it is generally believed that a system in a chaotic, non-equilibrium state cannot spontaneously form a stable, ordered structure. This is what traditional laws of thermodynamics state. However, the founder of dissipative structure theory, the physicist Ilya Prigogine, points out that an open system far removed from equilibrium, can, under certain conditions, organize itself to form a new, stable and orderly structure. That is, it can effect a transformation from disorder to order, from a lower to a higher level of order, by means of constantly exchanging energy and matter with the outside world. This new, stable and orderly structure within a non-equilibrium state has been called by Prigogine and others, the dissipative structure (sometimes referred to as a constant open system). The meaning of the word 'dissipative' is that the system will continue to consume energy. This orderly, stable structure is different from an equilibrium structure. Where there is a stable equilibrium structure (such as crystal) with no exchange of matter and energy with the outside world, and no change in the internal pattern (maintaining the number of variables and the relationship between them), we can say this is a static, stable, equilibrium state. This is a never-changing 'dead' structure. Dissipative structures, on the other hand, often exchange energy and matter with the outside world (otherwise, this structure could not be maintained). Since its internal movement patterns also change, we can say this is a stable and orderly structure. It is dynamic, a 'living', stable and orderly structure. Life is just this kind of highly organized, ordered structure far from equilibrium. It is only by continually metabolizing and renewing itself that it can continue to exist and develop.

### Evolution and entropy

Order and disorder are contradictory phenomena found everywhere in nature, society and the economy. In the past, people normally divided the motion of matter into two categories: one with a strict order and structure, such as crystal; and one which was chaotic, where was no fixed order and structure, such as the thermal motion of gas molecules (also known as molecular chaos). Modern science holds that this absolute division is incorrect. There is no unbridgeable gap between the ordered and disordered; they are closely linked, and can be transformed into the other under certain conditions.

In thermodynamics, the concept of entropy is used to measure the degree of order in a system. So, what is entropy? To answer this question, it is necessary to introduce the concepts of reversibility and irreversibility. All phenomena that occur in nature and human society, strictly speaking, are irreversible, or reversible only in approximate terms. The perceived meaning of irreversibility is that after changes occur, a return to the original state where all the conditions are the same is impossible. In fact, the evolution of human society is a typical irreversible process. For example, people are descended from apes, but do not revert to being apes; human society may have developed from the primitive society, but cannot revert to a primitive society.

In physics, reversibility and irreversibility are essentially different. For example, if a drop of ink is dropped on clothing, the ink spreads automatically outwards, but will not automatically contract to a point. This situation is described in the second law of thermodynamics.

The general principle of thermodynamics describes a macroscopic system made up of a large amount of molecular movement and change. The first law of thermodynamics focuses on the measure of movement, and demonstrates the conservation of energy. Any change of energy in the system must be the result of the transmission of the same amount of energy passing through the boundary. The second law of thermodynamics focuses on the direction of movement and discusses the distinction between reversible and irreversible processes. It states that under certain conditions, a system state will have a given direction of movement (as in the example of the drop of ink). In order to express this quantitatively, a new function has been introduced, called 'entropy'. Briefly, entropy is a function of the state of a system. This function can measure to what extent a system is organized (or disorganized).

## 86  Humans and entropy

Entropy, unlike energy, is not conserved, and is usually represented by the symbol S. Changes in entropy (S) within a very short time (dt) are written as dS, and called entropy change. Entropy change (dS) consists of two components: the first, $d_eS$, is the transmission of entropy through the system boundary, while the second $d_iS$ is the production of entropy within the system. From this we arrive at the following relationship:

$$dS = d_eS + d_iS \tag{5.1}$$

The basic characteristic of entropy production, $d_iS$ is that it can distinguish irreversible processes. The second law of thermodynamics states that, for the entire thermodynamic process, entropy production is non-negative, that is:

$$d_iS \geq 0 \tag{5.2}$$

When the process is irreversible, then:

$$d_iS > 0 \tag{5.3}$$

The mixture of gasses of the two different temperatures (see Figure 5.5) is a specific example. The assumption is that the system is isolated, that is, $d_eS = 0$ (that is, the transmission of entropy through the system boundary is zero). Thus, in this case, we arrive at:

$$S_2 - S_1 = \Delta S = \int d_iS > 0 \tag{5.4}$$

Above, $\Delta S$ is the amount of change in entropy (S) moving from state $S_1$ to $S_2$; $\Delta S > 0$ means that, with $S_1$ there is an energy difference within the system because $T_1 \neq T_2$ (that is, within the box, the temperature of the gas on the left and the right are different). This energy difference may be used to make work, which means that when the system is in state $S_1$, there is effective energy: $\Delta T = T_1 - T_2 > 0$ (and we may suppose that $T_1 > T_2$). As time passes, the energy difference within this system tends to disappear spontaneously (which can be imagined as the result of the continuous mixing of the hot gas molecules with the colder gas molecules). That is to say, effective energy $\Delta T$ with the passage of time tends to zero. Thus, the system changes from a state of low entropy $S_1$ (because it has effective energy $T_1 - T_2 = \Delta T > 0$) into a state of higher entropy $S_2$ (because its

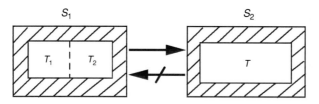

*Figure 5.5* Gasses of different temperatures mix.

Source: Author's own construct.

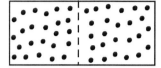 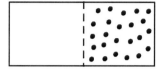

*Figure 5.6* Distribution of molecules.

Source: Author's own construct.

effective energy $T - T = \Delta T = 0$. So there is no energy difference within the system, where $T_1 > T > T_2$).

Thus, in this example, the second law of thermodynamics is expressed in the classic formulation: in an isolated system, entropy is increased. The formula for entropy change $\Delta S > 0$, is an expression of entropy increase. When $d_i S = 0$, only a reversible process can happen. Because entropy is a function of a state, where conditions are unchanging, the initial state begins to experience a process of change and then reverts to the initial state.

Entropy occupies a unique position, its changes being closely related to the direction of the process. The second law of thermodynamics, therefore, provides us with a universal law of macro-evolution. This is the entropy increase principle in an isolated system, or the principle that entropy production $(d_i S)$ is non-negative in a general thermodynamic system.

Now we have to ask what this entropy increase means for the molecular systems involved. In order to give a clear answer, we must study the microscopic significance of entropy. Let us take a look at the meaning of entropy and entropy increase using the example of a specific gas or liquid. In 1872, Boltzmann first stated that entropy is a measure of molecular disorder. The law of entropy increase, therefore, is a simple increase in the degree of disorder. For example, let us discuss a container with a permeable partition divided into two parts of equal volume (see Figure 5.6).

The contained gas has a total of $N$ molecules. Those $N$ molecules can be divided into $N_1$ and $N_2$ ($N_1 + N_2 = N$). There are a total of $P$ ways of dividing the number of molecules between the two equal volumes, and this can be determined by a simple formula for combinations where the quantity $P$ is called the number of complexion:

$$P = \frac{N!}{N_1! N_2!} \tag{5.6}$$

Beginning with any initial value derived from $N_1$ and $N_2$, we can see that, when sufficient time has elapsed, the gas container achieves equilibrium; apart from small fluctuations, the molecules in the two compartments are evenly distributed, that is, $N_1 = N_2 = N/2$. Obviously, this is equivalent to the greatest value of $P$, and moreover $P$ increases during the change process. This consideration ensures that the relationship between the number of complexion $P$ and entropy is:

$$S = k \log P \tag{5.7}$$

## 88 *Humans and entropy*

Here, $k$ is the Boltzmann universal constant. This expression of the relation makes it clear that entropy increase shows the increase of molecular disorder, as reflected by the increase in the number of complexion $P$. In an evolutionary process such as this, the initial state has been 'forgotten', that is, regardless of the initial value of $N_1$ and $N_2$, $N_1$ and $N_2$ both tend to $N/2$ in the end. Asymmetry will sooner or later be destroyed if, in the initial state, the number of particles in a room is greater than in other rooms, that is, the number of particles in the two rooms is highly asymmetric. In this example, the greater the asymmetry, the higher the degree of order in the state of the system. If we link the degree of order of a drop of ink, which has not spread and low entropy (or a high degree of order) in a system with energy difference, we can see that they have relatively great asymmetry or heterogeneity.

In the above example, we are talking about an isolated system. Now we let us look at a closed system. This is similar to the example of an isolated system, it is only necessary to introduce one new state function: the Helmholtz free energy $F$ or Gibbs free energy $G$, instead of the state function, entropy ($S$), and we can draw similar conclusions about the direction of motion of the system state. The definition is now:

$$F = E\text{-}TS \text{ or } G = E\text{-}TS\text{-}XY \tag{5.8}$$

Where $E$ is the internal energy of the system, $T$ is the absolute temperature, $X$ is the generalized displacement (for example, volume $V$), and $Y$ is the generalized force (such as pressure $P$).

The conclusion is: when $T$ and $X$ are constant, the closed system evolves in the direction of a reduction of $F$, with $F$ obtaining a minimal value when an equilibrium is reached, that is: $(\Delta F)_{T, X} \leq 0$. Or, when $T$ and $Y$ are constant, the closed system evolves in the direction of a reduction of $G$, with $G$ obtaining a minimal value when an equilibrium is reached, that is: $(\Delta G)_{T, Y} \leq 0$. This conclusion is the expression by the second law of thermodynamics of the closed system and shows the direction of transformation between order and disorder in a closed system. Roughly speaking, the evolution of the closed system evolves toward the direction of free energy reduction.

However, when the system is in an open, non-equilibrium state, the above result does not apply. Thus, dissipative structure theory has been created to describe non-equilibrium thermodynamics. Socio-economic systems are generally open systems, and often in a non-equilibrium state, so that it is necessary to employ dissipative structure theory to analyse the issues. However, the basic concept of entropy and its extended meanings remain relevant, no matter whether the concepts of $F$ or $G$ are introduced to deal with closed systems in equilibrium, or whether dissipative structure theory is employed to deal with non-equilibrium open systems. First, therefore, the concept of entropy must be extended into the domain of socio-economics. Entropy is usually used to measure the degree of disorder, and negative entropy to measure the degree of order. The latter concept is frequently employed in socio-economics.

In open systems, the crucial thing is that entropy transfer $d_eS$ (see above) can be greater than, equal to or less than zero; $d_eS$ is often termed negative entropy flow. If $d_eS < 0$, and its absolute value $|dS|$ is greater than the $d_iS$, then $dS = d_eS + d_iS \leq 0$. At this point, the total entropy $S$ of a system may be gradually reduced so that the system moves from disorder to order. Thus, where the second law of thermodynamics is not violated, non-equilibrium systems can reduce the total entropy through the increase of negative entropy flow, and reach a new stable ordered structure. In the case of living organisms, which are open systems, the evolutionary process is a process of increasing order. The result is a continuous reduction in the total entropy $S$, but requires a continual replenishment of order through a process of exchange with the outside world. For example, food intake and the digestive process in animals is an orderly process of exchange with the outside world. This can be visualized as 'eating one's way to order'. Conversely, if biological systems are in isolation, with no contact with the outside world, there is no source of negative entropy flow, the production of internal entropy accumulates and the system will eventually die, decay and fall apart, growing more and more chaotic and disordered.

A common feature of socio-economic systems is that their structures are created in an open system, and that these systems need a continuous exchange of matter and energy (and information) through the medium of the surrounding environment, in order to maintain their vitality. However, simply having an open system is not a sufficient condition to ensure the emergence of a dissipative structure (that is, a stable structure with a high degree of order within a non-equilibrium state). Dissipative structure theory states that all dissipative structures have three common characteristics: (1) they exist in an open system; (2) conditions far from equilibrium are maintained; and (3) between the various key elements within the system, there exist non-linear mutual interactions. Prigogine states, therefore, that non-equilibrium is the origin of order. This is a fundamental tenet of the theory of dissipative structure.

It is most important in connection with the second law of thermodynamics. This law states that, in an isolated system, in all reversible processes, the total value of the entropy does not change ($dS = 0$, that is, there is zero change in entropy $S$); and that in irreversible processes, the entropy value increases ($dS > 0$). The final outcome of changes occurring in the isolated system, therefore, is that entropy in the system grows until it reaches the maximum value, when differences (such as temperature difference) in energy within the system will disappear. This is the principle of entropy increase.

However, the second law of thermodynamics has been constructed through experiments, which are limited in space and time, and relies on generalizations drawn from those experiments. At least for the present, its significance for infinite space and infinite time is still very unclear.

## A plethora of ambiguities

The second law of thermodynamics, when extended to the whole of nature, produces some unexpected results. Changes in the natural world clearly cannot

## 90  *Humans and entropy*

wholly be seen in terms of periodic movements – cyclical, repetitive and also evolutionary, another kind of movement, which, for instance, moves things from the simple to the complex, or vice versa.

Unfortunately, however, the irreversible evolutionary development predicted by the second law of thermodynamics is not the kind of evolution from the simple to the complex that we would expect. On the contrary, what is predicted by the second law of thermodynamics is a general trend towards an equalization of temperature throughout the universe. This has historically been called the heat death of the universe.

Even if the dissipative structure theory is far from resolving the question of the heat death of the universe, we know that dissipative structure is dependent on order produced by the input of negative entropy flow from the environment. Thus, the price of this tendency towards greater order is increasing entropy in the environment. If we regard dissipative structure and its external environment as one system, then this system is still subject to the principle of entropy increase.

However, a few years ago, some studies on the expanding universe concluded that, according to thermodynamics, even if the original temperature is identical, temperature differences might still occur. The proof is approximately as follows: in the absence of gravitational force, the box of gas molecules evolves from non-uniform → uniform, structured → unstructured. In the absence of gravity, uniformity is a stable equilibrium state. But with gravity, this state of equilibrium becomes unstable because, in any localized area where slight increases in density fluctuations occur, the gravity will become stronger, attracting more matter and forming greater density. The reverse is also true. Thus, even small fluctuations can completely destroy a state of uniformity. It is clear that in systems with a strong gravitational force, the direction of evolution is from unstructured → structured, and from uniform → non-uniform. Within the circumference of the universe $\tau$, gravity is dominant, so even if the universe began as a uniform, disordered structure, it will automatically grow into a structured, non-uniform state. The process by which stars or stellar systems on any scale come together depends on this non-uniform process. Of course, for this process to be realized, in addition to gravity and the expansion of the universe, different types of material such as radiation and particles in the universe are also necessary (see Table 5.1).

Gravity is a long-range force, and one of the weakest interactional forces in nature. Thus, it is not possible to use it as the sole explanation for positive evolution

*Table 5.1* The theoretical basis of evolution

| *Theoretical basis* | *Whether or not evolution from simple to complex can be explained* |
| --- | --- |
| Pure gravitational force | No (circular motion) |
| Non-gravitational thermodynamics | No (heat death) |
| Gravitational thermodynamics | Possible (except heat death) |

Source: Author's own construct.

on a small scale (such as the generation of life). Here we must also draw on the latest developments in non-equilibrium physics and chemistry, such as the dissipative structure theory.

As the above discussion illustrates, the second law of thermodynamics cannot be unconditionally extended, even in the natural world. To extend it to the social domain requires the exercise of even more caution. However, even though the theory of evolution shown in the figure above affords some hope of avoiding the heat death of the universe, recent studies have seriously challenged the 'big bang' theory.[1] For the past 20 years, the 'big bang' theory has been taken as the best explanation of the origin of the universe, its expansion and ultimate fate. However, at a conference held in late February 1989,[2] plasma cosmology attracted the attention of physicists and astronomers. The meeting discussed some of the latest observations, which seem directly to contradict the basic principles of the 'big bang' theory. Some laboratory studies, computer simulations and new discoveries by astronomers appear to support this new theory.

The creators and supporters of the new theory are convinced that electrically-charged hot gases, called plasma, played a key role (though in a way which is not yet clear) in the process of formation of the universe, stars, galaxies and so on. They believe that the electromagnetic force of plasma and gravity together provided the basis for the galaxies and other cosmic bodies made up of matter. Plasma cosmology holds that the universe is ever-present, that is, we can see neither its beginning, nor its ending. By contrast, the 'big bang' theory believes that gravity is the major force in the formation of the universe, that the universe was formed instantaneously in a huge explosion 20 billion years ago and that from that point on, it has been expanding and will continue to expand until it finally collapses in on itself. Obviously, since the nature of this expansion is not generally established, the mechanisms mentioned above for avoiding heat death of the universe have no role to play. In short, it is premature to expect an answer to the question of whether the universe is tending towards heat death.

We should tread extremely cautiously in attempting to extrapolate the principle of entropy increase from the specific field of thermodynamics to the socio-economic sphere, in particular. Let us look at an example. Let us imagine three scenarios: a mineral is entirely concentrated in a particular region; it is evenly distributed in a dozen areas (in each case, in quantities many times greater than those required to mine it economically); or it is scattered in hundreds of regions (in insufficient concentrations to mine it economically). If we extrapolate purely from the second law of thermodynamics, the highest degree of order is clearly contained in the first of these three patterns of distribution, followed by the second distribution and then the third. But in social terms, the degree of order is clearly the highest in the second case, because the pattern of distribution helps reduce transportation costs. It is clear that if we extend entropy or the second law of thermodynamics to the social sphere, it has multiple meanings. The degree of order must be seen in combination with the purpose and effectiveness of human activities, otherwise it has little meaning. We can therefore see how the concept of entropy can be extended.

## 92 *Humans and entropy*

First, entropy which cannot be changed by human activity (because it is a purely natural process), is known as macroscopic entropy. For example, entropy change caused by the evolution of the sun, whether increasing or decreasing (or staying constant) is scarcely affected by human activities. Although this entropy change has a major impact on human survival, human activities are absolutely incapable of affecting or controlling it. We cannot diminish its adverse effects on us or increase its beneficial effects. All we can do is put up with it. This kind of entropy change remains strictly within the domain of physics.

Second, many processes are no longer purely natural, due to varying degrees of human intervention. We call entropy change in these processes, additional entropy or local entropy. These are processes of entropy change that human activities can influence and control. For example, assuming all other conditions are the same, over-grazing or deforestation has the effect, long term, of drastically reducing productivity and biodiversity and hastening the process of natural local entropy. Conversely, the appropriate control of forest fires reduces local entropy increase in the natural world.

Any discussion of this kind of entropy increase takes us some way from the concept of entropy in the strict physics sense. For example, with respect to the diversity of the ecosystem, this is no longer, strictly speaking, entropy as thermodynamics understands it. In general, however, such concepts (such as diversity metrics in information theory) can to some extent be appropriately linked with entropy in thermodynamics. For example, there is a positive correspondence between the diversity of ecosystems and their dry matter productivity. In this case, a few words of explanation are necessary to clarify the use of such concepts.

Third, entropy change linked to the purpose and effectiveness of human activities is known as conditional or significant entropy. This entropy change can be controlled by human activity. For example, when rainfall is too heavy and too concentrated within a short time frame, it is not conducive to crop growing. But water storage and water diversion projects, which are not destructive to the environment, can distribute this precipitation more evenly, thus benefiting crops.

It is this kind of entropy change that is most open to ambiguity. For example, using the Shannon information measure formula to measure the degree of order in organisms is of little real significance. In the following analysis, calculations show that the degree of order of an organism and the degree of order of a piece of rock of the same mass differs little in order of magnitude. One can calculate the amount of information and the corresponding entropy of cell biopolymers, but the calculation does not enable people to understand the characteristics of biomolecules. What is really important is not the amount of information in DNA, but the protein synthesis instructions it contains. To put it another way, in biology, what is important is not what the information contains but what it means. What counts is the value of information in the 'compilation order' and its quality.[3] This is the sense in which we can use the concept of conditional (or significant) entropy. However, since there is no agreed theory in this regard, in the following analysis we will confine ourselves within strict limits in order to avoid confusion about this use of the concept.

Sometimes, the third kind of entropy change intersects with the second kind. As an extreme example, in the physics sense, entropy decreases from the point of view of an increase in heterogeneity or asymmetry when rainfall tends towards ever increasing concentration. From point of view of effective use of the rainfall by humans, however, conditional entropy increases. If we assume that the sum of the two is zero, then if all other conditions remain unchanged, the sum of the three kinds of entropy change is zero. However, we sense intuitively that total entropy has increased, and that this undermines the extendible quality of entropy. When examining these questions, we can only deal with specific cases.

The first kind of entropy change, regardless of whether you make use of it, has no effect. For example, better use of solar energy not only does not accelerate the rate of increase of entropy of the sun itself, it may actually increase the degree of order on Earth. At this point, macroscopic entropy change does not change, while local entropy decreases, causing a relative reduction in the total entropy of the Earth–sun system. However, the authors of *Entropy* completely ignore this point.

With regard to the second entropy change process, over-use leads to local entropy increase (this is obvious), while under-use sometimes leads to local entropy increase (such as trees in a forest which are past their best). Moderate use leads to no change or a reduction in entropy. The third entropy change process, such as uniform use of rainfall, has no effect on natural entropy change (providing water storage projects do not affect the ecology), but conditional entropy, which affects humans, will decrease.

The above analysis shows that the problem is not as simple as it appears. Unless we exercise great caution in applying the second law of thermodynamics to an analysis of human society, it will be hard to avoid fallacious arguments. Below, we discuss the specific impact of human activities on entropy change.

## A multitude of barriers

We should not conclude the above analysis that the second law of thermodynamics is of no use in an analysis of human society. However, it is important to make clear the premises on which we are employing this law and its limitations.

*Assumption 1* (spatial restrictions): our discussion is limited to the solar system, and we must assume that the events which occur outside this system are neither affected by, nor can they affect, human activities (either in a positive, a negative or a neutral sense).

*Assumption 2* (time restrictions): since human beings cannot survive indefinitely on earth, let us set the upper limit at five billion years. Our sun may one day become very hot, making life on earth unsustainable. This means that we must assume that the period of survival of human beings on earth is limited.

*Assumption 3* (restrictions on the main source of negative entropy flow): Let us assume that for several billion years the sun can continue to work in our favour and does not turn into a new star, though this is entirely possible. (In that event, all life on earth will be destroyed, and our entire planet may even be vaporized.) After such an eruption, a star will just lose 1–2 per cent of its mass, after which

## 94 *Humans and entropy*

it will resume normal life. In fact, although some stars appear to have experienced several such outbreaks at repeated intervals, they still exist to this day.[4] In billions of years, therefore, whether entropy of the universe has increased or decreased, we can assume it will have no direct impact on our solar system.

*Assumption 4* (mobility restrictions): it is neither a practical option nor feasible economically for all human beings, within a million years or so, to leave the earth and fly to other planets.

*Assumption 5* (limitations on the interaction between different factors): let us assume the principle of short-term constraints. This means that the survival of humanity depends on a number of factors, and there cannot be limitless substitution between these factors. For example, the sun is not a substitute for air. Once the atmosphere presents a problem, however much sun there is, humans will not survive; at that point, atmosphere is the short-term constraint on the survival of humanity. Based on the above assumptions, we can draw several conclusions.

*Conclusion 1:* Within the time frame of billions of years we have established in assumptions 1 and 2, the solar system can exist as an isolated system from a human perspective. Thus, in terms of macro-entropy, that system is subject to the principle of entropy increase.

We can explain this idea as follows: We already know that the cyclical process of cohesion and dispersion of celestial bodies takes place over tens of billions of years. When, in billions of years' time, therefore, the sun becomes unable to work in a way that supports us, (let us examine the solar system here in combination with the surrounding universe, such as a galaxy), then it will take tens of billions of years for the movement of all celestial bodies to cause the sun to restart, so that macro-entropy decreases. Over billions of years, the sun will gradually consume its internal energy and its entropy will increase. This entropy increase dominates the solar system. We still do not know enough to conclude whether the movement of the universe outside this system can cause this entropy increase to be reversed.

*Conclusion 2:* We can draw a further conclusion from assumptions 1 and 2 and from the above conclusion: given limitations of human existence on earth, we do not have time to wait for those parts of the universe linked with our survival to condense once more, and bring together again energy dissipated by humans (such as burned oil).

*Conclusion 3:* by combining assumptions 3 and 4, and conclusions 1 and 2 above, and the definition of macro-entropy, we obtain the following: for human beings, which exist within the solar system, the key does not lie in macroscopic entropy changes (in the order of magnitude of billions of years, they do not constitute an effective constraint on the survival of human beings), but rather in how humans use the solar energy, and other stored forms of energy, which are a by-product of the process of solar entropy increase.

This conclusion means that the solar system is affected by entropy increase over billions of years, but in a smaller time scale (such as millions of years), this principle demonstrates no negative impact, nor does it constitute an effective constraint, on human survival. Thus, within this small time scale, it is changes in local entropy and significant entropy that humans can control and influence,

*Humans and entropy* 95

which are important, although these two kinds of entropy change (either decrease or increase) and are lower by several orders of magnitude, when compared with macroscopic entropy.

*Conclusion 4:* we know from assumption 5 that as far as industrialized societies, which only use stocks resources, are concerned, the earth can be treated more or less as an isolated system. The significance of this is obvious: because there are no other energy sources, however abundant sunlight is, it cannot replenish large-scale consumption of our stocks resources.

Now we can proceed to an analysis of a number of important issues with regard to human society and economic development in the long term, based on the above assumptions and conclusions.

Human society has become industrialized over a mere 300–400 years, while stocks resources (non-renewable resources) on which those industrialized societies rely for their survival have had to undergo a long geological process (tens of millions of years or even hundreds of millions of years) in order to form in sufficient quantities as to be economically exploitable. The amount by which these stocks increase over a few thousand years is negligible. Thus, as far as the formation of these resources goes, even if long-term changes in the natural world are a process of entropy decrease, the manner and extent of use of these resources through technology on a large scale during the era of industrialization, is clearly a process of entropy increase – a process whereby naturally abundant resources become dissipated. In terms of entropy change meaningful to humans, the latter process predominates. The rate by which existing resources accumulate is much smaller than the rate at which humans use them up. As a result, we can use the second law of thermodynamics to carry out an approximate analysis of the way in which these resources are used.[5]

Fusion energy can sustain an industrialized society for thousands of years (we will disregard here such side effects as the production of heat pollution). However, even the most wonderful machine in the universe cannot use energy alone to produce matter. If we reduce the assumed growth in material consumption rate in the calculation that appears at the end of the first section of this chapter, from 1 per cent to 0.1 per cent, the original 500 years is only extended to 5,000 years. In other words, after 5,000 years, global resource consumption is equivalent to 500 times that of 1970. Even if at this time, energy is not a problem, levels of non-energy minerals can simply not be sustained for such a long time. At the same time, resources can never be 100 per cent recycled, and the alternative is usually to substitute lower-grade minerals and greater expenditure of energy – which reproduces the same problems.

It is clear that, in terms of the production and consumption patterns in industrialized societies, the earth is an isolated system. There are two effective sources of energy on the Earth: one is reserves of energy from within the Earth itself, the other is solar energy. The former breaks down into two types: energy which is renewable within a time frame meaningful to humans; and energy which is renewable in a geological time scale, but which, as far as humans are concerned, is non-renewable energy. Renewable sources of energy on Earth are limited, and

## 96 *Humans and entropy*

once depleted, they become non-renewable. Although the total amount of solar energy is regarded as inexhaustible, nevertheless the speed and form in which it reaches the Earth is very limited.

A key point to make is that the sun and energy cannot, in themselves, create life. For life to thrive, the sun and energy must interact with a system that is composed of minerals, metals and others of earth's substances, to transform these substances into life, as well as into the nutrients necessary for life. Production and consumption patterns of industrialized societies ensure that this interaction accelerates the dissipation of limited amounts of matter, which make up the earth's surface. Thus, although the total amount of solar energy per second is in decline, energy resources on earth will have been exhausted long before the sun's entropy reaches the maximum value.

The different types of resources discussed above ultimately constitute a complementary system, which obeys the principle of short-term constraints. It is possible to conclude, therefore, that what is happening to industrial societies characterized by large-scale consumption of stocks resources, can be described by means of the second law of thermodynamics.

We can extrapolate further from the example mentioned above: by the end of the twenty-first century, the world's population will be five billion, and if this population achieves Japan's 1980 level of per capita GNP of material consumption, it will be equivalent to about 12 times 1970 levels of consumption in the USA. That is, by the end of the twenty-first century, the world's resource consumption will be four to five times 1970 levels. In 1974, Americans used 10 tons of minerals per capita – 20 tons, including fossil fuels and wood. From this we can project that by the end of the twenty-first century, total mineral consumption will be 26.4 billion tons, in addition to 53 billion tons of energy materials and wood.

Let us assume that from the beginning of the twenty-second century, the global economy continues to develop with an annual growth rate in material consumption of 0.7 per cent. At that rate, every 100 years, the total global rate of consumption will double. The total mass of the earth's crust is $5 \times 10^{19}$ tons, of which aluminium, iron and other elements constitute about 14 per cent, the total mass of these elements amounting to $7 \times 10^{18}$ tons. Accordingly, it can be calculated that in another 2,000 years from the beginning of the twenty-second century, these elements will be completely exhausted. On the basis of a population of ten billion, these elements will only last 1,000 years. If we assume that the principle of short-term constraints operates more broadly, then we can see that the lifespan of industrialized societies is only a few hundred years.

Thus, wealth-seeking, industrialized societies, based on the stocks technology of mass production and non-renewable stocks resources, cannot escape the constraints of the second law of thermodynamics. Stagnation is inevitable, and is only a matter of time. Attempting to sustain the system of production and consumption on the basis of new, high-level technology will only provide a temporary respite.

However, when material wealth ceases to grow, it does not mean the stagnation of human society. The fact that industrialized society is inevitably subject to the constraints of the second law of thermodynamics does not mean that a new model of development has to be similarly helpless. On this point, my arguments diverge considerably from those of the authors of *Entropy*.

## Which way forward?

Large-scale depletion of non-renewable resources and consequent serious environmental pollution caused by the 'classic' model of development can also be analysed using the principle of entropy increase.

Scholars such as Atsushi Tsuchida have examined reasons for the current crisis in the earth's ecology in the light of entropy theory. They start from the assumption that the earth consists of four parts: lithosphere, atmosphere, hydrosphere and the ecosystem, which includes human society. They then carry out calculations and analysis based on different situations.

Their methods are as follows. First, they assume that the earth consists only of the lithosphere. At this time, the average energy of the sunlight reaching the Earth's surface is $q = 257$ Kcal/year per square metre. If we take $q$ to be 100, 30 Kcal will be reflected back into space (that is, for the Earth, it constitutes useless energy). The remaining 70 Kcal warms the Earth, but will ultimately be radiated back into space. Calculated according to the $T^4$ law (the heat radiated by an object is proportional to the fourth power of the absolute temperature of its surface), the temperature of the Earth's surface should be $-18°C$ (equivalent to 255K, K being the absolute temperature).

Second, let us assume that the Earth has an atmosphere. Taking into account atmospheric absorption of direct sunlight, atmospheric absorption of surface radiation heat and heat returned to the Earth, as well as atmospheric convection, the average temperature of the Earth's surface according to $T^4$ law should be 28°C (301K). This is equivalent to a desert, too hot to sustain life.

Third, let us consider the Earth as it really is, with both atmospheric circulation and water cycle. Water encountering dry air evaporates and absorbs heat from its surroundings. The molecular weight of water is 18, and that of air is 29, so that moisture-laden air is lighter, and forms updrafts. However, during its ascent, adiabatic expansion will cause the temperature to drop, condensing the water vapour so that it forms rain or snow. This is the water cycle. Water in the upper atmosphere may emit heat when it forms ice or condensation and this heat is radiated outwards towards the universe. The heat sent out from the surface by the water cycle is four times the heat carried away by atmospheric circulation. The average surface temperature calculated according to $T^4$ law is 15°C (288K), which is consistent with the Earth's actual temperature. This endothermic process, where heat is absorbed from a high temperature (from Earth's surface), and released at a low temperature (towards the outer atmosphere), is a thermodynamic mechanism that is of great significance for entropy.

The entropy reduced by the circulation of water (and air) can be calculated as: $0.3 \times q \, (1/288 - 1/255) = 34.6 \, \text{cal/K} \cdot \text{cm}^2 \cdot \text{year}$ (where K is the absolute temperature). Motion and variation on Earth are carried out within the range of this discarded

## 98   *Humans and entropy*

entropy. Examples of this are the frictional heat generated when it rains, river flows, wind currents and life activities. All of these activities generate entropy, but the sum of this entropy does not exceed the above figure. In other words, because the water cycle exists, part of the entropy increase generated by all kinds of activities on the Earth's surface is discarded in space. In short, it is precisely because of the presence of the water cycle that our Earth became a planet with life on it, a world that has not reached the point of heat death.

Fourth, let us consider the ecosystem, including rocks, the atmosphere, water and human society. Only a small part of sunlight is used by plants in photosynthesis, while the remaining sunlight heats plants internally, that is, is turned into entropy. How is this excess entropy excreted by plants? It should be noted that plants have a mechanism for evaporating liquid into water vapour and that, as heat is carried away, entropy is carried away at the same time. In other words, in addition to requiring water for the manufacture of glucose, plants also need it for evaporation. If only plants existed on the earth, and these continuously carried out photosynthesis, then the $CO_2$ in the air would be exhausted, and plants could not survive. However, animals and micro-organisms use 21 per cent of the air that is oxygen, to break down what is generated by photosynthesis, thus maintaining the concentration of $CO_2$. Combining photosynthesis and decomposition gives a biological cycle. In this cycle, sunlight and water are absorbed, and water vapour and heat are emitted. The heat and water vapour generated by this biological cycle is carried to high altitude by water (or air), and heat is distributed outwards to the universe. Thus we can say that the biological cycle is part of the water cycle.

As we have seen, the biological cycle and part of its response satisfies the entropy increase principle, making it possible for the cycle to proceed. Whether or not these reactions exist in reality, however, is another question. In order for the biological cycle to be sustained, overall coordination is necessary. If intermediate stages of the process are interrupted, the harmony between plants, animals and micro-organisms will be destroyed, causing the biological cycle to stagnate. What is generally called biological pollution, such as eutrophication in lakes, belongs in this category.

Another type of pollution is the contamination of materials underground, a phenomenon unrelated to biological contamination. The history of collective disasters provides many such examples: one is long-term pollution of the water table caused by copper mining. This environmental pollution is connected to a civilization founded on oil. Many people believe that agriculture and industry alike are destroying the environment. Of course, this does happen. But humans can also make the biological cycle thrive and give it new vigour through agriculture, forestry and fisheries, for example, by preventing desertification, by planting plants and trees and by enhancing the soil's fertility. These are all instances of human beings strengthening the biological cycle. But generally speaking our petroleum-based civilization is damaging to the biological cycle. It appears that the decisive question is still whether or not human activities favour the recovery and strengthening of the water and biological cycles. (The destruction of topsoil in the lithosphere is not conducive to these cycles.)

*Humans and entropy*  99

The petroleum-based civilization of the modern age has resulted in the Earth's water cycle being unable to handle huge amounts of thermal entropy and physical entropy, as well as radiation entropy. What we call thermal entropy (also known as thermal pollution) is the emission of various forms of waste heat. We need to remember that nuclear fusion technology, even if it is commercially viable, produces thermal pollution, which is difficult for the water cycle and the biological cycle to deal with, if per capita energy consumption continues to increase. Physical entropy consists of all kinds of physical pollution (of air, water and organisms) in the process of mining and use of non-renewable resources. What we call radiation entropy refers to radioactive nuclear waste, which the water cycle and the biological cycle are unable to deal with. In other words, the water cycle cannot carry this entropy increase away to the outer atmosphere. Thus, sustaining the Earth – a subsystem of the Earth–sun system – continues to require the existence of an open, stationary system (that is, a dissipative structure). These entropies accumulate within the earth's subsystems, but a necessary condition for the existence of an open, stationary system is that entropy within the system must continuously be discarded to its exterior. The gradual accumulation of entropy is bound to threaten the continued existence of mankind.

This presents us with a very serious global crisis, which no past civilization has ever faced. The solution depends on whether or not we can immediately begin to reduce the number of technology-dominated areas in which we consume large amounts of non-renewable resources, such as oil. Using water, soil and biotechnologies places humans within the biological cycle. Human activities should be conducive to the recovery and even the strengthening of the water cycle and the biological cycle, rather than vice versa. We should create new economies, societies and civilizations that are founded on a diverse range of collaborative human relationships.

## Notes

1 〈等離子體宇宙論向「大爆炸」理論提出嚴肅挑戰〉,《科戰日報》 1989 年 3 月 7 日。 ('Plasma cosmology seriously challenges the "big bang" theory', in *Fight for Science Daily* newspaper, 7 March 1989.

2 The first International Conference on Plasma Cosmology, held in La Jolla, California, 20–22 February 1989.

3 M. V. Volkenstein, *An Introduction to Physics and Biology*, Academic Press, New York. (M. V. 伏爾更斯坦:《現代物理學與生物學概論》,復旦大學出版社 1985 年, 第 104, 105 頁。 [Fudandaxue Chubanshe Publishers, 1985, pages 104–5]).

4 Asimov, I., 1972, *Asimov's Guide to Science*, Basic Books Inc., New York. (I. 阿西摩夫:《宇宙、地球和大氣》, 科學出版社 1979 年。 [*The Universe, the Earth and the Atmosphere*, Kexue Chubanshe Publishers, 1979].

5 槌田敦等:〈水、生物、人類與熵的理論〉,《世界科學》 1986 年第9期。 (TSUCHIDA, Atsushi *et al.*, 'Water, life forms, humanity and entropy', in *World Science*, 1986, issue 9.)

# 6 Making a fresh start

The basic problem facing an industrialized society is that, while we treat stock reserves formed through geological processes as if they were limitless, the natural replenishment of such resources lags far behind the rate at which human beings have consumed them over the past three or four centuries. At the same time, levels of pollution are seriously damaging the Earth's water and biological cycles. In other words, the cost of human 'progress' has been greatly underestimated and net progress is far less than is commonly believed.

Moreover, human beings are resistant to change, meaning that we are under the illusion that the 'classic' development model is the only, the universal, way. Not only does this belief obscure the fact that there are alternatives, the superficial effectiveness of the 'classic' development model in a small number of countries of the world makes it more difficult, and more painful, for people to make rational choices of alternative modes of development.

The truth is that when people have satisfied their basic needs for food and clothing, an infinite variety of development models present themselves. I will demonstrate this below with a detailed analysis of the superficial success of the 'classic' development model.

## Grossly over-rated

The 'classic' development model relies basically on deficit spending, which makes it attractive to people who focus on short-term aims at the expense of long-term aims. For those who are not prepared to look beneath the surface, it is all very clear and logical that Western mainstream economics is the only orthodox theory, and it is beyond argument that that fine-sounding system, GNP, should be the core of national accounting systems. The Chinese have a saying: people need clothes; horses need saddles. The 'successes' of the 'classic' model of development are nothing more than a garment whose many colours blind people to the fact that it is full of holes and hides the crudest of flaws within it.

Christine Lepatte (*sic*)[1] states that the current, environmentally-harmful industrial system should be replaced by one more favourable to the environment; and that the current practice of taking GNP as a measure of national welfare completely obscures the fact that currently economic activities not only have a

*Making a fresh start* 101

damaging effect on the environment and society, but are actually increasingly counter-productive to the aims of production itself.

We have seen the devastating consequences of the 'classic' development model on the environment and resources, and the way in which national accounting systems have been used to exaggerate economic growth both past and present. I will now further explore the way in which this growth is expressed – the concept of GNP.

According to Lepatte, there are three ways, today, in which the concept of economic growth and of GNP as its measure, are inappropriate. First, economic growth is measured in terms of goods and national income, but ignores their impact on the environment. Neither our use of natural resources (energy, raw materials, water, air and land) nor the damaging effects of waste products and pollutants are reflected in the economic balance sheet.

Second, economic growth is a very broad concept. All currency-related economic activities are included in GNP, regardless of the purpose of these activities, or what role they play in production and consumption. As a way of evaluating the contribution of industrial production to a society's quality of life, GNP is clearly inappropriate because it is one-dimensional. It is increasingly necessary to include within GNP calculations, those business activities which cannot be given a positive value but which can compensate for the damage caused by 'classic' economic activities.

In addition, economic growth is measured in terms of 'flow' rather than 'stocks'. 'Flow' (referring to GNP) has, in recent decades, increasingly been seen as a means of measuring economic and political success: the higher the GNP and national income growth rates, the greater the achievements on economic and political fronts, the more the flow increase is equated with social welfare. In the 1950s and 1960s, commercial and economic development tended to ignore the effects of the exponential growth of the flow rate (of such things as total output, consumption, consumption of raw materials and energy and industrial waste emissions) on natural and human resources. They totally ignored the fact that, in the final analysis, flow requires a steady supply of resources.

According to Lepatte, Herman Daly has suggested that three new accounts – costs, profits and capital (or assets) – be set up on the basis of resources (stocks) and consumption (flow). The problem with GNP is that three very different areas are clumsily subsumed within this one concept. The three areas are: (1) the growth figure in resource reserves; (2) the amount of material consumption (wastage – pollution – consumption); and (3) the services provided by the resource reserves. These three different areas should be subdivided into different accounts: (i) the profit account (including the services provided by the environment); (ii) the loss account (including wastage, pollution and ineffective labour); and (iii) the assets account (including natural assets). Bundling costs, profits and added value all together into total assets does not make sense. Daly views it as necessary to divide national accounting into three types of accounts, because each category included within GNP should have a different explanation: when resource reserves are adequate, and the ecology is in balance, then reserves should be 'sufficient for what is needed' and material consumption should be at a minimum, while services

## 102    *Making a fresh start*

provided and satisfaction with them should be at a maximum. An economics–environment accounting system can be created from this, with the aim of setting up costs, profits and assets accounting for these three accounts. By using the notion of 'compensation', we can differentiate those special reserves that may not produce net profits and can only have a preventative role (compensation for damages). Additionally, this is the only way to distinguish genuine profits from profits, which are actually society paying an additional price.

Lepatte explicitly states that the traditional concept of economic growth should be abandoned because the chief characteristic of traditional GNP is that consumption in the negative sense is also included in the positive calculation. Traditional measures of economic growth, therefore, should not be taken as a real indication of the results of economic policies. The growth targets of the once-generally accepted macroeconomic thinking are no longer appropriate in the present era. On the contrary, the goal of economic growth tends to work against improvements in the quality of the environment and living and working conditions in industrial society.

Lepatte suggests that, in order to ensure that future development focuses on quality, a different standard of measurement is needed, one that finds a way of distinguishing between compensatory production and consumption in GNP, so that we can prove what the full costs of economic activities are. These costs include not only actual resource consumption costs calculated according to market prices, but also the burden imposed on the economy or elsewhere by production activities. For example, occupational diseases and industrial accidents are consequences which must be borne by society, and the cost of these negative consequences of the production process should appear on the debit side in assessing cost-effectiveness in the economy, rather than, as now, being attributed to the credit side.

Lepatte divides the costs of production and consumption into four categories: (1) Compensation either for past losses, or to prevent a future recurrence of such losses. Within GNP, these can be described as loss-compensation costs; (2) the economic costs of pensions and health insurance paid from total income in order to maintain human assets in good condition. These can be described as depreciation of human assets; (3) loss of assets that have an economic value (natural resources, buildings, works of art and so on), as well as losses caused when workers cannot work due to disability; and (4) actual losses caused to individuals, the natural environment and works of art (although the degree of loss may be hard to quantify). In principle, the first three categories can be calculated by price. Lepatte has made a calculation of the costs of the first category based on the situation of the Federal Republic of Germany.

I have used these estimates to examine the growth of the Federal Republic of Germany from 1970 to 1981. At 1970 prices, GNP in the Federal Republic of Germany was 675 billion marks and in 1981 it was 1,543 trillion marks, so that the annual growth rate of nominal GNP was 7.8 per cent. After deduction of the increase in the first category of compensation, for the same period, of 230 billion marks, the value of nominal national ecological production (= GNP – depreciation of fixed assets – compensation) grew annually by 6.2 per cent. If we assume that the total expenditure of the last three categories are equal to the first category of expenses, and we deduct them from the nominal GNP, then the net national welfare (= GNP – depreciation of fixed assets – the four categories of expenses) grew by only 4.4 per cent. If we further deduct commodity price increases over the same period, then the actual growth rate of net national welfare is close to zero or negative. (Annual inflation in the Federal Republic of Germany was as follows: 1971, 7.5 per cent; 1972, 5.3 per cent; 1973, 6.3 per cent; 1974, 6.5 per cent; 1975, 5.8 per cent; 1976, 3.3 per cent; 1977, 3.5 per cent; 1978, 4.2 per cent; 1979, 3.8 per cent; 1980, 4.4 per cent; 1981, 4.2 per cent.)[2] This means that the net growth of economic activity over 11 years was zero or negative, in other words, there was either no real growth, or the economy suffered a real setback. This is what we might call using one hand to claw back all progress made by the other hand. What kind of progress is that, may I ask? No sane, sensible person would act so stupidly. The only explanation is that people nowadays earn profits from deficit spending, while the costs of this deficit will be borne by future generations. That is, the gains come first, and costs follow, an unbalanced arrangement. Herein lies the secret of the problem.

When the deficit is eventually paid off (in other words, by future generations), the flow growth figures over these 11 years – costed in terms of consumption of stocks resources – do not add up. There may even be a drop below 1970 levels, since people enjoyed the same quality of life in 1970 compared with 1981, and they also had more stocks resources than in 1981. This false idea of growth really should be abandoned, and the sooner the better. It is not only unnecessary for developed countries, but it is a heavy burden on developing countries.

## Time flies and waits for no one

If we want to rid ourselves of the burden imposed by this false concept of growth and get back on the right track, correct accounting and rational analysis are only the first steps. We must also rid ourselves of worthless cultural concepts, which the 'classic' development model has brought in its wake and instilled in us. This is a more difficult task, but, without this, we cannot complete the leap to a new development model. The following section briefly discusses three basic stages of human development and the chief characteristics of corresponding systems of resource use and technical systems. I will further analyse the impact of western civilization as expressed through the medium of the 'classic' development model.

### *Resource utilization in three models of development*

In terms of production and lifestyle, human society has developed through the following stages: hunter-gatherer society, agricultural society, industrial society and what has recently come to be called post-industrial society. However, resource utilization can be roughly divided into three kinds.

## 104  *Making a fresh start*

Hunter-gatherer and agricultural societies are basically characterized by the use of renewable resources, and these are renewable within a human time scale. Other than for land, there is no difference in order of magnitude between use and renewal of resources. Humans can only use the flow portion if they want to ensure that these resources remain renewable. For simplicity, we call these 'flow resources'. Pre-industrial society is based on old flow technology and uses basic flow resources to support the development of human society. This is a fundamental characteristic of hunter-gatherer and agricultural societies and the basis of their survival.

As populations grew and standards of living improved, old flow technology and flow resources proved unable to cope with the requirements for further growth and so models of development began to change. In the transition from hunter-gatherer to agricultural societies, it was millions of years before flow resources obtainable in the wild were finally depleted and replaced by flow resources created by the labour of agricultural societies and their corresponding flow technology. When, after a few thousand years, these flow resources and technology were once again inadequate to meet the demands of population growth and improved living standards, models of development changed again.

This time the transition was to an industrialized society. This transition was fundamentally different from previous transitions in that it involved the large-scale consumption of non-renewable stocks resources through modern scientific and technical means. These are stocks resources in terms of a human time scale. For the first time in millions of years since human use of natural resources, there appears, with the transition to industrialized society, a huge discrepancy between the time scale for the formation of resources used by humans and the time scale of human life – a fundamental change, which has had an enormous impact on human development.

One of the most important consequences of the large-scale use of stocks resources is to separate the rhythms of human life and production from the rhythms of the natural environment. For the first time, humans discovered solar energy reserves, accumulated over billions of years and seemingly inexhaustible. But as they plundered this substantial energy wealth, concepts of the seasonal cycle were gradually forgotten. Both in production and also in their daily lives, humans make every effort to disconnect themselves from the environment. Take, for example, air-conditioning units for offices and houses: for more than 99 per cent of human history, we have been able to endure summer heat and humidity, yet now some people find it unendurable. Solar energy is the goose that lays the golden egg – and humans no longer have to wait for the sun to shine every day in order for energy and life to be produced. Everything has been speeded up. There is no doubt that these stocks reserves and stocks technology are the basis for the existence of our entire industrial society and the 'classic' development model.

However, nothing good lasts forever, and it has become clear, after only a few hundred years, that stocks resources are not only limited but are being rapidly depleted. The rock on which industrialized society and the 'classic' development model are built – stocks resources – is disintegrating and, indeed, stocks technology is also deeply flawed. This has led people to talk in terms of a post-industrial society.

### The crisis of Western civilization and the plight of developing countries

The famous British historian Arnold J. Toynbee states in his article 'Who will inherit the West's position of world dominance?' that, by 1974, the West will undoubtedly have sickened and that its dominance will seem as fleeting as that of the Mongols or the Muslims.

Western dominance is the result of the Industrial Revolution. This revolution essentially opened up the floodgates of human greed. The greedy have been told that their pursuit of personal gain is the best way to ensure that the whole community obtains the maximum benefit. However, two centuries of experience have shown this doctrine to be completely untenable. Only a few emerge victorious from the struggle.

The victims of the Industrial Revolution were industrial workers, who were not only exploited by society but also excluded from it. This is an inherent weakness in Western society. Moreover, the pursuit by the West of GNP growth has brought it into conflict with most non-Western societies and, indeed, with the Earth's environment. It seems that the world is moving towards a 'post-Western' era. Be that good or bad, the new era cannot escape the inheritance bequeathed it to it by the West.[3]

What new thoughts occur, re-reading this article a dozen years after it appeared in Chinese? It is a common view in China that oriental civilizations repress the individual in favour of the collective, while the West focuses on the individual. I do not propose to discuss the rights and wrongs of this view; instead I will investigate the relationship between development models, the resource base and the cultural background against which this development is played out.

It is precisely because they could commandeer stocks resources worldwide, that the first industrialized countries focused on the individual. These few countries had access to almost unlimited resources, which they could exploit to their heart's content, and this gave rise both to laissez-faire policies and extreme individualism. Just a few countries have evolved industrialized societies in their most mature form on the basis of this combination of ideology, stocks resources and modern science and technology – the United States is typical of these. In the USA, per capita resources are plentiful, competition between individuals is not likely to reach excessive levels, and this has led to the belief that the (sum total of) interests of the individual equate with the interests of the community.

In other words, individual and social values in the West evolved in a world that seemed to have no limits. In this world, there was no contradiction between getting more and more today and using more and more tomorrow. If we think about how the pioneers penetrated the vast expanse of the American west, with all its natural wealth, this is not difficult to understand. Social patterns and cultural values in this context inevitably focus on the individual because, when per capita

## 106  *Making a fresh start*

resources are unusually plentiful, people rarely need their neighbours. Thus, the relationship between individuals can be simplified to purely economic relations – money dealings. However, times have changed. In a world where short-term interests often cause long-term damage or vice versa, continuing to base our actions on Western ethics could well be the wrong route for the rest of us to take.

In some developing countries in the East, by contrast, there have been age-old constraints on flow technology and flow resources, and much lower levels of per capita resources, with the result that competition between individuals has had brutal consequences to society as a whole. In order for these societies to continue to exist, a strong sense of community and curbs on excessive competition between individuals have been necessary. For example, even though Japan has entered the ranks of the most developed countries, the status of the individual in Japan is much weaker than in the United States.

There is no space to discuss here why countries of the East, with their age-old cultural traditions did not take the lead in industrialization. But one thing is very clear: economic expansion, together with pressing resource and population problems, means that the earth has become increasingly crowded. This throws into doubt the assumption that the 'classic' development model is still feasible. First, most developing countries will never achieve modernization by adopting the 'classic' development model (although, of course, I do not exclude the possibility of the occasional success story). Second, since the basis of the 'classic' development model – unlimited stocks resources – is crumbling, it is highly questionable whether this development model and its cultural trappings – Western civilization – can survive intact. Endless discussions about 'post-industrial society' reflect to a certain extent the deep crisis facing Western civilization both internally and externally.

This sense of crisis was thrown into sharp relief at a conference on the theme of 'ideology and economic development' held at Harvard University in January 1981. The conference started from the following premise: individualism cannot shoulder the sole burden in developing a country's economy; the group, and team spirit, are needed to complement the individual; and the free market no longer works in the United States. Participating scholars took the view that individualism has become a modern disease in the United States, and that individualism, as a dominant way of thinking in Britain and America, has proved unable to adapt to a changing environment. The effect, when thoughts and behaviour diverge, is to weaken countries. To achieve increased competitiveness, strong rapid economic growth and social stability, they should look to Japan and other countries of the East, which put the emphasis on team spirit and social consensus.[4]

Those developing countries with ancient civilizations hope that they can follow in the footsteps of the developed world to modernize, yet they lack the necessary preconditions – large quantities of stocks resources and a cultural affinity to this model. They have found it a painful process to transform their civilizations in a hurry and have suffered repeated setbacks as they follow the 'classic' development model. For decades it has been clear that only the lucky few will succeed by this route. The much-discussed problem of the North–South divide has not only not been resolved, it grows ever more acute.

It seems that humankind as a whole is facing a stark choice: the collapse of our civilization or making a new life for ourselves. It is one or the other. However, there are differences due to different initial conditions, boundary conditions and internal infrastructure, and thus the transformation process, the form it takes and its costs will also be different.

## The phoenix rises from the ashes

Toynbee asked: who will lead the world after the decline of the West? He believed that Japan or the Soviet Union have been eliminated from the race for dominance because they have become so westernized, and been infected by the faults inherent in the Western model. Black Africa and India are not in the race either: Africans are preoccupied in dealing with local problems and the Indian subcontinent is split along religious and linguistic lines. People must look to the societies of East Asia, he believed, to inherit the West's legacy and take over world dominance. To do this, these societies will have to deal both with the legacy of the West, and with the problems inherent in agricultural societies. In short, they will need to open a new page in the history of humankind.

China has an ancient civilization, yet it is now a large, developing country endowed with the smallest quantities of per capita resources – depriving it of the necessary preconditions for the 'classic' development model. As we have seen, per capita levels of key resources are all lower than average, with the exception of tungsten and rare earth, which China possesses in higher than average quantities. With many resources, China has less than one-third of the global per capita average, and it has less than half the global per capita average of things like fresh water, arable land, energy and iron ore, on which long-term economic development depends. This makes it particularly pressing to adopt a new long-term development model. Is such a model possible?

China's ancient and splendid civilization led the world for thousands of years. However, this civilization and its ancient flow technology can no longer support development in the modern era. For a variety of reasons, China in the modern era has never been in a situation where stocks technology was complemented by almost limitless material stocks resources. Thus, the 'classic' development model of the past is not repeatable and modern stocks technology cannot be used to its best advantage. Moreover, the external costs of this technology have, in recent years, proved to be so extravagantly wasteful as to be unaffordable for long-term development. What, then, is the way forward? To find an answer to this question, we must accept that preconditions for the old model no longer exist, and accordingly look for new preconditions and a new development model that fits them.

Under this new model, society's material consumption must not exceed that rate at which those resources are produced or renewed in nature. The new model should govern our use of non-renewable natural resources, which represent fixed, ecological 'capital' that can be used once only: we should cut our use of these non-renewable resources to the minimum, particularly where they are also non-recyclable, and should limit our consumption of renewable resources to levels at

## 108 *Making a fresh start*

which they can be replenished. Only then can we redress as far as possible the deficit between society's consumption of resources and the production of those resources in nature, and ensure that this imbalance does not threaten humankind in the long term. We must root out the fatal flaws inherent in the 'classic' development model.

It has been said that this would push us back to the pre-industrial era, but I believe that such conclusions are over-hasty. It may appear that the kind of resource utilization I propose is similar to that of pre-industrial societies, but there is one fundamental difference: we have new kinds of modern flow technology at our disposal, which ancient societies did not have.

There have recently been rapid developments in solar energy. We should rely on this kind of modern flow technology, absorbing the kind of modern stocks technology appropriate to a new development model, clean up the legacy of Western culture and abandon its superficial temptations, and then the spirit of our ancient civilization will rise, phoenix-like, from the flames, and shine with new splendour. This is what the new development model for China is really about. In implementing a new approach to development and the use of modern flow technology, we will not only develop the strengths of Chinese civilization, but can also be effective in overcoming its weaknesses.

The reason why Chinese civilization is mute is inextricably linked to its inability to find and put to use flow levels in modern technology. It is therefore helpless in the face of the challenges posed by Western civilization and stocks technology. However, new technology rooted in modern flow technology supplemented by modern stocks technology, may have the effect of slackening the iron grip of repression, which Chinese civilization has historically exerted over the individual in order to protect society as whole. (In fact, this iron grip is merely superficial, the reason being that competition between individuals is by its very nature intense and difficult to regulate.) Such technologies can provide a solid foundation for making the most of the strengths of oriental civilization while overcoming its weaknesses and effectively integrating the relationship between individuals and groups. Moreover, this new technology can ensure that, in the process of implementing a new development model, we are not over-burdened with stocks technology and its attendant cultural baggage and can minimize the technological, economic, social and psychological costs of change.

For example, solar energy as an energy source has obvious advantages – it is clean and exists in inexhaustible amounts (the sun has continued to burn for a few billion years). But solar energy also has a drawback: low-energy flux density. This makes it ill-suited to sustaining the 'classic' development model. Solar energy is necessarily dispersed into many small units, unlike non-renewable resources, making it difficult to adapt to the needs of highly centralized industrial societies.

Solar energy technology is most economical when used in smaller economic units. In an industrial and urban setting, solar energy systems are rarely suited to the complex technical structures necessary to contemporary society, and existing industrial systems are completely unsuited to the requirements of a solar energy age. For example, in order to provide power for New York City, it would be necessary to build an installation many times the size of the city itself for the solar collectors. In fact, it is almost impossible to use solar technology to maintain the existing infrastructure of an industrialized society, its mode of production and way of life.

However, the future of humankind, in post-industrialized or post-Western societies, lies in solar energy. There is no doubt about that. The key issue is whether, stubborn to the end, we waste our energy on building a solar energy infrastructure for existing technology systems, which consumes large amounts of energy and will accelerate the earth's decline, or whether we build a new energy infrastructure that uses the minimum amount of energy and resources at every stage of human life and production. This question means something quite different to the minority of developed countries and the majority of developing countries.

For the developed world, making the latter choice means accepting a lower standard of living than that which they have reached, and abandoning or modifying a culture, which is too heavily biased towards individualism, in favour of reviving a belief in public duty and social responsibility. Whichever choice they make, the necessary adjustments must be in a downward direction, so that both options are painful, because industrialized societies, and the inertia of their models of production, have grown too big.

For most developing countries, only the latter route to development is open to them. Since this is an upward adjustment, the price they pay is much smaller. A more difficult problem is whether they can relinquish the seductive temptations offered by the developed world and the 'classic' development model and adopt a new development model, which will enable them to take a historic leap into modernization with all possible speed.

My readers may well question whether this kind of modernization, if not actually retrograde, is not synonymous with the stagnation or death struggles of human society? The following two chapters will be a comprehensive answer to such questions.

## Notes

1 克里斯汀·雷帕特: 〈經濟增長的社會代價〉,《經濟學譯叢》1987 年第 3 期。(Christine Lepatte [or Lepeter?], 'The social price paid for economic growth', in *Economics in Translation*, 1987, issue 3.)
2 Hall, Robert E and Taylor, John B, *Macroeconomics: Theory Performance and Policy*, W W Norton & Co, New York, 1986. (羅伯特·E.霍爾等:《宏觀經濟學 — 理論、運行和政策》中國經濟出版社, 1988).
3 湯因比: 〈誰將繼承西方在世界的主導地位〉,《外國哲學歷史經濟摘譯》, 上海人民出版社 1975 年, 第 4 期。(A. J. Toynbee, 'Who will inherit the West's position of world dominance?' in *Translated Extracts from Philosophy, History and Economics*, Shanghai Renmin Chubanshe publishers, 1974, issue 4).
4 田一摘編: 〈「美國病」需東方藥〉,《當代思潮》1986 年, 第 6 期。(TIAN Yi, extracts, '"American disease" needs an Eastern remedy', in *Contemporary Thought*, 1986, issue 6).

# 7 Engel's Law

This chapter and the next will provide the philosophical background and the theoretical foundation of a new development model. First of all, the underlying micro-foundations and the mechanism by which it takes effect will be shown through an analysis of Engel's Law. Then we will extend this to encompass material needs and derive from it a generalized Engel's Law.

One of the most important consequences of this law is that once China, as a developing country, has succeeded in meeting the basic needs of its people, it can adopt a variety of low-consumption approaches to satisfy their material needs, without reducing the level and quality of national development.

The practical significance of this for China as it manages the twin pressures of material constraints and consumerism, is self-evident. It is to be hoped that a generalized Engel's Law can give a theoretical answer to the questions raised in the first chapter of this book.

## Micro-foundations

Engel's Law is formulated as follows: with the rise of per capita income levels, the proportion of the total expended on food (the Engel coefficient) drops, and non-food expenditure rises proportionately. In other words, the Engel coefficient is a decreasing function of per capita income (see Figure 7.1).

This law has been broadly substantiated. It has been shown that long-term economic growth, whether in socialist countries or capitalist countries, in developing or developed countries, invariably obeys this law, to the extent that the Engel's coefficient has been used as a yardstick of a country's development. However, the micro-foundations and the mechanisms by which this law takes effect are still worthy of further exploration. In this chapter, I hope to extend Engel's Law in such a way as to draw from it further useful analytical concepts and conclusions. The three micro-foundations of Engel's Law and associated mechanisms will be stated below.

### The biological foundation

As far as humans are concerned, food consumption satisfies needs for survival, enjoyment and growth. Humans need a basic intake of energy to survive, just

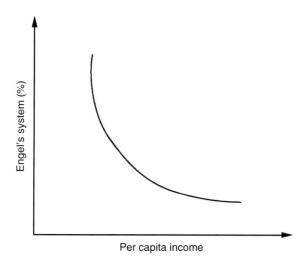

*Figure 7.1* Engel's curve.

Source: Author's own construct.

as other living creatures do. Thus, the rules of both physics and biology apply in this discussion.

The heat generated by animals is a product of a biochemical reaction whereby tissues emit heat. This energy ultimately comes from food. All living systems are subject to the first law of thermodynamics (conservation of energy), so this law can be applied to the body's energy balance. Thus, total intake of energy = heat + work + energy storage.

The human basal metabolic rate (BMR) differs according to age and gender. (Basal metabolic rate is the measurement of heat production when the body is at rest.) It is highest in infants and reduces with age. At any age, it is slightly higher for men than for women. In people who are suffering from malnutrition, starvation and hypothyroidism, basal metabolism is low. By contrast, hyperthyroidism and increased body heat cause basal metabolism to rise. To maintain BMR, a man of medium build requires about 2,000 Kcal (about 8,400 KJ) of food energy every 24 hours. In general, people lose weight where there is insufficient calorific intake, and gain weight when food intake exceeds energy needs.

Certain factors raise heat above the basic level. First, manual labour (labourers need to eat more than office workers. For example, a plumber requires an additional 3,000 Kcal (13,000 KJ) of daily food intake above the basal metabolic requirement of 2,000 Kcal while a sedentary college student only needs an additional 500 Kcal (2,100 KJ)). Second, mental work: however, the process of thinking only needs a negligible extra amount of food energy. It has been calculated that the extra energy per hour needed for completing a very difficult mental arithmetic sum can be supplied by just half a salted peanut. Third, eating: eating

## 112   *Engel's Law*

can increase heat production, (this is known as a specific dynamic action, or SDA), as does the heat generated by food. One hour after eating, heat production begins to increase, reaching a peak about three hours later and maintaining this raised level for several hours. This heat helps to maintain body temperature. The SDA of protein is the highest, with 30 per cent of its calorific value taking the form of heat loss. Thus, if an animal needs a daily 100 KJ of food to maintain its energy balance, if the food is pure protein, it needs a daily supply of 143 KJ in calories. The corresponding figures for carbohydrates and fats are 106 and 104 KJ daily.[1]

It has been calculated that humans require on average 2,250–2,750 Kcal per person per day. This is not particularly lavish, just sufficient to meet basic needs. The minimum appropriate to ensure that a moderate amount of physical and mental work can be done effectively, is probably 2,400 Kcal/day per person. The average person also needs a minimum of about 53 grams of protein per day, of which about 20 grams should be animal protein, as well as essential fatty acids and, especially, a sufficient quantity of various vitamins and minerals.[2]

In short, the amount of food required to keep humans alive and well is limited. In actual fact, the large amount of food consumed by the wealthy is far from good for them. Excessive nutrition contributes to a number of diseases and raises the mortality rate. It is for this reason, doctors say, that the most serious health problem in the United States is neither cancer nor poliomyelitis, but obesity – the total biomass of Americans is more than 250 million kilograms in excess of the optimum.[3]

Clearly, according to the laws of physics and biology, a person cannot continue to eat indefinitely without reaching the critical point at which needs have been basically or fully met. This is a precondition for Engel's Law. It is also obvious that if population growth were zero, food production would not grow indefinitely either. Hence the biological basis of Engel's Law: when per capita income rises, food consumption (expenditure on food) will reach capacity and will then be subject to the S-curve (see Figure 7.2). This curve is the macro-economic statement of Engel's Law. When other consumption is growing, the proportion of food expenditure is bound to decline. When the population is constant, not only does food expenditure fall in line with income growth, it also ceases to grow in absolute terms.

### *Economic constraints*

Engel's law, in a general sense, illustrates the relationship between levels of per capita income and per capita consumption. There is a big difference between this law of economics and general laws of physics and biology. Humans cannot violate the laws of physics, chemistry or biology. For instance, the fact that humans cannot create a perpetual-motion machine of the first or second kind is determined by the first and second laws of thermodynamics. But these laws alone cannot guarantee that the Engel's Law will come into effect naturally; for example, we can imagine someone consuming an infinite amount of food. Of course, this undermines Engel's Law, but does not contradict the laws of biology.

The above scenario is generally restricted by limits on income and the cost of food. Even though the biological need for food intake is limited, it is still possible

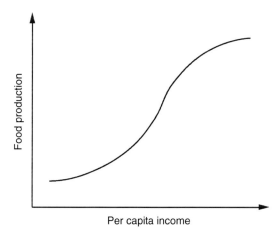

*Figure 7.2* S-curve.

Source: Author's own construct.

that existing resources may not be able to meet all food and other needs. In addition to the laws of physics and biology, therefore, establishing Engel's Law is also subject to technical and economic conditions. For example, it is well known that demand declines as prices rise. That is to say, under certain technical conditions, the limited nature of resources imposes constraints on food needs, through the law of supply and demand. We call this the technical and economic constraints on Engel's Law.

## *Making a reasoned choice*

We should not leave our exploration of Engel's Law here. As technology advances, the scope of human resources available also expands, and once people's income has substantially exceeded the level at which food needs can be fully met, the latter are no longer subject to economic constraints. At that point, what stops people wastefully consuming food? The answer is that people see the clear advantages of non-food consumption, so they make a reasoned choice to stabilize their spending on food and to increase other kinds of consumer spending. Thus, food expenditure is bound to decline proportionately.

This reasoned choice is certainly not made purely on the basis of the relative scarcity of resources (as shown by price levels) at a specific time. This condition is neither necessary nor sufficient, indeed since the price elasticity of food requirements is low (for example), lower prices do not create increased consumption.

We can verify this by imagining a group of people who, for their entire lives, have received a superlative education and engage purely in leisure activities, not production. They consume whatever they want and resource constraints do not exist for them. Will they waste limitless quantities of food products? Of course

## 114    *Engel's Law*

not. What they will do is find a constant stream of new consumer needs, for the outside world to supply them with. The reason is that, once their consumption of food reaches a certain level, they will obtain more mental and physical satisfaction by consuming other things. It is clear that reasoned choices are needed in order for people to discover new preferences. The role of economic constraints is purely to enable these preferences to take shape (especially when a variety of preferences are equally reasonable).

At any given time, economic restrictions are still necessary because reasoned choices are limited and also incomplete. However, with the development of reason and understanding, people may change their spending behaviour for other reasons. For example, when they realize that eating too much rich food can make them ill and shorten their lives, they may reduce their expenditure on food even though they do not need to save, or indeed have an increase in income. There is a certain critical point where income levels have abundantly exceeded what is necessary for human survival and progress, and economic restrictions on the enjoyment of food no longer apply either. At this point, the need to enjoy food is subject to the constraints only of biology and reasoned choice. When a high degree of rationality prevails, there will be less irrational enjoyment of food.

In short, there is necessarily a microbiological foundation for Engel's Law. Additionally, within certain income levels, a combination of reasoned choice and economic constraints will bring this law into effect. Finally, when income reaches a high level, economic constraints no longer apply and biology and reasoned choice will constrain how much food is consumed.

## An elementary extension

Human beings' need for food is primary. Since we all know that food is essential to human survival, and can further be classified as either basic foods (those which meet basic energy needs, such as coarse grains), or standard quality food (required for further physical and mental activities, such as refined grains and small quantities of meat), or luxury food (to meet the need for enjoyment, such as large quantities of meat and fine cuisine), we can make a quite natural extension of Engel's Law. First, however, a few words of explanation about the concept of income elasticity.

### Classification and extension

Income elasticity refers to demand for certain products. The income elasticity of demand means that, as per capita income increases, there is an increase (or decrease) in the demand for a social product relative to growth in per capita income. The formula is as follows: the income elasticity of a social product = growth in product demand/per capita income growth rate.

$$e_Y = \frac{\Delta Q}{Q} \bigg/ \frac{\Delta Y}{Y} \qquad\qquad (7.1)$$

Of which: $Y$ is the per capita income, $\Delta Y$ is the increase in income; $Q$ is the demand for a product when the per capita income level is $Y$, and $\Delta Q$ is the incremental demand for the product when the increase in income levels is $\Delta Y$.

The income elasticity of a product is less than 1 (or greater than 1), meaning that for every 1 per cent increase in per capita income, the demand for the product increases by less than 1 per cent (or more than 1 per cent). Thus the proportion of income growth, which goes on expenditure on the product, declines (or rises) compared with previously. For example, consumer durables are called high income elasticity products because demand for them increases in line with the rise in per capita income and the growth in demand exceeds the growth in income (that is, income elasticity is greater than 1). Conversely, coarse grain is a low-income elasticity (less than 1) product.

At any given level of per capita income, we can classify products according to whether their income elasticity of demand is large or small. Those with an income elasticity of less than 1 are defined as basic goods, those with an income elasticity of around 1 are standard quality goods, and those with an income elasticity greater than 1 are defined as luxury goods.

The above definition is non-structural because it does not state what specific products constitute basic, standard and luxury products at a given income level. But this is unavoidable because given income levels cannot be specified. Moreover, it is impossible to find anything more basic than food products. Now let us look at extending Engel's Law in accordance with the above definition.

To say that the proportion of expenditure on clothing shrinks in line with the rise of per capita income is a commonplace extension of Engel's Law. Although it is undoubtedly correct, and, indeed structural, the amount of information it provides is too small to be of any interest. A further natural extension of Engel's Law is that, given a certain level of per capita income, and assuming that basic, standard and luxury goods have been determined in relation to that income level, then the proportion of expenditure on basic and standard products drops, and that for luxury goods will rise in line with a continual rise in per capita income levels.

The corollary is that the proportion of expenditure on any type of material goods will sooner or later see an irreversible downward trend with the rise of per capita income levels. This extension of Engel's Law and its corollary has now been empirically verified. In other words, the growth of any one specific class of material production is subject to the macro S-curve. There is an even more useful and obvious corollary: the amount of any one specific kind of product which people can rationally need in order to ensure human survival and progress, is limited. The micro-foundations that enable these inferences to be made are still subject to natural constraints (those imposed by the laws of biology, chemistry and physics), as well as technical and economic constraints and the constraints of reasoned choice.

For example, as regards clothing, the need for survival requires nothing more than protection against the cold, imposing natural limits on per capita requirements. Anything more than protection against the cold is clearly surplus to requirements. For clothing to satisfy evolving social norms and the requirement for enjoyment (of

116  *Engel's Law*

comfort and beauty, for example), technical and economic constraints and those of reasoned choice apply, so these needs cannot be infinite either. Even when income levels are high and there are no economic constraints, how often we change our clothes will still be constrained by the reasoned decisions we make simply on the grounds of convenience and aesthetics. We all know that that time could be spent on other activities, which provide more satisfaction and benefits.

In fact, it is not difficult to see from the history of material production and consumption that demand passes through successive stages from high-income elasticity down to low-income elasticity. This clearly indicates that the need for specific categories of material goods is limited. At different income levels, the characteristically low price elasticity of essential goods shows that people will not buy more necessities, however low the price. Clearly, this sort of buying behaviour is not motivated purely by economic considerations. This fact is another way of illustrating the limited nature of these needs.

### *Characteristics of constraints at different stages*

We will now use these three Engel's Law mechanisms to analyse the relationship between food needs, and demand and supply at different stages of human society. In Figure 7.3, the curve RS is the growth curve of the rational need for food per capita. The curve DS is the growth curve of the ability to meet this need. In the long term, if we assume supply is equal to demand, then DS can also be seen as the growth curve for demand for food per capita.

It has only been in the last few hundred years of human history that the per capita expenditure on food has fallen to below 50 per cent of income in a few countries. Thus, in the pre-industrial era (and even during the early stage of industrialization), most people primarily worked to feed and clothe themselves (see Figure 7.3, stage I). During this time, the growth in rational food needs will be greater than the growth of the ability to meet this need (supply). The difference (see shaded area I) must be eliminated by means of technical and economic constraints (that is, through restricting rational needs by means of effective demand).

With the development of science and technology, the growth of our ability to do this begins to exceed the growth of rational need at point A where stage I and II intersect. At this point, technical and economic constraints no longer apply (relative to needs), and the remainder will be eliminated by means of reasoned choice. This is implemented by reducing effective demand, such that the DS curve behind point A moves down to the RS curve.

However, in Figure 7.3, we can see that the DS curve behind point A is much higher than the RS curve, which indicates that effective demand is greater than rational need. Far from being a mere fiction, this is a true reflection of a fairly common situation, especially in developed countries. As has already been mentioned, the total biomass of Americans exceeds the optimum by more than 250 million kilograms. A more general analysis of the problem of effective demand exceeding rational need follows below. To highlight its importance, we will look at a concrete example, tobacco consumption.

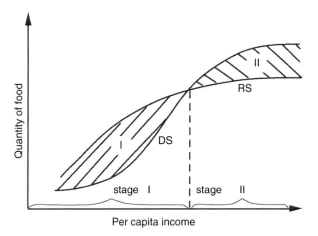

*Figure 7.3* How constraints function.
Source: Author's own construct.

William U. Chandler, in an article called 'Banning Tobacco', presents the following figures:[4] by 1986, tobacco consumption had grown by 20 per cent from the beginning of the anti-smoking movement in 1964. At that time, nearly 2.5 million people were being killed every year due to smoking, accounting for almost 5 per cent of all deaths. Smoking kills 13 times as many people as drugs and eight times as many as car accidents. Smoking is an epidemic with an annual growth rate of 2.1 per cent, which is faster than world population growth. The increase in tobacco consumption slowed briefly in the early 1980s, mainly for economic reasons, but now is rapidly regaining its former momentum. At present, there are no less than one billion smokers worldwide, consuming five trillion cigarettes annually, or more than half a pack per person per day. In the USA, the cost of smoking each year is about $30 billion, to which must be added the loss of income from deaths and economic losses caused by disease, totalling between $38 billion and $95 billion.

We can make further projections from these figures: five trillion cigarettes are equivalent to 250 billion packets. If these are priced on average at 30–40 cents per pack, the total output of the tobacco industry worldwide is worth between $80 and $100 billion. If we add in additional damage caused by smoking (calculated at a low one-for-one basis), we arrive at a total of $200 billion.

The fact is that smoking is not only damaging, it provides absolutely no benefits at all. If no one in the whole world smoked, we would all be $200 billion better off. If we used these extra resources for activities beneficial to humans instead, such as growing food on tobacco land, then there would be an estimated increase in revenue of $300–400 billion – no small sum. This specific example clearly shows that technical and economic constraints alone are not enough. If people made wiser choices, the result would be a better quality of life at a lower GNP per capita.

118  *Engel's Law*

## Social intervention

The case of tobacco clearly shows how, in many cases, it is not sufficient to rely solely on these three micro-constraints to ensure rational consumption and production, and that a degree of social intervention is necessary. In fact, Figure 7.3 still describes the situation too simply. Even in stage I, when rational need is greater than effective demand (that is, the fulfilment of needs), there is still an element of irrational demand within the rational, even though it emerges in economically achievable form. For example, in the lower income brackets, many people smoke poor quality tobacco, which is even more harmful to the body than better quality tobacco. Thus, there is great potential for raising the quality of life, even where there is a low per capita GNP. The reasons for the failure to achieve this cannot only be ascribed to a lack of rationality on the part of humans. There is much about human psychology that remains unknown. Apart from ignorance, there are other important reasons that we should not ignore.

The first is connected to needs and the means by which they are satisfied. For example, peasants living in poverty, going hungry and dressed in rags, have to resort to over-exploiting the land to ensure their own survival. They do not have the luxury of considering what future generations will inherit. In this case, it is not enough to develop new ways of meeting their needs. It is also necessary to impose controls on the growth of the human population as a whole.

The second reason has to do with the mechanisms by which resources are allocated and property rights. We have already looked at this area in some detail. Take, for example, the distortions caused by economic constraints, which underestimate the value of resources and encourage the inflation of irrational effective demand.

The third reason is related to unsound personal choices, for example, conspicuous consumption and the ostentatious flaunting of wealth. However, I am limiting myself here to individual incomes that fall within the range of reasonable. Another, frequently-seen factor is a greedy concern to maximize immediate profit and ignore the situation of resources in the future.

The fourth reason is connected to conflict between partial and global rationality. Take, as an example, two privately-owned livestock farms belonging to two different farmers: let us assume that (1) they know that over-stocking will lead to degradation of their pasture, (2) there is no control over market prices and (3) they are not greedy and are content with their standard of living. But due to fierce market competition, both farmers have to ignore long-term consequences, such as damage to pastures and loss of long-term productivity, in order to maintain high profit margins and withstand the competition. Edward C. Wolf, in 'Pasture Management' provides many such examples: stock-rearing in countries like the United States and Australia, where land and livestock is privately-owned, has given rise to widespread and severe over-stocking and environmental degradation.[5] In fact, this example can be extended from two competing individuals to competing collective groups. This situation arises where resources are non-exclusive in the long term (or where exclusivity is uncertain) or where resources are vertically non-separable, and leads to conflict between the rationality of partial and global choice.

Market price liberalization, privatization and even strict partial public ownership cannot be relied upon to eliminate these problems. Wide-ranging social intervention measures are necessary. For example, in order to save on fuel consumption, Japan has implemented mandatory fuel efficiency standards. Some Western European countries have implemented high fuel taxation, where the taxation element is even higher than the pre-tax cost.

Such mandatory efficiency standards for energy or resources can play a huge role in curbing unreasonable demand. See, for example, the 'public trust law' mentioned in Chapter 000. Such measures are collectively referred to as social intervention; they can also be termed a fourth constraint. In the long term, with humans facing great uncertainty and the possibility of serious and irreversible changes in their environment, this fourth constraint can play a huge role, one which none of the other three constraints are able to play, at least within the time available.

## Notes

1 Hardy, R. N., *Temperature and Animal Life*, Edward Arnold, London 1979. (R. N. 哈迪: 《溫度與動物生活》科學出版社, 1984 年, 29 頁 [Kexue Chubanshe Publishers, 1984, page 29.])
2 Duvigneaud, P., *La Synthese Ecologique: Populations, Communautes, Ecosystemes, Biosphere, Noosphere*, Doin, Paris, 1974. (P. 迪維諾: 《生態學概論》, 科學出版社 1987 年, 227–8 頁. [Kexue Chubanshe Publishers, 1987, page 227–8]).
3 Ibid., page 230.
4 Brown, Lester R., *State of the World 1986: A Worldwatch Institute Report on Progress Toward a Sustainable Society*, WW Norton & Co, New York, 1986. (萊斯特 R. 布朗等: 〈取締煙草〉, 《經濟社會科技 — 1986 年世界形勢評述》科技文獻出版社, 1987 [Kejiwenxian Chubanshe Publishers, 1987]).
5 Ibid.

# 8 The principle of equivalence

I have shown how Engel's Law can naturally be extended to any kind of material goods, and have analysed the micro-foundational factors on which this extension is based: natural constraints, technical and economic constraints and reasoned choice constraints. It is the existence of these constraints, which ensures the growth in production and consumption of any kind of product; regardless of the specific characteristics of the product and production process, all are subject to macroscopic growth laws described by the S-curve.

In this chapter, I extend these arguments to all material needs and the production associated with them. Here, the fundamental question arises as to whether human material needs are unlimited. The following discussion addresses that question.

## Specious arguments

It is, by now, generally recognized that the growth in production and consumption of any particular kind of material goods obeys the S-curve. It is clear that the need for these goods is limited. However, most people would oppose any claim that there are limits on material needs (but not on demand) in their entirety, and indeed there is little evidence to support this proposition. It is generally believed that human material needs are unlimited, the basic logic being that with changes in the technology, economics and culture, material needs become more diverse – while some disappear, new needs constantly emerge. The only possible conclusion seems to be that people's material needs are unlimited – but is this really the case?

### Natural constraints

First, the time resources of any individual are limited because there are only 24 hours in a day. Second, an individual's activity per unit of time is limited. These two premises are basic to an analysis of the relationship between the amount of material needs and natural constraints. They are based on a series of physical, chemical, and biological laws, so they are incontrovertible. Any consideration of material consumption – as a type of human activity – cannot get around them.

*The principle of equivalence*   121

For people to take action to meet their material needs, they need time. The amount of consumer activity that can be fitted into a unit of time is, however, limited. If a factor of a 24-hour period is multiplied by the maximum amount of human biological activity per unit of time – let us say, the energy needed by a man engaged in heavy labour for one hour – we get a finite value, which we can call the index of the greatest extent of material consumption activity. This value will fall between 5,000 Kcal/day and 6,000 Kcal/day. If this value is multiplied by the total population, it gives a figure for the greatest extent of material consumption by the whole population.

The limited nature of this value shows that, even without considering limits of income, there are necessarily limits on the overall real ability to consume of any individual or limited population (this equals the material consumption activity index multiplied by the amount of consumption/kcal. Even though the latter factor changes over time, it is nevertheless clearly limited). This conclusion is obvious because, although people have a belief that the type and quantity of their material needs are infinite, those needs are constrained by their capacity for consumption, so that actual material needs must also be limited. It should be pointed out that consumers must have both objects to consume and the ability to consume them. One without the other will not do. For example, people with hearing loss will not be able to engage in consumer activities that involve the enjoyment of music. It is meaningless to talk about material needs over and above our capacity for consumption. Material needs that exist within the constraints of consumption capacity are known as intrinsic material needs.

In normal economic analysis, it is generally accepted that constraints are imposed on material needs by effective demand or actual income; however, the constraints that intrinsic material needs impose, have been almost ignored.

### Economic constraints

Despite the fact that any individual's consumption capacity or intrinsic material needs are limited, that does not mean that this need can always be met at a given time. For example, when the population is large, those needs may still, under certain technical conditions, far exceed resource constraints at a given time, even if the needs are limited. In such circumstances, if there are no technical or economic constraints, the conflict between consumption capacity or intrinsic needs and actual supply or production capacity cannot be resolved. Thus, consumption capacity (or intrinsic need) is further constrained by actual income or effective demand, in the guise of technical and economic constraints, and is connected to actual supply or production capacity. Sometimes non-economic social distribution is necessary in order further to regulate the satisfaction of individual needs, as well as to resolve the conflict between individual needs and the needs of society.

### Partially rational constraints

In the above analysis, we have seen what happens after specific material needs have been fully met: technical and economic constraints become ineffectual and

## 122    *The principle of equivalence*

natural and reasoned choice constraints become major constraint factors. This chapter will be devoted to extending this discussion to material needs as a whole (where not specified below, material needs refers to intrinsic material needs).

### Needs and demands

Let us look first at the situation where rational needs are greater than effective demand – generalized malnutrition among hungry people in Africa is a typical example. It is clear that the basic survival needs of these people are entirely rational, but a variety of factors have led to extreme economic underdevelopment and their needs are far from fully met. This problem must be resolved by improving or weakening supply constraints in different ways.

What is more noteworthy is what happens when rational material needs are smaller than effective demand. Over-eating by the rich in developed countries is a classic example. For instance, the biomass of all Americans is more than 250 million kg in excess of the optimum value (more than one kg per capita). If we take into account the fact that the population includes a considerable number of people who live in poverty, then we can see how the material needs of other sectors of the population are based on deeply irrational choices.

This example reminds us that technical and economic constraints do not guarantee that people will be able to make reasoned or effective choices. For individuals and society, this not only represents waste, it also confers no benefits, either direct or indirect. In this regard, we propose a new concept: reasoned intrinsic material needs, which are smaller than intrinsic material needs.

Everywhere in the developed world excessive material consumption is rife, showing that economic constraints alone are not sufficient to ensure that people will make reasoned consumption choices. It also shows how we still have much to learn about how consumers reason their choices once income constraints have been surpassed. Understanding this can help us exercise self-restraint and appropriate social intervention.

### Material and non-material needs

The reality is that the reasoned need for (or consumption of) things such as food cannot grow indefinitely. For example, the principle that more is better does not apply to such items as housing, refrigerators, televisions and cars. Instead, just as eating too much rich food can cause physical discomfort and disease, so owning excessive material goods not only does not increase comfort, it also leads to unnecessary trouble and expense. For example, living in a big house can make people feel lonely, and, when it is too big to clean, the accumulated dust can cause illness. And then there are the air-conditioning-borne diseases, which are prevalent in Western society.

Thus, as food consumption reaches a certain level, people may find that consuming non-food products is more conducive to physical and mental health and self-development. When people's material consumption reaches a certain level,

*The principle of equivalence* 123

and the disadvantages become increasingly obvious, the question inevitably arises as to what to do next. Because of limits on the frequency, quantity and time spent on human activity, even if technical or economic constraints are ineffective, people will realize that spending more time on consuming non-material products is more advantageous. This is not only a function of the relative scarcity of resources reflected in their price at a given time, but has much deeper roots in people's increasing understanding of the relative levels of wealth in different areas of life.

We have seen how, after food consumption reaches a given level, humans will certainly engage in various activities that are healthy for them, although too much will be harmful. In just the same way, after material consumption reaches a certain level, it can be guaranteed that humans will engage in a variety of non-material activities. For example, outstanding scientists and scholars at different periods of history have numerous significant achievements to their credit, even though their material standard of living was not of the highest.

A study[1] of such historical figures leads us to an important conclusion: there are clear limits on the rational intrinsic material needs (quantitative and qualitative) necessary to guarantee sufficient stamina, energy and intelligence to effectively engage in a variety of material and mental activities. In the rest of this chapter, this point will be addressed from a variety of perspectives.

### Global rationality constraint

In order to limit the irrational part of the effective demand for certain products, the three constraints mentioned above should be complemented with a fourth – social intervention, also known as the global rationality constraint. This is especially true for the irrational element of the aggregate effective demand for material goods. This aggregate can come to an alarming amount and have extremely adverse consequences. For example, global spending on illicit drugs today amounts to more than $100 billion. The United States is the world's largest 'drug kingdom', consuming about 65 per cent of the total output of world drug consumption. Drug-trafficking, drug abuse and consequent urban drug wars have become the number one domestic issue in America. Needless to say, the ranks of American drug addicts include large numbers of the jobless and homeless but also, more seriously, students, teachers, workers, managers, government employees and other highly-educated professionals. According to a special report published by the US government in July 1989, at least 72 million Americans have tried a drug at least once in their lifetime. That is one in every three of the population. In North America, the relentless demand for drugs has provided a strong stimulus to maintaining drug production in South America and a steady supply to the North. In Latin American countries such as Colombia, Bolivia and Peru, the drug economy accounts for a significant portion of the national economy.

If we calculate its value in the same way as we did for tobacco in the previous chapter, this industry adds up to between $150 and $200 billion. Most alarmingly,

124    *The principle of equivalence*

current global military spending totals trillions of dollars. This has all happened under the auspices of effective demand. If, one day, the irrational element of aggregate effective demand could be estimated, it could well add up to trillions of dollars. Cutting down on this expenditure would lower per capita GNP globally, but rather than reducing people's quality of life, it would actually raise it. These examples of irrational demand clearly show that it is hard for economic constraints or free market mechanisms to effectively regulate rational supply and demand, and they are particularly powerless to push supply and demand in a different direction. The most ridiculous thing is that, in Western economics, such examples are attributed to reasoned choices made by individuals. It is believed that social intervention will distort individual preferences, leading to low efficiency. In fact, social intervention can play an important role in curbing irrational demand, reducing resource consumption and improving quality of life.

## An analysis of need

In order to analyse more thoroughly how irrational demand is formed, a more in-depth discussion of human needs is required. For convenience, let us divide human needs into three categories: basic needs, and the needs respectively for self-development and pleasure. These three kinds of needs, and the form in which they can be satisfied, will be discussed below.

### *Characteristics of these three kinds of needs*

The key characteristic of basic needs is that they are necessary to human existence, so they are met mainly or entirely through material consumption. However, the materials that enable these basic needs to be met can be very different.

For example, it is known that basic human nutrition needs cannot be met by an all-plant food diet; proteins and fats are also needed, thus, animal products must also be ingested. However, there is a marked difference between the customary diets of different societies. Animal products are the principal component of European and American-style diets, but only form one-half of a Japanese-style diet. The GNP per capita in Japan in 1980 was the same as in America in 1970, about $5,000 (at the 1970 dollar value). But the 1970 per capita consumption of animal products in the United States was 164 kg more than in Japan in 1980. (This will be addressed in more detail below.)

Different patterns of material consumption mean that the consumption of resources differs greatly. Based on the above example, we can see that, to meet human nutritional needs, an American-style diet annually requires at least 1,000 kg of grain per capita more than a Japanese-style diet. (Plants convert into animal food at a ratio of 3:1). A whole series of consequences derive from this: a need to expand arable cultivation, as well as demand for fertilizers, machinery and pesticides, all of which have unavoidable effects on a country's mode of production.

Survival itself is not the sole purpose in life for human beings. We need not just a healthy life, but to be able to work, study and play healthily as well. For

*The principle of equivalence*   125

human society to progress, humans need to develop better ways to put their physical strength, energy and intelligence to use to achieve a variety of objectives. The main difference between basic needs and those for self-development, is that the former can be satisfied by consuming widely varying amounts of resources.

For example, one person may play Chinese chess as a way of using their leisure time to improve their IQ and the speed of their reactions; another person may learn to drive to achieve similar purposes. If both are outstanding in their respective fields, to the extent that they are regarded as equally good, then those two people have equal capability, and each has reached their maximum level of satisfaction. However, the significant difference between the two is that the level of material consumption required for each form of leisure activity is very different. The resources required for the former are almost negligible, while the quality and quantity of resources needed by the latter are considerable.

Another example is physical exercise and the development of human strength and physical skills. Any form of exercise requires the same amount of energy and nutritional supplements, but the material resources expended in carrying out these different forms of exercise vary greatly. Martial arts and qigong, for example, require hardly any space or equipment, while equestrian sports and motorboats cannot be enjoyed without the necessary space, equipment and resources.

Obviously, if we turn our attention from the micro to the macro level, there are not only marked differences in the overall levels of consumption of material resources by the social groups who partake in these different leisure activities, but also in the production and supply systems designed to meet these resource consumption models.

Pleasure needs are very similar to self-development needs, but there are subtle differences: the need for self-development is more directed and purposeful, while the need for pleasure is less so. Although self-development needs (for example, the need to develop physical stamina and skills) may well have inappropriate aspects, problems of choice usually arise only during the specific process of fulfilling this need and the levels of material consumption that arise therefrom. Pleasure needs, on the other hand, may generate a number of irrational needs if participants are simply filling their leisure time and have no specific objectives.

### Choices and how they are realized after basic needs have been met

Now that the nature of these three needs has been clarified, it is easy to answer this question. Meeting basic needs requires a pattern of material consumption, which enables survival and a certain standard of living. The form this pattern takes largely derives from the specific form that economic and natural constraints take. Once basic needs have been met, the situation is very different. It then becomes crucial to make choices between a variety of mutually substitutable non-material and material means to satisfy needs for self-development and pleasure.

It is not enough to make these reasoned choices on the basis of economic constraints alone. For example, economic constraints cannot effectively solve the

126 *The principle of equivalence*

problem of excessive per capita biomass in the USA. Careful observation of the societies in which we live will reveal much irrational supply and consumption, even though these societies are still subject to economic constraints.

For example, there is increasing evidence that, in Western countries, excessive consumption of beef and saturated fat is a factor in causing heart disease, obesity and other disorders. In fact, the evidence repeatedly shows that unless the human ability to reason has developed to a certain level, and without social intervention underpinned by an understanding of social consumption, we cannot rely on technical and economic constraints alone to provide a fundamental solution to the problem of irrational needs.

## A paradox

Hawken, in his book *The Next Economy*, states very clearly that the macro-economic economy of material production as a whole is also subject to the S-curve.[2] However, his viewpoint is restrictive in that he ascribes this fact purely to resource constraints. He believes that because of limited material resources, material production will, sooner or later, come to a standstill when we run out of resources. However, if advances in science and technology mean that solar energy can be employed better and more cheaply, can material production continue to grow? This is a question he cannot answer.

The very fact that material production as a whole is subject to the S-curve shows why his viewpoint is too restrictive. Take growth in the production of specific goods for example: as technology continues to progress, constraints of resources and supply can be ignored (that is to say, when all resources have been used to produce those goods, resource constraints can be regarded as non-existent). At that point, demand constraints are primary; demand constraints are non-natural resource constraints, operating internally and determined by people's income and intrinsic characteristics.

In order to go beyond the narrowness of Hawken's theory, we have to extend Engel's Law in a more generalized way and to clarify the general mechanism by which the growth of material production as a whole is also subject to the S-curve. The concept of generalized income is first discussed below, then a generalized Engel's Law is described and analysed. Finally, some useful corollaries of a generalized Engel's Law are discussed.

### *The concept of generalized income*

The economic activities of any individual can be seen as subject to the following two constraints: that individual's income and 'time allowance'. The two taken together comprise the total social income, which the consumer can use to meet personal objectives.[3] We are going to amend this description of total social income as follows: the algorithm states that the value of time is equal to the time that individual devotes to work, and the additional financial income that accrues therefrom. The problem arises because it is impossible for a person to work for

24 hours to earn more income. For this reason, it is necessary to deduct the portion of the time allowance necessary just to survive:

- Survival time is defined as the time necessary for simple regeneration of a given amount of stamina, skills and intelligence.
- Self-development time is defined as the time necessary to increase and improve stamina, skills and intelligence.
- 'Pure leisure time' is defined as the time remaining after hours spent on the above activities have been deducted. This definition is very vague because the purpose and effect of leisure time are neither obvious nor direct and may, or may not, be conducive to survival and self-development. Without further specific analysis, this can only be treated as neutral time, that is, time which, at least in the short term, has no obvious, direct implications for survival and self-development.

Obviously, in real life, these distinctions are necessarily blurred. For example, work time is not only necessary for survival; it may also meet the need for self-development and pleasure. However, theoretically, time may be divided into three, simply classified as above. This leads to the following definition: 'generalized income' can be broadly defined as an individual's financial budget plus their pure leisure time allowance and some of their development time allowance.

The reason for this definition is obvious. First, survival time (such as sleeping time) cannot be an extra value, as that would be double counting and would contradict reality. Second, part of self-development time is necessary to maintain a certain level of renewal; it has to be spent, so it is not completely 'disposable income'.

### Description of a generalized Engel's Law

Human society over the past few centuries has been characterized both by a continuous increase in income (calculated in constant values) and a gradual reduction in time that is spent working (part of survival time). This has led to a commensurate increase in leisure time (see Figure 8.1).

This, of course, has meant a growth in generalized income. These concepts can be employed to express a generalized Engel's Law as follows: the increase of per capita generalized income will lead to an irreversible trend – the proportion of generalized income accounted for by material consumption will decrease while that for non-material consumption will rise.

This is because there is no requirement here for material production to stagnate; it is only stated that, with an increase in per capita generalized income, non-material consumption grows faster than material consumption after a certain critical level is reached. This is similar to Engel's law, which does not require the absolute level of food consumption to stagnate or decline. At the same time, this extension does not require there to be an absolute limit to natural resources.

128 *The principle of equivalence*

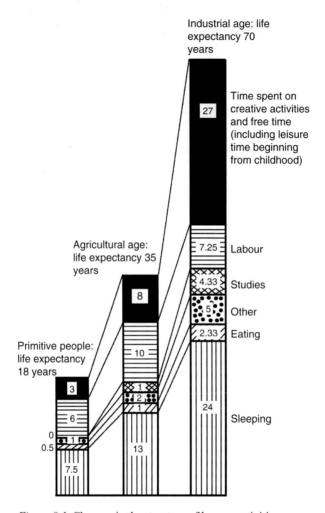

*Figure 8.1* Changes in the structure of human activities.

Source: Author's own construct.

Source: cited in（罗）格.普.阿波斯托尔主编:《当代资本主义》，三联书店 1979 年 (G. P. Apostol ed, *Contemporary capitalism*, Sanlianshudian Publishers, 1979).

The subtlety of the generalized Engel's Law is that it is no longer limits the argument to material resources within a given period of time. In so doing, it transcends the optimists' objection that humans need not limit their use of materials in the long term. This law takes natural constraints (transformed into technical and economic constraints) as its base but also bases itself on social constraints (on the making of reasoned choices) by focusing on the visible disadvantages of excessive material consumption, as well as the advantages and

The principle of equivalence    129

enriching nature of non-material consumption. There is something counter-intuitive about this extension, but it is clear from the preceding analysis that it is as solid and reliable as Engel's Law.

### Further discussion of material and non-material needs

Scholars have divided human needs into two categories: the needs of the human body for survival fall into one category; the other category is the need for accumulated human knowledge and knowledge arrived at through individual, ethical and moral needs, linked to strong desires for such experiences as social contact, knowledge, love and social status. Interactions in the second category are necessary to human social existence and are characterized by the fact that they are not physical but are met through the process of activities.[4]

Of course, meeting the needs for social existence requires material goods and facilities. But this is very different from the pattern and extent of material consumption when meeting people's physical needs. First, very different patterns of material consumption can give ample expression to the same non-material needs. Second, in the process of meeting non-material needs, material consumption plays an auxiliary role, which is fundamentally different from the way in which physical needs are met. Third, with an increase in per capita generalized income, once rational, intrinsic material needs are no longer subject to technical and economic constraints, it is finally possible for humans to give consideration to rational modes of material consumption.

Once per capita generalized income passes a certain critical level, the amount of pure leisure time and how it is used increasingly becomes a prime element in human life. At this point, meeting physical needs becomes a less important part of life, and reasoned choice constraints play a greater role. This is the basis on which a generalized Engel's Law can be established.

### Empirical evidence and experimental evidence

Now that we have completed the theoretical derivation of a generalized Engel's Law, it is necessary to provide empirical evidence for this law since, without convincing evidence, my readers may regard it as pure conjecture.

*Development of the tertiary industry sector*: according to 1983 data, the total employed population in the United States was 100.8 million people, of which primary sectors like agriculture accounted for only 3.5 per cent. Employment in the secondary sector – manufacturing, civil engineering and building – had dropped to 26.8 per cent and the proportion of the working population within the manufacturing sector was only 19.8 per cent. The remaining 69.7 per cent of the employed population were concentrated in the tertiary industry sector. It is very striking that there has been little increase in the number of workers engaged in transportation, retail and wholesale trade employment while, in the last decade, the working population as a whole has expanded by about 20 million, with most going into information technology, advertising, fashion design, entertainment

## 130   *The principle of equivalence*

and the tourism industry. Of these, industries that create 'knowledge value' accounted for a large proportion.[5] This is indirect evidence for the decline in material needs (though we must exclude here the abnormal development of tertiary industries in the developing countries).

*Recession in basic resources industries during the 1980–3 economic crisis*: during the crisis in the global economy between 1980 and 1983, resource consumption industries (known as 'foundation industries'), in the petroleum-based economies, were the most severely affected. Post-war, petroleum-based economies and their production systems are founded on the belief that more material consumption is a good thing. However, in recent years, the contrary belief, that it is not necessarily a good thing, has grown and a gap has resulted between market demand and the production capacity of resource consumption industries. In the global economic crisis from 1980 to 1983, sales of natural resources, agricultural products and raw materials stagnated.

In the summer of 1983, the world economy, triggered by a recovery in the US economy, was restored to health. But a number of phenomena unknown to pre-1970s petroleum-based economies were now apparent. First, there was no corresponding increase in demand for raw materials. Second, agricultural products and raw materials were stagnating in international commodity markets. Generally speaking, with a boom in world markets, international trade commodity prices should also rise. But this time they did not. And 1984, a year when market economies experienced a significant recovery, produced an anomaly: prices for most commodities actually fell.[6]

If we then consider the fact that in most developed countries over the past decade, visible growth has been slow, it must be concluded that this stagnation cannot wholly be explained by resource constraints. In the above example, there was economic recovery with no corresponding recovery in commodity prices, and there was continued weakness in the market for raw materials. This shows that the material economy in these countries is moving towards maturity and stagnation.

*A growth in demand for a good 'cultural life'*: by the latter half of the 1970s, and especially since the 1980s, the situation has changed with the emergence of environmental issues. Attitudes have changed in Europe, the United States and Japan; people feel satiated with material wealth, and increasingly demand a good cultural life. In seeking to add richness and variety to life, they demand quality over quantity. Rather than material wealth, which can be calculated in figures, they seek an unquantifiable sense of well-being, enjoyment of beautiful surroundings and a rich and varied cultural life.[7] This is direct evidence in support of a generalized Engel's Law.

*Changes in reasoned choices*: according to the 1976 annual report of the Stanford Research Institute, between four and five million adult Americans have voluntarily taken a substantial reduction in income. In so doing, these people, who used to be enthusiastic participants in the high-entropy industrial consumer economy, have shifted from their original position. The lifestyle they have adopted could appropriately be called 'spontaneous simplicity' and is a low-entropy mode of existence, which is based on reducing material consumption and materialism, stresses the development of the individual's inner world and gives increasing importance to the state of the environment. The Stanford report estimated that as many as 8–10 million Americans have to some degree adapted to a simpler way of life.

In May 1977, a Harris Poll found that 79 per cent of the American public approved of their leaders promoting the simple life; only 17 per cent emphasized attaining a higher standard of living; 76 per cent were in favour of 'learning to get our pleasure out of non-material experiences'; only 17 per cent were concerned with 'satisfying our needs for more goods and services'; 59 per cent believed that they should make real efforts to eradicate the causes of pollution, rather than simultaneously pursuing development and identifying ways to clean up the environment; 82 per cent of people were willing to 'improve our existing modes of transportation'; while only 11 per cent of people believed that 'we should strive to go further faster'; 77 per cent were willing to 'spend more time on increasing mutual understanding between human beings'; only 17 per cent of people wanted to 'to enhance and speed up our capacity for interpersonal relations through more advanced technology'. Finally, nearly two-thirds of the public believed that seeking individual satisfaction from work was more important than 'expanding the scale of industry and raising productivity'. 'We should first learn to appreciate human values rather than material values'; and 'producing more goods and creating more employment opportunities' was secondary to this.[8] These facts provide statistically significant evidence for a generalized Engel's Law.

## A new way

As we have seen, by eliminating pervasive and harmful economic activities such as tobacco and drugs, living standards and quality of life can be improved without raising per capita GNP. Japan and Western Europe have reached the same per capita GNP as the United States, with only half the consumption of energy. There is a great disparity between the consumption of grain with which different countries achieve the same level of health in its citizens. And outstanding figures of different eras have achieved major creative successes under very different material living conditions of life. We can abstract from this the following principle.

*Equivalence principle*: there are very different levels of material consumption required to satisfy basic human needs and needs for self-development and pleasure, in terms of quality and quantity. As the level of needs rises (especially once survival needs have been met), more ways will be found to meet them, and the difference in the amount of materials that are consumed in order to to satisfy those needs, will also continue to grow.

This principle is illustrated in Figure 8.2. To a certain extent, the equivalence principle has more universality than a generalized Engel's Law. The former takes into account a variety of material constraints, while the latter may well be distorted when levels of material constraints differ, for example, by the prevalence of harmful consumption and production behaviour.

I believe that a generalized Engel's Law and the equivalence principle provide a sound theoretical foundation and philosophical background for a new

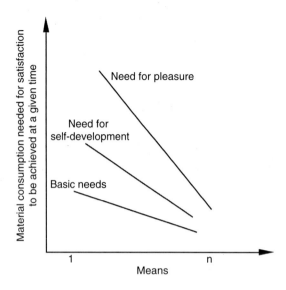

*Figure 8.2* Equivalence principle.

Source: Author's own construct.

development model. I summarize below some of the most important conclusions to this chapter.

First, the rational, intrinsic material needs (quantitative and qualitative) necessary to guarantee that people have adequate physical strength, energy and intelligence effectively to engage in a variety of material or cultural activities, is clearly limited. Second, with the growth of per capita generalized income, an irreversible trend will sooner or later make its appearance, that is, a proportionate decline of material consumption. The proportion expended on non-material consumption will rise commensurately. Third, once the stage of meeting basic needs has been passed, there will be ample ways to lower consumption in fulfilling people's needs for self-development and pleasure. Indeed, the required level and quality of satisfaction may be achieved with a broad range of means. Fourth, the fundamental reason why actual material consumption far surpasses rational, intrinsic material needs, both qualitatively and quantitatively, is that inappropriate ways of satisfying all kinds of needs have been chosen, with no guarantee that the desired satisfaction will be achieved. Fifth, purely technological and economic constraints cannot, on their own, ensure that humans will make reasoned choices.

Three interesting deductions can be made from a generalized Engel's Law. They have important implications, and their influence on changes to the way we live now cannot be ignored:

1   As material consumption or expenditure rises in line with the rise in generalized income, a point is reached when the marginal effect of that expenditure on the long-term development of human society diminishes.

The principle of equivalence    133

2   As generalized incomes rise, the proportional fall in material production and consumption, requiring fewer natural resources, is highly beneficial to human quality of life and can also reduce material consumption levels. This point should be obvious because, by then, such activities as travel, hiking and enjoyment of nature will have assumed a relatively important role in people's lives. All of these benefit from fresh air, unspoiled natural landscapes, limpidly clear lakes and rivers, blue seas, towering forested mountains, green fields, beautiful flowers and bird song. This kind of social and self-development not only does not exact a destructive price from the environment; it actually benefits nature just as nature benefits humans. At the same time, it reduces the need for anti-pollution measures and directly increases social wealth, and thus average per capita 'income'.
3   Future human development will be characterized by a full and effective use of leisure time and a rich cultural life.

We only need give a thought to the unimaginably rich cultural achievements of such great scientists as Euler, Newton, Maxwell, Einstein and Boyle, in times when levels of material consumption were far lower than they are today. These achievements (still, half a century later, scarcely known by the vast majority of people) allow us to imagine how great human potential is in the future.

If we add together these conclusions and implications, we can draw a further, extraordinarily useful conclusion: now that China, as a developing country, has passed the stage of meeting the basic needs of its people, it is in a position to choose a variety of means to satisfy their other needs, which require relatively low consumption levels and do not hold back national development and quality of life. These choices must not employ technological and economic constraints alone but should, as far as possible, use other constraints.

### Some additional thoughts

Once we accept the generalized Engel's Law, then an even more interesting question presents itself: since people's rational, intrinsic material needs are limited, are cultural activities also limited? A comprehensive answer to this question is beyond the scope of this book, but I will present a few simple points for the consideration of my readers.

First, both cultural and material needs alike require time, so that cultural activities are obviously limited by the time available. Second, before humans can engage in creative, cultural activities, they have to devote a considerable amount of time to study, absorbing the ever-increasing wealth of knowledge accumulated by their predecessors. Moreover, certain universals exist, such as maximum speed and smallest activity. Thus, what people are able to observe is necessarily limited and incomplete. Finally, once research has become sufficiently sophisticated, the complexity and accuracy of its conclusions leaves no room for doubt.

Starting from these premises, it is clear that creative, cultural activities are necessarily subject to limits, at least as far as the scope and level of current

## 134    *The principle of equivalence*

research is concerned. Thus a study of the form that cultural activities take (including intuitive activities), when they happen and how they are distributed, will surely increase the effectiveness of these activities, thus promoting self-development.

What we cannot know at present is whether human cultural activities will ever reach saturation point and consequent stagnation.

## Notes

1  Goble, Frank G, *Third Force: The Psychology of Abraham Maslow*, Grossman Publishers, New York, 1970. (弗蘭克·戈布爾: 《第三思潮》上海譯文出版社, 1987 [Shanghaiwenyi Chubanshe publishers, 1987]).
2  Hawken, P., 1983. *The Next Economy*, Henry Holt and Co., New York. (保爾·霍肯: 《未來的經濟》1985 年 , 科技文献出版社 , 第 92 頁。 [Kejiwenxian Chubanshe publishers, 1985, page 92]).
3  Henri Lepage, *Demain le Capitalisme* ('Capitalism Tomorrow'), Le Livre de Poche, Paris, 1978 (亨利·勒帕日: 《美國新自由主義經濟學》第 239 頁。).
4  《現代外國哲學社會科學文摘》, 1987 年第 2 期 , 第 6 頁。
5  堺屋太一: 《知識價值革命》, 東方出版社 1986 年 , 第 205 頁。 (SAKAIYA Taichi, *The Knowledge-Value Revolution, or A History of the Future*, Kodansha International, Tokyo, 1985).
6  Ibid.
7  Ibid.
8  Jeremy Rifkin and Ted Howard, *Entropy: A New World View*, The Viking Press, New York, 1980. (杰里米 里夫金等《熵: 一種新的世界觀》 1987 年, 第 192–195 頁, 上海译文出版社 [Shanghaiyiwen Chubanshe Publishers, 1987, pages 192–5]).

# 9 Overcoming barriers

Chapters 6, 7 and 8 have discussed the possibility of a new development model in general. The following three chapters focus on how China should construct a solution specific to its particular circumstances, providing a comprehensive overview of how a new development model can be implemented. We may employ a set of rules here – the safety rule, the minimum rule, the equivalence and priority rules. From these, a series of further rules compliant with a new development model can then be extrapolated.

## The safety rule

A feature of renewable resources is that they have a maximum sustainable yield (MSY). If human beings restrict their use to this limit, they may continue to enjoy them freely, year-on-year. Conversely, if utilization consistently exceeds this limit, and renewable resources turn into non-renewable resources, then permanent damage will result. The fact that the ecosystem has these kinds of limits shows us that, within those limits, the ecosystem is capable of recovery, that is, it can absorb all kinds of harmful, polluting substances, allowing human beings to make use of these resources freely. Conversely, if pollution or damage exceeds a certain threshold, the environment's absorption capacity is reduced or lost altogether, causing permanent damage. It may even be necessary for humans to pay additional costs (such as the compensation I have discussed above) to achieve equivalent levels of pollution control.

Staying within MSY limits brings a positive benefit, while exceeding it represents a negative cost. In both cases, these resources are gifts of nature and are connected with the water and biological cycles. Acceleration of the 'classic' development model is achieved by exhausting stocks resources and their annual flow rate. This is vividly represented in Figure 9.1.

Line A represents the utilization of natural resources within the threshold of renewability. It is clear that with the extension of time ($t$), the area below line A continues to expand, that is, area A = $t$ × threshold (MSY). Curve B shows over-exploitation: in the interval between $t_0$ and $t_1$, the area below the curve is a finite constant and with the passage of time ($t$), the area under the curve will become a negative. Additional costs are incurred to compensate for this. The logic of the

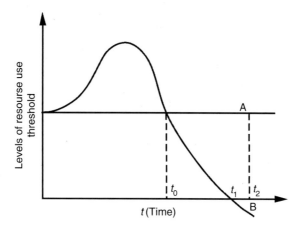

*Figure 9.1* Two models of use.

Source: Author's own construct.

'classic' development model is that over-use leads to the eventual extinction of renewable resources and, as exploitation accelerates, non-renewable resources are used to compensate for the adverse consequences that this entails.

Even though during the time up to $t_1$, the area under curve B is greater than that under line A, when $t$ reaches a certain point, the area under B will sooner or later become smaller than the area under A, regardless of how great the area under B at $t_1$. Obviously, with any given constant $a$, a time ($t_2$) can always be found, such that $a \leq t_2 \times \text{MSY}$. Thus, model B is the one most appropriate if the earth is likely to be destroyed quickly (that is, within 500 years) because we only need have regard for immediate benefits. However, if we assume that humans have a few hundred thousand years of existence left, then model B should clearly be abandoned, and model A should be adopted.

As far as we know at present, the time for adopting model B is still in the distant future. (Of course, it is conceivable that, at some point, the earth will no longer be suitable for human habitation, and before that moment arrives, it is desirable for all the earth's natural resources to be used to the maximum in order to enable as many people as possible to leave the earth and fly to another habitable planet). The best choice, therefore, is to use model A, that of sustainable use of renewable resources and environmental capacity, in such a way that the compensating expenditure of non-renewable resources can be put to other uses. It will also become clear that, with sufficient time, and as long as there are no cataclysmic changes in the earth or the sun, this choice does not mean that we will never have the opportunity to adopt model B. In fact, an intuitive understanding of Figure 9.1 is that, as long as the curve B moves parallel and towards the right, we are free to take the opportunity to switch to model B even if model A has previously been adopted.

*Overcoming barriers* 137

The above analysis reminds us that the protection rule ought to be established with regard to the use of renewable resources and environmental capacity, and this should ensure that the use of such resources is not allowed to exceed maximum sustainable yields, resulting in irreversible losses. Essentially, this protection is a necessary condition for sustained and effective use of these resources. Thus, as long as there is no conflict between protection and sustainable use, the effect of both is the same, that is, the protection rule (also known as the 'vertical optimal efficiency rule') is consistent with sustained optimal efficiency. We can draw a corollary from this: for such resources, a discount rate higher than the natural growth rate is inappropriate for sustainable development. It is easy to verify, for example, that at a discount rate of 3 per cent, stocks resources kept for 100 years and valued at $100 will only have a discounted present value (PV) of $5. The protection rule, therefore, means that it may become necessary for certain resources to be exploited at a discount rate close to zero. For example, requiring the sealing off of tropical rainforests to protect the global atmosphere requires a zero discount rate; so do regulations which allow only a maintenance level of felling in forests used for water conservation on the upper reaches of a river.

Under certain conditions, the protection rule may come into conflict with short-term or horizontal optimal-efficiency rules. However, such conflicts between global and partial efficiency, long-term and short-term efficiency, if they involve horizontal or vertical external diseconomy, are likely to demonstrate that partial or short-term optimal efficiency is actually inefficient. This is a good reason for adopting the protection rule.

In previous chapters, we have discussed the process by which human society has made the transition from the use of pre-modern flow technology and limited flow resources, to modern stocks technology, and large-scale use of non-renewable stocks resources and resource allocation mechanisms. We have also analysed fundamental problems and the prospects for resolving them.

The future of humankind ultimately involves a system where the focus is on new flow technology (such as bio-engineering, solar engineering) and large-scale use of a variety of flow resources (tidal energy and wind energy), and this is supplemented by the economical use of stocks resources through modern stocks technology. During the transitional period, it may be that new flow technology and modern stocks technology will be equally important. Emerging advanced technologies should, however, be treated as a separate topic. They include both stocks technology (coal gasification and liquefaction, and nuclear fusion, for instance), and flow technology (such as solar and wind power).

Modern stocks technology requires huge investment, its purpose being to meet requirements for high levels of resources, albeit at a huge cost to the environment and society. Thus, this type of technology will inevitably have adverse effects, such as unacceptable levels of environmental pollution and environmental degradation, social and political structures, which are detrimental to human values, and a continual rise in costs caused by shortages of non-renewable resources. There will also be an increase in the range of serious and pressing problems we have to resolve.

138 *Overcoming barriers*

Investment in new flow technology can play a role in the long run, because flow technologies such as solar and wind power are energy-saving and do not deplete natural resources, have few adverse effects on the environment and may even have a beneficial influence. The risks to society and the political systems are therefore minimal, and these flow technologies are unlikely to soar in price in the same way as stocks resources. In contrast to the wasteful practice of depleting non-recyclable resources, flow technology employs resources that are inexhaustible.

While we should not ignore Western advanced technologies, therefore, we should adopt a pre-emptive approach and actively take the lead in developing high-tech flow technology. The reason is very simple – there is an increasingly urgent need for it. Conversely, we should adopt a cautious approach to advanced stocks technology. Again, the reason is simple: the relative opportunity costs of this type of technology are too high for us, because China's per capita resources fall far short of average per capita levels globally. Flow technology cannot be completely separated from stocks technology, however. The correct approach for China is systematically to 'tail' high-tech stocks technology; or, as Sun Zi wrote in *The Art of War*, to 'gain control by attacking from the rear'.

What this actually means is that we should take advantage of China's vast population, wealth of resources and huge market potential: first, we should focus on those more mature stocks technologies and establish a few pilot plants benefiting from economies of scale; and, second, we should make detailed observations of the environmental and social consequences of their operations globally. If we find that they are harmful to China's economy and society, then we should call a halt to them. If we find that they are compatible with flow technology and the protection rule, we can push rapidly ahead. This 'tailing' strategy focuses, therefore, on the development of factories.

In the short term, this strategy will not cause us to lose out on economic benefits, and will enable us to remain sensitive to and familiar with modern stocks technology. (Those few pilot plants can be used for training and observation so that, when the time is right, they can spread rapidly throughout China.) In the long term, it will enable us to be fully informed about the environmental and social consequences of large-scale use of modern stocks technology by developed countries. We will also have avoided astronomical opportunity costs because we will not have applied it on a large scale or over a long period; we can minimize our learning costs without losing any significant opportunity to benefit from this technology. We are therefore employing a flanking manoeuvre, allowing the adversary to make the first move and gaining control by attacking from the rear.

But, I hear you ask, suppose the prospects for the future are not as dire as you predict? If, for example, stocks resources are found that are more abundant and cheaper than oil, would this strategy result in China lagging passively behind and being dominated by the competition? Leaving aside the likelihood of finding new stocks resources, let us apply the following analysis. This is a classic uncertainty problem; uncertainty means that the future will not always be a repeat of the past. Of course, any forecast must be based on existing knowledge, understanding and experience. Once a completely new situation occurs of which we have no past experience, and no theories to help us, we may refer to this as uncertainty. Uncertainty is different from risk, where recurring events obey statistical laws. The latter may be predicted by those laws, while the former refers to events which have never happened in the past, but which may occur in the future. In this case, what kind of countermeasures should be taken? See Figure 9.2.

In Figure 9.2, A shows a future state of affairs. $A_1$ indicates a good outcome and $A_2$, a bad one. B shows what we expect will happen in the future, $B_1$ being expectations of a good outcome (optimistic expectations), $B_2$, expectations of a bad one (or pessimistic expectations). There are a total of four possible outcomes: (1) $B_1A_1$ means that good expectations are fulfilled; (2) $B_1A_2$ means that, despite good expectations, a bad outcome results, that is, the actual outcome is worse than expected; (3) $B_2A_1$ means that, despite bad expectations, there is a good result, that is, the actual outcome turns out better than expected; and (4) $B_2A_2$ means pessimistic expectations are fulfilled. The pessimists (assuming they live as long as other humans) may be onto a winner in either case, while the optimists have only half a chance of success, and have no way of dealing with a $B_1A_2$ situation. From this, we can deduce another rule, the 'insurance' rule; one which may not be universally appropriate for different individuals, but which must be complied with in order to ensure the longest possible survival of the human race.

The best approach to dealing with a situation, which may have irreversible destructive consequences (such as the extinction of a biological species and large-scale, irreversible damage to geological, hydrological and ecological systems), is caution, restraint and risk-averse behaviour. Additionally, in making choices that may have disastrous consequences in the future, even if the likelihood of such consequences is very small, we should exercise extreme caution and restraint. Two things must be pointed out here: there is no such thing as a zero-cost reversible choice; and many so-called irreversible choices are actually reversible, if at an almost infinitely great price. The meaning of irreversible

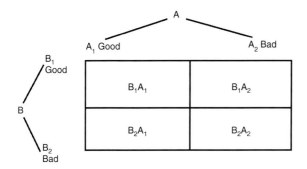

*Figure 9.2* Countermeasures to uncertainty.

Source: Author's own construct.

## 140    *Overcoming barriers*

change is therefore that the change is still hard to reverse even after a high price has been paid.

Thus, it is only when the results will only have an effect in the near future, and the range of possible outcomes will happen basically within the same time frame, that applying the discount rule to calculate the maximum net value is a rational method of resource allocation. In this case, the insurance rule is relegated to second place. Nevertheless, it can also be seen from Figure 9.2 that when pessimists encounter a $B_2A_1$ situation, they may regain the initiative without much difficulty as long as they have sufficient mental and physical reserves, and spot an appropriate opportunity. This corresponds to the strategies of 'tailing' factory development, and gaining control by attacking from the rear, which I have talked about above.

The protection rule and the insurance rule are collectively known as the safety rule. Specifically, in flow technology, we should strive for innovation and preemptive strikes. In new stocks technology, we should adopt 'tailing' tactics and gain control by attacking from the rear. This should be our basic strategy and should also form the basic principle on which we deal with the relationship between trail-blazing and 'tailing' other people's innovations.

## The minimum rule

Although China is still a developing country, modern stocks technology is in widespread use here, and has penetrated every corner of our lives. Thus, the fundamental issue that needs to be tackled, without delay, is how to transform this technology, combining it with new flow technology, and how to pave the way for new technology systems which put the latter in first place.

There is a difference between stocks resources and flow resources. Within given critical values (MSY or threshold values), we can make infinite use of the latter, while in the case of the former, once a quantity is used, there is that much less of the resource remaining. This is true too of recyclable, non-renewable resources since 100 per cent re-use is either impossible or unprofitable. However, it is important to grasp the differences between recyclable and non-recyclable, non-renewable resources. This is particularly important when we consider that fossil fuel resources may be replaced to some extent by renewable resources.

### *Principles of use of Class II resources*

Let us first consider those numerous products made from recyclable, non-renewable resources (for convenience, these will be referred to as Class II resources, while renewable resources will be referred to as class I and non-recyclable, non-renewable resources as Class III resources). If these are properly designed and manufactured, they can be used for decades, after which they can be almost completely recycled. Basic items whose functions do not change, and which are basic necessities in people's lives, should be designed and produced to last as long as possible; we should avoid the throw-away, high-consumption, high-wastage

*Overcoming barriers* 141

society and mode of production for these products. In other words, consumer fashions typical of the 'classic' development model are undesirable.

The reasons for this are obvious: first, Class II resources are limited and non-renewable, and it is uncertain whether in the future more abundant, cheaper alternative resources can be found. Thus the safety rule dictates that they should be used prudently. Second, with basic, functional goods needed for human survival, there is very little need for frequent changes in their design. The longer the life of the product, the fewer items need to be manufactured annually, and the service flow they provide remains unchanged. Extending the life of these items, therefore, is consistent with normal cost-saving rules. Third, the smaller the annual flow, the smaller the consumption of Class II resources. This also creates savings in energy consumption and other Class III resources, reduces pollution and saves on pollution control. From the second point above, we can deduce another rule, that of the minimization of unnecessary or harmful redundancy, (or minimum rule, for short). When the minimum rule is applied to products made from Class II resources, considerations of safety and frugality dictate that their service life should be extended as far as possible. The long-term cost of following fashion for such articles is extremely high, and the satisfaction provided both in the long and short term is very low.

The idea of extending the life of products is often criticized by those who question the need for this in the present day. The obvious riposte is to ask: how many of the latest articles to appear on the market truly reflect the needs of consumers? In fact, the desire for such products is, in part, manufactured by the producers, who then use means such as advertising to seduce consumers into buying them. Additionally, in the deficit economy, consumer desires are also stimulated by the effect on income produced by consumer overdrafts.

The truth is that using the same basic machine or product for many years does not impede technological innovation. Products can be designed and manufactured in such a way that improved parts can replace the original parts and there is no need to replace the entire product. In a flexible manufacturing system it should be possible to adapt speedily to the need for product updates. For example, interchangeable lens cameras have been designed, where all that is required for the camera to acquire a new function is to add a new, improved lens, rather than replacing the entire, original camera.

A second situation is where products made from class II resources can be recycled. There are differences between this and the first scenario, although there are similarities too, such as with the recycling of milk bottles, where the cost of recycling is low because essentially no energy is consumed. Another category of recycling incurs higher costs, such as paper and metal. The following discussion only concerns the second category.

In modern industrialized societies, goods made of materials such as metal, glass and paper are often used once and then thrown away. The result is to reduce stocks of the world's high-grade ore, to fill city garbage dumps to overflowing, and to increase pollution, in many communities, to intolerable levels. Another by-product of this wastage is double-digit inflation. The pursuit of fashion and

## 142 *Overcoming barriers*

wastefulness are habits formed when oil cost $2 a barrel and the car industry was booming. Since then, waste has become a virtue and frugality a bad habit, and this is exacerbated by the unending pursuit of so-called modern conveniences.

However, attitudes have begun to change, as people perceive that using items once and then throwing them away is equivalent to throwing away energy, minerals and security. By contrast, recycling can reduce energy and materials consumption in the national economy and promote healthy economic development. For example, the energy required for recycling aluminium is only 4 per cent of the energy required to produce aluminium from raw bauxite; the energy required for recycling copper is only 10 per cent of the energy required to produce copper from copper ores; and energy-savings of 47 per cent can be achieved if only scrap iron is used in iron and steel production. If newsprint is recycled, the equivalent saving in paper production is 23 per cent and, additionally, the pressure on forests is reduced. Recycling a ton of newsprint can save a ton of wood, or 12 trees. Recycling glass containers achieves energy-savings of 8 per cent, and more energy can be saved if they are re-used.[1] Table 9.1 shows how recovery and recycling has multiple advantages.

Of course, the best way to solve the waste problem is to reduce the amount of waste. Legislation on containers is one way to make this happen – by means of a mandatory deposit on recyclable bottles, or an absolute prohibition on the use of non-recyclable containers. The US Environmental Protection Agency estimates that nationwide legislation enforcing recycling of containers could achieve annual savings of 500,000 tons of aluminium, 1.5 million tons of steel and 5.2 million tons of glass. At the same time, it could reduce consumption of crude oil annually by 46 million barrels (about 6.3 million tons), almost equal to eight days' worth of America's crude oil imports in 1980. The Danes have come up with the best solution for the problem of containers. In Denmark, the beverage container is designed to meet general needs; there are five standard containers so, for example, juice, milk and beer all share the same bottle design. This greatly simplifies container recycling. All companies selling bottled products need do, is change the label or the logo. If stocks of bottles were to be controlled by a national computerized system, this could greatly reduce the energy needed for transportation and manufacturing.[2] Thus, a serious effort to expand and improve the system of recovery and recycling of products made with Class II resources would, in the long term, produce excellent economic benefits, even though in the short term increased costs may be incurred.

*Table 9.1* Benefits to the environment of recycling in the USA (%)

| Benefits to the environment | Paper | Aluminium | Iron and steel |
| --- | --- | --- | --- |
| Reduction in energy expenditure | 30–55 | 90–95 | 60–70 |
| Reduction in scrap and solid waste | 130 | 100 | 95 |
| Reduction in air pollution | 95 | 95 | 30 |

Source: cited in 《萊斯特·R.布朗等: 《縱觀世界全局》, 中國對外翻譯出版公司1985年, 第153頁 [Zhongguoduiwaifanyi Chubangongsi Publishers, 1985, page 153.] Lester R. Brown, *et al.*, editors, *Comprehensive Survey of the World* (Original not identifiable).

The third basic situation is where damage or wear to Class II, resource-based products represents only 1 per cent or less of the entire product value, but the product is designed and manufactured deliberately to be non-reparable. Such a system has led to a squandering of resources and increased production of waste, with the resulting increase in pollution. In short, the focus of the current economic system is production and processing, which leads to large-scale use of resources. We must therefore shift our focus to service and repair.

Opponents of this strategy often put forward the argument that to change the principles of mass production would be uneconomic and would lead to unemployment. It is true that this change would greatly reduce the number of production workers, but it would also provide increased job opportunities in service and maintenance departments. In fact, new jobs generated in the service and maintenance sector would outnumber jobs lost in production and processing because the labour required in service and repair is greater than that required in highly automated production systems. And just as many goods would be available as before because the decrease in production of some commodities would be balanced by an increase in services and maintenance enabling products to be re-used. Finally, service and maintenance work demands greater, all-round skills than highly automated production line work and includes far more interaction between people. Thus, the shift towards a service-maintenance economy benefits not only the environment but also society.

However, the current economic system is built on an entirely contrary logic, whereby new technology is linked to exterior design modifications. In order to achieve this improvement in product appearance, a new product is substituted for the entire product; in many cases it is difficult to buy parts for the old product, which forces consumers to buy new products. In order to reverse this trend, the maintenance-service system needs to be greatly strengthened and expanded.

The three principles outlined above can be extended more generally as follows: with products made from Class II resources, when the service function of the product is the principal objective, and there is no accompanying consumption of the materials from which the product is made (as is the case with food, for example), at a given moment in the service flow provided by the materials (unit reserves), we should recycle or repair the product, or modify its function, thus extending its useful life as far as possible. This will reduce to a minimum our consumption of Class II resources and of stocks resources, while maintaining the same service flow. This is the general expression of the minimum rule that should be applied to Class II resources, in order to minimize the consumption of stocks of materials from which the products are made, while maintaining a given service flow.

### *Principles of use of Class III resources*

Unlike Class II resources, Class III resources are not characterized by durability, and are often consumed the first time they are used. Thus, it is difficult, or infinitely costly, to recycle them because the services they provide are intrinsic to the consumption of the resource itself. For example, heating is the direct consumption

## 144  *Overcoming barriers*

of heat, and the service flow it provides is directly proportional to its consumption. Additionally, because of the limitations of the second law of thermodynamics, the decline of that proportion has a lower limit. The following formula graphically illustrates the difference between Class II and Class III resources:

The services flow provided by Class II resources = $\alpha \times$ unit stocks
The services flow provided by Class III resources = $\beta \times$ unit flow     (9.1)

The upper limit of coefficient $\alpha$ is very uncertain, while the upper limit of coefficient $\beta$ is relatively certain. Thus, $\alpha, \beta \geq 0$, but $\alpha \gg 1 \geq \beta$. In the first formula, after the unit flow has provided a given service flow, the degree of wear and tear is minimal (a few percentage points), and they can continue to provide service. In the second formula, after unit reserves have provided a given service flow, they will have been wholly, 100 per cent, consumed and new Class III resources will be required to continue to provide services. Nevertheless, there is still much that can be done to improve the efficiency of use of Class III resources. Different scenarios are discussed below.

First, we can make our existing activities more efficient. For example, we can use less energy to heat a building by insulating it. We can replace the open stove common in many Third World countries with more efficient sealed stoves manufactured using local materials. This has been estimated to cut fuel consumption by 50 per cent, thereby doubling energy efficiency.[3]

The second type of energy-saving measure is to reduce some activities, or to change activity patterns to achieve the same purpose. For example, in the United States, a car weighing 2 tons is often used to transport 10–15 kg of food from the supermarket to the home, or even just to fetch a litre of milk or a loaf of bread from a few miles away. If we can reduce the amount of car driving, we can improve energy efficiency. In 1975, private cars accounted for 89 per cent of motorized passenger miles in North America, 78 per cent in western Europe, 68 per cent in Latin America, but only 11 per cent in the Soviet Union, where buses and trains accounted for 89 per cent of passenger miles, exactly the reverse of the United States.[4]

In a city, buses and trains have a potential fuel efficiency of up to 150 passenger miles per gallon (PMPG). For transportation between cities, buses can achieve 200 PMPG, while trains, if full, can achieve double that. By contrast, the American car, which carries on average 1.4 passengers, only achieves 24 PMPG. Thus the former is equivalent to six to eight times more energy efficient than the latter. Now let us look at Table 9.2.

Energy intensity and energy efficiency in Table 9.2 are opposite quantities: the lower the energy intensity, the higher the energy efficiency. The average occupancy of American cars in the city is about 1.4 passengers, equivalent to a 28 per cent load factor (assuming the car can carry five people). The purpose of passenger traffic is to move people through space. Table 9.2 shows that the energy-efficient way to do this in a city is to ride a bicycle or to go on foot; but any mode of transport is at least 25 times more energy-efficient than cars, whose the energy efficiency is only between 4 per cent and 2.4 per cent of the former.

*Table 9.2* Energy intensity of various transportation modes in the USA

| Traffic | Energy intensity | | Energy efficiency | | Load factor % |
|---|---|---|---|---|---|
| | *(BTU per passenger mile)* | *(BTU per ton mile)* | *(passenger miles/gallon petrol)* | *(ton miles/ gallon petrol)* | |
| *Urban* | | | | | |
| Bicycle | 200 | — | 630 | — | 100 |
| Walking | 300 | — | 420 | — | 100 |
| Group passenger transport | 3800 | — | 33 | — | 20 |
| Car | 8100 | — | 15 | — | 28 |
| *Intercity* | | | | | |
| Pipeline transport | — | 450 | — | 280 | — |
| Rail | 2900 | 670 | 43 | 188 | 35 |
| Water transport | — | 680 | — | 185 | — |
| Bus | 1600 | — | 79 | — | 45 |
| Lorry | — | 2800 | — | 45 | — |
| Car | 3400 | — | 37 | — | 48 |
| Plane | 8400 | 42000 | 15 | 3 | 50 |

Source: Wade, Charles G., *Contemporary Chemistry: Science, Energy, and Environmental Change*, Macmillan, New York, 1976. (G.韋德：《能源與環境變化》科學出版社, 1983, 第162,163頁。 [Kexue Chubanshe Publishers, 1983, pages 162, 163]).

Note: The figures in the second column for energy intensity and energy efficiency are for intercity freight traffic and the load factor is for passenger traffic.

The third type of measure works by combining energy-saving (that is, reducing useless energy emissions to the outside world), and energy matching. Let us first look at the example of an electric heater. If heat is created by an electric induction furnace, and this heat is all given to the electricity user to heat the house, which then retains its heat, then a traditional evaluation of energy use and energy-savings gives us a thermal efficiency of $\eta t = 100$ per cent. However, a comprehensive evaluation of energy use and energy-savings must go beyond $\eta t$ to include the energy-matching principle. That is, it should assess the energy process not just quantitatively, but also qualitatively. For example, when the room temperature is 20°C and the ambient outside temperature is 0°C, we can see that there is a wide discrepancy between the energy level of electricity ($\Omega = 1$) and that required by the user ($\Omega = 1 - 273/293 = 0.068$, where 273 and 293 are absolute temperatures): $\Delta\Omega = 1 - 0.068 = 0.932$. Thus, from the energy-matching point of view, energy levels supplied are unreasonably high.[5]

Experience tells us that to heat a house, heating systems need only reach 40 to 50°C (a temperature which serves for little else apart from heating) yet the heat produced by an electric induction furnace (so called high-quality heat) is several hundreds or thousands of degrees higher – appropriate to a much higher class of work. Obviously, using high-quality energy (such as electric furnaces) to do low-quality work, such as heating, makes no sense. This is the essence of the

## 146 *Overcoming barriers*

energy-matching rule. Combined heat and power (CHP) uses the energy-matching principle: thermal electricity is used to make steel (where a high-quality supply for a high-quality product is required), and the waste hot water (or steam), as it cools, is used for bath water (where a medium-quality supply for a medium-quality product is required). The waste hot water can also be used for heating (where a low-quality supply for a low-quality product is required). Electricity accounts for only 13 per cent of end-use needs in the USA, but it consumes 29 per cent of its fossil fuels.[6] CHP usually improves energy efficiency by 15 to 20 percentage points.

Let us look again at Table 9.2 from this point of view. In the table, assuming that we can increase the efficiency of cars fourfold (for instance, by reducing their weight), then cars are close to their maximum energy efficiency, and there is no further potential for saving energy. But cars use high-quality energy, so that a mismatch of energy is created when someone drives 2 km to do a job, instead of making the same journey using low-quality energy (such as muscle power, peddling a bicycle). The wastage generated by energy-mismatching is often even greater than this.

The three principles outlined above can be extended more generally as follows: with regard to the services provided by products made from Class III resources, when the physical and chemical properties of the resources which supply those services are irrelevant (for instance, chemical, electric or thermal energy can all be used for heating purposes), when a given service flow is reached, its energy efficiency should be maximized, so that the levels of energy supplied and users' energy requirements match as closely as possible. In other words, the flow rate of consumption should, as far as possible, be minimized. This is the general expression of the minimum rule for Class III resources. If people still insist that a service should be supplied by a process with specific physical or chemical characteristics, for example by using electric furnaces for heating, then they should be asked to pay an additional fee (a wastage or extravagance tax).

### The equivalence rule

These concepts of energy intensity, energy efficiency and energy quality can naturally be extended to the intensity, efficiency and quality of matter. In this way, we can extend the energy-matching rule to Class I, II and III resources and other resources (such as fixed assets, human resources and scientific and technological knowledge). In other words, the use of material resources should be assessed not only quantitatively, but also qualitatively. We can call this the generalized energy-matching rule, or matter-matching rule.

From the equivalence principle (see Chapter 8) and the generalized energy-matching rule, we can derive an equivalence-matching rule (or equivalence rule, for short). This means that, in our material lives, it is possible to achieve the same goals with the same effectiveness by means of different processes with very different levels of material intensity and efficiency. In pursuit of a goal with any given quality requirements, the lowest grade of materials should be chosen when the individuals or groups pursuing that goal have said that they do not mind what specific materials or processes are used to achieve their purpose. The difference between the grade of

*Overcoming barriers* 147

material assumed to be needed to carry out this purpose and the material actually used during the implementation process should be kept to a minimum.

In economies where constraints on materials are severe, this rule has serious, wide-ranging significance for all resources use. The irrational nature of the process whereby the United States uses 90 per cent of its grain production to feed livestock, and then humans eat the meat of the livestock, is perfectly obvious. First, food intake in the United States exceeds desirable levels, meaning that its thermodynamic efficiency, $\eta_t$, is low. Second, the matching rule shows us that using high-quality beef to meet low-quality caloric needs in humans creates a differential of $\Delta\Omega = 0.9$. According to the 'ten-to-one' rule, if it takes 10 llb of grain to produce 1 llb of beef, and if the energy level of 1 llb of beef = 1, then that of 1 llb of grain = 0.1, while there is hardly any difference in the calories they produce. The energy level difference is 0.9, which is totally irrational. The only possible conclusion is that food intake should be reduced both in quantity and quality.

We can now use this rule to analyse two examples, the first of which is energy-saving by producers. See Table 9.3 and Table 9.4.

*Table 9.3* Total costs of energy (free energy) needed to produce a car

| Item | Energy (kilowatt hours) |
| --- | --- |
| Metal used in manufacture | 26,185 |
| Other materials used in manufacture | 865 |
| Auto parts production and assembly | 9,345 |
| Transportation of materials | 655 |
| Transport of assembled motor vehicles | 235 |
| Total | 37,275 |
| Ideal thermodynamic energy requirements | 1,035 |

Source: Wade, Charles G., *Contemporary Chemistry: Science, Energy, and Environmental Change*, Macmillan, New York, 1976. (G.韋德：《能源與環境變化》科學出版社, 1983, 第255頁。[Kexue Chubanshe Publishers, 1983, page 255]).

*Table 9.4* Methods of car recycling, and service life

| System | Costs of car energy (kilowatt hour) | Energy-savings per single car (%) |
| --- | --- | --- |
| Car manufacture using only new raw materials and no recycled materials | 37,275 | — |
| 15% steel from recycled scrap vehicles | 35,600 | 4.5 |
| Crushing and recycling a vehicle to make a new car | 24,635 | 33.9 |
| Annual energy costs – currently (10-year vehicle life) | 3,728 | — |
| Annual energy costs (when vehicle life is doubled) | 1,243 | 66.7 |

Source: Wade, Charles G., *Contemporary Chemistry: Science, Energy, and Environmental Change*, Macmillan, New York, 1976. (G.韋德：《能源與環境變化》科學出版社, 1983, 第255頁。[Kexue Chubanshe Publishers, 1983, page 255]).

148　*Overcoming barriers*

From both tables we can see that using different materials for the same purpose (to manufacture a car), can achieve huge potential savings of energy and materials. For instance, if a giant crusher is used, all the metal can be extracted from an old vehicle and the new car can be made wholly from recycled iron.

Let us now look at another example. This is a question of how consumers save energy through changes to their lifestyle, and is related to the generalized energy-matching rule. The following proposals show that energy consumption for passenger and freight transport can be reduced by 50 per cent if lifestyle changes are made which ensure a match between consumer needs and the energy required to satisfy them, without reducing total passengers and freight miles. This is how it can be done:

1　shift half of current intercity goods transport from lorries and planes to rail;
2　shift half of all intercity air passengers and one-third of private car passengers onto trains and buses. Change the design of cars, aircraft and trains to improve their efficiency by 33 per cent;
3　switch half of car passengers travelling within a city to public transport. Increase the load factor of public transport and private cars within the city by 10 per cent. Improve the design of city cars to increase miles per gallon by 33 per cent.

The purpose of these proposals[7] is to illustrate the significant reduction in transport energy consumption that it is possible to achieve. The technical requirements are all entirely feasible, as they are by no means sophisticated. However, whether or not we can improve the efficiency of the transport system depends less on technological breakthroughs than on human willpower and judgment. Viewed from this angle, one of the major causes of the kind of consumption rooted in the 'classic' development model stems from wrong use of stocks technology, that is, generalized energy mismatching, where high-quality energy and materials are regularly used for low-quality work.

We have applied the equivalence rule above to aspects of material life, but it can also be extended to the realm of nature and to intangible aspects of life, so long as we can find a correspondence in the latter areas. For example, if we compare surfing and motorboat sports, the former is much less 'materials-intensive' than the latter, although both require participants to train to similar levels of skill, speed of response and courage. In another example, hiking and climbing are just as much adventure sports as car racing, but the first two are not only more sparing in their use of materials, they also help to achieve another purpose: protection of the environmental and natural diversity, and protecting resources increases our wealth. Car racing, on the other hand, takes a very circuitous route to achieve the same objective, that is, participation in an adventure sport. First, exploitation of natural resources is necessary, then comes refining and processing, and finally the manufacture of the object, the racing car, required in order to engage in this sport. This process has the effect of reducing and/or destroying natural resources and is a low-efficiency way of creating material wealth. It is clear that another

Overcoming barriers 149

shortcoming of the 'classic' development model is the excessive or inappropriate use of manufactured objects instead of the use of natural means to satisfy human needs. The wasteful practice of excessive use of air-conditioning is another example.

Social welfare means not only improving material living standards (that is, increasing ownership of manufactured possessions), but also increasing spiritual, cultural and other forms of intangible wealth. In other words, for the sake of the environment and of human beings, two things must be improved: the social environment and the material environment in which we live. Figuratively speaking, welfare = standard of living + living conditions + living environment.[8]

The living environment created by the climate, in terms of land, plants and animals, can provide us with three major types of wealth, both intangible and material: (1) physical health and comfort, (2) the aesthetic enjoyment of beauty, and (3) cultural and moral education, the enjoyment of heritage sites and scientific research. If you think I am exaggerating, read on.

In order for people to enjoy recreation and beauty, a variety of natural landscapes is indispensable. Nature is an asset in itself. If people enjoy the wealth of nature instead of consuming the wealth of manufactured products, this will not only slow the reduction in intangible wealth brought about by the production of material wealth, but will also increase people's total wealth by reducing the expenditure needed to control pollution, a dual benefit to humankind.

As society progresses, leisure time will increase, but without a good environment in which to enjoy it, people will fritter away their time uselessly. A high-quality living environment (in terms of climate, land, flora and fauna) is fundamental to meeting a variety of psychological needs, such as for art and entertainment, and scientific and other knowledge, all of which are consistent with a happy and fulfilling life.

As more and more people take advantage of increased leisure time, beauty spots and the tourism industry in general should be strictly managed, to protect natural resources while at the same time enabling more people to travel to these areas and to enjoy the beauty of nature. In the rush to go back to nature, our most wonderful scenery must be protected because in today's world, natural scenery is also a kind of 'national income'. We must educate people in ecology and the environmental sciences, because this is the only way to make people understand that human activities change the natural environment. People also need to understand that natural resources are a real source of wealth, which should be treasured by us all.

If our moral view of the world is founded on co-existence with nature, the result may just be a world where everyone can lead a healthy and happy life – each person developing their talents to the fullest extent. This moral view is rooted not just in objective knowledge and understanding, but also in harmonious relations between humans and the ecosystems of which their environment is made up.

People are beginning to feel their way towards a new concept of environment, which includes physical, chemical and biological factors as well people's

150    *Overcoming barriers*

economic, cultural and social needs. We should look at the environment in terms of human ecology, keeping in mind the overriding principle that the conservation of natural resources is a way of making better use of those resources for the welfare of humanity.

## The priority rule

This chapter has summarized the features of natural resources and manufactured resources and the links between them, and has abstracted from the discussion three rules: the safety rule, the minimum rule and the equivalence rule. The following section leads us on to a brief discussion of human resources as part of resources in general.

### *Long-term advances in the development of education*

The major difference between human resources and knowledge resources, and the two kinds of resources discussed above, is that the former increase as they are used and developed, while the latter remain constant qualitatively and quantitatively. (The relationship between natural resources and fixed assets resources is mutually competitive because fixed assets are generally created from natural resources.) Human resources are both key elements of production and the purpose of that production. The growth of scientific and technological knowledge resources, as well their embodiment in fixed assets, however, must also pass through the 'hub' of human resources. The development of human resources, therefore, is of special importance.

For underdeveloped countries, the first consideration in order to accelerate the development of national economy is usually to bring in foreign experts and advanced technology and equipment. But some economists think that it is more important to develop that country's own human resources, especially technically-skilled human resources, otherwise it will be difficult to throw off dependence on foreign technology and experts. Technically-skilled human resources can be divided into the following levels: inventors and innovators, managers and engineers, technicians, craftsmen and skilled workers, semi-skilled and unskilled workers. Apart from semi-skilled and unskilled workers, the remaining four categories require 15–20 years or more of training. It takes even longer to train a scientist.

Thus, human resources are the limiting factor, relative to natural resources and fixed assets, in the composite structure of the production process. This is because natural resources are readily available, and production equipment can be purchased, but there are no substitutes for human resources. The principle of short-term economic constraints dictates that it should be a priority to develop them. When we take into account how fast scientific knowledge is increasing and being incorporated into the production process, it is clear that we must continue to make human resources a priority. This is what is meant by the priority rule.

Without high-quality human resources, neither of our two economic strategies, pre-emptive strikes and coming from the rear to take control, is possible.

*Overcoming barriers* 151

This is easily verifiable through an examination of the facts. The formation and growth of robust, high-quality human resources is inseparable from the process of education.

Japan provides a classic example of this process. Since the Meiji Restoration, Japan has never failed to prioritize universal education. To this end, its government has carried out three major reforms of its education system in the past 100 years. In 1872, the Japanese government promulgated the Education Act, promoting real-world knowledge and education as the foundation for building Japan. All villages were required to have educated families and all families to have some members who had been to school. In 1907, six years of universal compulsory education was enforced, and enrolment of school-age children reached 97.38 per cent. In March 1947, at the behest of American occupying forces advisors, the Japanese government enacted the Fundamental Law of Education and the School Education Law. These two decrees abolished the system of centralized education administration, implemented local control, and extended compulsory education to nine years. This, the second educational reform after the Meiji Restoration, happened under extremely difficult economic conditions following the carnage of World War II. The government adopted watchwords such as 'equality of educational opportunity' and 'training up talent for development' and enacted a series of basic measures to promote economic development in modern Japan. As a further step to ensuring that education met the needs of industrial and socioeconomic development, the Japanese government enlisted the help of more than 200 education specialists and spent a full four years in drawing up basic guidelines for a comprehensive expansion and reorganization of school education, enacted in June 1971. This was Japan's third educational reform.[9]

It is only long-term prioritizing of the development of education that has provided the necessary conditions under which Japan's post-war economy has marched forward. Continuing improvements in the levels and penetration of education have undeniably made a great contribution to Japan's economic miracle. Some economists have even reached the conclusion that, for a very long time after World War II (until the early 1970s, more or less), the average level of education in Japan was actually much higher than was required by the economy at the time.[10] With such robust intellectual resources, Japan could seize all opportunities that presented themselves, and successfully adapt in the face of unforeseen events.

Turning to China, the situation is very different. In the sixteenth and seventeenth centuries, China led the world in average levels of education, after which a decline set in. After the Liberation in the 1950s and 1960s, there was rapid improvement, followed soon thereafter by decline once more. Today, China has the lowest literacy rate in the entire Asia–Pacific Rim region, at only 69 per cent.[11] China now has more than 200 million illiterates and there is an increasing disdain for book knowledge. This sorry state of affairs casts an ominous shadow over China's development in the long term.

The key factor hampering China from creating a new development model is neither money, nor resources, but knowledge. In this, it is not alone: developing

## 152    *Overcoming barriers*

countries commonly lack adequate numbers of highly skilled technicians, managers and skilled labourers, yet it is precisely these people who are crucial to developing and putting to use new kinds of flow technology.

The most advanced technology, such as microprocessors and photovoltaic cells suitable for use in all areas of the country should become the core of new types of flow technology. These technologies are suitable for developing countries with fewer per capita resources because they use smaller quantities of stocks resources, are cheap and promote the use of widely-available flow resources, providing millions of households with energy and access to knowledge. However, levels of utilization of these new technologies depend largely on the general level of education of the people in those countries.

For developing countries, therefore, it is the education of their entire populations, above all else, which is the key to a new development model. This is true even if it initially causes the economic growth rate to slow down. Post-war Japan, for example, extended compulsory education from six to nine years in the face of extremely difficult economic circumstances. It is clear that advancing the development of education is not only possible, but necessary – even when a country faces economic difficulties.

It is only when a nation has robust, high-quality human resources that it can take the long view, and make a real choice of economic strategies, whether to take pre-emptive action, or to gain control by attacking from the rear when the moment is right, as Sun Zi put it.

### *Structures for the future*

The four rules outlined above form the basic structure of a new development model. Let us call them the four basic laws of the new development model. The first law (the safety rule) links long-term, global efficiency and short-term, partial efficiency, showing clearly that sustaining long-term advances in human society can only be carried out to the extent that the environment (a Class I resource) permits. Short-term partial efficiency can only achieve best results within these constraints, which ensure the integration of safety, efficiency and development. The second law (the minimum rule) defines the relationship between Class II and III resources and manufactured fixed assets, as well as the principles of utilization and partial optimization. It can also be referred to as the partial equivalence law. The third law (the equivalence rule) provides the criteria for overall optimization of these relationships through a comprehensive description of the relationship between natural resources, fixed assets and production/consumption models. The fourth law (the priority rule) focuses on an analysis of a unique element of our socio-economic system – human resources – establishing the principle of development and utilization of these resources.

These four rules provide the definitive argument for the new development model, given that it is increasingly difficult to extract minerals and fuels, and that resources are limited, as is the ability of the environment and humanity to absorb the damage caused by pollution, and they show that economic objectives should

*Overcoming barriers* 153

be determined on the basis of reserves of natural resources. These objectives cannot be achieved by endlessly increasing consumption of energy and raw materials. On the contrary, a successful economy is one that ensures a standard of living necessary to a civilized society, while minimizing demand for mineral, energy and environmental resources.

It is clear that a new development model structured on these four rules is just such a successful economic system. We can easily deduce from them a series of principles, which should inform our choice of development model after we have gone beyond the stage of meeting the basic social needs of our citizens. They are:

1   Controls on consumption should immediately be imposed on the rate at which stocks resources are consumed, once needs for food and clothing have been met. We should not wait until difficulties have already arisen and then be forced to adjust.
2   Once these basic needs are met, we should actively slow down the manufacture of products made from stocks resources and use, instead, intangible and natural wealth (such as landscapes and greenery).
3   There should be a focus on short-term constraints on flow resources (such as water) to ensure that overall levels of use of those resources do not overstep short-term limits and damage them.
4   We should exploit new flow resources, and recover the use of damaged flow resources.
5   New-style flow technology should go hand in hand with new technology systems, lifestyle changes and new educational approaches.
6   The consumption of non-renewable, non-recyclable resources should be carried out in accordance with the principle of short-term constraints on flow resources, so that the consumption of stocks resources is reduced and flow resources are used as effectively as possible.
7   We should increase levels of re-use of recyclable, non-renewable resources wherever this is economically viable, and economize as far as possible on the use of such resources.
8   A systematic study should be made of the way in which all our needs are being met, and a series of standards proposed, the lowest possible, which strictly prohibit unnecessarily wasteful use of resources. Excessive consumption of non-renewable resources should be subject to appropriately heavy taxes, and supply and demand should be kept within limits, although producers and consumers should also be offered a degree of choice.
9   Population growth should be limited, and tireless, long-term efforts should be made to improve the cultural and educational level of all citizens.
10  Citizens should made ever more aware of the nature of the world in which they live so that they gradually learn how to co-exist harmoniously with nature.

If we choose a development model in accordance with the above principles, we can at least keep the adverse effects of the second law of thermodynamics to a

154 *Overcoming barriers*

minimum. This will allow us to find solutions to the challenges of industrialization, and the long-term prospects for the development of our society will be bright.

## Notes

1 Brown, Lester R., *Building a Sustainable Society*, W W Norton & Co, New York, 1982. (萊斯特·R.布朗 《建設一個持續發展的社會》科技文獻出版社1984年, 第152頁。[Kejiwenxian Chubanshe Publishers, 1984, page 152]).
2 Ibid., page 154.
3 Ibid., pages 158, 203.
4 Ibid.
5 楊東華:《火用分析和能級分析》, 科學出版社1986年, 第4, 5頁。 (YANG Donghua, *Analysis of Exergy and Energy Levels*, Kexue Chubanshe Publishers, 1986, number 4, page 5).
6 Brown, Lester R., *The Twenty Ninth Day*, W. W. Norton & Co, New York, 1978. (L. R. 布朗:《第29天》科技文獻出版社, 1986年, 108頁。[Kejiwenxian Chubanshe Publishers, 1986, page 108]).
7 Wade, Charles G., *Contemporary Chemistry: Science, Energy, and Environmental Change*, Macmillan, New York, 1976. (G. 韋德:《能源與環境變化》科學出版社, 1983, 第164頁。 [Kexue Chubanshe Publishers, 1983, page 164]).
8 Duvigneaud, P., *La Synthese Ecologique: Populations, Communautes, Ecosystemes, Biosphere, Noosphere*. Doin, Paris, 1974. (P. 迪維諾:《生態學概論》科學出版社, 1987年, 326頁 [Kexue Chubanshe Publishers, 1987, page 326]).
9 蘇真:〈富國強民之道 — 日本教育改革簡述〉,《百科知識》1984年第11期。 (SU Zhen, 'Rich country, strong people – outline of Japan's educational reform' in *An Encyclopedia of Knowledge*, 1984, issue 11).
10 Patrick, H. and Rosovsky, H., eds, *Asia's New Giant: How the Japanese Economy Works*, Brookings Institute, Washington, 1976. (休·帕特里克等人:《亞洲新鉅人 — 日本經濟是怎樣運行的》上海譯文出版社, 1982 [Shanghaiyiwen Chubanshe Publishers, 1982]).
11 〈太平洋沿岸國家和地區 — 全球的重大經濟力量〉,《世界經濟科技》1988年4月5日。Patrick, H. and Rosovsky, H., eds, ('Pacific Rim countries and region – a great global economic power' in *World Economy, Science and Technology*, 5 April 1988).

# 10 A blueprint for reconstruction

The rules and principles discussed in Chapter 9 provide us with an answer to the fundamental question raised at the end of the first chapter of this book, 'Is China capable of implementing the third choice successfully?' The answer is, yes. Starting now, China can, by adopting a new development model, take appropriate, far-sighted steps to enable it to achieve a high level of modernization.

It has been noted that other countries undergoing the modernization process have chosen different lifestyles and modes of production, resulting in a different burden on their natural resources. Facts such as these have greatly strengthened my confidence that we can find ways to overturn the 'classic' development model. In order fully to understand what may happen as society and the economy progress, we should start by taking the ultimate human goals of survival and progress as our point of departure; we should then revert to considering the system of production. That is to say, we should start from the end-point, and derive from it the necessary changes to patterns of consumption, which, in turn, lead to adjustments to the mode of production (our starting point). The final steps are to bring our end point and our starting points together to form a closed loop, and to study how well-matched they are, by means of the generalized energy-matching rule.

## The truth in all its clarity

In this section, I will refine my description of a future socio-economic system by assessing a number of different lifestyles. Due to the lack of systematic, comprehensive data, the following projections will inevitably contain errors. But my purpose here is only to explore the possibilities for a new approach to modernization, which does not follow the 'classic' model and the uses we might make of it. All the following projections, if not otherwise stated, take the US dollar (1970 value) as the unit of calculation, and the 1970 US per capita annual consumption of $3,020 and per capita GDP of $4,794, as a basis for comparison.

### *Food and clothing*

The main purpose of human food consumption is to provide the quantity and quality of nutrition required to enable effective physical and mental work. The

156    *A blueprint for reconstruction*

diet we eat is the means by which we achieve this end. There are three main types of diet in the world: the first one is based on animal products and is common to such countries as the United States, Canada, Australia and the Soviet Union. The second is based on a mixture of animal and plant products, and is prevalent in Japan. The third diet is largely plant-based and is eaten in China and India. Why do we have three different diets to achieve the same purpose? Below I will compare these three dietary models.

For comparisons to be made, we must use common standards. Calories, protein and fat in the diet are three internationally accepted indicators used to measure a country's nutritional levels. It is generally believed that the daily per capita diet needs to provide 2,400 Kcal: 75 grams protein and 65 grams of fat, to meet basic individual requirements. In 1970, the US daily per capita diet consisted of 3,514 Kcal: 106 grams of protein and 159 grams of fat, which exceeded the international standard respectively by 46.4 per cent, 41.3 per cent and 144.6 per cent. In 1980, Japan's GNP per capita was equivalent to US 1970 levels, and per capita daily intake was 2,853 Kcal: 86.7 grams of protein and 80.6 grams of fat, respectively and 18.8 per cent, 15.6 per cent and 24 per cent (respectively) higher than the international standard. In other words, the United States consumed 661 Kcal: 19.3 grams of protein and 78.9 grams of fat per capita more than Japan, the difference being mainly due to America's higher annual consumption of meat and dairy products. In 1970, this was 164 kg higher than that of Japan in 1980.

Insufficient or poor quality nutritional intake is, of course, not conducive to effective physical and mental activity, in other words, it deprives us of the means to achieve our end. However, we have seen in previous chapters that over-eating can also lead to poor nutrition, and is similarly not conducive to the realization of our goals. In other words, in the latter case, the means to achieve the end have been abused. Thus, in terms of international standards, the US dietary pattern (the first kind of diet mentioned above) is irrational, whereas the Japanese way (the second kind of diet) is more rational.

What would happen if the per capita food intake in the USA were adjusted downwards? In 1970, Americans spent about $900 per capita on food. If we multiply this by two-thirds, $900/1.5 = $ 600, savings of about $300 per capita are achieved. This shows that, as far as the ultimate goal of food consumption goes, there are not only health benefits in achieving a more rational way of life, but other indirect benefits too – energy is saved, material consumption and pollution are reduced, and consumers save about one-third of their food expenditure.

China's diet is based on plant products. The 1982 National Nutrition Survey results showed that daily per capita calorie intake was 2,484 Kcal and 67 grams of protein; (the former is above the international standard, the latter, 8 grams below).[1] Compared with 1982, China's per capita meat consumption for the year 1986 was 5 kg greater than 1982; consumption of eggs was 2.5 kg greater per capita; and milk was 1.34 kg greater.[2] It can therefore be calculated that by 1986, daily per capita intake of protein had only risen to about 70 grams. In 1985, per capita daily calorie intake had reached 2,620 Kcal.[3] Therefore, to improve the

*A blueprint for reconstruction* 157

Chinese diet, it is necessary to increase the intake of high-protein plant foods (such as soy) and meat and dairy produce.

From the point of view of improving the national diet, it is clear that we should move towards the second type of diet (an equal stress on meat/dairy and vegetables), while avoiding the first, meat- and dairy-based type of diet. From the point of view of China's resources, during that transition, a slight preference should be given to plant foods, that is, we should make the maximum use of soy products, and increase the quality and quantity of protein in the national diet by ensuring that everyone receives an appropriate share of plant- and animal-based foods. If China chooses the second type of diet, its agriculture will diverge from the path taken by the United States, Canada and the Soviet Union. This choice will also affect the development of agricultural sideline products and processing methods, the proportion of the population engaged in agriculture and patterns of urbanization.

Humans need clothes as well as food. The basic purpose of human clothing, apart from simply to protect us against the cold, is to conform to social norms. A few years ago, a conference of nutritionists, architects, fashion designers and sociologists was held at the University of Pennsylvania. The purpose was to make comparisons between lifestyles in different countries, and to examine which country was doing it best. As far as dress was concerned, the conference came out in favour of the British way. A clothing expert reported that the wardrobe of the British man-about-town held only two outfits, plus two or three extra pairs of grey trousers. The same went for British women, who often wore dark-coloured outfits, and had one or two evening dresses as well. Although Britain was a country where attention was paid to dress, the British as a whole were far less extravagant in that respect than the French, Italians and Americans. The British made each outfit last 8–10 years, whereas the French and the Americans bought new outfits on average once a year.[4]

Americans spend about $420 on clothing and other personal items. If they adopted the British way (and taking into account that British garments are better-made), we could divide $420 by two, giving an expenditure of $210, and a saving of $210 per capita. The raw materials for clothing come mainly from three sources: plant products (such as cotton), animal products (such as wool), and petrochemical products (such as synthetic fibres). In recent years the trend has been for a proportionate decline in use of the first two products, and a rise in the third.

In 1986, China's per capita synthetic fibre consumption reached 10.6 kg, far higher than the developing countries' average of 3.8 kg.[5] We have therefore solved the basic problem of keeping our citizens warm. To improve on this situation requires a choice in two main areas: first, whether to use plant-based or petrochemical-based products; and, second, what style of clothing to adopt and how often to replace items. The first choice will affect the internal structure of China's large-scale farming and its use of petroleum resources; the second choice will affect the position occupied by the textile and clothing industries in the national economy. When we take into account modern technical developments in plant products, the first choice is especially important. I will discuss this further

## 158   *A blueprint for reconstruction*

below. As far as the second choice goes, we should learn from the British way of doing things.

### *Housing and articles for domestic use*

Housing meets a number of basic human needs: it is a place where we can rest and recover mental and physical strength, and where we can study and pursue a number of other activities fundamental to the human community. The Pennsylvania Conference particularly praised the Soviet way of solving the housing problem: in the Soviet Union, people rarely have single occupancy of a house with a garden; most live in blocks of flats of four or five storeys and without lifts. These flats are generally quite spacious and accommodate from two to five people. Each block or cluster of blocks shares a small garden, with a gardener employed to look after it. This is different from America, where people spend a huge amount of time every weekend gardening in their own small plot. The Soviets, therefore, have an environment no worse than the Americans, and also avoid the loneliness so prevalent in modern society. The reason why the Soviet housing solution is better than the American one is that the former can accommodate 300 people in an area occupied by only 100 in America.

Soviet-style flats are ready-furnished, with such items as beds and tables, so that moving house is simple. The Soviet Union has developed a variety of solar-powered domestic appliances, such as colour TVs, air-conditioning units and refrigerators.[6] The combination of Soviet-style accommodation and solar-powered household appliances, including domestic heating and hot water, can create significant savings in the quantity of land, energy and materials used for housing.

For the year 1970, per capita housing costs in America were $918, five-sixths of which went on rental or mortgages, and the rest on fuel, utilities, furnishings and domestic appliances. If savings in the order of two-thirds are made on rental, fuel and utilities, and of one-third on furniture and appliances, then per capita savings of $546 could be made annually. The combination of Soviet-style housing and solar power for domestic use, can reduce spending to less than half that of American-style housing. Such a choice would have a huge impact on the production of building materials, on urban construction, the production of consumer durables and on energy consumption.

In 1988 in China, per capita living space was 8.8 square metres in cities, and 16.6 square metres in rural areas, double the figures for 1978.[7] In the long term, we should aim for something similar to Soviet-style housing. In 1988 in China, there were 13.2 TVs per hundred people, 6.2 washing machines and 1.8 refrigerators.[8] These figures are growing fast. The commensurate increase in electricity consumption has exacerbated the shortage of electrical power. The issue of converting solar energy for use in the home is therefore crucially important.

### *Transport and medical care*

The purpose of transport systems is to take people to and from work, to enable information exchange, and to facilitate recreational travel. The detailed analysis

*A blueprint for reconstruction*   159

of different transport systems designed for the same purpose in Chapter 9, shows that energy consumption can double, depending on the mode of transport and that, when bicycles are used for intercity transport, costs can be reduced by half.

In 1970, US per capita expenditure on transport was about $338. These costs may vary greatly, depending whether the single vehicle/household model is used, or a system that combines bicycle use and good-quality public transport. In the latter case, the figure of $338 can be divided by four, to give $84, giving a saving of $254 per capita. This choice of bicycle use and good-quality public transport would have a huge impact on the production and consumption of cars, steel, energy and raw materials, as well as on roads, land use and pollution. If the average household car (exchanged for a new one every five years, weighing 1.5 tons, one per household of three people) were shared, instead, between ten households, then per capita steel consumption alone could be reduced by 90 kg.

The basic purpose of health care is to maintain physical and mental health. The main factors that have a negative impact on human health are the following: first, contagious diseases; second, cumulative internal pathological changes, usually related to people's working lives, the environment in which they live and their psychological state; third, non-infectious sudden-onset diseases, such as appendicitis; and fourth, common minor ailments like colds. We have seen, in a previous chapter, how contagious diseases have been effectively controlled by vaccines and preventative care; they are no longer as dangerous for humans as they once were. Minor ailments can usually be cured through the body's ability to heal itself, improved basic standards of hygiene and self-diagnosis and treatment. Non-infectious, sudden-onset diseases always require hospital treatment.

That leaves the second type of illness, internal pathological changes. These are often difficult to cure with drugs and hospital treatment, are usually chronic and cumulative, and are best prevented or treated by looking after oneself, maintaining mental health, and making gradual daily adjustments to ones environment and working life. For this type of illness, hospital-based health care is exorbitantly expensive especially in modern high-tech health care systems. In terms of future trends, the second type of illness is set to become a major threat to Chinese people's health.

The generalized matching rule shows us that using sophisticated technology to treat this type of disease is not only prohibitively expensive, but also gives poor results. These four categories of disease should therefore be treated by different means, all of which should be integrated into a comprehensive and effective prevention and research system. Contagious diseases should be treated by means of improvements in basic nutrition, vaccines, antibiotics and other preventative measures; internal pathological changes should be treated through universal access to basic medical knowledge, simple and effective self-care methods (such as the practice of qigong and tai chi exercises) and changes in ways of working and the living environment to promote mental health. Health posts equipped with only simple medical technology should be established to deal with the second and fourth category of ailments; and hospitals equipped with complex medical equipment should deal with the third category (non-infectious, sudden-onset diseases) and carry out research that draws on the practice outlined above and

## 160 *A blueprint for reconstruction*

provides a new basis for the promotion of better health care. This structure forms a pyramid of preventive health care, ensuring highly effective, low-cost basic health care. By contrast, the unthinking pursuit of ever more, high-tech means to deal with the whole range of diseases (an inverted pyramid) not only fails to meet people's physiological and psychological needs, but is also proving impossibly costly and inefficient.

This illustrates the phenomenon described earlier in this book: since the 1950s, US per capita health care costs have spiralled, while average life expectancy has scarcely increased at all. The basic reason is that the available means have been misallocated (that is, means and goals are mismatched) or misused. US per capita health care costs reached $208 in 1970 (triple that of the 1950s). Measures could be taken to reduce this expenditure by two-thirds, to $69, a saving of $139 per capita in medical expenses.

In 1988, there was on average one doctor in China per 676 people, a figure somewhere between the average in developed and developing countries, and much better than the average figure of 4,940 patients per doctor in middle-income developing countries. China's predicted life expectancy in 1987 was 69 years, higher than the 64 years average life expectancy in middle-income developing countries; and infant mortality rate was 3.2 per cent, lower than the 5.6 per cent figure for middle-income developing countries.[9] As China continues to develop, we should ensure that we avoid the inverted pyramid model of medical treatment. Instead, we should improve on the existing pyramid model by, for example, promoting universal access to health care knowledge.

### *Other costs and totals*

In 1970, per capita spending in other areas in the USA was $236. If this figure were adjusted downwards as outlined above, dividing the original figure in half would create a saving of $118 per capita.

In total, the above cost savings per capita would total $1,567, or 52 per cent of the original $3,020 per capita consumption expenditure. This means that if a reasoned choice of alternative patterns of consumption is made, expenditure can be reduced by half and yet substantially the same purpose can be achieved. Reduction in personal expenditure will inevitably influence other areas of per capita GDP, reducing government spending, investment and stocks of materials. If we assume that personal expenditure continues to account for 63 per cent of per capita GDP, then this can be reduced from the original $4,794 to $2,306. However, this does not mean reducing the current standard of living and indeed, if we take into account reductions in pollution, it may well lead to an improved quality of life.

### Blazing new trails

The following section is based on the above analysis and the rules and principles outlined in Chapter 9. In it, I examine what adjustments should be made in modes

A blueprint for reconstruction   161

of production in order to achieve the best match either in part or overall. For convenience, the system of production is divided into primary, secondary and tertiary industries. It should be noted that I do not intend to provide a comprehensive description of the future of these industries; instead, I will focus on the kind of major changes that need to be made, with particular emphasis on adapting to China's resource constraints.

### *Primary industry*

First, in order to achieve a balanced mixed (meat/vegetable) diet with a relatively low grain content, we need first to change what farmers grow – this involves increasing soybean output. In protein content alone, 1 kg of soybean is equivalent to 2 kg of lean beef, 3.5 kg of eggs and 4 kg of pork (mixed fat and lean meat), all of which require 9–18 kg of grain to produce. Additionally, the nutritional value of soy protein and animal protein is very similar. It has been calculated that if we could raise China's acreage of soybean cultivation from currents levels, 120 million *mu*,[10] to 1935 levels (the highest in its history, at 220 million *mu*), and if the per-*mu* yield was 77.5 kg, this alone would be enough to increase our per capita daily protein intake by about 7 grams.[11] The main problem with the diet of China's population is the low quality of the protein, which has insufficient amino acids of the kind the body needs. The most economical and nutritionally balanced protein is to be found in legumes, especially soybeans. 77.5 kg of soybean, the yield of one *mu*, produces the same amount of protein as 620–1,400 kg of grain, and has the additional advantage of fertilizing the soil at the same time. A rapid increase in legume cultivation can bring about significant improvements in the national diet, making this a measure that is both feasible in the near future and strategically important.

Second, cultivating protein-rich strains of rice, wheat and corn also has great potential. It has been calculated that, in the medium term, the wheat and rice produced in China could add 2.5 billion kg of protein to the national diet,[12] so raising China's per capita daily intake of protein by 5.5 grams. In addition, biotechnology offers great prospects for improving nutritional levels. For example, the use of growth hormone can increase crop yields many times over, in some cases even more than tenfold. Other biotechnology applications, such as genetic engineering, breeding new varieties, improving the efficiency of photosynthesis, and artificial nitrogen fixation in non-leguminous plants, also deserve serious attention.

Third, we should focus on producing the correct proportion of cereals, animal feed and cash crops. More than 90 per cent of China's major livestock-derived products come from farmed land, and the factor limiting this production is the lack of feed grain. But it is uneconomical to use grain for animal feed. The solution is to switch to growing high-yield and high-quality animal feed. In an area of 30 million *mu* in South China, we could gradually switch from double-cropping rice and low-yield paddy rice to growing rice in rotation with maize, beans, forage and other feed crops. Hunan province has already demonstrated that is

162  *A blueprint for reconstruction*

possible by extending this system to more than 200,000 *mu*, and, overall, has achieved 50 per cent higher productivity than double-cropped rice. Throughout China, there are 150 million *mu* of land growing green manure and nearly 300 million *mu* of corn, potatoes and yams, sorghum and barley, which could gradually be switched to grain and animal feed, expanding feed crops to 500 million *mu*, and creating a crop system combining grain, animal feed and cash crops.[13] This is an effective way of increasing meat and dairy production, as well as being a key factor in moving away from continuous cropping of a single crop, in combining crops and livestock-rearing, maintaining soil fertility and improving crop production and utilization of the land.

Primary industry was once regarded as a 'twilight industry', gradually declining with the rise of biotechnology and oil-related industries, but there is now some scepticism about this view. There is huge potential for the development of forestry, for example. It has been calculated[14] that the world's annual production of timber amounts to more than $1.2 \times 10^{13}$ tons, equivalent to twice the annual consumption of fossil fuels. With the steady decline in supplies of oil and gas, trees may supplement and eventually replace them, providing us with useful chemical products, such as raw materials for textiles, plastics, pharmaceuticals and dyes. Not all chemical products are manufactured from petrochemicals, even now. Wood supplies the raw materials for some fibres, such as rayon. There are accurate statistics that prove that trees are quite suitable for making chemical raw materials. Every individual only needs the products of five trees in their whole lifetime to meet their clothing needs; a tree can supply a family with clothing, carpets and curtains for a year. Rayon produced from wood is a substitute for petrochemical-based textiles, such as polyester and polypropylene fibres. Emsley, in his article, calls for tree planting to supply the chemical industry.

Although trees are an important chemical raw material, only about half of the component parts of wood can be used as raw materials in industry at present and are mainly limited to use in the manufacture of cellulose, paper and textiles. If trees are to be a real substitute for petroleum, then all the elements that make up wood must be developed. The structure of trees is very complex, its four most useful components being cellulose (about half), hemicellulose (one-fifth); lignin (a quarter) and resin or oil (about one-twentieth). In China, universities and research teams are already exploring the use of effective methods of using the component parts of wood. It has been suggested that innovations in the chemical industry could enable us to take advantage of this important resource.

Of all major ecosystems, forest ecosystems have the highest biological productivity. Their annual biomass production is 31.7 kg/metre$^2$ per year, whereas farmland only produces 1 kg/metre$^2$ per year. Their net primary productivity is 1.4 kg/metre$^2$ per year, more than twice that of farmland.[15] One can imagine that technology breakthroughs in the exploitation and use of forest resources will eventually have a revolutionary impact on large-scale farming, with forests assuming a central position in the air-water-organisms-soil biosphere. As a result, the forest will no longer be something to be cut down but to build up. With technological breakthroughs, forests will provide tremendous conservation benefits

*A blueprint for reconstruction* 163

as well as great economic ones, giving life to entire ecosystems and eco-agriculture globally. The strategic significance of forests cannot be exaggerated. China has more than 4 billion *mu* suitable for afforestation, of which about 40 per cent is currently tree-less. If these areas are planted with trees, it will increase China's forest cover to 30 per cent of the country, an increase of about 1.3 times on the current area. Based on the calculations above, each family will then have half a *mu* of forest to meet their lifetime needs for clothing, carpets and curtains. Only 200 million *mu* of China's forests will be sufficient to meet the clothing and textile needs of its entire population for 60 years.

China has 1.2 billion *mu* of productive coastal waters, but is using only one-seventh of the area. It has 75 million *mu* of freshwater, but is using only half. These vast areas of water could be developed for breeding algae. The protein content of algae is more than that of legumes, with *spirulina platensis*, for example, containing up to 60 per cent (dry matter) protein and a variety of amino acids essential to humans and animals. *Spirulina* makes good fodder and is also edible for humans. Promoting the cultivation of algae is a key way to solve the problem of feeding ourselves[16] and, additionally, algae may also become an important biomass resource. The single-celled algae *Botryococcus braunii* also appears to have attractive prospects for development, with between 15 and 75 per cent of the dry weight being long chain hydrocarbons. Temperate and tropical regions all have algae, in freshwater and brackish water, which can be cultivated in great quantities. Experimental results show that, under certain conditions, 60 tons of hydrocarbons per hectare (that is, four tons per *mu*[17]) of *Botryococcus braunii*, can be cultivated annually, in either natural or artificial water areas. These can be used as energy and as raw material for the petrochemical industry. From China's 37 million *mu* of unexploited freshwater areas alone, it would be possible to produce 148 million tons of hydrocarbons, almost the same as China's annual oil production.

In short, in the context of agriculture as a whole, including forestry, animal husbandry and fishing, we have ample scope for new developments. If we combine the latest advances in water-saving technology and biotechnology resources (such as drip-feed irrigation, and ammoniated straw for cattle-rearing), with new plans for China's arable land use, such an ecosystem (including water, living organisms, land and the atmosphere) not only has the potential to protect humanity, enabling us to survive and progress, but will also be imbued with a fresh vitality, providing us with new sources of wealth. The use of these natural resources will go far beyond agriculture – they will provide us with clothing and food, energy and chemical raw materials, thus breaking down the barriers between primary and secondary industries. Just as the agricultural revolution was followed by the Industrial Revolution, the decline of the Industrial Revolution may be followed by an Eco-Industrial Revolution.

### Secondary industry

This kind of industry consumes a far greater proportion of energy, raw materials and other resources than other kinds of industry; indeed, it is here that the

## 164   *A blueprint for reconstruction*

squandering of resources typical of the 'classic' development model is largely found. Secondary industry should therefore be the focus of changes, which the new development model will bring about.

As one of the world's biggest energy consumers, China has for decades been faced with a conflict between energy supply and demand. Astonishingly large quantities of energy are consumed or wasted annually. Overall energy consumption per ton of steel produced in China is 58.6 per cent higher than Japan; energy consumed in supplying electricity and coal is 31.6 per cent higher than in the Soviet Union and 28.7 per cent higher than Japan; while that consumed in boilers is 31.7 per cent higher than advanced types of boilers used overseas.[18] Energy conservation is therefore of great significance, not only to mitigate China's energy shortages (energy-saving has been called a second energy), but also to reduce pollution and consumption of raw materials. In this regard, circulating fluidized bed boiler technology has strategic significance for energy-saving, and for transforming the structure of China's fuel consumption, reducing environmental pollution and the problem of acid rain.

Combined heat and power technologies are particularly worthy of our attention. More than 90 per cent of China's condensing power plants are simply used to generate electricity and, although this is high-quality energy, its energy utilization efficiency is only 30 per cent. Scientists at Qinghua University have been successful in producing combined heat and power at a cost per kilowatt/hour of only 3 cents. Such small-scale, high-efficiency energy-saving technology is particularly important for improving energy efficiency in the innumerable village and township enterprises scattered all over China, even if it cannot confer economies of scale. Cogeneration technologies can combine with circulating fluidized bed combustion in a mutually complementary way.[19]

Advanced technologies in such areas as new types of materials also have huge potential for energy-saving and pollution control. The excellent new high-strength, heat-resistant silicon nitride and silicon carbide ceramics, for example, can give fuel savings of 8 per cent in gas turbines, while increasing generating capacity by about 20 per cent. The manufacture of ceramic car engines not only gives energy-savings of up to 30 per cent but can increase efficiency by 15–20 per cent.[20] The very low costs of innovative practical solutions (advanced technology is not always necessary) should also not be ignored. For example, Chinese scientists have recently invented a method of preserving the freshness of eggs, which does not require electrically-powered refrigerated warehouses and equipment and which only costs 0.4 *yuan* per ton of eggs per month to run. After ten months of storage by these means, the yolks and whites of 98.3 per cent of the eggs were still intact; conversely, the cost per ton of eggs stored by the conventional refrigeration methods was up to 30 *yuan* per month, and after only five months of storage, the egg yolks were breaking up.[21] Another example is a new kind of household vegetable storage cabinet, patented in China in 1989. This vegetable storage cabinet does not run on electrical power or use chemical preservatives and is more effective than a refrigerator.[22]

It has been reported that resources worth as much as 25 billion *yuan* are wasted annually in China in the form of wastewater, exhaust gas and industrial

*A blueprint for reconstruction*   165

slag, with industry responsible for about 20 billion *yuan*, and commerce for about 5 billion *yuan*. Statistics are incomplete but the indications are that about 400 million tons of tailings and slag are discharged annually, making a cumulative total of 5.6 billion tons, covering an area of 900,000 *mu*, and causing environmental pollution costing 9 billion *yuan*. Inadequate recycling of scrap steel means that 1 million tons are lost through oxidization each year.[23] The recycling of wastewater, gasses and slag wastes saves energy and reduces the consumption of resources, as well as reducing environmental pollution. On the basis of the above figures, I estimate that efficiency can be increased by more than 35 billion *yuan* annually.

China's wastewater discharge totals 33.9 billion tons per year, of which 26 billion tons is industrial effluent. By 1985, 80 per cent of China's rivers were polluted to varying degrees. With economic development, wastewater emissions are increasing every year. Bold attempts are currently being made to change this situation and to transform wastewater into useful resources. For example, Tianjin Hangu Chemical Plant's bio-sludge uses eco-technology to treat wastewater, producing water of a quality better than the quality of wastewater treated in tanks, and clean enough for fish-farming.[24] In 1990, it was reported that Japan's Ministry of International Trade and Industry (MITI) was launching a seven-year programme of research into the development of a comprehensive water cycle system. A sequence of processes will ensure a closed system with no access to an outside water supply, where the water is in a permanent loop.[25]

The outlook for the development of new types of flow energy and mineral resources is very bright. As has been mentioned in the previous chapter, solar energy for household use is one example. The most promising development is solar-powered hydrogen technology. This is one kind of energy that does not pollute the environment. The world's first pilot plant producing hydrogen from water, which includes electrolysis using solar power technology, was established in Nuremberg, Germany. It has been estimated that if the Federal Republic of Germany had $11,000\,km^2$ of solar panels and coupled this with hydrogen energy technology, it could produce 40 per cent[26] of its continuous electrical energy requirements, (equivalent to 10 per cent of China's requirements) per annum. In addition, with a combination of solar energy technology and high-temperature metal phase change energy storage technology, storage temperatures of up to $800°C$[27] can be achieved. This is crucial for improving the energy utilization efficiency of solar energy, which has low energy flow density, and is greatly affected by night-time darkness.

China has a vast 'maritime territory'. In addition to the $18,000\,km$ of coastline and more than $300,000\,km^2$ of territorial waters, it also has over $3\,million\,km^2$ of exclusive economic zone and continental shelf. This vast expanse of waters is not only rich in fish, shellfish and algae resources, it is also estimated to contain 9 billion tons of offshore petroleum resources, coastal sand reserves of 430 million tons and stores of wave and tidal energy of 1 billion kilowatts. Polymetallic nodule resources on the seabed are particularly worthy of our attention. It is estimated that the Pacific Ocean floor contains 1.7 trillion tons of polymetallic nodule resources, of which about 15 billion tons are economically viable.

## 166 *A blueprint for reconstruction*

As regards transport, we should learn a lesson from the way in which cars have developed in Western developed countries, and should prioritize public transport. We should make full use of bicycle traffic in the city, take advantage of the great flexibility offered by taxi and minibus services and ensure that private car use is severely restricted. For freight transport, we should give priority to rail and waterways.

As for new materials, the development of optical fibres provides an excellent opportunity for the communications industry in China to take a leap forward. Optical fibres not only have technical advantages compared with traditional coaxial cables – their greater capacity and higher call quality – they also cost half as much and save on steel and other raw materials. Experts believe that optical fibre communications and other advanced means of digital transmission, combined with digital exchanges, will enable China to proceed directly to advanced levels of modern communication without needing to build a complete analogue communication network followed by digitization, as in the developed countries.[28]

In secondary industries, it is worth taking a close look at China's machinery industry, the technological equipment that drives each sector of the national economy. The quality of our existing machinery lags behind international standards by about 20 years and, to develop the national economy, we need to move fast to renew it. Group technology (GT) and flexible manufacturing systems (FMS) are particularly useful in this regard. FMS overcomes the shortcomings of traditional assembly line production because, with the latter, updating the product requires replacing specialized equipment and fixtures wholesale and re-arranging the production layout. This not only lengthens the production cycle and consumes much capital and labour, it also brings the production line to a halt for long periods. FMS uses computerized controls and production automation. Computer programmes offer flexibility because they are easily modifiable, and thus suitable for a variety of small batch production lines. The currently most advanced production systems are computer-integrated manufacturing systems (CIM), which consist of FMS, CAD (computer-aided design) and CAM (computer-aided management). The machinery industry is the heart of any national industry and should be the first to achieve international levels of excellence. China today can make advances in at least some key sectors of its machinery industry.

### Tertiary industry

China's tertiary industry lags far behind its primary and second industries, but it also has the greatest development potential. In this regard, Italy provides us with a very instructive example, having put great efforts into developing its cultural heritage.[29] Italy has made this heritage into an important part of its strategic resources and economic structure and has also developed related industries. An initial investigation of its cultural heritage concluded that exploiting it would require only a small investment but would bring great economic benefits. Italy currently spends less than 200 billion *lire* (about US$160 million) annually, but

*A blueprint for reconstruction* 167

levies as much as 4.5 trillion *lire* (about $3.6 billion) in VAT on cultural tourists. Initial estimates suggest that if the entire country's cultural heritage were developed to the maximum extent (three-quarters of it remains undeveloped), the economic benefits would far outstrip those from manufacturing. Second, the cultural economy is an important way of solving the employment problem, providing far and away more jobs per unit of investment than other industries. Third, a thriving cultural economy also benefits the construction industry, commerce, transport, and indeed the entire tertiary sector, helping to develop the country's most backward areas. China's cultural heritage is far greater than Italy's, so we should attach great importance to protecting and developing it.

In the decade from 1979 to 1988, China's GNP annual growth rate was 9.6 per cent, much higher than the 2.7 per cent for same period globally, making China one of the few countries with a fast-growing economy. At the same time, however, the numbers of school dropouts and illiterates remains persistently high, with over 50 million primary and secondary students not completing their studies, an annual average of more than 15 million. Adult illiteracy has not yet been eliminated, and illiteracy amongst the young is re-appearing. Of China's current population over the age of 15, a total of 238 million are illiterate, an illiteracy rate of 31.9 per cent.[30] This ratio is not only much higher than in developed countries, is but significantly higher than in some developing countries.

In human resources, quality is what counts. As with poor-quality ore deposits, the lower the quality of human resources, the less their value. Quantity is no substitute for quality; in fact, the reverse may be true. The fundamental way to improve the quality of human resources is to develop education. The quality of China's education system is poor at all levels, and has largely left its population wallowing in ignorance. Even primary education is by no means universal: only 76.7 per cent of 6–14 year-olds currently attend school. And secondary education enrolment in 1985 was only 39 per cent, ranking us as number 80 in the 139 countries of the world; 1.7 per cent attended higher education in China in the same year, putting us at 110 out of 139. In secondary education, 92.4 per cent of schools provided a general education, with vocational education still lagging behind. In 1985, China spent only 2.9 per cent of GDP on education, ranking us as number 120 in the world's 154 (*sic*) countries.

About 70 per cent of China's population lives in rural areas. This is where illiteracy is largely concentrated, and the backwardness of China's education is most clearly demonstrated. For example, in 1988, about 13 million school-age children in rural areas (99 per cent of the national figure for non-attendance) were unable to go to school. It is the countryside, therefore, where we have to focus on getting children into primary education and eradicating child illiteracy. In 1988, about 65 per cent of rural primary school children went on to lower middle school, and about 10 per cent of lower middle school children went on to upper middle school. Compared with a decade earlier, these figures are down about 20 percentage points. In the same period, the number of secondary schools in rural areas fell by 77,000, a decrease of 53.7 per cent, and there were 694,000 fewer teachers, a decrease of 29.4 per cent.

168    *A blueprint for reconstruction*

Surveys have shown that poor education in the countryside is a fundamental factor in hindering the rural unemployed from finding jobs outside agriculture. Of those who had completed secondary education (lower or upper middle schools), 17.5 per cent succeeded, compared to only 4 per cent of primary school graduates and 1.5 per cent of those who remained illiterate or semi-literate. For children born in contravention of the one-child-per-family policy (that is, second and subsequent children in a family), education is an even bigger hurdle. China's third national census shows that in 28 provinces, municipalities and autonomous regions, the birth rate of second or subsequent children was on average 17.9 per cent, of whom 26.75 per cent received a primary and middle school education, 40.19 per cent remained illiterate, 3.41 per cent attended upper middle school and 1.23 per cent went to university.[31]

China therefore has to grasp the nettle of culture and education. This is of paramount strategic significance, not only for the development of the tertiary sector, but also for China's overall modernization and a balanced development of the whole industrial structure. If we allow the backward state of China's education to continue, then it is bound to have an extremely negative impact on the entire process of modernization in China, and on the long-term development of our economy and society.

In this respect, we can learn from the experience of South Korea. Education and training in South Korea is formed of complementary systems: standard schooling is divided into six years of elementary and three years of lower middle school; then, during three years of upper middle school, students can either take regular or technical classes; this is followed by four years of university undergraduate education (or two years of junior college). The second system is comprised of vocational training which begins after lower middle school and lasts either for three months, six months, one year, two years or three years; additionally, technical colleges and universities offer two- and four-year courses, (training those who will teach skills and technical courses). The first system comes under the Ministry of Education and the second system is managed by the Ministry of Labour.

In the short and medium term, China should gradually build up a solid vocational training system, focusing on developing technical education whose content meets production needs, and operating in parallel with university and graduate education. Particular attention should be paid to developing education in rural areas, and the structure should gradually be changed from a system offering general education only, into one that combines basic education, vocational and technical training and adult education. We should take active steps to promote vocational and technical education at basic and intermediate levels, as well as different kinds of after-school technical training. Basic rural education should focus on increasing locally-based course content, and vigorous steps should be taken to strengthen education in work-based skills. At secondary level, elective vocational technical courses can be offered where appropriate. This is the only way to adapt education to the needs of rural areas, and to the economy and society as a whole.

In the new development model, the best resources are human resources, and this is the area where our efforts will be most cost-effective. As we face a future

_A blueprint for reconstruction_   169

of growing uncertainty, the best strategy is to make sure we have reserves of human resources, which are adaptable, of excellent quality and which match national needs. It is both necessary and beneficial to have surplus reserves of human resources.

## Some thought-provoking general comparisons

Writing in the late 1960s and early 1970s, the American scholar, Alex Inkeles, proposed a number of indicators to define modernized society: (1) per capita income of $3,000; (2) an agricultural sector worth no more than 20 to 25 per cent of GNP; (3) a service sector valued at more than 45 per cent of GNP; (4) non-agricultural employment, which accounted for more than 70 per cent of total employment; (5) literacy levels of more than 80 per cent of the total population; (6) 30 to 35 per cent of any one age group of young people in higher education; (7) more than 50 per cent of the total population living in the cities; (8) one doctor for every 800 people; (9) an average life expectancy of more than 60 years; and (10) one out of every three people buying a newspaper.

These indicators were developed on the basis of the situation in the world's most developed countries. Per capita income is an important standard to measure a country's modernization, but not the only one. For example, Kuwait's per capita income is among the highest in the world, but Kuwait does not meet all of the other indicators, and thus cannot be included in the list of modernized countries.

As I have shown above, using GNP as an indicator raises many questions. Let us assume for the time being, that we have deducted all the social costs, enabling us to take Inkeles' indicators as a rough frame of reference and measure how far China is from modernization. Between 1980 and 1988, China's GNP growth grew, in real terms, by 116 per cent.[32] The annual growth was, on average, 10.1 per cent, but if we take into account a population growth rate during the same period of 1.3 per cent, then real GNP growth was 8.8 per cent. In 1980, China's per capita GNP was $205 (at the 1970 dollar rate, see calculations in Chapter 1 of this book), and in 1988, it was $403 (at the 1970 dollar rate, or $806 if converted into the 1980 dollar rate). If we compare this to Inkeles' indicator (1), then this figure is only 13.4 per cent of his stipulated $3,000 – a yawning gap.

China's primary industry as the proportion of GNP in 1988 was 27.7 per cent, close to the lower limit (25 per cent) of indicator (2). Also in 1988, China had one doctor per 676 people, 18 per cent better than indicator (8). Similarly, average life expectancy in 1987 was 69 years, 15 per cent better than indicator (9). In other words, of the ten indicators of modernization in 1988, China came close to or exceeded three of the indicators. For a country that had only reached 13.4 per cent of indicator (1), per capita GNP, this was a remarkable achievement. It shows that China's nutrition levels and health care system are exceptionally effective. Obviously, this is inextricably connected with an insistence on fair distribution of wealth, which is a characteristic of socialist countries. That is, when estimating GNP, the way in which wealth is distributed has a huge effect on how effectively wealth is used.

## 170   *A blueprint for reconstruction*

In 1988, China's tertiary sector was 25.7 per cent of the total economy, which was about 20 percentage points lower than Inkeles' indicator (3), or 57.1 per cent of his stipulated figure, and 10 percentage points lower than 35 per cent of low-income countries. (However secondary industry in China is about ten percentage points higher than low-income countries, equivalent to levels in middle-income countries.) In 1988, only about 40 per cent of people in China were not employed on the land,[33] 30 percentage points below his criterion (4) (and only 57.1 per cent of his stipulated figure). At present, 31.9 per cent of China's population aged over 15 is illiterate (see p. 185), while in Vietnam, Thailand and Laos, which are far from being modernized countries, it is 20 per cent or lower. China's figure is at least 12 percentage points lower than the figure stipulated in indicator (5). The number in higher education in 1985 accounted for 1.7 per cent of the population, and is estimated to be no more than 3 per cent in 1988, more than 27 percentage points lower than the lower limit in indicator (6), or only 10 per cent of the required level. In 1988, only one in 19 people in China buy a newspaper,[34] 28 percentage points lower than indicator (10), or only 15.8 per cent of the stipulated figure.

It is clear that in five of the seven indicators where China falls short of the criteria for modernization, there is a direct connection with the underdevelopment of our tertiary sector. In three of those five cases, the shortfall is connected to cultural and educational backwardness. The basic reason for this distortion in China's development is over-extension of our secondary industry, leaving the tertiary sector behind, particularly in so far as culture and education are concerned.

The proportion of China's population living in cities and towns in 1988 was 51.3 per cent,[35] apparently more than indicator (7) above, but this figure is not a true comparison. I have re-calculated it as follows, adjusting it in line with pre-1983 figures. Between 1978 and 1983, China's urban population grew by about 70 million,[36] an average annual increase of 14 million. Let us assume that the increase in the following five years (between 1983 and 1988) was double this (an estimate which is probably on the high side); then, in 1988 the urban population was 380 million, or 35 per cent of China's total population in 1988, 15 percentage points lower than that for indicator (7) or 70 per cent of the stipulated figure. This figure is probably more reliable.

If we take indicator (1) to be a function (or result) of the other indicators, then it is clear that to achieve modernization through continuing expansion of secondary industry is impossible. The only way to modernize faster is to raise those levels that currently fall below Inkeles' indicators. This means that it is the backwardness of our tertiary industry and the fact that China is insufficiently urbanized, which is holding China back. In fact, these two factors are not independent of each other: the city is the vessel that contains the tertiary industry and the latter, in turn, is the catalyst within this vessel. More specifically, it is only well-educated surplus labour from rural areas that is able to survive in the expanded city, because only such high-quality human resources can service the demands of this diverse and rapidly changing environment. Rapid improvements to education in rural areas are, therefore, crucial to future development.

*A blueprint for reconstruction*    171

However, if there is no corresponding progress in urbanization, this catalyst will not work efficiently. So how should the new development model confront the challenge of urbanization in China? This is a final and crucial technical issue that we have to answer in this book.

Judging by current trends, we will continue to see the development of major cities with populations of millions. However, there has been dramatic growth in new technologies suitable for decentralized use. For example, the development of solar power for household use has made large-scale centralized energy supplies to the civilian population a less economically attractive proposition. Another example is the combination of cogeneration and the recycling of waste materials like iron and steel, which make small-scale production and power supply systems an increasingly competitive option. (The surplus heat from smelting iron and steel can be used to heat hothouses and domestic housing.)

Even traditional industries dominated by large-scale technology are changing. In the long run, the emergence of new polymer materials and the development of membrane separation technology may cause a fundamental shift in the basic technologies and production processes of chemical and other industries. For example, membrane separation processes can be used with materials whose physical and chemical properties are very similar and have hitherto been difficult to separate, such as anisotropic and azeotropic mixtures. In this way, petrochemical facilities, which, in the past, depended on large-scale distillation columns, can use small-scale equipment instead, saving energy in the process.[37] When the chemical industry has switched principally to biotechnological micro-organisms and enzyme reactions, we will see the development of value-added industries which save on energy and resources, and a consequent decentralization to local and small and medium-sized cities.

Let us consider agricultural and forestry resources, which renew themselves annually: the huge amount of discarded methylcellulose, in particular, which the human stomach cannot digest, can instead be 'digested' with biotechnology and turned into monosaccharide syrup. This, then, can provide raw materials for new food processing systems, which will pave the way for the factory production of fruits and vegetables. At that point, agriculture will no longer consist of the annual planting of crops, but the exploitation of forests to produce food, clothing and energy. The combination of the sustainable use of decentralized flow resources and new small-scale technology may also give rise to new forms of economic organization and social communities such as corporations or regions, which engage in a mixture of industry and agriculture. One can imagine small or medium-sized cities, surrounded by trees, with chemical plants, food factories and energy supply and water circulation systems that use forests as their raw materials, such that the city and the natural cycle become one. Not only would such cities not destroy the natural cycle, they would actually strengthen it, to their own benefit.

In short, urban systems under the new development model will be reconstructed. Small and medium-sized cities based on renewable resources and the technology described above, will take centre stage, while the city based

## 172 *A blueprint for reconstruction*

principally on the exploitation of non-renewable resources remains typical for the present time.

### *Affirming our beliefs and making careful choices*

These are not merely fanciful predictions. In Stockholm, Sweden, the Institute for Futures Studies, which is directly responsible to the Prime Minister's Office, has proposed phasing out the use of the private car. This would be accompanied by a considerable expansion in and improvement of the public transport system and taxi services (the latter for use in exceptional circumstances).[38] In one small town in the American state of Wisconsin, most of its 600 or so families do not turn the heating on, even when even the temperature drops to minus 15°C. Instead, they use natural resources like sunlight for heating. A family whose home is equipped with solar heating equipment pays $900 per year for heating, the same amount that would be paid monthly by a family entirely dependent on central heating.[39] The Quan Ji Sun Building in Gangcha County, Qinghai province, which doubles as the Quan Ji post office and staff living quarters, has never used fire for heating since its completion in October 1979, nor does it have any auxiliary heat source. However, it is so well insulated, and conserves solar heat so efficiently, that it is warm in winter and cool in summer.[40] Machida City, in Japan, has a 'recycling centre' which, in addition to sorting and recycling material objects, also refurbishes furniture, mends clothing and bicycles and sells them cheaply, or gives them to the needy.[41]

All this has made people of vision in developed countries reflect seriously on their lifestyles and modes of production. It should be emphasized that the small number of developed countries that modernized first, command a substantial technological lead, and have put global resources to use for their own purposes without being constrained by any material restrictions. This may, at the time, have appeared to be an economic choice, but in fact the rational basis of that choice has never been established. Now that conditions have changed, especially since the 1970s oil crisis, resource constraints have had a severe impact on the way the 'classic' development model works. As many serious scholars point out, if changes are not made to this model, humanity will inevitably face trouble.

Abandoning the 'classic' development model depends as much on our collective will and judgment as it does on scientific and technological breakthroughs. The world is undergoing major changes. The real difficulties lie not only in deciding how to deal with the challenges of the new technological revolution but, even more importantly, on waking up to the fact that the existing model for modernization is not wholly suited to China and therefore we need to respond to this challenge with all possible speed. The relative abundance of resources enjoyed by Western countries when they industrialized, is no longer available to China. As for the advantage we enjoy in terms of scientific and technical advances, this is a double-edged weapon, which can both benefit and harm us. For a large country as undeveloped as China, therefore, it is crucially important to make a comprehensive and serious reappraisal of the way in which we modernize and develop, on the basis of the facts and the changing trends that we see around us.

*A blueprint for reconstruction* 173

Paul Hawken in his book *The Next Economy* (1983) makes this issue very clear. He writes:

> What are we growing in our economy? Do we absolutely need all things to grow? If we use fewer drugs or X-rays or spare parts in our bodies, are we a failing economy? Once our sons and daughters are adults and not growing any more, we don't complain that they're not still growing, because once they're adults we completely change our attitude to their physical growth. Can't we reassess our definition of the economy in the same way?

Of course, China is still far from having a mature economy. However, we surely do not need to wait for our economy, under the existing development model, to mature before re-appraising current problems. When we see the USA, which accounts for 6 per cent of the world's population, consuming 50 per cent of the world's resources, why on earth would we follow that model to resolve our own problems?

If, by the end of the twentieth century, China's GNP per capita has reached $800, then it certainly should not prove difficult to achieve a per capita GDP of $2,400–2,500 and a high level of modernization after a further 20 to 30 years. Crucially, we must reject the way in which the developed world has modernized, and we must do it now. We must absorb only those parts that are rational, and discard others, however superficially attractive. The entire population must be armed with a conviction that this is the right approach and must address this problem conscientiously and far-sightedly. We must mobilize to the maximum all the wisdom, strength and courage of the entire Chinese nation. We must begin this transformation smoothly, so as to avoid shocks to a system that is still fragile, and use the potential offered by scientific and technological advances effectively. Only in this way will it be possible to complete this unprecedented breakthrough to a new development model.

The last two chapters can be summarized as follows. As we choose a long-term development model, we should focus on using renewable resources, and the consumption of non-renewable resources should be reduced. As regards food consumption, we should adopt a balanced diet of mixed meat/dairy and vegetable products, avoiding a largely meat-based dict. Our transport system should be made up of a combination of bicycle transport, public transport systems and taxis; and private car use should be discouraged. Agriculture should be labour-intensive and knowledge-based, and managed along ecological lines, avoiding a reliance on fossil fuels. Both cities and rural areas should be re-planned; vigorous efforts should be made to expand, and improve on, the recycling of materials and resources, and we should refrain from consuming, then discarding, vast quantities of materials. We should put more efforts into restoring and protecting the environment, rather than waiting until the damage has reached intolerable levels before intervening. We must prioritize universal education, improving all-round skills in the whole workforce. Our health care should be based primarily on prevention and self-care, and we should reject a large-scale, high-tech health care system. We should employ a variety of economic, administrative and legal means to limit the consumption of resources on which there are currently severe

174  *A blueprint for reconstruction*

constraints. We should adopt the use of new communication technologies to enhance social integration and reduce communication costs. All of these measures should take full advantage of advances in science and technology, enabling us to make great improvements to the existing infrastructure on which our long-term development will be based. This will also put us in a position where we can take advantage of new opportunities and meet new challenges.

But we must understand that it is only when the long-term development model has begun to have real effects on economic process that we will see a positive impact on China's drive for modernization. A number of countries have already accumulated a wealth of practical experience in their implementation of long-term economic goals. A serious examination of these experiences reveals that there are two possible results. (1) Consumer demand creates unbearable pressure on the national economy and restrictions are imposed to inhibit both demand and concomitant supply. South Korea is a typical example: colour television production technology was developed here at an early stage, but the demand for colour TVs in Korea was suppressed as premature and transmitters were only made available domestically a full ten years after Korea had begun exporting colour TVs. Another example: Britain, Germany and other countries have resorted to legislation on fuel economy in an attempt to stop the production of high-fuel consumption cars, no matter what the price. The Soviet Union's strict vigilance as regards consumer goods is well known. The negative impact of this cannot, of course, be ignored, but the positive factors are still worth noting. (2) The other strategy consists of actively discouraging consumerism by promoting a more rational lifestyle, educating public opinion and inculcating public morality, and accompanying this by practical measures such as regulation of taxation and imports, eventually bringing about a change in the national consciousness. In this way, everyone learns to resist the blandishments of a throwaway, wasteful, consumer-focused culture, and there is a growing enthusiasm for an economical, rational development model more suited to the demands of modernization. We can see how this works by looking at the Japanese sense of pride in its own food culture. Most Japanese people believe that they eat more plainly than Americans, but enjoy better health and live longer.

It is undeniable that, in the short term, we will encounter many difficulties in implementing such long-term development goals. As use of market mechanisms becomes more extensive and market demand is formed, how are we to ensure that we do not lose sight of long-term goals, inexperienced in this area as we are? It is crucial that we act with a conviction based on the grasp of indisputable facts. Developing countries must be guided by a visionary strategy as they enter a new stage of consumer demand. There is an arduous struggle ahead, in the social, political and economic domains, and we need to be convinced of the rightness of our cause. We need to take the entire population with us, convincing them of the need to balance the books in a rational way. In this way, we can effectively influence the formation of market demand and consumer preferences.

It must be clear that only with a visionary strategy for this new stage of development in the national economy can China ensure sustained and effective growth and healthy development towards modernization.

*A blueprint for reconstruction*    175

# Notes

1　賈曉慧、張風莎：〈正確的食物結構與營養 —— 提高全民身體素質的保證〉,《科技日報》1989 年 5 月 11日。 (JIA Xiaohui and ZHANG Fengsha, 'Correct food structure and nutrition guarantees improved physique in the entire population' in *Science Daily* newspaper, 11 May 1989.)

2　《農村問題論壇》1987 年 12 月 15 日 (125)第 25 頁。 (*Discussion of the rural problem*, 15 December 1987 (125, page 25))

3　〈我國人民生活質量高於發展中國家平均水平〉,《北京晚報》1989 年 10 月 15 日。 ('Quality of life for Chinese people better than average in developing countries' in *Beijing Evening News*, 15 October, 1989).

4　梁厚甫：〈各國「生活模式」的比較研究〉,《世界經濟科技》 1985 年 1 月 8 日。 (LIANG Houfu, 'Comparitive study of lifestyles in different countries' in *World Economy, Science and Technology*, 8 January 1985).

5　〈我國人民生活質量高於發展中國家平均水平〉,《北京晚報》 1989 年 10 月 15 日。 ('Quality of life for Chinese people better than average in developing countries' in *Beijing Evening News*, 15 October, 1989).

6　凌征均：〈太陽能家用電器〉,《中國青年報》 1989 年 12 月 8 日。 (LING Zhengjun, 'Solar-powered household appliances' in *China Youth Daily*, 8 December 1989).

7　中國統計局編：《中國統計摘要 1989 》, 中國統計出版社 1989 年。 (China Statistics Bureau, *Digest of China Statistics 1989*, Zhongguotongji Chubanshe Publishers, 1989).

8　〈我國人民生活質量高於發展中國家平均水平〉,《北京晚報》 1989 年 10 月 15 日。 ('Quality of life for Chinese people better than developing countries' average in *Beijing Evening News*, 15 October, 1989).

9　〈我國人民生活質量高於發展中國家平均水平〉,《北京晚報》 1989 年 10 月 15 日。 ('Quality of life for Chinese people better than developing countries average' in *Beijing Evening News*, 15 October, 1989).

10　One *mu* is one-sixth of an acre, one sixteenth of a hectare. *Trans*.

11　余永龍：〈食物結構問題是個國策問題〉,《人民日報》1988 年 3 月 2 日 (YU Yonglong, 'Food structure is a national policy issue', in *People's Daily* 2 March 1988).

12　Ibid.

13　《中國科技關於合理調整我國食物結構的建議》, 1988 年 (*Scientific and Technical Proposals for a Rational Adjustment to China's Food Structure*, 1988)

14　John Emsley 〈為化學工業植樹〉,《世界科學》1988 年 第 10 期 第 15 頁。 (Emsley J., 'Planting trees for the chemicals industry' in *World Science*, 1988, issue 10, page 15).

15　夏偉生：《人類生態學初探》第120頁。 (XIA Weisheng, *An Exploration of Human Ecology*, Gansu Renmin Chubanshe Publishers, 1984, page 120).

16　余永龍：〈食物結構問題是個國策問題〉,《人民日報》1988 年 3 月 2 日。 (YU Yonglong, 'Food structure is a national policy issue', in *People's Daily* newspaper, 2 March 1988).

17　Sasson, Albert, 1984, 'Biotechnologies: challenges and promises', Unesco, Paris. (阿爾貝·薩松：《生物技術——挑戰與希望》科技文獻出版社, 1986 年 第 267 頁。 [Kejiwenxian Chubanshe Publishers, 1986, page 267]).

18　劉怡：〈節能降耗必須靠技術進步〉,《科技日報》1989 年 9 月 21 日。 (LIU Yi, 'Technological progress is necessary to reduce energy levels' in *Science Daily*, 21 September 1989).

19　梁沂濱：〈謝行建與能源的階梯開發〉,《經濟日報》5 月 8 日 (LIANG Yibin, 'Xie Xingjian and development of energy' in *Economics Daily* newspaper, 8 May *[sic]*.

20　甘道初：〈陶瓷新秀〉,《科技日報》1990 年 3 月 4 日 (GAN Daochu, 'Ceramics – the new star' in *Science Daily*, 4 March 1990).

21　顧健：〈不用冷庫不耗電, 照樣可以貯鮮蛋〉,《農民日報》1990 年 2 月 22 (GU Jian, 'Keeping fresh eggs without the need for cold storage or electricity', *Farmers Daily* newspaper, 22 February, 1990).

22　〈新型蔬菜保鮮儲存櫃問世〉,《光明日報》1989 年 9 月 1 日 ('New–style vegetable storage cabinets', in *Guang Ming Daily* newspaper, 1 September 1989).

176  *A blueprint for reconstruction*

23 郭培章等人:〈增產節約中的一個重要課題〉,《經濟參考》1987 年 2 月 18 日。 (GUO Peizhang *et al.*, 'An important task in increasing production and practicing economy' in *Economic Reference*, 18 February 1987).

24 黃玉瑤:〈污水資源化的生態學途徑〉,《百科知識》1989 年 第 8 期。 (HUANG Yuyao, 'The ecological route to making resources from waste water' in *An Encyclopedia of Knowledge*, 1989 issue 8).

25 〈日撥鉅款開發新型完全水循環系統〉,《科技日報》1990 年 2 月 7 日。 ('Japan invests huge sums in developing a new-style, complete water circulation system' in *Science Daily*, 7 February 1990).

26 周美瑛譯:〈氫氣─未來的燃料〉,《世界科學》1988 年 第 11 期。(ZHOU Meiying, trans, 'Hydrogen – fuel of the future' in *World Science*, 1988 issue 11).

27 黃志光:〈令人矚目的高溫金屬相變貯能技術〉,《科技日報》1989 年 12 月 12 日。 (HUANG Zhiguang, 'Astonishing high temperature metal phase change energy storage technology' in *Science Daily* newspaper, 12 December 1989).

28 《經濟日報》1988 年 9 月 10 日,王玉玲的報道。 (*Economics Daily* newspaper, 10 September 1988, report by Wang Yuling).

29 《光明日報》1986 年 5 月 13 日。 (*Guang Ming Daily* newspaper, 13 May 1986).

30 陳冰:〈2.4億文盲: 亟待高度重視〉,《經濟日報》1989 年 4 月 12 日。 (CHEN Bing, '240 million illiterates – awaiting urgent attention' in *Economics Daily* newspaper, 12 April 1989).

31 陳冰: 2.4億文盲:亟待高度重視〉,《經濟日報》1989 年 4 月 12 日。 (CHEN Bing, '240 million illiterates – awaiting urgent attention' in *Economics Daily* newspaper, 12 April 1989).

32 中國統計局編:《中國統計摘要(1989)》第6頁。 (China Statistics Bureau, *Digest of China Statistics 1989*, Zhongguotongji Chubanshe Publishers, 1989, page 6).

33 Ibid., page 10.

34 Ibid., page 91.

35 Ibid., page 14.

36 Ibid.

37 〔日〕野村綜合研究所:《新時代的尖端產業》,科技文獻出版社 1987 年, 第 149 頁。 (Nomura Research Institute (NRI) 1982. Shinjidai no sentan sangyō: asu o hiraku seichō sangyō o tenbōsuru. Nomura Sōgō Kenkyū Jōhō Kaihatsubu, Tokyo, 1987, page 149).

38 Brown, Lester R., *Building a Sustainable Society*, W W Norton & Co, New York, 1982 (萊斯特·R.布朗:《建設一個持續發展的社會》科技文獻出版社 1984 年, 第 207 頁。).

39 春梅:〈太陽城〉,《新觀察》1985 年 第 13 期, 第 15 頁。 (CHUN Mei, 'Sun city' in *New Perspectives*, 1985, issue 13, page 15).

40 木村建一:《太陽房》譯序, 新時代出版社 1986 年, 第 iii 頁。(Ken-ichi Kimura, *Solar House*, Xinshidai Chubanshe publishers, 1986, page iii).

41 Brown, Lester R., *et al.*, *State of the World 1985: A Worldwatch Institute Report on Progress Toward a Sustainable Society*, pub. W. W. Norton, New York, 1985 (萊斯特·R. 布朗等:《經濟社會科技─1985 年世界形勢述評》科技文獻出版社 1986 年, 第 329 頁 [Kejiwenxian Chubanshe Publishers, 1986, page 329]).

# 11 Desperate measures are called for

In the preceding chapters, we have looked at the new development model from every angle. This chapter first gives an overview of its basic framework and then discusses ways in which we can make the transition to this model and achieve our ultimate goals. Finally, we will analyse some popular misconceptions, which stand in the way of progress.

## Making a U-turn

The new development model and the 'classic' development model are different, indeed opposite, in every aspect. I will summarize these differences below:

1   The basic premise of the new development model is that both the sustainability of the environment, and the quantity and quality of available resources are limited. (The term 'limited' is used here not only in the absolute sense, but also in a relative sense, relative to the overall capacity of human beings in the present day to consume these resources, a fact that is not, at first sight, obvious.) A good, clean natural environment is a necessary precondition for the survival and progress of human beings, as well as being important to the quality of their lives. Economic and social progress cannot, in the long term, overstep the limits of sustainability without incurring serious consequences for resources and the environment. However, we see examples everywhere of the ability of the 'classic' development model to disregard this premise either overtly or covertly.

   The changes necessary to implementing the new development model are not random nor can they happen in a vacuum. The 'classic' development model has had devastating consequences in terms of air pollution, deterioration in water quality, and desertification. There is a growing awareness that this poses a threat to humanity's very existence, and that we can no longer act on nature with impunity. It is precisely on the ruins created by the 'classic' development model that the new development model will be established. Understanding this fact has far-reaching consequences, and will result in a transformation of the economy and society.

2   This transformation will lead to corresponding changes in overall priorities. The new development model gives top priority to a clean and healthy natural

## 178 *Desperate measures are called for*

environment. In second place come basic human needs (such as for food and housing). The short-term efficiency of economic activity comes in last place. By contrast, the 'classic' development model puts the short-term efficiency of economic activities in first place, while the state of the natural environment in the long term is the last thing to be taken into account.

To understand such changes in priorities, one need only look at the following facts: without food, human life can be sustained for five weeks; without water, life can be sustained for five days, and without air, for only five minutes. In the past, we never realized how well off we were. Today, people have begun to sense the power that the environment holds over our very existence.

3    For the two reasons mentioned above, the new development model will be based on renewable resources, and will protect these resources by means of effective and sustainable utilization. This resource base is sound enough to sustain human survival long-term. By contrast, the resource base of the 'classic' development model is the large-scale consumption of non-renewable resources and a blinkered pursuit of short-term, high-speed economic growth leading eventually to serious resource depletion. By the same token, this model also wreaks havoc on renewable resources.

It is clear that non-renewable resources like oil, coal and other minerals will eventually be used up even if we use them in the most economical, non-polluting way. This means that the only solution for humans is to extend and enhance the use of renewable resources, such as solar and wind power, to the maximum. In addition, we should take vigorous measures to develop new materials to replace traditional non-renewable resources; for example, using silicon carbide and silicon nitride ceramic matrix composites to replace carbon steel and high-alloy steel, since silicon accounts for 26 per cent of the earth's crust, while iron accounts for only 4.2 per cent.

4    Changes in the resource base will significantly alter the way we live. Under the new development model, material consumption will no longer be allowed inexorably to increase. We need to ensure that our people are physically strong, highly-skilled, intelligent and wise and that they engage in work that is beneficial to the community, to future generations and to the environment. In order to achieve this, levels of consumption must be rational and moderate, and strict limits need to be imposed on population growth. By contrast, the 'classic' development model is characterized by reckless consumption, and the production of harmful levels of waste.

It is clear that, where the resource base is static, or indeed declining, the only way forward is to transform the way we live, cutting out excessive wastefulness, so that improvements in our standard of living are sustainable within the limits of available resources and the environment.

5    The new development model will primarily be based on new-style flow technology (including technology for the recovery and recycling of resources), supplemented by the economical use of stocks technology. By contrast, the 'classic' development model relies on large-scale consumption of non-renewable resources and highly-polluting stocks technology.

The new development model has only minimal effects on the environment, almost none of which are cumulative. Additionally, it is based on the matching rule and the principle of equivalence and can thus meet reasonable requirements for improved living standards even within established resource constraints. The 'classic' development model, on the other hand, is characterized by overkill. That is, instead of asking what the purpose of the product or service is, it delivers everything by means of high-quality resources and expensive equipment. This system is the root cause of excessive and harmful redundancy.

6    The new development model will create a progressive economic system based on the 'maximum sustainable yield' of the natural world, keeping 'capital' loss to a minimum and ensuring that waste (materials or energy) re-enters the natural cycle, or is limited to levels, which the natural world is capable of eliminating. By contrast, the 'classic' development model has constructed a growth economy based on using up natural resources.

To re-build the economy under a new development model, systems of property rights and methods of resource allocation must be reorganized, according to whether resources are recyclable, separable or exclusive. In particular, priority should be given to the design and construction of a system of effective public property rights.

7    Collaborative social relationships should be the core of the new development model and these should focus on common rights and an increasingly equitable enjoyment of the environment, education and the economy. By contrast, social systems under the 'classic' development model are focused on competition between people and favours the interests of the current generation, that is, partial interests.

The need to transform the social system in this way should not surprise us. As the earth becomes increasingly crowded, and theoretically everyone can engage in 'free and fair competition', it is likely that the result will be a handful of winners and a majority of losers, who lack the resources to earn their livelihood and are reduced to dire poverty. In most of the world, poverty and the social systems associated with it are the main culprits in destroying the environment. As damage to the environment reaches critical levels, for example, when tropical rainforests disappear, the implications globally will be very serious. No one will survive unscathed. Those who were the winners initially will be long gone. Selfish behaviour, which once furthered people's own interests, will, in the future, harm those individuals as well as others. The space each of us has in order to exist will diminish and, in a social system that relies on excessive competition, there will be no ultimate winners. At that point, the only way for people to serve their own interests will be through cooperation and consensus.

The above is a brief summary of the new development model. Each feature of this model is applicable to China's future development. However, since China faces more severe constraints on per capita resources than other countries, we must put even more efforts into developing this model, showing even greater creativity and imagination.

## 180  *Desperate measures are called for*

I have outlined a frame of reference for China's long-term development, but there are many intermediate steps, which we must also take. We face great uncertainty and must address the issue of how to achieve this transition. There are currently two popular approaches. The first neglects long-term goals and espouses piecemeal, stop-gap measures. This approach applies to inertia-based systems – things carry on in the same old rut, only minor changes are ever made and the system is incapable of making a complete transformation when it is needed. In the second approach, exhaustive, comprehensive plans of action are drawn up, in a kind of 'testing' approach; everything is regarded as wholly determined and problems will be solvable simply by acting according to the plan. When the system faces huge uncertainty, as ours does, this approach is useless.

It is my belief that a third approach is more appropriate: we should establish certain basic goals necessary to long-term human survival and progress – although not in any great detail. Then we should establish the means by which we can achieve these goals (see below) and identify the deviation between the *status quo* and our goals. We can then ensure that the transformation of the system is consistent with survival of the species, we can revise and improve the specific structure and details relevant to achieving our objectives, and we can apply these methods to a gradual reduction or correction of the deviation, in order to approach our ultimate goals.

The safety rule will prove extremely useful in dealing with the difficulties created by transforming the system and the huge uncertainties we face. Goals established now may prove inadequate or incorrect in the future, but as long as they do not run counter to the safety rule, then any errors will be minor and reversible, and we will have sufficient leeway to correct them. For example, it is better to under-exploit resources rather than make the mistake of over-exploiting them, because the former can easily be remedied and has very few after-effects while the latter is not only difficult to remedy, but will also bring a string of disasters in its wake.

The following, highly practical proposals show just how this approach works. Since China faces severe resource constraints as it modernizes, the new development model dictates that we should take the following steps: (1) We should bring an end to destruction of renewable resources and economize as far as possible on the use of non-renewable resources, in line with the safety rule and the minimum rule. We should identify which of these two types of resources have been most seriously depleted and most wastefully used, and which are crucial to national survival and progress in the long term. (2) We should identify those sectors and technologies most closely implicated in the destruction and waste of these resources. (3) We should identify the most advanced resource and energy regulations in force both within China and overseas, and impose such standards on the exploitation of key resources and the energy they produce, giving them the force of law. (4) We should focus our efforts on devising means of enforcement, which gradually close the gap between the actual consumption of resources and energy by those sectors and technologies and the mandatory regulations that we have put in force.

*Desperate measures are called for* 181

These steps are not sufficient to enable China to achieve high levels of modernization, but they are nevertheless necessary. It is only by beginning with these necessary steps that we can avoid making irreversible mistakes and can minimize the costs of learning from them. So long as this process is allowed to continue uninterrupted, then we will assuredly achieve our ultimate goals.

I will now analyse the twin goals of modernization, the establishment of indicators for material consumption and energy consumption in an advanced society, and the relationship between them. I will not use the GNP per capita indicator to measure the degree of modernization (I have discussed its failings in some detail above) but, instead, I will use indicators similar to Inkeles' in Chapter 10, to examine China's progress towards modernization: (1) average life expectancy of over 70 years; (2) one doctor per 700 people; (3) literacy and education for more than 85 per cent of the total population; (4) more than 40 per cent of young people in higher education; (5) one in every three people reading newspapers; (6) over 70 per cent of the total workforce in non-agricultural employment and over 45 per cent in the service sector; (7) more than 60 per cent of the total population living in the cities; (8) per capita living space of more than 20 square metres; and (9) per capita daily nutrient intake of 2,700 calories: 80 grams of protein and 75 grams of fat.

Having established these indicators, the next problem is what kind of energy consumption and material consumption levels will enable us to meet these standards. It has been calculated that a modern lifestyle requires an energy consumption per capita of at least 1.6 tons of good-quality coal,[1] a figure that we may take as the standard required for achieving modernization. For other major materials (such as steel, iron, cement and copper), we may use one-sixth to one-seventh of the per capita consumption in 1970's America as the requirement.

These can be used as initial values in the process of achieving modernization, and can then be continually iterated through the four steps outlined above. For example, as we use renewable energy more, and more effectively, a proportion of that energy consumption of 1.6 tons of coal can be replaced with solar power reducing the need for coal, for example, to only 1 ton per capita. We can treat other requirements in a similar way. Thus we can establish another set of values as a second step towards our goal. With the benefit both of domestic and international experience, we may continue to revise our base criteria for modernization, making them both more specific and more comprehensive. By repeating this process, it is entirely possible for us to achieve a high level of modernization by using the new development model.

## The means to achieve this end

Economic, legal and administrative means must be employed to shape supply and demand. Economically, consumption can be divided into two categories: productive and non-productive. The former refers to the consumption by enterprises of raw materials, semi-finished products and fuel; the latter mainly refers to consumption for personal use and community services. If the consumer items

## 182   *Desperate measures are called for*

produced vary, then the structure of production and the impact that that production has on its surroundings, especially in terms of waste, will also change.

Take the problem of waste. Many current production processes are far from eco-friendly. An increase in production is often followed by the production of large amounts of hazardous waste, and the construction of purification facilities requires huge investment often costing between 20 and 40 per cent[2] of the fixed capital of enterprises. One way to solve the waste problem is to incorporate it into the stream of consumption. Production technology can be transformed in such a way that hazardous waste from industry is turned into raw materials. This process, whereby the waste component is transformed through changes in patterns of consumption, is often referred to as a circular system of production. Changing the supply process not only achieves a reduction in waste harmful to the environment, but also a reduction in the sources of pollution and the consumption of non-renewable resources, thus killing two birds with one stone.

Measures taken to alter demand, so as to limit environmental pollutants, can also play a significant role in addressing other environmental problems and, indeed, may be the only feasible way to protect nature. For example, statistics show[3] that in cities with a population of more than 50,000, vehicle exhausts along transportation corridors have caused intolerable air pollution. When the urban population doubles, air pollution increases nine-fold. Measures designed to reduce vehicle emissions such as adjusting carburettors, using gasoline additives and installing exhaust gas absorbers, will fail fundamentally to improve the quality of urban life, and so it is crucial to limit demand for the private car in large cities.

It is entirely feasible to do this if we ensure that people live close to their place of work, if there is an increase in the numbers using public transport and an expansion of car taxi and motorcycle taxi businesses, if new communication technologies are used to bring people together virtually, thereby reducing transport costs for goods and people, and if there is an increase in and diversification of non-motorized individual transport such as touring bicycles, racing bicycles, multi-seat bicycles and cargo bicycles.

In addition, vigorous steps should be taken to develop consumer demand for eco-friendly products by promoting an informed awareness and love of nature and all living things. A peaceful and healthy existence for humans depends largely on a peaceful and healthy natural environment.

We may adopt a variety of direct or indirect measures to shape supply and demand and to stimulate the economy as we implement the new development model. Some of these are under discussion or have already been implemented in the West; for instance: tax credits or tax cuts to promote the insulation of buildings, tax increases on petrol, price rises for natural gas, 'efficiency labelling' on equipment, which spells out initial costs and running costs (to enable consumers to identify and compare the economic benefits of each item) and 'energy taxation', which reflects the amount of energy consumed in the production of all new products.

In addition to the adoption of ingenious measures to stimulate the economy, it is possible to enforce energy-saving through legislation. For example, laws can require cars to be more efficient – the US Energy Policy and Conservation Act of 1975 required car fuel efficiency to reach 20 miles per gallon by 1980 and 27.5 miles per gallon by 1985. However, whether such legislation can be passed and enforced depends on public acceptance and willingness to comply with the law. For instance if people refuse to downsize and insist on buying big, fuel-inefficient cars, then it will be impossible to enforce fuel-efficiency regulations.

If, on the other hand, consumers become more aware of the need for energy-saving and change their behaviour accordingly, then the same effect can be achieved without the need for legislation. For example, they may change their shopping habits to show a particular preference for durable goods that can be repaired when necessary, instead of goods which can only be thrown away and replaced with new ones. In this way, we can move towards a service-maintenance economy.

It must be recognized, however, that it will take some considerable time to fundamentally change direction to an energy-saving, low-consumption economy. For example, even if people are willing to insulate their homes, and the equipment and labour is available so that it is possible to make everyone do it immediately, this is only a small part of what needs to be done. Industrial restructuring to enable re-use of waste heat, a major shift towards a service-maintenance economy and the re-development of cities to reduce freight transport and increase public transport will take much longer.

We should not underestimate the importance of a well-designed system of public ownership honed to optimum efficiency. This will be crucial in determining whether China can achieve the Four Modernizations (of agriculture, industry, defence and science) through adopting a new development model. This touches on an aspect of the three-body problem: namely, the relationship between China's internal structure and its development model, and it must be the subject of a further, special study.

## China at the crossroads

I have made approximate estimates of needs for clothing, food, housing, transportation and medical treatment in previous chapters, and analysis shows that the new development model can meet people's basic needs, while reducing levels of consumption that are common under the 'classic' development model by at least half. If we compare the per capita energy consumption of 1.6 tons of coal, proposed as a standard for a modernized economy, against actual per capita consumption of 10 tons in the USA and 5 tons in Japan, then the potential for savings is indisputable.

Although some people acknowledge this, many more still labour under misapprehensions with respect to the developed world's 'classic' development model. This confusion manifests itself particularly in the current enthusiastic discussions around 'concept innovation'. It is worth analysing such misconceptions briefly, because they have a direct bearing on how, and how well, we choose the path to development, which in turn has practical consequences.

## 184 *Desperate measures are called for*

For example, when we talk about an agricultural population of less than 7 per cent, and car ownership of one per household, as the height of modernization, we are really talking about the problem of how to measure living standards in the abstract, and whether per capita GNP is the appropriate measure for such a purpose.

At the point when a society is still working to meet its people's basic needs for food and clothing, GNP per capita can be used as an approximate measure of living standards, but once this stage has been superseded, the applicability of GNP is increasingly doubtful. Chapter 6 has a detailed discussion of this question, and a further specific example follows below.

GNP per capita is determined by the flow rate of production and consumption in a specific year. In the classic calculation, the higher this flow per capita, the higher the standard of living is assumed to be, and vice versa. In fact, this flow is generated from two sources: the first from stocks resources, and the second from flow resources. In the former case, the higher the GNP per capita, the fewer stocks resources remain as surplus. In the latter case, the more abundant the quantity of flow resources used up, the higher the GNP per capita. (Although once the threshold of sustainable use is passed, flow resources are in a similar situation to stocks resources.)

Until that sustainable use threshold is reached, the more abundant the quantity of flow resources used up, the higher the GNP per capita and the higher the standard of living. This is the case both in the short term and the long term, but it is not the case with regards to stocks resources, which have a different source. Here, the relationship is different – the higher the per capita GNP in the short term, the higher the short-term standard of living. But in the long term, as available stocks decline, so long-term per capita GNP is likely to decline also, resulting in reduced average living standards. This has complex implications, which are not always readily understood.

Let us look at a concrete example, the recycling of glass bottles. Suppose that a glass bottle is worth 1 *yuan*, where materials and labour make up 0.80 *yuan* and profit 0.20 *yuan*. Now imagine that bottles are used once only and then thrown away, and that each individual uses on average one bottle annually. This corresponds to per capita GNP of 1 *yuan* per person. Now consider bottle recycling: suppose that a bottle has an average service life of five years, and that each instance of recycling and re-use has a cost plus profit of 0.5 *yuan*, that is 2.5 *yuan* over five years. Add to this the original cost of 1 *yuan*, making a total of 3.5 *yuan*, and the corresponding annual per capita GNP is 0.7 *yuan* per person. If we assume that other items making up per capita GNP have not changed, then the overall GNP per capita shows a net decrease, although in fact per capita living standards have not declined and per capita resource consumption shows a net decrease. If 0.2 *yuan* per person of the 0.3 *yuan* per person saved is used on measures to protect the environment, then per capita wealth has actually increased. Thus a lower per capita GNP (0.9 *yuan* per person is less than 1 *yuan* per person) can achieve a standard of living that is higher than a GNP of 1 *yuan* per person. In other words, by improving the quality and extending the life of goods made with stocks reserves the flow rate of stocks resources can be reduced.

*Desperate measures are called for*  185

In fact, the logic of this simple example is that by extending the life of goods and improving maintenance and services, we can achieve the same or even higher standards of living, and reduce the consumption of resources at the same time as we reduce per capita GNP – per capita annual production flow rate. Such conclusions apply both in the long and the short term. Saving on stocks resources and abundant use of flow resources can be called 'combining high standards of living with low per capita GNP'.

However, it is not at all clear what impact other ways of economizing will have on living standards. The car is a very good example. About 25 per cent of total American oil consumption is in the form of vehicle fuel. The efficiency of a car engine is about 25 per cent, not too low in terms of the energy conversion itself. This efficiency rate includes both running the motor and carrying passengers. However, using a car weighing 2 tons to carry passengers is less than 1 per cent efficient, and more than 99 per cent of the energy is wasted. That is, only 1 per cent of the energy is used on the ultimate goal – transporting people through space – while 99 per cent of the energy is consumed by the means to achieve that goal. This is a typical example of energy-wasting transport.

The internal combustion engine was developed about a hundred years ago, and it will be very difficult to increase its basic efficiency even by a few percentage points. However, that efficiency can easily be increased many times over by means of reducing vehicle size, weight and power. If our aim in driving a car is to travel from one point to another point, then it is clear that using a smaller or lighter car not only does not lower our standard of living, but also saves energy (and lowers per capita GNP). However, if we regard a large saloon car as a status symbol, then the choice of an energy-saving, small saloon car does indeed lower our standard of living.

With regard to transport, ensuring that people who live in densely populated residential areas travel by means of efficient public transport can achieve even greater energy-savings. Similar measures for heating and cooling buildings can be equally effective. The energy required for heating and cooling inner-city flats is only 75 per cent that required for homes of the same size, but geographically scattered. For many people, living with others in a block of flats represents a substantial decline in their standard of living. If, on the other hand, appropriate improvements were to be made to such residential blocks (for example, through the provision of public green spaces in front of them), this could promote neighbourliness and might even be regarded as raising living standards.

In summary, a low GNP per capita may, or may not, mean a low standard of living. Put simply, if we look at this question in the context of the implementing the new development model, it is clear that even if GNP per capita is low, real standards of living will by no means be low.

Once people's basic needs have been met and society moves to the next stage, therefore, concepts of quality of life may differ widely, and these differences will have real consequences to the environment and society. For example, historically, thrift was considered a virtue and an economic principle. Now it is largely ridiculed as the sign of a backward and blinkered mentality – yet recently, in developed

## 186 *Desperate measures are called for*

countries, thrift is making a comeback. It is thought provoking to realize that many supposedly 'new' concepts are actually old concepts recycled.

It is inevitable, when China's situation is assessed by comparison with developed world standards, that people will come to a very pessimistic view of our economy and society. For example, one car per household (of three people, the car costing $12,000 and replaced every five years) compared with an average of one car per ten households, represents an annual difference in GNP per capita of as much as $800. No wonder that many Chinese who have been to the US are convinced that China will never catch up with that country. If we measure modernization purely in terms of levels of per capita consumption, then this gap is inevitable and will never be closed, thus justifying that pessimism.

However, there is a problem with such comparisons, and it can be illustrated by means of the scientific principle of simplicity, also known as Occam's razor: theories that reach the same conclusion under the same circumstances are compared, and the simpler the theory, the more universally applicable and the better it is. The above comparisons, however, run precisely counter to this, confusing the relationship between ends and means, turning the means into the goal and making it thereby unattainable.

We need, therefore, to adopt a different perspective, one that starts from the ultimate goals of life and production, and compares the means to an end according to its effectiveness in achieving that purpose. This is a truly positive attitude, consistent with the modern scientific spirit.

Per capita GNP (in reality, this is per capita material consumption, or consumption of non-renewable resources, which is the same thing), is clearly an inadequate measure to assess an individual's mental and physical well-being, and this becomes all the more obvious once the population's basic needs have been met.

We only have to think of the most illustrious statesmen, military strategists, writers, philosophers and scientists down the ages, (always bearing in mind that rapid growth of the developed world's per capita GNP dates back less than 100 years), and we will find that it is not only entirely possible to assess human society other than through GNP, it is also highly desirable in practice.

This new perspective begins by examining the question against the benchmark of levels and the quality of our physical and mental activities. For example, an individual's particular skill level can be reached by means of very different levels of consumption. Again, where people have an abundance of physical stamina, their mental and spiritual activities may take very different forms. It is virtually impossible to give an adequate explanation of social development simply by measuring per capita GNP. The new criteria should therefore be stated as follows: in striving to achieve a given standard of physical strength, skills and intelligence, the lower the per capita material consumption, the higher the level of modernization.

Research into the lives and achievements of major historical figures has shown (and this is corroborated by my personal observation of the developed world) that per capita consumption devoted in developed countries to achieving standards of mental activities equivalent to the physical energies of a population, is not only excessive but also harmful. This conviction essentially underpins the new development model. Armed with this knowledge, I believe that it is by no means unimaginable that China will catch up and surpass the developed world (including America) and that there is scarcely any reason to be pessimistic.

In conclusion, it is clear that both renewable and non-renewable resources are finite, and limits will inevitably be enforced on their use in the not too distant future. However, this does not necessarily mean that human civilization is doomed. If we can rise to the challenge, there are many effective ways to adapt to these limitations and, through effective use of scientific advances, to ensure that our own and further generations have a bright future. Put simply, relying on the new development model to achieve modernization presents developing countries with a historic opportunity. Will China be able to seize this opportunity? We not only can, we must. There is no other way!

## Notes

1 馬洪、孫尚清等:《中國經濟結構問題研究》, 人民出版社 1983 年, 第 293 頁。 (MA Hong, SUN Shangqing *et al.*, *A Study of China's Economic Structure*, Remin Chubanshe Publishers, 1983, page 293).
2 王興成: 〈社會生態學與社會發展問題〉,《國外社會科學》1888 年第 1 期, 第 18 頁。 (WANG Yucheng, 'Social ecology and social development' in *Social Sciences Outside China*, 1988 issue 1, page 18).
3 Ibid.

# Appendix

## Differential pricing, Pareto efficiency, property rights

### Differential pricing

For the same commodity, different buyers may be willing to accept different price levels. For example, some people are willing to pay 4,000 *yuan* for a 20-inch colour TV, whereas others are only willing to pay 2,500 *yuan*, or even 1,500 *yuan*.

Now assume that a colour TV manufacturer sets their prices in the following way: the seller sells the product to the buyer who is willing to accept the maximum acceptable price (such as 4,000 *yuan*); then the seller lowers the price slightly (for example, to 3,800 *yuan*) and sells the product to some other buyer willing to accept this lower price; and the seller carries on in this fashion until reaching the point (for example, 1,500 *yuan*, the cost price) of selling at a loss. This is differential pricing, that is, different people (depending on their income, preferences and so on) receive different pricing treatment.

With non-discriminatory pricing, by contrast, no matter who the customer is, they pay the same price (2,500 *yuan*). Obviously, the seller whose sales are made entirely on the basis of differential pricing will sell more than the one who implements non-discriminatory pricing. The latter is equivalent to a price tag, while the former is akin to bargaining with each customer.

The seller would obviously prefer to implement differential pricing, because with non-discriminatory pricing, s/he is selling to some customers who would have been willing to pay the higher price, and may lose some customers who were only willing to pay a lower price. Equally obviously, however, it is difficult to prevent purchasers from exchanging information about prices, which makes it almost impossible to fully differentiate pricing.

### Pareto efficiency

Pareto efficiency is defined as a state where the economic situation of each individual is the best it can possibly be, while, at the same time, other people are not made to suffer as a consequence. At this point, no more effective allocation of resources and goods can occur. Not only are there no more possibilities for such voluntary transactions, but also peak economic efficiency has been reached. Pareto efficiency is optimally efficient, to the point that efficiency cannot be

*Appendix* 189

increased through the redistribution of resources and commodities. Once Pareto efficiency is achieved, one person gaining further advantage will inevitably lead to others suffering.

A Pareto improvement is when there is an increase in income (or benefits) of at least one person, which does not make any other individual worse off. Any improvement that can achieve this effect is called a Pareto improvement. According to the definition of Pareto efficiency, when there is room for Pareto improvement in an economic system, it is axiomatic that the system has not achieved Pareto efficiency, in other words, it is Pareto-inefficient.

## Property rights

### *Ownership*

Ownership is a legal means that determines the right of use. The market economy is based on the concept of private property, where payment results in ownership. A variety of possible restrictions may operate, where ownership brings with it the right to use. The least restricted kind of ownership is exclusive ownership, which confers the right to use on the owner, and excludes anybody else under any conditions from using the object of ownership. In law, exclusive ownership is the precise opposite to property, which does not belong to anyone.

Ownership is an essential prerequisite to transactions. Who in their right mind would be willing to pay for a commodity with no guarantee that they can use it? Conversely, who in their right mind would want to pay for a commodity which no one can prevent them using for free? Obviously, however, certain restrictions on ownership must apply. If everyone was free to do whatever they pleased with anything they owned, this would produce great confusion.

### *The definition of property rights*

Property rights define the proper relationship between people when they use goods, and the punishment to be imposed when those relationships are infringed.

### *Non-attenuated property rights*

In economies which, in other aspects, are highly efficient (for example, there is no monopoly, no non-separable consumption and no decreasing cost curves), non-attenuated property rights can ensure Pareto efficiency. Characteristics of non-attenuated property rights are as follows:

1　They must be completely clearly defined. This forms a complete system, which includes all of the rights on the property, including restrictions on those rights, and the punishment for infringing those rights.
2　They must be exclusive. Here all the rewards and losses arising as a result of an action are given to the person who has the right to take this action, that is, the owner.

190 *Appendix*

3    They must be transferable. These rights can be absorbed into the most valuable forms of use.
4    It must be possible to implement them and implement them fully. Without the ability to implement such rights, they do not exist.

In other words, non-attenuated property rights should have four characteristics: they should be clearly defined, exclusive, transferable, implementable and fully enforceable. If property rights lack one of these characteristics (for example, they are not transferable, or their provisions are not clearly defined), then they are known as weakened property rights.

# Afterword

*Translated by Phil Hand[1]*

Deng Yingtao spent the final year of his life in hospital. During this time, Wang Xiaoqiang recorded the following interviews with Deng Yingtao. They place this book in the wider context of Deng Yingtao's lifetime of research.

Wang Xiaoqiang is the author of numerous studies on different aspects of China's political economy. He collaborated closely with Deng Yingtao over many years, including their path breaking research on China's western region. The results of their joint research were published in the two books *Rebuilding China*, and *Opening up the West.*[2]

Interview recorded and edited by Yang Ying. Titles, sections in bold and footnotes added for clarity.

## Modernization for the many

WANG XIAOQIANG: There is a question that has been going round in my head for a number of years now. I read your book in 1992, while I was at Cambridge. Peter Nolan pressed it on me in a state of great excitement. He also told me about every detail of your visit to Cambridge – how you seemed, the way you acted. He said you were like a child, and as the Confucians say, a child's heart follows the Way.[5] I read the book, and was stunned by what it said. When Peter and I discussed it, we both thought that *the questions you'd raised were not just questions for China, but issues that would affect the future of the whole human race.*

But at that time, there were not many economists who could understand your book. The Soviet Union had just collapsed, and plans for reform of the old bloc were everywhere. 'Shock therapy' was the prescription du jour. My doctoral thesis was a critique of Kornai and Sachs.[6] No-one seemed to have realized what you stated at the very start of your book: that *(1) economic reforms, (2) the selection of a development model, and (3) international systems of economy, politics and strategy are all interlinked, part of an irreducible 'three body problem'. You have to address all three together, and find an integrated solution.*[7]

Ever since then, I've been wondering where you got these ideas. Everyone was absorbed by China's move towards a market economy and by how we

192  *Afterword*

were going to join the world economy. In China we used to talk about 'overtaking the UK and catching up with America'. But there you were, insisting that there is no 'overtaking', no 'catching up'. We can't do what the West does. We can't even have the lifestyles and industries that the West has! You were a very lonely voice amid all the hype of the reforms. And in the book, you say that you started thinking about these issues as far back as the end of 1984.[8] How did you come up with this extraordinary analysis?

DENG YINGTAO: It was quite by chance, actually. At the beginning of the 1980s, the Party set some targets: eradicate absolute poverty by the end of the twentieth century, and fully modernize by the middle of the twenty-first century. I was thinking about this at the time, looking at some of the literature, and I found some things that didn't seem quite right. At the time, China was only just achieving subsistence. Our economy was very small – in 1980, China's per capita consumption of energy was just 0.6 tons of coal equivalent per year [about 17.5 gigajoules]. So doubling or quadrupling the size of the economy wouldn't be a problem. But modernization? When I looked at the developed nations – the USA, UK, France, Germany, Japan – even if you added them all together, their total population was still less than China's. They represented 10–20 per cent of the world, but they were consuming 60–70 per cent of the world's energy.[9] So I thought, if we develop to a level comparable with these countries, given China's huge population... I did the calculations, and the numbers were enormous! World energy consumption would more than double. At the time, US energy consumption was 11 tons of coal equivalent (tce) per capital. In Japan, Germany and France it was nearly 6 tce, and Italy was more than 4 tce. If we take Japan as our reference (because Japan is the most efficient energy user of all the developed countries – its energy is shipped in, and the population is highly concentrated in the flat part of the country, so there's little wasted on overland transportation), it is absolutely inconceivable that we could reach that level.[10] So in 2010, when President Obama was in Australia, he said this:

> ... if over a billion Chinese citizens have the same living patterns as Australians and Americans do right now then all of us are in for a very miserable time, the planet just can't sustain it...[11]

And it is not just China. There's India, Brazil, Vietnam and the other Southeast Asian nations, African nations like Egypt... The world population is now seven billion people, and by the middle of this century, it will be ten billion. Everyone wants to modernize, so if we assume consumption of 5 tons of coal equivalent per person per year, that's 50 billion tons. That number's not even in the right ballpark. It is five times global energy consumption today! Thinking about these issues, it was hard to keep the relative levels clear in my mind. In that situation, the price of oil would probably hit $1,000. And then who could afford it? It wouldn't take a huge amount of resources to eliminate poverty and ensure that China has enough food and basic commodities to supply its population. But would modernization be feasible? Could China support that kind of development?

So I proposed the idea of 'dual pressures'. The first pressure is easy to understand: we are less advanced than some, and we want to modernize. The second pressure is that the world's resources are already tight. If the many, 70–80 per cent of the population, want to modernize, then energy consumption is going to quadruple, go up sixteen-fold. The planet can't bear that kind of pressure. So I started thinking then that *modernization should not be the same as westernization.* So is there another model; A model of resources, production and lifestyle, which would allow the many to modernize, not just the few? *The classic model of Western modernization is: I modernize, you don't.* We can't choose that model.

I wrote a paper in 1986 exploring how shortages of resources can place constraints economic development in the short term.[12] Then Lu Liling, from the Chinese Economic System Reform Research Institute (CESRRI), asked me to write a paper for her. I told her that there was no point in writing the same paper twice. I'd been thinking about these issues since 1985, reading up on the literature, finding out about mineral reserves and resources. I had the ideas ready, so I wrote a paper for her institute's journal,[13] and that was the seed of *A New Development Model and China's Future.*

WANG XIAOQIANG: Of course, like so many things, it seems obvious once somebody says it. In the early 1980s, oil was still one of our biggest exports,[14] so you seemed to be worrying about nothing! But 25 years have gone by, and China all of a sudden is an oil importer, more reliant on foreign oil than the USA. Before long we'll be the world's biggest consumer of oil. One American source estimates that '[d]omestic oil, for example, will provide only about one-quarter of [China's] anticipated requirement by 2030, with the rest being imported'.[15] We start doing deals overseas, but things are difficult in the Middle East, so we look to Africa ... But wherever we look for oil, trouble follows: Syria becomes unstable,[16] South Sudan secedes,[17] there's regime change in Libya.

And it is not a problem of insufficient democracy. Kuwait is an emirate; the UAE is a nation of emirates; Qatar is an emirate; Bahrain is an emirate; Jordan is a kingdom; Oman is a sultanate; Saudi Arabia is the only country in the world that is still named after its royal family! And all of these countries enjoy the protection of democratic America. They are locked together in the great Pax Americana.[18] Meanwhile, the media, apparently unaware of the painful irony, celebrates the emirs of the Arab League paying studious attention to the current wave of 'democratic' elections. And then, following an intervention by Sarkozy, 30,000 Chinese citizens have to be evacuated, and the media fawn over our government's 'decisiveness'. Put yourself in the place of these African nations: who would dare make a deal with us now? No matter how good a deal it was?[19]

Even today, very few people understand the idea of selecting a development model. But you never stopped working on research into this question.

194  *Afterword*

You looked at the use of biogas in rural China, and pig farming techniques. You tested the waters of the Yarlung-Tsangpo River. You produced *Remaking China, Strategies for the Development of the West, Notes from Surveys of Development in the West I* and *II, Remaking China, Moving Forward* and *The New Energy Revolution and Shift in Development Model.*[20]

DENG YINGTAO:  It is a very important question, but during the 1980s and 1990s there were many other pressing questions on economic reforms and rural development that needed research, too.[21] But the way I work is to keep the problems I'm interested in bubbling away at the back of my mind, and every now and then I add some more data, until eventually I have enough information and my ideas are properly mature. Then I can write something.

By 1986, I was at the Research Department of Rural Economy, part of the State Council's Development Research Council, and I got funding for a big piece of research, so over the course of '87 and '88 I wrote up five case studies. The first report, I remember, was a critique of something Song Guoqing had said: I demonstrated that we didn't owe China's farmers anything. Since the revolution, what the state had given the farmers, and what it had extracted in the form of the 'price scissors', were roughly in balance. Cui Xiaoli added up the two sides, and found that the state had taken a little over $500 bn from farmers in artificially cheap food; but had given them over $500 bn in cheap fertilizer, farm equipment and other subsidies. So there was no exploitation. The fourth case report was the one I gave you. I expanded it a bit, and it became *A New Development Model and China's Future.* It was published in September 1988.[22] In 1989, I returned to the Rural Development Institute (RDI) at the Chinese Academy of Social Sciences (CASS). I thought that some of the work I'd done was still a bit rough. There were some key ideas that needed to be researched in greater depth. But I was very busy as our liaison with other research institutions, so I didn't have the time to work through it systematically. I just kept the questions at the back of my mind, the way I always do, and gradually gathered more data and sharpened my concepts.

During this period I remember doing one survey on use of the water hyacinth to improve farming efficiency. I took a team to do work in the field, and we produced a report. Pig farming produces a lot of manure, and dealing with this manure is a big problem everywhere in the world. The report was about planting water hyacinths, and the problem is how to help the plant survive the cold winters of northern China. You can spray the pig-pens clean, and channel the run-off water to the water hyacinths, which would break down 80 per cent of the organic waste. Then you could use an azolla water fern from Germany to break down 80 per cent of the remaining organic matter, and at that point the water was virtually clear. And the water hyacinths produced enough plant matter to feed the pigs! So in 1992, the farm was put on the UNEP's Global 500 Roll of Honour.[23] This was a sustainable agricultural cycle, and it was a strengthened cycle, stronger than what you find in nature. The azolla also produces feedstock, a complete feed providing all the pigs' essential nutrients. We wrote a book on it called *The Xi'an Eco-Animal Breeding Farm*.[24]

At the time, in addition to my work at the Institute, I was thinking a lot about finding more real-world examples. Theory is not enough. If you rely on theory alone, you get problems. For example, I've talked about using biogas in Liaoning. Originally, I was going to commission a report on a biogas/greenhouse system that was called '4-in-1'. *The technology involved is practically free.* The temperatures get very low in the winter in northern China, so biogas was only available for four or five months of the year. If you set up pigsties in a green house, they provide you with sufficient biogas year round. You use the biomass to fertilize horticultural crops, and you can use the biogas for cooking. Traditionally, Chinese hobs have been very smoky, but we would go to the houses of farmers using this system, and there was no smoke at all. The kitchen stayed much cleaner. The houses would also be built with large windows to capture the sunlight, so even in the depths of winter, the temperature indoors would stay at about 15–16 degrees. That made a big difference in Liaoning. I was very interested in these example projects. I had an intuition back then, *that as these elements developed, they would support a new kind of modernization: modernization for the many, for ordinary Chinese people.*

At the beginning of 1991, CITIC Press published a series of books containing work we had done. An editor had discovered all of these reports produced by the Rural Development Institute, and asked me to edit them into shape, expand them a little. Not three months later, they were all officially published. The ideas in these reports were still new technologies back then, still laboratory-stage ideas: things like forest chemical products. Today there are whole industries using these ideas. Forests can supply almost everything humans need to live: food, clothing, shelter, transport… rayon, or artificial cotton, can be made from wood. I was in charge of research at the RDI, so I couldn't spend all my time out in the field. I just collected together reports and data of this type that we already had.

WANG XIAOQIANG: I have another question to ask you. At the end of '87-early '88, I went with Zhao Ziyang[25] and Du Runsheng[26] as they visited Guangdong, Jiangxi, Shanghai and Jiangsu. That entire trip, we were talking about flows of international trade. We were thinking about what message we could take from the Asian tiger economies that would be applicable to the 200m people living along China's coast. We never guessed that the economy of the coast would become the engine of Chinese growth, or that it would become the middle link in a supply chain, taking raw materials from overseas suppliers, processing them, then sending finished products to overseas markets. This model has meant that we've built up $3 trillion in foreign currency reserves, and that the renminbi has risen. A strengthening currency should have made our raw material imports cheaper, but the cost of energy and mineral commodities has skyrocketed beyond any reasonable level. Even with a trend that should have benefited us, we still managed to lose out, and it is hard to

196    *Afterword*

see how this can be sustained. But you foresaw all of this in this book, written in 1991. You not only foresaw it, you seemed to be writing a critique of these distant future events. The very striking image you use of the flea and the elephant makes explicit that the experience of the Asian tigers is not applicable as a development model for China.

DENG YINGTAO:  Right, China can't follow the Asian tigers model. Of course the coastal regions can import some materials, do some export processing to make some foreign currency. At the time we were desperately short of foreign exchange. But the model cannot be reproduced across the whole of China. There is no way that the whole country could modernize using this model. It can't bring modernization to the majority. But, they say, Japan has an export-oriented economy! I think the problem is one of orders of magnitude. Just as with the flea and the elephant: the flea can jump to 200 times its own height; but with the same musculature, an elephant could not even dream of jumping to half of its height. The two things are chalk and cheese. An elephant absolutely cannot jump to the same relative height as a flea. This is a way of looking at the question from side on. What it means is that all of China can't be an export-processing zone. It is an error of composition: a single example doesn't necessarily generalize. It is like in a cinema, if the seats aren't well designed. Some people can't see the screen, so they stand up, and then they can see better. But then their neighbours stand up, then their neighbours. In the end, everyone is standing, and no one can see any better than before. What succeeds in a limited area may fail when it grows to encompass the whole. That's the logic that I see as key to understanding this problem.

At the time, everyone was very excited by the prospect of growth. All the local governments were hoping for quick technical fixes that would catapult them into modernity overnight. Perhaps in reaction to that, I became rather sceptical. *I think a more interesting way to look at it is this: tigers and lions are predators, at the top of the food chain. They are the law of the jungle, feeding off the weak. Of course, the elephant is a rather peaceable herbivore, and it does no deliberate harm to any other creature. But funnily enough, none of those savage predators would ever dare attack an elephant!*

So I thought, developing a system for full modernization is a long-term project. It will take years to work out a programme for modernizing industry and lifestyles, so there's no rush. I could go on just collecting my materials bit by bit, writing my ideas as they took shape. As to whether I'd ever finish – well, the success of a universal modern economy doesn't depend on me alone. Others will carry on my work. So during this period, I was all the time gathering data, collecting case studies, bit by bit and piece by piece.

WANG XIAOQIANG:  You brought together a lot of small case studies illustrating how sustainability could be achieved on the micro level. I think this concept has existed in China for a long time. It is symbolized by the mulberry fish pond: you dig a pond and use the excess earth for a dyke where you plant mulberries; silkworms grow on the mulberry; worm droppings feed the fish; pond water is used to irrigate the trees and wash the silk cocoons...that's the kind of sustained cycle that you can get when you observe and learn from nature. The problem is that all these cases were limited in scope. You needed to link them together, and that required some larger-scale thinking. Was that why you set up research group to look at the allocation of water and land resources?

## Key technologies for water in western China

DENG YINGTAO: That was really by chance, as well. I've always just gone where I'm told, you know!

In 1997 I saw the paper Guo Kai had written about diverting water from the Yarlung-Tsangpo,[27] and I thought that this was a very worthwhile idea, whether it ever came to fruition or not. So I wrote a paper on it: 'Creating another China: the value of the Shuoma-Tianjin canal'.[28] As you can tell from the title of the paper, it was an attempt to gain more publicity for this idea, to help out Guo Kai. The Buddhist teacher Nan Huai-chin read the paper, and thought it was interesting, so he asked to see me. Wang Qishan sent me from Guangdong to Hong Kong, and I stayed with Master Nan for a few days. He agreed to pay for a survey to look more deeply into the idea. I invited Guo Kai to come to my home and talk about how we should organize this survey. When someone is paying for work to be done, you have to produce tangible results for them, right? So we had to write up a research proposal, a survey action plan, set milestones, etc., etc. But Guo Kai didn't want to get involved in all that work, so he withdrew.

Luckily, Li Danlin got me an introduction to Qian Zhengying and Wang Shucheng. Qian is one of China's leading hydrologists, and Wang later became Minister of Water Resources. If this project were to go ahead, the Ministry of Water Resources would of course be taking the lead. But as it turned out, despite a number of very friendly meetings, neither of them was at all interested in the project. It was all very awkward. Finally, both Wang Qishan and Nan Huai-chin said to me, in separate meetings,'This is hugely important for China's future. You take the lead!' After all this back and forth, somewhat against my better judgement, I decided I would just have to go ahead and do it myself, so it got started in earnest at the end of 1998.[29]

To begin with, I didn't make a direct link between water diversion and my ideas about new development models. I was thinking about it from a resources perspective. I used to say: China is a paralysed giant. Sociologists say this is a mystery, but I don't think there's anything mysterious about it. It is just common sense. Draw a line marking off the areas that receive 400 mm or more of rainfall a year, from north to south. Start at the Ejin River in Heilongjiang, and draw a diagonal down to Tengchong in Yunnan. In terms of area that line cuts the country almost exactly in half, but 90 per cent of the population and the productivity is in the east, while most of the water and mineral resources are in the west. *We're a big country, resource poor, and we're like a stroke victim, paralysed down one side.*

198  *Afterword*

We've got nearly 10 million square kilometres of land, but you still hear people saying that we don't have enough land for all our people. You know why that is? Qian Zhengying said it: 90 per cent of the population and productivity is squeezed into a floodplain of just one million square kilometres. And we use huge amounts of manpower on maintaining dykes and dealing with flooding. Out in the northwest, Xinjiang covers 1.66 million square kilometres, equal to all fourteen coastal provinces put together. And it is not as high as the Tibetan plateau. Most of Xinjiang is inhabitable: it is flat, has reasonable elevation, temperatures, sunlight, minerals, oil and gas... there's everything you could ask for. They actually had to develop techniques to stop excess sugar building up in their cotton plants! These big northwestern plains are boundless, and they have everything – except water.

The one thing about China that's not big is our water resources. But is the problem that there isn't actually enough water? China's water resources are mostly in the southwest. In almost all developed nations, you see 90 per cent usage of water resources. In China, it is always been about 10 per cent. The Yarlung-Tsangpo, the Nu,[30] the Lancang[31] – all of these major international rivers flow through China, carrying 600 billion cubic metres of fresh water per year, and we use none of it. *It is like ten Yellow Rivers going entirely to waste.*

China basically slopes downwards from south to north and from west to east. The Tibetan plateau, in the southwest of the country, is the roof of the world, so they say. Water flows downwards, and that's why water transfers from the west of China seem so attractive. But the terrain prevents most of the water on the Tibetan plateau from flowing north. There are the rising folds of the Himalayas, the geologically changeable Hengduan mountains, and the Bayan Har mountains right in the middle of China, so only the Yellow River actually flows northward, and almost nothing flows to the dry northwest. The rest of the water goes either east or south. Back in Mao Zedong's time, when he passed through the upper reaches of the Yangtze and the Yellow River on the Long March, he saw how hard life in those areas was. He talked then about bringing water from the south up to the dry north. But it is easier said than done. There are mountain ranges in the way.

WANG XIAOQIANG:  I just wish you wouldn't say 'against your better judgement'. I know that you went first to Guo Kai, then Qian Zhengying and Wang Shucheng. But if your project had just a 1 per cent chance of waking our 'paralysed giant', then it is worth 250 per cent of our effort; *250 per cent of our heart and soul.* The problem was that when I went to the west with you, we saw how much labour, resources and time big hydrological engineering projects take there. We got into the survey, pre-feasibility and feasibility study stages, and I just kept thinking: it doesn't matter what we see. It might look feasible to us, but there are so many different specialists who have to come and take their various technical measurements – hydrologists, geologists, engineers – all of this work has to be done before we can really know if the project will be possible or not. If those engineers wouldn't come, then

*Afterword* 199

it wouldn't matter how well we put our case. We couldn't do without their expertise. You said to us a few times, in all seriousness, 'We have to understand the key technical issues ourselves!' I know you were thinking of the story of Mao Zedong learning geology so he could discuss the foundations of a dam on the Three Gorges with Lin Yishan.[32] But with Mao, that was a decision-maker making sure that he could follow the debates of his advisers. For you, learning these subjects was pointless. Even if you really did understand them, you still wouldn't have any authority.

DENG YINGTAO: *I'm sure that as long as a few developed countries continue to dominate the world's oil resources, as long as there is no change in the global power structures, the Chinese people will have to undertake major hydrological engineering projects in western China if they want to modernize.* Back when we were sent out to the farms to work on in the production teams, there were no artificial divisions between economists, political scientists, historians…. If you wanted to know something, you learned it. You didn't have to have gone to a hydrology university and learned every detail of hydrological engineering. *When decisions had to be made, the decision-makers understood the key technologies, and then applied common sense. That was enough.*

Of course, with a massive enterprise like this, you have to be professional about it. Speaking of which, I should thank Xu Xinyi, who liaised with all the local hydrology departments for us. He was an old friend of Cui Heming, and he went above and beyond the call of duty. He was head of the water diversion bureau in the Ministry of Water Resources, so he had to respect his organization. But he wasn't at all intimidated by Guo Kai's attitude, and for years he helped us contact local engineers, arranged meetings, supported our research, and spent a long time discussing the project with us. Everywhere we went, we'd sit with the local hydrology department, and get the locals to take us to see rivers, reservoirs, channels, planned dykes, run off points, etc. They would explain the local conditions to us onsite, so that the features we'd seen in books and maps came alive right there in front of us.

I should also thank Lin Yishan. He was injured fighting against the Japanese, and after the Liberation he served as head of the Yangtze River Committee for life. The Jingjiang Dam, the Danjiangkou Reservoir, the Gezhouba Dam, the preparation for the Three Gorges Dam – all of Lin Yishan's projects were successes. Not a single one of his major technical decisions was ever shown to be wrong.[33] Mao Zedong called him the 'king of the Yangtze'. Me, I say he's the successor to Yu the Great.[34] Lin had been blind for many years by that time, but he had visited every major stream and channel in the region, and he had the entire Yangtze mapped out in his mind. *He saw a river as a living thing*, and wanted to make full use of all of its resources.[35] Over the course of seven years, I met more than 50 times with Lin. As he saw it, *water diversion in the west of China was a mission handed to him by Mao himself. He had devoted several years to researching and promoting the idea, and he believed it was completely feasible.*[36] I was doing

200   *Afterword*

everything I could to learn the subject, reading hydrology books, getting advice from experts like Chen Chuanyou of the Academy of Sciences, looking back over historical water engineering projects....

WANG XIAOQIANG:  After working on this for more than a decade, with your natural intelligence and the applied and theoretical expertise you'd picked up, you were way ahead of all the hydrology 'PhDon'ts' that we met. You published *Lin Yishan on Water Controls and Developing the Country*. And you also managed to edit Lin's last important publication, *Diagnosis of River Conditions and Flood Control for River Plains*. That was a long process of dictation and reading, editing, re-editing, getting referees.... The Yangtze Hydrology Committee even organized an expert conference to finalize the text. Finally, a month before he passed away at the age of 96, you were able to place a fully printed and illustrated copy in Lin's hands, complete with your two theoretical appendices containing the maths and diagramming techniques that the book relies on.[37] It was an extraordinary collaboration between two scholars with 40 years between you. It reminded me of Ch'ien Mu.[38] It was historic. But could you tell us the main conclusions in less technical language, without the equations? What are the key technical problems in diverting water in western China, and why are they solvable?

DENG YINGTAO:  There are three main conclusions.

*One is the use of very cheap wind power to lift water.* A lot of hydrologists are very dubious that Guo Kai's idea of a channel running right from Shuoma to Tianjin can be achieved. To bring 200 billion cubic metres of water from the Yarlung-Tsangpo to the north, you have to build a channel that runs downhill nearly the whole distance. Before you can even think about constructing the channel, you have to work out how to get the water high enough. There's a contradiction here, because the higher you follow the Yarlung-Tsangpo, the less water it has in it. Guo Kai's solution was to build a high dam where the flow rate is high enough. But that massively increases the difficulty of the project.

So raising the water is the key to making the whole thing easier. But where do we get the energy to do that? Obviously we can't use hydroelectric – it takes more power to raise water than you can extract from it as it flows downwards. Otherwise it would flow upwards itself! And it would definitely be uneconomic to haul any other energy source up into those remote mountains, especially if you count the cost of getting people to work up there. You couldn't get out more than you put in. This problem stymied me for many years, right up until 2007. I'd been criss-crossing the west for many years by then, but one day I saw something that made me jump up in excitement. It was a breakthrough in wind generation. I quickly tracked down all the information I could, read up on it to confirm what it was. This new technology transformed the way I was thinking about this water transfer project: we could use wind power to raise the water!

China has highly developed wind generation technologies, but they haven't been exploited on an industrial scale yet. Particularly vertical-axis wind turbines: they offer 360 degree generation, i.e. they can use wind from any direction, which increases their efficiency by five times! And because the stresses are different, come from a different direction, the mechanical demands on the structure are not the same at all. They're much cheaper to construct. Using the older technology, wind generation equipment cost RMB 10,000 per kilowatt. Thermal power stations typically cost RMB 4–5,000 per kilowatt, so wind is about twice the price. With vertical-axis wind turbines, the cost of a turbine comes down by half, so it is about the same as thermal power. If wind power is used to raise the water, designing a pump that works well with the type of electricity generated by wind turbines could cut the cost by another half. So we're talking a quarter to a fifth of the original cost. And if we take out the cost of connecting to the national power grid, the transmission cables and the human resources costs, then it looks a lot cheaper still. *There is a lot of wind on the Hengduan mountains.* On one square kilometre of land, you can put about five 2,500 kilowatt vertical-axis wind turbines. Chinese wind turbines never used to last more than 2,400 hours, but today they can operate continuously for nearly 4,000 hours. And what's the load variation? This is an astounding Chinese technology. It is unique in the world – foreign turbines can only produce a few dozen kilowatts.

*This idea of using wind power to raise the water is truly amazing. It is turning water into wine.* Wind power is known as 'garbage power' because there's so much variability. Loads can go from 20 per cent to 250 per cent. No transmission network can cope with that – they need constant loads. Just recently the Inner Mongolia power grid was paralysed because of wind power. It is too unreliable. So in any major network, wind power cannot make up more than 12 per cent of your supply. But if you're using it to raise water, there's no problem. The turbines don't have to be linked to the national grid. They can be placed wherever we need the power. Installing a few extra water pumps wouldn't matter. Imagine one turbine produces 1 kilowatt, starts to operate at just 0.2 kilowatts of power, and keeps operating right up to 2.5 kilowatts. When we have a 20 per cent load, one pump starts. When the wind is strong, we get more power, and another pump switches on. We don't have to switch the power in or out, we don't have any transmission losses. We can use virtually 100 per cent of the power produced immediately. It would be unprecedented use of this natural resource. When the wind is strong, we would get more power, and raise more water; when the wind is weak, we would get less power, and pump less water. All over the Hengduan mountains, there are valleys which channel strong winds. The resource is plentiful, so we can generate sufficient lift. That means we can extract the water from the Yarlung-Tsangpo down at an altitude of 2,000 metres. We don't have to worry about whether there's sufficient volume any more. We can place our wind turbines and raise water wherever the easiest route takes us. Once you get over the watershed, the water can flow as normal. And when it is flowing, we can extract hydroelectricity from it. Then wherever the water comes to a suitable piece of ground, we can build a reservoir, and provide a

## 202 *Afterword*

reliable water supply for a community that lives and works there. The most straightforward would be Chen Chuanyou's scheme based on two lakes: raise the water with wind power to Ngoring Lake and Gyaring Lake, then let the water flow naturally down. Now that would be something![39] If we use wind power for a water diversion project, build gigawatts of capacity of vertical-axis turbines, manufacture them on an industrial scale, then place them wherever they're needed without worrying about grid connections or transmission or transformers - then the cost of the electricity could come down to just a few RMB cents.

If we can use this incredibly cheap electricity to raise water, then build reservoirs wherever we find the right type of land along the course of the river, we'll be turning 'garbage electricity' into usable hydropower. It would be the equivalent of pumped storage. This is a key benefit. And wind turbine technology keeps on advancing. There are many more possible ideas. One suggestion is using blimps with multiple turbines attached to them. Another thing that is being tried is stringing up a network of high voltage cables between two mountains, and installing a series of fan turbines on them. And there are experiments using kites and balloons to hold up cables with lines of turbines attached to them. When you get up several kilometres off the ground, the wind never stops. It is dozens, even a hundred times more powerful than it is at ground level. *There's more capacity to develop in wind power than we can possibly imagine.* It is orders of magnitude more than we are thinking. Thinking about it, in the future, wind power could be linked directly with energy-intensive industries. They wouldn't connect to the grid at all, they'd just have their own local grids. If they can resolve the issue of syncing variable supply and variable demand, then energy-intensive industries like aluminium smelting could cluster in western China, wherever there is abundant wind and good roads.[40]

*The second main conclusion concerns long tunnels and aqueducts.* There isn't much to say about this – the technology is developing very fast. Japanese tunnel boring machines can dig tunnels with diameters of 16–17 metres. There are Chinese machines that can do 13 metre tunnels. They make big, roomy tunnels, which are certainly good enough as water channels. With this elevated water and the ability to dig long tunnels, we can follow the geography of the mountains. We can dig tunnels where appropriate, or lift the water over saddles in the mountains. Because we'll have this ability to supply cheap electricity, we can skirt around any areas where the geology makes digging tunnels difficult. Aqueducts allow us to run a channel from mountain to mountain. We don't have to follow a flat line around the contours of the land. That makes for a long channel, hard to maintain. We can just bridge the low points along the way instead. In all the construction of motorways and railways over the last few years, these two types of engineering have progressed in leaps and bounds. A lot of long new tunnels and new bridges are now carrying traffic. And tunnels and bridges can both be made earthquake proof up to a certain level. Without these new engineering possibilities, water diversion would be much more difficult. But today we have these capacities, and they are tried and tested. We can be confident.

So if you put together these two technical advances, then you get the third conclusion: *a distributed project approach. What we call the 'western channel' should be renamed just the 'western water transfer project'.* Guo Kai proposed a single channel running right from Shuoma in Tibet down to Tianjin, of which 70–80 per cent would have to be dug as new canal. It would carry 200 billion cubic metres of water, the equivalent of three or four Yellow Rivers. Conceived as a single project, winding through thousands of kilometres of mountains, it is hard to imagine with our current technology. Long canals are vulnerable to geological conditions: instability and geological faults make construction difficult. Moreover, the channel would have to traverse many existing waterways joining the flow, then branching off again towards the next river. This would make maintenance excessively hazardous. But if we could make use of cheap wind energy to raise water, and build long tunnels and aqueducts where necessary, then we could turn the whole project into a network of many smaller projects. We could place wind turbines wherever the wind is strongest, build reservoirs wherever the geology allows. We don't have to build one mega-dam holding trillions of cubic metres, have one single channel bringing all the water to the north. That kind of talk is rather terrifying, I understand. Instead, we can break it up into many much smaller reservoirs and shorter channels, linking up phase by phase and step by step. Big dams where the natural conditions allow them; small dams where they don't. Long canals where we can; shorter ones where necessary. They can connect together, or even run in parallel between rivers, so that *there can be multiple channels into and out of existing watercourses.* With a water network like this, if there is a problem on one part of the watercourse, it won't destroy the whole project or cause a major disaster.

So the reason that I've named these technologies – wind power and the engineering of tunnels and aqueducts – as key conclusions is this: they allow us to break up a forbidding mega-project into a series of small projects, which are quite feasible with our existing technical resources. Suddenly, the project seems much easier; the danger of accidents is much reduced; and construction can go ahead much more quickly. A distributed, multi-channel system of water pumps and channels using wind power and generating hydroelectric power. Each section could generate returns alone. We wouldn't have to wait for the water to reach Tianjin. *The project would start to generate returns during construction.* One of the reasons we were pressing so hard to get started on the western channel project is that there is a lot of preparatory work to be done in the very remote, uninhabited areas. A lot of basic hydrological data gathering has yet to be done. So we were very impatient. Even if the government decides to do it and the Ministry of Water Resources starts work, even if we move to writing geological investigations, the pre-feasibility studies…. As with the Three Gorges, there would have to be a period of research. It would be 20 to 30 years before we started the actual

## 204 *Afterword*

construction. It now looks as though China's high-speed economic growth may not be sustainable. When China has 1.6 or 1.7 billion people, is the growing young workforce from Xinjiang going to spill down into Guangdong? To find work? To get into brawls?[41] We have the key technology now, with these wind turbines to power water pumps. We're ready to go!

And there's another benefit: *it could reduce international frictions.* With the Guo Kai scheme, if we proposed a high dam or a large reservoir, the countries downriver would certainly get in a state about it, and no doubt the Americans would stick their oar in, in the name of 'fairness'. But our way, it wouldn't be one single effort. It would be a lot of separate projects or small or moderate size. Of course, when I say small I mean in comparison to the Guo Kai 'Shuoma-Tianjin channel'. In reality, all of these would be sizeable projects. But they would all be similar to the 'mini-western channel' that is happening already.[42] They may link up; they may cross over; they may run parallel. But who could protest about more mini projects the same as is already happening? We divert from the Yalong River, from the Tongtian, from the Jinsha, from the Lancang, from the Ang, from the Nag, from the Yu and the Wei, from the Parlung Tsangpo, the Nyang, the Lhasa River and the Nyangchu... these aren't international rivers, are they? Even if we do end up taking water from the Yarlung-Tsangpo, we wouldn't need to put a mega-dam across it. We could break the whole enterprise up into small projects wherever we find the right hydrological and wind conditions. We wouldn't necessarily even have to build a dam at all to channel water off. We could just build a channel and pump water along it. What could other countries do about that?

At the end of the day, with these three technical capacities – wind, tunnels, aqueducts – the whole water diversion project becomes much more manageable. I summed it all up in a few phrases: *Gao shui bei diao* (divert high-altitude water to the north), *di shui dong diao* (divert low-altitude water to the east), *feng shui hu ji* (integrated use of wind and water), *ti yin bing zhong* (use of both pumping and channelling), *dong xi dui jin* (starting from the east and the west), *diao bu jian chou* (both diversion and replacement). The idea of diverting water to the east to replace lost water comes from Deng Deren. I think it is very important. If significant amounts of water are diverted from the Yangtze, that will affect the lower reaches. That would spark serious opposition within China. The lower reaches of the Yangtze are the heart of China's economy. They are too important to risk. In the Three Parallel Rivers area on the border of Yunnan, you have three major rivers flowing just 70 kilometres apart, and the land sloping down north–south. We went to Bingzhongluo on the Nu River, and to Deqin, where the Lancang and the Jinsha flow. Deng Deren has been surveying that area for years, and his conclusion is that lower altitude rivers from Tibet can be diverted into the Yangtze system, to replace water diverted out of Yangtze tributaries higher up.[43] 'Starting from the east and the west' means that even if we can't work

*Afterword*   205

simultaneously on all parts of the project, because of the difficult terrain, we can at least start at both the eastern and western ends. All in all, this redistribution of water resources will be rather scattered. Five or six hundred billion cubic metres diverted in total, one or two hundred billion cubic metres to the north, it'll take decades, and that's pushing it!

WANG XIAOQIANG:   This combination of wind power and hydrology is the keystone, I think. With that, everything else falls into place. Wind is *feng* and water is *shui* – it seems the feng shui is right for this project! Smart technology gives us the tools we need. *And the distributed approach would allow us to tackle the easier sections first, build up experience, and leave the more difficult engineering challenges until later.* With a rolling process of surveying, design and construction, we could develop expertise as we go, and at the same time the project will act as a catalyst for Chinese industry: road building, transport, support services, heavy machinery...

I remember when we first started talking about water diversion; the investment required was a major stumbling point. But China is a lot richer now. We have money. When the US financial crisis hit, China found four trillion RMB to inject as a stimulus. With one trillion, we could complete the diversion, stimulate Chinese industry and build an engineering monument that will last for generations.

DENG YINGTAO:   Yes. The irrigation system at Dujiangyan was a rolling project, too. There was no complete plan before the work started. But Li Bing and his son built a system that has watered the Chengdu plain for 2,000 years, dozens of generations. And the area irrigated by that water has been expanded in modern times. At the Liberation it was two million *mu*, but now it is 13 or 14 million, and it could grow further to 20 million *mu*. This scale of irrigation is unique in the world. The Dujiangyan system was made possible by three innovations: the Fish Mouth Levee, the Flying Sand Weir and the Bottle-Neck Channel. The Grand Canal was also a rolling project. They started with the sections where there was greatest need, and where the construction was easiest. They gradually solved local technical issues, and then after generations of work, linked all the sections together, finally forming the continuous north–south link.

The Great Wall was the same. Back during the Warring States, the Xiongnu in the north became a threat, and each state built its own wall. An earth wall was completed during the Han Dynasty, but it wasn't until the Ming that the present continuous brick wall was finished. The resilience of the Chinese race lies in these huge projects, great walls built over thousands of years. There has never been a people who worked on a project for such a long time. Thousands of years, it is unimaginable. Dynasties rose and fell, generation after generation after generation went by, and they were still working at it. *And the entire process of construction was driven by need: wherever the problems were most urgent, they would build, then gradually extend and expand, until finally the full edifice was complete.*

206    *Afterword*

## The environment: from protecting to building

WANG XIAOQIANG:    The Yellow River carries 58 billion cubic metres of water per year. Water diversion projects bringing 100–200 billion cubic metres would be the equivalent of bringing two or three new Yellow Rivers to the north of China. That water could irrigate untold expanses of the Gobi Desert – we could flood the desert plain. All of those development cluster patterns you've researched over the years could spring up wherever the water flows. It would be a storm of new development. Just thinking about this vision, it is incredibly inspiring.

DENG YINGTAO:    This is the other important finding of our work. While researching the complex issues around water resources, water usage and population, I realized that diverting water to north China could stimulate a new type of development on a grand scale. Think of the northwest: billions of square kilometres of dry earth. It is at a perfect altitude, it has sunshine, it has a good range of temperature, it has mineral resources. It has everything you need for a revolutionary shift in development model. I've been all over the northwest, and what I saw there helped me radically refine my thinking about the selection of development models.

Some have suggested that China can really only support 600–700 million people. This is absolute rubbish. Qian Zhengying said it: 90 per cent of our population and our economic activity is squeezed into a plain of one million square kilometres. If we had enough water, and we could develop the northwest, then how much more land would China have? In 1998 I wrote my first paper with the title 'Creating another China'. The title means making another million square kilometres of usable land - it is the equivalent of making a whole new China. Then when we published the book, you were worried that people wouldn't understand, and insisted on changing it to *Remaking China*.[44] I thought about it, and of course 'remaking China' is also correct. We are not just talking about creating a new fertile plain of a million square kilometres, we are talking about creating a new mode of development. If we can resolve this problem, then we can have modernization for every one of China's billion or more people. *The key is not protecting the environment. It is creating environments. If we can create new environments, that will be a huge leap forward in human development.*

WANG XIAOQIANG:    Environmentalists are a source of a lot of the noise, which has been whipped up against river diversion projects and the development of the west. I call it noise, because a lot of people haven't really thought it through. They are just reflexively opposing the old form of development, from the old days when we couldn't even feed ourselves: the mass production of iron and steel and the cutting down of the forests, the planting of grasslands with crops that ruined their ecology. We are in favour of protecting the environment. The Tibetan antelope of Hoh Xil should be protected; and there should be no farming around the headwaters of the Yangtze. But places like the Ordos Desert and the Horqin Desert used to be verdant grasslands. The question is what do you want to protect: a desert or a rich grassland? The name of the Taklamakan Desert means 'sea of death'. Is that what you want to protect? Even if you wanted to, deserts can't be protected in their present state, because they are remorselessly advancing, driving the people out.

The real protectors of our country are Niu Yuqin and Shi Guangyin. One a widow, one an ex-con, *neither of them able to read. But they stabilized the desert across 300,000mu, planting nearly a hundred million trees.*[45] We should go and listen to them for a change! We've seen farmers on the Shiyang River in Gansu getting nothing but mud from their dried up wells, and having to use it to cook. We've seen row after row of abandoned houses, whole villages of them. *If we don't divert more water to the north, the population and economy of the northwest cannot be sustained.*[46] Simple passive protection is not enough. You can't just fence off the 'environment' and stop people from going there. You have to give people a livelihood. People want to make money. They want to modernize. *The environment today is not getting better, it is deteriorating. Stasis is not an option. Either the desertification gets worse, or we take action to reverse it.* And the first priority is to get that clear in our heads. We want to move forwards, not backwards.

DENG YINGTAO: Our idea of 'building up the environment' is planting – planting grass, planting trees. We don't use slow-growing species that churn the soil up. *We pick species that bring fast ecological benefits and economic returns, so we can develop biomass energy as well.*

For a long time now, I've been thinking around two particular topics: one is the right distribution of water resources; the other is the distribution of energy. Redistributing water resources requires enormous investment and mobilization of labour, but the infrastructure created is permanent. Dujiangyan, the Lingqu Canal, the Grand Canal… many of these ancient waterworks are still in use today, and are still being expanded and improved. And the massive water engineering projects since the Liberation have played an obvious role in the last 30 years of economic growth. But it is not enough simply to redistribute water resources. Even if we focus all the efforts of the nation on water, redistribution will still take us decades to complete. China is also rich in coal. We've done a lot of work on coal technologies, clean burning coal, etc. We also have exploitable reserves of oil and gas. But we do have to accept that we will be the world's biggest importer of oil. And of course these energy resources will eventually run dry. Wind is a sustainable resource, and can be used locally for water pumping. However it is too unreliable to link into the national grid. Another option is solar power. That is also sustainable. *Over the long term, solar power and hydroelectric are the most sustainable energy resources. They will be the solutions that break China's energy bottleneck and power our modernization.* Once those resources are tapped, China will be unstoppable. No one will be able to contain us.

I wanted to write something on this: 'Distributed energy grid and local urbanization'. Solar power is fairly universal. There are differences across China, but basically there is solar power everywhere. I estimate that only

208 *Afterword*

about 20 to 30 per cent of Chinese counties can modernize through the energy and chemical industries. Most counties can't, and so we've seen tens of millions of farmers flooding into the cities, which have heavy industry infrastructures. Seventy to 80 per cent of counties can't urbanize because they don't have the industrial basis. For example, a lot of petrochemical products can't easily be transported long distances overland, so the petro-chemical industry is basically concentrated along the coast. The vast majority of Chinese regions couldn't make these products; even if they did, they would be uncompetitive. So the limiting factor for urbanization in most areas is secondary industry. Agriculture isn't a problem; and of course, terti-ary industry, retail and services, is not an issue. What's missing is the infra-structure of the intermediate industries: manufacturing, energy or chemicals. Agriculture used to be highly distributed, but it is moving towards a more Western model now. It is becoming reliant on petrochemicals; uses enor-mous quantities of chemical fertilizer. Agriculture is now our biggest source of pollution, because of nitrates.

So how can most Chinese regions resolve this need for an industrial infra-structure? By planting their own energy resources in the form of quick-grow-ing grasses. In round numbers, when you plant crops, a single person's output over the course of a year is about 400–500 kilograms, or 0.4–0.5 tons. A modern economy involves the consumption of at least 4–5 tons of coal equiv-alent per person per year. If you look at it in terms of monetary value, the difference is even bigger. Grain costs about RMB 2,000 per ton; oil is about RMB 5,000 per ton. But if you plant grasses, plant energy, then agriculture is no longer just supplying food, it is supplying energy, usable by most small towns and cities. The possibilities for the productivity of agriculture sud-denly grow by an order of magnitude, and as a result, modernization becomes possible for the majority.

Solar power technology is progressing in leaps and bounds, and China is at the forefront. In Shandong they have electric solar tiles that go on house roofs. They are extraordinarily cheap, the same as ordinary tiles, and they last for decades, even a century. They're in production now.[47] But I won't go into that here, the point is that active regeneration of the environment is the new development model. *The key technology here is capturing hydrogen energy. Methane is going to be the most fundamental energy resource in the future.* Methane can be used to generate electricity. In the form of natural gas, it can be used directly; biogas produced on farms is 60–70 per cent methane, and needs purifying before it can be used for electricity. With a catalytic reaction, liquid fuels can be synthesized from methane. They can be used for heating and cooking, and these processes can form a carbon industrial cycle that is effectively unconstrained. The chemical formula of methane is $CH_4$ - that's one carbon. Single carbon molecules can be proc-essed into vinyl chloride, and thence to PVC.[48] *Most importantly, this proc-ess can happen on any scale.* This is a wonderful quality. *Properly understood, the kind of large-scale industrial production we've seen in the past, benefiting a small minority, was really based on economies of scale.* Small-scale, distributed industry does not exist; if it does exist, it is inefficient, and it cannot survive market competition.

Once we are freed from the constraints of the scale economy, we no longer have problems of centralized monopolies. No monopoly can form. In 2010, I saw a report on a farmer who had excess biogas, so he went and got a portable biogas generator. It was just a small thing, 20 or 30 kilos, but when he attached it to his biogas tank, it was sufficient to power the lights in his house. Using methane to generate electricity is actually highly efficient. And it has another very useful quality – it is very quick to start. The electricity grid makes heavy use of hydropower and pumped storage for load balancing. It is very quick – generation can start in less than a minute. Methane is even quicker – under 20 seconds to get started. In developed nations, natural gas and hydroelectricity account for 50 per cent of the load balancing capacity. And dry grass for biomass is everywhere. With these technologies, 60–70 per cent of Chinese counties could develop green energy and bio-industries. Urbanization could happen anywhere. There will be jobs for everyone.

We used to have a housekeeper called Zhang. She never meant to stay in Beijing. She just wanted to work for a few years then go back to her hometown. The problem was that there were no jobs back home. Seventy to 80 per cent of counties in the west of China don't have any jobs to offer. If we had a distributed energy network, all counties could build their own industries, and could urbanize themselves. Back at the start of the Han Dynasty, Liu Bang gave his generals titles and land all over China, to stop any palace intrigue from gaining critical mass and turning into a plot to kill him. We have the same situation now: wherever the resources exist to build large-scale industry, the monopolists move in, and everyone is drawn in, because the industry has critical mass. In future, everyone's home town will have its own industry, and they'll be gone.

There is one very bad habit that needs changing: in China, farmers only irrigate crops. They never irrigate grassland. I looked up the figures, and we have over six billion *mu* of grassland; our forests are expanding toward the 4 billion *mu* mark; and we have just between 1–2 billion *mu* of arable land. *China is actually one of the world's great grassland nations.* Our six billion *mu* of grassland produces 300 million tons of straw a year, just 10–20 kilos per *mu*. But if we had managed grasslands – if we could manage 10 per cent of our grasslands, then we could produce 600 million tons; another 10 per cent, and we'd have a billion tons! These days a pound of straw is worth the same as a pound of grain. The whole plant is being used, which is amazing. Imagine producing a billion tons of grain! It won't happen in our lifetime – we only produce 500 million or so tons today. So there is amazing potential in these four billion or more *mu* of dry grassland in the north, if we can only manage them and increase the yield.

210   *Afterword*

Farmed grasslands will require some irrigation, and some localized changes in the species of grasses. But once these changes are in place, they will become an unimaginably rich agricultural resource. Along the Yellow River, in the western regions, China's agricultural problems would be solved. Now I need to stress at this point that when I talk about grass, I'm not just talking about pasture and silage. There are plenty of technologies that will advance animal husbandry: factory farming, compound feeds, bio-engineering.... Livestock farming will not need the whole six billion *mu* by any means. The grass will be used in the same way as Americans use all the corn they grow: as biomass to produce methane. It is the stalks that are valuable – an entirely new agricultural product, and an entirely green source of energy. *This is a revolution in agriculture.*[49] I've collected a lot of data on high-productivity grasses. Chinese elephant grass, for example, once it is mature, can produce 2 tons of biomass per *mu*. Some of the mega-grasses imported from Africa can grow to 4–5 metres, sometimes even 7 metres. In the hills of Zhejiang, these grasses can grow at a rate of 45,000 kilograms per *mu* per year. That produces 5 tons of straw, and it is rich in protein. You can feed fish with it, and cows are addicted to it! Or there's samphire, which can be irrigated with seawater. That can produce 2.5–3 tons per year of dry biomass. Or Jerusalem artichokes: they block the wind and stabilize sandy soils, and they are high producing. They contain large quantities of fructose, and can be processed into 2-methylfuran, which burns as well as petrol....[50]

WANG XIAOQIANG:  You're imagining agriculture that is not just about planting grain for food and cotton for clothing. You're not talking about meat. You're talking about actually planting grass as an energy resource.

DENG YINGTAO:  That's right. So we need to distribute our hydroelectric capacity and our electricity effectively. What's the situation with thermal electric power today? They now use ultra-supercritical steam, and they are constantly working on new ways to increase working pressure. Of course, that's helped to reduce coal consumption. But heavy industry requires high levels of clustering; and organic mineral energy sources will one day be exhausted. They're not sustainable. Using methane to generate electricity is still efficient even when you only generate a few Watts. This technology is completely free from the constraints that economies of scale impose. In summer, air-conditioning represents 30 per cent of China's total electricity demand. In the big cities like Beijing and Shanghai, peak load can be more than twice the base load. If it is 1,000 at peak, then it is 500 when there's nothing going on. With that kind of variation, you get a lot of wasted equipment. If methane generation becomes common, then every household will be able to store its own electricity. There are proposals that supermarkets should install natural gas cylinders in their basements. If you get a power cut during peak usage, the air conditioning goes, and it gets very hot inside a shop. Every person in there is a walking 200 Watt heater. It gets so you can't stay in there any more. If you have natural gas to power the air conditioning, then power cuts aren't a problem any more.

## Progress through changing the development model

WANG XIAOQIANG: Productivity is the basis for all economic relations. It is the foundation for our economic superstructure. The capitalist industrial revolution, at its base, was a revolution in the use of fossil fuels to process mineral resources. Inorganic minerals give us bricks to build houses (from earth); silicon to make computer chips (from sand). The supplies are inexhaustible, and they can be recycled. The reason for the unreasonable spike in the price of iron ore is that for years, the developed nations have been getting 80–90 per cent of their iron from recycled steel. But energy is different. Coal, oil, gas – these organic deposits have been formed by geological processes. They are distributed very unevenly around the globe, so extraction has to be concentrated in small areas. They cannot be recycled, and using them depletes our reserves. They continue to grow ever more scarce, so we have to haggle over the price of every drop. And we even mobilize our political and military resources to seize fossil fuel resources. By way of comparison, water is a sustainable resource. Dujiangyan has been in continuous use for thousands of years. Solar and wind power – they're available everywhere. You don't have to compete for them, you don't have to occupy them, and you couldn't trade them on any market, even if you did. So you can see that if we achieve a leap forward in our development model, it will bring about a historical advance in our social model: from one that requires a market and requires a fight for resources, to a society that does not need a market, and in which we do not need to compete so much.

DENG YINGTAO: I have a theory, just something that I concocted, called the 'GDP equipartition theorem'. It says that when our non-renewable energy resources have been exhausted, and we are left with solar power and water, available to everyone – in the future, this will apply to any country that has enough resources to support itself and have a little left over, perhaps China, for example, or India, though India is a little lacking, because it doesn't have the same land area that China has, and it can't retain its water resources (it has plenty of rain, but the soil doesn't hold water well, so it is at the mercy of any drought that hits it) - then the equipartition theorem says that the GDP of a country will be in proportion to its population: if a country has 20 per cent of the world's population, it will produce 20 per cent of the world's GDP. The equipartition theorem is actually a concept from quantum physics.

WANG XIAOQIANG: In *The New Energy Revolution and Shift in Development Model*, you go into detail on how new resources will move us onto a greener developmental path. It is very clear. The book offers us a montage of the 'sea of death' – the Taklamakan Desert – in 2050. The desert's oil has been exhausted; in its place are vast expanses of extremely cheap solar panels. High altitude wind generators hum hundreds of metres above the desert surface. And 400,000 square kilometres of desert have been turned into an irrigated, managed grassland. The high-yield grasses grow thick as a forest, swallowing up all the wildlife that now lives here. Irrigation works cover the

## 212  *Afterword*

area, providing a sustainable water supply.[51] Every household has solar panel roof tiles, and uses methane to provide all the electricity they need for household consumption – lighting, heating, cooling, cooking etc. Methane also powers their vehicles and other heavy machinery. Horticulture is practiced in sustainable cycles: mulberries and silkworms surround the fish ponds; pigs live in 4-in-1 greenhouses. Economic activity is distributed as evenly as the sunshine and water. The natural landscape is unpolluted, the natural economy rich and self-sufficient. There is no need for competition over resources, so human relations are much friendlier and more relaxed. It is what Laozi imagined when he wrote:

> The greatest achievement of a ruler is: the people of different countries live close enough to see each other, to hear the cock crows and barks from each other's farms; the people believe their food to be sweet, their clothing to be beautiful; they are peaceable in their habits and enjoy their work that they enjoy; but never in their lives do they engage with the people of another state.[52]

DENG YINGTAO: 'Never in their lives do they engage with the people of another state' doesn't mean that they don't communicate. It means that they aren't reliant on each other. You don't have regions that can't feed themselves without support from others. Everyone does their own thing and makes their own living. You work when the sun comes up, you relax when the sun goes down. *There's no need for any emperor any more.*

WANG XIAOQIANG:  That really is the Way! The sun warms, the rain brings moisture. Everything is in the great cycle, and can play its own role. Everyone has their own living, and no one is beholden to any ruler. Our non-renewable mineral energy resources are dwindling. They were saying we only had 50 years' worth left. They may last longer than that, but even so, one day they will run out. And nuclear energy is too dangerous for the environment. Whatever safety measures you take, there is always the possibility of a problem. And once there's a leak, the contamination lasts millennia. *And uranium is a non-renewable resource as well.*[53] As long as human economic activity is chained to these mineral resources, it is going to be unevenly distributed. There will be haves and have-nots, and when the haves consume more, that will leave less for the have-nots. It is a recipe for destructive competition. In the modern world, all of the disputes, sanctions and wars among rich countries – particularly World War I and World War II – all their 'geopolitics' and 'strategic interests' – are bound up with this uneven distribution of mineral energy resources.

But in two or three generations from now, fossil fuel resources will run out. And the majority of people in developing Asia, Africa and Latin America will be using water, wind and solar power. They will make sustainable use of resources available to them on the spot, and never need to compete or dispute with their neighbours. The international commodity markets, where every ounce of material must be haggled over, will fade into secondary importance. Wouldn't that be the kind of Great Unity that communism envisages?

DENG YINGTAO: That's what they say: 'soothe the material desires, and you can end strife in this world'.[54]

## Markets, bureaucracies, reciprocity

DENG YINGTAO: I've been thinking over this for many years. *In the broadest possible sense, the allocation and use of resources in a society can be achieved through three kinds of mechanism: markets, top-down bureaucracies and reciprocity. The structure of social organizations depends on the mix of these three mechanisms in the particular field that an organization serves.* Anthropologists talk about the 'clan system', which is a type of reciprocity mechanism. Clan means tribe, and in primitive Communism, within the tribe there was no trading, no haggling, no calculating of prices. The simplest example would be building houses in rural communities. It is still done this way today: when farmers want to build a house, they call on the village carpenter to help design it, choose the lumber, direct construction, raise the roof beams. The tiler and the day labourer play their part, and finally the paperer papers the walls. That's another skill that not everyone possesses. No one demands wages, or starts complaining because my skill is more valuable than your skill. Everyone works together, and in exchange, the farmer feeds and entertains them. But there is a condition: when the next person wants to build a house, the farmer has to help, and may not request payment, because the community didn't take any for helping with the farmer's house. That's how houses get built in the villages. It is a classic reciprocity mechanism.

Humanity's earliest approach to allocating and using resources was through reciprocity. As tribes got bigger, and as more tribes sprang up, bureaucratic mechanisms emerged, with systems of seniority and authority. We call these systems 'bureaucratic', which has rather negative connotations, but we can also call them hierarchies or rank systems. The earliest systems were leadership by acclaim. Tribal chiefs were chiefs because they were accepted by the tribe. If they did not perform, they would be replaced, so there were real constraints on them.

Reciprocity started as a clan-internal mechanism. It then extended into inter-tribe relations with the exchange of gifts. Your tribe hasn't got this resource, so we give you a bit; we lack that resource, so you give us a bit. Gradually, this turned into a market mechanism for trading. *Strictly speaking, every system in every society is a mix of these three different mechanisms. They vary only in the proportions in which they are present.* In the earliest societies, reciprocity played a relatively large role in their systems for allocating and using resources. For example, when hunting, you can't have someone who's just wasting time on the sidelines. Even if you say, that

214  *Afterword*

person only gets the bones anyway, it still doesn't work. When you hunt, everyone has to be fully engaged, has to try their hardest, otherwise the prey is going to escape. As time goes by, the tribe grows, and it develops its own processes. It has its own code, its systems. Some people do this; some do that. If every little question has to be discussed, then they never get anything done, so someone has to assign tasks, as the head of a production team does in Chinese villages. The leader is trusted by everyone, and is highly constrained. A tribal chief can't just do whatever they want.

There are also three principles of social interaction that correspond to these three mechanisms of resource organization.

*Reciprocal systems are governed by the golden rule.* The golden rule is golden because it is not easy to put into real practice. In terms of game theory, it represents a highly unusual equilibrium. It is the situation where a company and its staff identify completely with each other – it is the equivalent of a group of friends, who make no distinction between each other, who feel a sense of ownership, so the interests of the company are precisely their own interests.[55] Obviously, this only happens when you have very close relationships among the people in the group. And there must be a low turnover of new people. A reciprocal arrangement demands memory: today you help me, so next time I will help you. It has an ongoing temporal dimension. It is not like the market, where you can find hourly labour, based purely on how much money you have. The relationship there is bounded: at the end of the day you settle up, and both employer and worker go their separate ways, without any further obligations.

WANG XIAOQIANG:  So reciprocity is the same as mutual obligations, so it develops into relationships that have a moral element and that constrain our actions.

DENG YINGTAO:  Right. Why were reciprocity mechanisms initially called clan mechanisms? Within the tribe, you grew up together; you knew each others' backgrounds. No one could escape: everyone knows what everyone else has done, good deeds and bad, going back for years or even generations. *There is actually often a kind of guilt by association, which can be very serious.* If you don't pull your weight, then it is not just the men who hunt with you that will shut you out; your wife will be socially shunned as well, and no one will play with your children. The children are dishonoured because of the crimes of their father. On the other hand, acts of valour or great worth by the children bring honour to their parents and grandparents.[56] Thus reciprocal arrangements have reward and penalty mechanisms, and *these mechanisms are maximized both vertically (in time) and laterally (by association with relatives).* So the Golden Rule maximizes the efficiency of the group.

WANG XIAOQIANG:  We worked in production teams in very poor, very remote areas. We've seen these reciprocal mechanisms at first hand. Like in the TV show, *This Chinese Land*, there are always one or two people that no one wants to mix with. You ask why, and it's all – oh, a time ago they did this or that, maybe even their grandfather did this or that. Most of the time, unless it is something that is fairly specific to one family, the whole community pitches in for jobs that require time and labour: digging furnaces, building houses, weddings, funerals, looking after widows and orphans, harvesting.... If someone calls, everyone comes together to help each other.

DENG YINGTAO: There's a book called *X-efficiency*, which looks at a lot of companies in different countries around the world, and how they use their assets, their market monopoly position, their pay structures, and so on. For each of these elements, it works out how productive they are. But at the end of all the calculations, there is a still a lot of efficiency that can't be explained, and so the author calls it 'x-efficiency'.[57] This is just like the current research that has found that the matter and energy that we can see only makes up 20 per cent of all the matter in the world. The rest is dark matter and dark energy. There's been an experiment in China, under the Yalong Dam, where no external radiation can enter.

WANG XIAOQIANG: Some of the concepts in Chinese medicine are the same: meridians, acupuncture points, *qi*.... Just as concepts commonly used in Chinese medicine cannot be explained by Western medicine, 'x-efficiency' can be found in companies everywhere. Companies may be the same in terms of products, size and level of technology, but some pursue profit margins, some market share, others brand name, still others employee care. In economics, we abstract away from all of these differences through the unitary concepts of 'rational economic actors' and 'suppliers'.

DENG YINGTAO: And so this 'x-efficiency', which can't be explained by economists, is everywhere. The logic of the markets is to *allocate* resources to where they are most efficiently used. But when you're talking about efficiency, when you're talking about the differences between the internal *processes* of different organizations, the theories of economists don't explain it. The idea that people do more for more money only holds in situations where the calculation is simple: where wages are paid by piecework, or where you have timed shifts. But the incentives and constraints that exist within a human organization cannot be as simple as a transaction in a shop with a shopkeeper who you don't know, and do not need to know. And even there, we still have to think about the value of service with a smile. So 'x-efficiency' can also be called 'non-allocative efficiency'.[58]

Actually, Japanese companies have gone a long way towards maximizing both allocative efficiency and operational efficiency with their tight collective spirit, lifetime employment, seniority systems, on the job training, employee housing, etc. They form durable reciprocity relationships between company and employee and between employees: tangible benefits create emotional ties, and emotional ties produce tangible results, in part because the relationships help to impose a form of regulation and discipline. Today, it is widely recognized, particularly by large companies, that market and bureaucratic mechanisms such as stock ownership, wages, bonuses and career opportunities are not enough. They also expend significant amounts of time and resources building a sense of belonging and identification among

216    *Afterword*

their staff, through leisure activities and team-building activities. They are trying to create reciprocity relationships, including mechanisms for incentives and penalties, in order to achieve maximum operational efficiency.[59]

*The obvious limitation of reciprocity mechanisms is that they do not work for large groups, and the group membership must be relatively stable.* When a tribe or a team grows beyond a certain size, or if the turnover of membership increases above a certain level, people don't know each other well enough. You spend the time to forge bonds with new members and before you know it, they've moved on. Under these circumstances, the likelihood of free riders grows significantly. As the group grows larger and larger, you get less direct contact between members, and reciprocal support happens less and less often. The number of people in the group that you know well decreases – relatively speaking. The Golden Rule gets corroded to a silver rule, and before long it is a tin pot rule. So scale and stability form the two main natural constraints on reciprocity.

WANG XIAOQIANG: But then the Industrial Revolution brought large-scale, mechanized production, with its powerful economies of scale. Market mechanisms do not require any memory at all, and even encourage churn. They are the diametric opposite of the organizations that encourage traditional reciprocity mechanisms.

DENG YINGTAO: That's exactly right. As soon as we get into economies of scale, bureaucracies spring up. *Bureaucratic mechanisms have an obvious benefit in that they can function in enormous organizations.* In sociology there's a one-to-eight rule: one person can effectively manage eight other people. Any more than that and you are stretched too thin. Of course, this is not universally applicable, it is just a rule of thumb. If you do a simple calculation, one person can manage 8–10 people, and each of those ten can manage another ten, so on and so forth down to the fifth layer, then your organization can be as large as 10,000 people. If you have six layers, you can have 100,000 people; seven layers, a million. So bureaucratic organizations can be very large indeed.

Of course, they lack the very strong incentives and monitoring that reciprocity mechanisms create. There aren't the same horizontal and vertical pressures (association and time), or the glue of everyone knowing each other. So efficiency is naturally rather lower. There has been a lot of criticism of the problems with bureaucratic mechanisms, particularly since the emergence of IT-driven 'flat organizations'. Information does not flow easily between layers, and you get information asymmetries up and down the organization. That has a very negative effect on efficiency. But bureaucracy does allow you to impose order on a very large group of people, and *that's what large scale mechanized industry needs. That's how you achieve economies of scale.* That's not all: churches, political parties, governments, militaries, even the UN – all large organizations are classic bureaucracies.

*During the process of expansion, vertical mobility (promotion) is the incentive for growth within bureaucracy.* This feature helped to make bureaucracies more competitive, particularly during the era of mass production, where scale was the deciding factor in an organization's success or otherwise. When a company grows from 8–10 people up to 100, 1,000 or even 10,000 people, those initial 8–10 people climb higher up the ranks. It doesn't matter whether the expansion is through hiring or by merging with other companies. Thought of in the abstract, this kind of vertical movement is just the same as direct sales, missionaries spreading a religion, building a political party or expanding an army. Though the restrictions on vertical mobility within the organization may be strict, if the external conditions permit expansion, a priest (or commissar or captain) can achieve promotion through the ranks to bishop (local secretary, lieutenant) or archbishop (party secretary, major).

Of course, headcount is not the only factor in an organizational expansion. Market share, assets, industry rankings are also factors. A department head 30 years ago might have had control over assets worth tens of thousands of renminbi; today, it would be hundreds of millions. There is no comparison in terms of the quantities of assets. Similarly, back in the 1950s, Liu Qingshan and Zhang Zishan were executed for embezzling a few thousand renminbi.

But the very features that make bureaucracies successful are also their Achilles heel. Bureaucratic mechanisms promote growth in an organization, but when the growth stops, the limited prospects for promotion are no longer a sufficient incentive to members, and *the Peter Principle* starts to bite: in a sclerotic bureaucracy, *every person rises to their level of incompetence.*[60] In other words, when the cost of real work and expanding the organization becomes higher than the cost of being a yes-man to the boss upstairs, the organization will become all about politics and covering your ass. For companies, as long as there is market competition, covering your ass will not be enough. The company will fail, and that's the end of you. For militaries, if they are tested in battle, then covering your ass will fail: you lose in battle, and that's the end of your army. Political parties also face competition, and can be defeated. So the Peter Principle is often seen most clearly in the civil service, where there is little chance of losing your job or benefits. Government agencies just have to follow their rules, make sure they dot the Is and cross the Ts. That's why they are so renowned as breeding grounds for petty obstructionism – the kind of bureaucracy that gives bureaucracy a bad name. There used to be a joke that being a bureaucrat is the easiest job in the world. You just need to be able to say two things: 'yes, boss' and 'right, boss'. Once you get to this point, you find that the chain of command above you is nothing but dead weight. There's virtually no one left who's really competent at their job.

WANG XIAOQIANG: Haha! I've experienced that. When I was at the CESRRI, Chen kept asking me, how come you never come to internal committee meetings? I told him that the good folks were putting 120 per cent of their efforts into building our political consciousness in committee. Even though I only had to expend 10 per cent on actual research, a measly 90 per cent of me could never compare with their organizational fervour, so I'd better leave

218  *Afterword*

it to them. That way I even managed to free up more time to do, you know, my job!

DENG YINGTAO:  Lin Yishan said to me that he had worked with the Ministry of Water Resources for decades before the revolution, and you could divide the bureaucrats into three groups: a third of them did good work, a third of them did no work, and the last third undid all the good work. They didn't actually go around smashing public works with hammers or blowing them up, they just wasted their time on schmoozing, sophistry and trying to climb the greasy pole. Anyway, the result was that two-thirds of the people in the ministry didn't get anything done. Lin told me a story as an example. He said there was a meeting at the ministry, and one of the people there represented the Yangtze Planning Office. The minister made a few comments, and then this engineer stood up and said, that's not right, there's a serious problem with that idea. After the meeting, the minister took Lin aside and made a joke of it: those engineers are a bit presumptuous, aren't they! Some guy from a technical department contradicting the minister in public! Lin just smiled and left. He thought that actually, the minister had got off lightly. This was a rather cheeky thing to think by the standards of bureaucratic life. As I understand it, the reason was that Lin saw exactly what this meant for the ministry. When a 'guy from a technical department' points out a technical problem, and the minister can't see past his own rank and ego to engage with the issue on a technical level, then you know what the result will be.

This is why Mao Zedong disliked bureaucracies so much. The Peter Principle is a terrible thing. Ideas come from those at the bottom of the heap, but the more ability someone has, the sooner they get pushed out of the organization. Pretty soon all you have left are the incompetents. That's the weakness of bureaucracies, arising out of the Peter Principle.

Of course, in reality, there are no purely bureaucratic organizations. Every system for allocating resources has varying proportions of the three types of mechanism. For example, militaries are bureaucratic by necessity: 'always follow orders' is the first commandment for a soldier. But a military's fighting spirit is extremely important. You remember they said nothing scared the Yuejia Army.[61] And it is a line from *The Art of War*: 'He will win whose army is animated by the same spirit throughout all its ranks.' This is the spirit of reciprocity. Yue Fei, leader of the Yuejia Army, didn't win just through his brilliant military strategy. He won because they were all brothers, all in it together. No one talked about property then, did they? I join up with you, fight with you against the enemy, don't you have to give me something in return? That's how it is in a lot of very able armies; they all have this sort of system. When Zuo Zongtang joined the communist Gelaohui organization in Xinjiang, he used this system to motivate his troops, and they dominated the local Hui fighters, who were no slouches themselves. Reciprocity affects every aspect of life. The Mohists had a reciprocity system, and so did the secret societies of imperial times like the Cao gang and the salt smugglers.

Markets are governed by rules, just as reciprocity mechanisms are. But *the 'Randall Proposition' for efficient allocation of resources only applies to a very limited subset of resources.* I wrote a lot about this in this book in 1991. Randall divides the world's resources up into four types. The first type is separable and exclusive. These kinds of resources are allocated most efficiently by a market. For example, if we have a piece of bread, for every mouthful you take, I have to take one mouthful less. This is called both separable and exclusive, and market mechanisms apply here. There are three other types of resource: separable non-exclusive, exclusive non-separable, and non-separable non-exclusive. To a greater or lesser extent, none of these are best allocated through a market. Or, to put it another way, if you insist on allocating them through a market, you won't achieve maximum efficiency. There will be inevitable waste. Markets are only right for one kind: separable, exclusive resources. The Randall Proposition can be mathematically shown to be correct.[62]

WANG XIAOQIANG: We can understand it without using maths. For example, if we carry our water home from the river every day, we pour it into our own tanks, and there it becomes ours. You can't drink from my tank unless I give you permission. Or the use of solar energy: if you have bigger solar panels on your roof and generate more electricity, am I in a position to complain? Can I compete with you for those sunbeams? Or if one person hears the weather forecast, that doesn't stop other people from using that weather information as well. If I tell you an idea of mine, it might be that my idea becomes clearer in the very telling.

DENG YINGTAO: Then I took the idea further. At this point, it won't be long before the world's 'separable and exclusive' energy resources, like coal and oil, are completely used up.[63] The scope over which market mechanisms are relevant will become much smaller. Imagine a tree that I've planted. The tree's branches, leaves and roots are all separable assets, and they all belong to me, exclusively. But a tree breathes valuable oxygen into the air around it. Can you own that exclusively? I will breathe it in when I just walk by. What are you going to do, charge me for it? That sounds like the beginning of a bad Nasreddin joke! Or think of Shi Guangyin, who spent years planting 60 million trees, which were then designated a protected forest. If he was given 'separable and exclusive' ownership, then he'd be in the absurd position of having a theoretical right to the trees and any benefits accruing from them, but in practice he would be unable to cut down a single one. Even thinning the saplings would be a violation of the Forest Law. He could end up in prison for touching his own property![64] With oil and coal it is the same. In the past, it was your property, and you could do what you wanted with it. It was nobody's business but your own. Today, that's changed. If you pollute, you get fined. In other words, trees and coal both produce gases of different types. What type of gas they produce determines how large the 'externality' is, as they say in the language of economics. An externality is something beyond the scope of market controls. And large externalities can make a big difference.

220   *Afterword*

WANG XIAOQIANG:  The best example is the intellectual property rights that they go on and on about. When you use market mechanisms to incentivize invention, my invention earns a return dependent on its market share. Fine, so you pass laws and you enforce them, and the costs of all this regulation are pretty much endless. So-called intellectual property rights present an enormous theoretical challenge for market mechanisms.

DENG YINGTAO:  Right, but the people who beat the drum for markets will never admit it. I saw one very good paper on this, saying that Americans have finally achieved communism online. Any website which attempts to charge for its content is immediately abandoned by readers. Any website that wants to generate cash flow can do so only by attracting advertising. As soon as it tries to charge fees, internet users defect in droves. And what's strange about that? There is a large group of people who are happy to hack and share popular music and videos just because they like it. Come and get it for free, everyone! There are a lot of people doing that, it is very interesting. So, as the oil and gas gradually run out, the portion of the economy to which market mechanisms are relevant will become gradually smaller. Once it falls below a certain threshold, then markets will no longer be the dominant idea in the way we run our social relations.

Because reciprocity mechanisms, market mechanisms and bureaucratic mechanisms are not just ways of allocating resources, they are the fundamental mechanisms in the way we use resources. I originally wanted to write a paper on each of these three types: their specific features, preconditions, limitations, scope of application, the organizations they apply to and how they interact as organizational structures change. I wanted to take some time to map out all of the functional pathways for each type of mechanism, then add in a reading of history, to produce a work of real economic history. All that is easy to say, but when I sat and thought about what would be involved, I realized that this wasn't a one-man project. Just looking at the way these different mechanisms were intermixed in dynastic China, you'd have to go through the historical sources, gradually building up evidence.... It would be a massive task – not something to be undertaken lightly.

WANG XIAOQIANG:  Wow, that would be fascinating! Just think of the family: some farmers lived in nuclear families, with the man doing the heavy farm work and the woman weaving. They formed an economic unit, husband and wife happily combining their resources. Some lived in extended families, with strict hierarchies – men took precedence over women, elders over juniors. Among wealthy merchants, spouses' finances were sometimes kept separate: whatever you bring to the marriage remains yours, to dispose of as you will. But whatever the form, no family was an absolute and unalloyed commune, without any trace of bureaucracy or market process; no family was a pure market, with no bureaucracy or reciprocity; and none was a pure bureaucracy with no reciprocity or market. Thinking about it in your terms, every family was a mix of varying levels of reciprocity, bureaucracy and markets. Some were weighted more this way, some tilted more that way; some used this kind of mechanism for one particular set of issues, some would have that kind for another set.

*Afterword* 221

From this perspective, the 'rational economic actor' that economists love is too simplistic. It is such an abstraction that it no longer bears any resemblance to a real person, and as a result, it doesn't produce persuasive economics.

DENG YINGTAO: That's right. In real life, you'll never find a *homo economicus*. I once wrote a paper comparing two different types of incentive system. One type I called 'discrete incentives'. They include capital returns, which go to the capitalist. They are a function of his ownership, and his incentive to manage his assets well. There are wages, which incentivize workers. And there are things like options, which incentivize executives and managers. These are all discrete incentives. In addition to these, I suggested that every organization has another type of incentive, that I called 'compound incentives'. It is a function of the interaction of all of these different discrete incentives, and it includes x-efficiency. If you don't balance your incentives, they don't work as well. For example, if you give your managers too much authority, then your workers end up as slaves, and you get zero x-efficiency, or even negative x-efficiency. It can cancel out whatever gains you might have got through the discrete incentive that you offered the managers.

WANG XIAOQIANG: That's excellent. This is just like the way you approached the water diversion issue: wind power for water pumping plus tunnels and aqueducts = a multi-route solution. One plus one does not equal two, it equals three. This is a very Chinese way of thinking. It is right there in the *Dao De Jing*: 'One gave birth to Two, Two gave birth to Three, Three gave birth to all the myriad things.' Human relationships and organizations are an evolving mixture of market, reciprocity and bureaucratic relations. It is true of families, companies, government agencies, local communities and local governments, nation states and international organizations. All of human society functions this way, from the smallest to the largest units. This idea was an absolute inspiration to me. I wrote a series of papers called 'Only socialism can save China'. In historiography or meta-history, the biggest conceptual problem is the binary relations created by uni-dimensional terms like 'modernization' and 'progress'. This straight-line view of historical 'progress' can be traced in western thinking right back to Darwin, the Bible and the ideas of redemption and the Day of Judgment. I'm not sure if I can explain it clearly, but it is something that I sense: if you project the mixture of these three mechanisms onto a plot with productivity determining economic relations and economic infrastructure determining the social superstructure along the y-axis, and humanity's increasing control over nature through ever greater technological capabilities over time on the x-axis, then the idea of social progress naturally thickens into a three-dimensional, realistic picture of history.

Throughout history, all of the different social configurations that we see have been a mixture of market, bureaucratic and reciprocity mechanisms. Sometimes it is more of one, sometimes more of another. That is to say, in primitive times, clan-style reciprocity mechanisms were standard. In dynastic China, and in capitalist systems, markets and bureaucracies occupy a

222　*Afterword*

leading role, and clan reciprocity is sometimes condemned as being a backwards tradition. Now, fast technological change and the rise of new reciprocity-based organizations like NGOs have given reciprocity a new life. Now we are approaching what you wrote about in another book: *The New Energy Revolution and Shift in Development Model* (2011). These changes will again reverberate through our social structures. Market transactions and bureaucratic organizations will gradually shrink, and more equitable reciprocity mechanisms will bring us closer and closer to Marx's 'community of free individuals'. This kind of society could be called communist, or it could be called 'post-capitalist'. It may once have been an impossible dream, but as the oil runs dry, it is becoming closer and more tangible by the day....

## Is communism so unrealistic?

WANG XIAOQIANG: From what you're saying, reciprocity mechanisms appeal to you as a Communist Party member because they are close to, perhaps even the same as, the communist social ideals. They represent the Golden Rule.

DENG YINGTAO: You could put it that way, but I think it is a bit more nuanced than that. We try to avoid this sort of absolute, black-and-white approach. That falls into the same trap as the claim that the only way to sort out the problems of public ownership is privatization. We, on the other hand, may not agree with someone like Wu Jinglian's slavish admiration for markets, but that doesn't mean that we are anti-market.[65] Like I said, when I published the book in 1991 it had this all laid out, with figures and charts and mathematical demonstrations. For separable and exclusive resources, markets offer the most efficient allocation – they produce a Pareto-optimal result. Similarly, the Communist Party of China went from tiny to enormous; the People's Army scaled up from small to very big. That wouldn't be possible without bureaucratic systems and the scalability they bring. As you say, every household is different, but you can always find these three mechanisms co-existing and interlocking in the way they work.[66] In other words, markets, bureaucracies and reciprocity mechanisms will always be present in the way people allocate resources, even after we've used up the last scrap of mineral energy and the lock of capital monopolies has been broken. Markets will still be the most effective for separable, exclusive resources. Organizations that need economies of scale will still have to use bureaucratic systems. Perhaps this is what Mao Zedong meant when he said that even once we achieve communism, there will still be disagreements and conflicts.

But going back to your idea, that reciprocity is the same as communism – I said that that was too absolute. *But it does remind us that if we look at the way the three basic mechanisms combine, look at what's happening now, look to the future, then we see communism isn't such an exotic, unattainable ideal.* Reciprocity mechanisms are always present, everywhere. We are all caught up in them, they are inside our families, inside our organizations, and they are becoming more important as time goes by. For example, Elinor Ostrom, an American economist who researches public governance and sustainable development, and the only woman ever to win the Nobel Prize for economics, mostly researches this issue. Her core idea is 'polycentric governance'.[67] People used to think of socio-economic organizations as falling into just two categories: governmental, official institutions; and private, competitive companies. Ostrom believes that institutions today are very mixed. NGOs and non-profit organizations are neither companies nor governmental. They have a very broad range of concerns, objectives and functions, and to a great extent, they are communities of free individuals. She has surveyed many organizations and institutions of this type, and has looked at how they allocate and use resources. I've read a lot of these surveys, and she finds reciprocity mechanisms everywhere, in places where no one thought they could possibly exist, in places where everyone thought the problem of free riders made them impossible. Smart institutional set-up, positive relationships, incentives and constraints all combine to produce effective, functioning systems. In some places, you see systems that local societies have used for thousands of years, and which allow for sustainable development. She calls these types of human organization 'organisms'.[68]

WANG XIAOQIANG: Reciprocity is there to be seen in many areas of life, so long as you don't blind yourself to it with irrational trumpeting of markets, like Wu Jinglian, with his hatred of the Communist Party's planned economy. Reciprocity plays an irreplaceable role, and it must not be ignored. I've lived in small town America (Boulder) and in a village in the UK (Quy), and these places have a lot in common with rural China. It doesn't matter what job you do or how much money you make, come the end of the year, there are a series of events where the community expresses its reciprocity.

DENG YINGTAO: The USA is a classic example. It is an immigrant country, with a large land area and a low population. A lot of things are dependent on self-governing, quasi-governmental and non-governmental organizations, to the point where they have a massive influence on formal government bodies. Ostrom and her husband wrote a book called *Local Government in the United States*, in which the title of the first chapter is, 'Is there a system of local government in the US?'

> American local government is distinctive for being so varied. There are enormous differences across the country. In terms of absolute numbers, of course, it is very big. The 1987 U.S. census records 83,166 local government authorities. These local authorities are organized in fifty different ways, because the laws that define and regulate them are mainly the state constitutions and state laws. Plus, nearly half of the states have passed local autonomy statutes, allowing local residents to draft their own charters for certain local government institutions. Local autonomy leads to even more diversity in the structures of local governments, so even within a single state you can get very marked differences.

## 224   *Afterword*

So there are 3,042 counties, 19,205 cities, 16,691 towns, 14,741 campuses and 29,487 special zones with their own local system of government,[69] and they are not at all consistent. Plus, you have public institutions and administrative zones for things like utilities, police departments, fire departments, education boards and airports, which spill over various jurisdictions. If we try to understand this purely in terms of markets and bureaucratic mechanisms, as Wu Jinglian might, then we'd have to say we have excessive bureaucracy, we have monopolies; it is not fair, it is not competitive; it is certain to produce 'rent-seeking' and corruption. There must be vast efficiency losses. But the Ostroms find that incentives and efficiency in any organization are not just about 'following the money'. In a well-constructed organization, reciprocity can create all sorts of 'x-efficiency', which economics fails to capture. This efficiency far outweighs what fair market competition and rigid bureaucracy can create, and it is much more sustainable and much more adaptable![70]

Of course Elinor Ostrom's husband, Vincent Ostrom, took this line of thinking a step further. In his books *The Intellectual Crisis in American Public Administration* and *The Political Theory of a Compound Republic*, he explicitly questions whether the US Congress is really democratic. There's no way you'd get a Nobel Prize for that![71]

WANG XIAOQIANG:  That's very interesting. If we look at the past in terms of stages, communism is equivalent to paradise, to the Garden of Eden. There is no abuse of authority, no exploitation; resources are allocated according to need. Everything is good. That's why it is so hard to achieve now. If we look at the world through the kaleidoscope of your three mechanisms, then it is like looking at different families: we can find examples everywhere of highly successful reciprocity mechanisms.

DENG YINGTAO:  Could it be any other way? Do you know what I thought when I went to Nanjie, the village that still operates as a collective? I thought communism isn't so hard to achieve as we think. Go and look at Nanjie, then go and look at Huaxi. The wealth is shared equally in those villages.[72] I've been collecting examples like this for many years. There's Mondragon in Spain. That has been the textbook case for many years of a modern workers' cooperative. Every worker in Mondragon has his/her own capital account. In addition to their salaries, they also receive dividends on their share of the capital. If you want to leave, you can – there are no restrictions. But the cooperative has no external shareholders, so you have to progressively sell your stock back to the coop. There are nearly 100,000 people working there, often multiple generations of the same families. It is a huge group of companies with its own bank. Because of the way we live now, that's the largest example that I know of a group run on the basis of reciprocity.[73] In China, as we try to develop our reciprocity systems, I think we should introduce the cooperative system into a lot of our companies. Every worker should have his/her own capital account. This is the best way of regulating capital.

WANG XIAOQIANG:  Ha, that's a good idea. Regulating capital is not about stopping capital from developing, rather it helps it to develop much further!

DENG YINGTAO:  Capitalists used to say, I contribute by managing my capital; as the company gets bigger and the value of the capital grows, the contributions at the margin are mine. The problem is that the efficacy with which capital is managed includes 'x-efficiency'. At the very least, we aren't hurting you with negative 'x-efficiency' are we? And given that we are being so nice to you in terms of x-efficiency, those profits can't really belong entirely to you. We made a contribution to them as well, so some of the capital returns should be ours.

The biggest problem in all of this is free riders. That's what Olson's *The Logic of Collective Action* is all about.[74] That latest paper that I photocopied for you is a rebuttal to Olson. It argues that the problem can be resolved.[75] People have always had strategies for stopping free riders. The most powerful and effective is mutual surveillance – put in its ugliest terms, guilt by association. It can be done in many different ways.

In the debate today, we conflate a lot of things, which produces a lot of incorrect ideas. We imagine that public ownership is the same as having no owner, which is incorrect. Ostrom specifically criticized this idea. *She says free riders are not associated with public ownership.* We used to say that when something is everyone's responsibility, no one takes responsibility. But in reality free riders only appear when public ownership is not handled properly. Public ownership does not mean no one's in charge. This applies to the 'tragedy of the commons', too, which privatization advocates love to raise as their classic case study.[76] Actually, it is been known for a long time among Western researchers that throughout the Middle Ages, there was in fact no over-grazing on the shared grasslands around feudal manors. So the problem was not a tragedy of the commons, it was a problem of lack of stewardship, failure to properly define resources, lack of rules. The grass was over-grazed only when no one managed it.[77] *Both private and public ownership allow of many different ways to define and divide assets.*

WANG XIAOQIANG:  Land in Hong Kong isn't privatized, but they still managed to let a small minority take most of the value. Similarly, privatization is never absolute. Separable and exclusive resources are easy to allocate. You stuff that whole piece of cake into your mouth, and then there's none left for me. It is allocated! But when the issue is 'resources', it is more complex than that. For example, the land in Hong Kong's New Territories is privately owned. But it is zoned so that farmland can only be used for agriculture. Agriculture isn't economic here, so the land is left fallow. It is deserted. It just sits there. Residential land is also privately owned, but you need government approval to build on it, and you have to follow planning regulations: no higher than three storeys; no more than so many square feet; if you don't want to use all of the property yourself, you can't sell the extra space, only rent it out. There are regulations covering every detail. Apparently, a Hong Konger's home is not his castle. And there we were, thinking that private property was inviolable; regulated only by the market.

DENG YINGTAO:  Right. It is true from whichever direction you approach it. If you insist on me defining exactly what communism should be, I can't do it.

226  *Afterword*

But if you look at what happens today, even in capitalist societies – in the USA, in Sweden – there is some regulation by markets, some administrative regulation, and some reciprocity mechanisms. Mostly, these three types of regulation combine in various ways. There's loyalty to one's home area, team spirit, common interests, public works...none of these can be explained just in terms of *homo economicus*. And as society advances, personal relationships and collaboration are becoming more important and more frequent. Teamwork and reciprocity are necessarily becoming even more prominent.

## Modernization for the many: making it happen

WANG XIAOQIANG: In the past, we used to talk about stages of history. We used to say it was a scientific law, that society would progress through various stages, leading inevitably to the final outbreak of world revolution that would usher in world communism. That is why the revolutions in Eastern Europe and the break up of the Soviet Union were seen to be the nail in the coffin of Marxism. Socialism has failed, they said. The belief in communism was an illusion. History is the only standard against which we must test our theories, and there was the conclusion of history. It seemed like there was no more discussion to be had. This was reality. In 1987 I went to Germany, and the first thing that people said to me there was: our political system and yours spring from the same source. I was shocked at first, but when I thought about it, they were actually right: of course there's Eduard Bernstein and the Second International, and Germany's famously strong social security, but even on the boards of German companies, workers' representatives have to have one-third of the seats! So after that, I would ask anyone who told me that socialism had failed, why is socialism so well developed in developed, capitalist countries, including the USA? Why do they have systems, which are in some ways more socialist than my own country? Who exactly is it who has failed here, and how? The way I see it is that the failure of Eastern Europe and the Soviet Union is a bit like our Great Leap Forward. They show that you can't over-centralize and force the pace of socialism. But you look at the examples people have found in the West. Giving the Nobel Prize to Elinor Ostrom is a real victory for solid, grounded progress.

DENG YINGTAO: The failure of the Soviet Union and Eastern Europe can be looked at in a number of ways. Stalin won the war against fascist Germany, took Berlin, and dragged his country up from a serf economy to a socialist counterbalance against the Western powers. Can markets achieve that? Is that a failure or a victory? The so-called failure of the Soviet Union was that their amazing technological progress outstripped their political ability. They turned into socialist imperialists.

WANG XIAOQIANG: Yes, I completely agree. At the heart of Marxism is the idea of working class uniting, that it is only the working class who can set themselves and all of humanity free. Without this core idea, all you're left with is narrow nationalism, which is exactly what Western capitalism/imperialism produces. That is the argument I was making in the 'Only socialism can save China' series (Wang 2010–11). And it is actually what a lot of people worth listening to have been saying lately, including Nan Huai-chin. The question of China's survival and the question of where the world is moving are in fact the same question. Returning to our topic of 'modernization for the many', you give calculations in your book which cover not just the many in China, but the population of the entire planet.

DENG YINGTAO: I did the calculations for the world population, but the questions were those that arose out of China's reform and opening up. A few developed countries in the West have taken control of the majority of the world's energy. If we can't find another way to achieve our Four Modernizations, then we're stuck.

WANG XIAOQIANG: 'No saviour from on high delivers/Our own right hand the chains must shiver!' So when you present this concept of blending markets, bureaucracy and reciprocity, you are really saying that *humanity has a range of options that it can choose from as it meets its challenges.* To deal with some particular external environment or pressure, we can select an institutional apparatus that is light on markets and bureaucracy but relies heavily on reciprocity; or we can choose systems with significant market and bureaucratic elements, and little reciprocity.

Of course, it is easiest just to follow the path of least resistance, using whatever systems we have and applying patches where necessary. Fighting for the country to rise up is much harder. So people easily slip into just waiting for the stages of history to roll by and for world revolution to bring about true communism. But the ideas that you developed are tools to help us break out of this passivity. Because if you're interested in 'material abundance', today's productivity, and our supermarkets, far exceed anything that could be imagined in Marx's time. And a lot of people have used this fact to argue that Marxism is unrealistic. But back in 1991, in this book, you had two chapters called 'Detrimental effects of redundancy' and 'The economy of waste'. *'To each according to his need' had become 'to each more than his needs' a long time ago!* Clothes artificially distressed? A fashion for buying old watches, furniture, cars? Lifestyle diseases? Rowing in a gym? Running or cycling until the sweat soaks right through your clothes, without ever actually moving? Eating so much that you have to lose weight by starving yourself, taking pills to make yourself vomit or even paying a surgeon to cut open your perfectly healthy flesh? These are insane things to do. With all this going on, can you really say that we do not live in an age of material abundance?

DENG YINGTAO: So the theory says that productivity determines economic relations. But you have to fight to actually make it happen. In Germany, worker representation makes up a third of company boards. Did that come about naturally? Was it easy? Luxemburg and Liebknecht were shot, remember? All of the little improvements that help ease tension between groups within developed countries came about only through fierce fighting by workers'

228  *Afterword*

movements. They suffered plenty of violence along the way. And part of the reason they were successful is because Western governments were scared that a communist revolution really would sweep over the world. After the break up of the Soviet Union, the world became a single capitalist market. And the division between capital and workers became suddenly much larger than it had been. The middle classes in developed nations were the first victims.

So really Mao had it right when he said, 'Where the broom does not reach, the dust will not vanish of itself.'[78] Even if the oil runs out, have you seen the American film *Blood Diamond*? Diamonds have no practical value beyond being used to show off someone's wealth. Most people can't even tell the difference between diamonds and cut glass. Even so, people kill and die for them. Or here's another example, have you heard of canned air from Mt Fuji or the Alps?[79] It really exists. There will be a Chinese brand soon enough.[80] The point is that whether it is reciprocity, markets or bureaucracy, there are always vested interests and power games in existing social institutions. Here we are, investing our time in the question of how to bring modernization to more people. And at the same time, without any fuss at all, canned air has become the next big thing. If they can make a fortune off air, you can imagine how much more there is to make from dwindling stocks of oil and gas.

WANG XIAOQIANG:  In other words, you think that the mix of the three mechanisms is something that a society decides. It is not a natural historical process.

DENG YINGTAO:  That's right, it doesn't happen by itself. Those big companies are pushing their agenda, aren't they? When you've got someone like Bill Gates, as rich as a small country, and you say in the future, you'll be allocated an equal share of GDP along with everyone else – well, would you like it? I don't think so. *That's the situation in developed countries, and it is even more true of developing nations.* Do colonies and semi-colonies count as modernized? For a few bureaucrats and the comprador class, of course colonization is progress. It is modernization. Vested interests and conspicuous consumers get to live even more extravagant lifestyles than the rich in developed countries. The majority remain poor, so labour remains cheap. It is a situation that rich country investors can only dream of. What's not to like? So the GDP grows, the cake gets bigger, but modernization for the majority is absolutely not a natural process. The barriers to shared wealth are in fact larger in developing countries than they are in rich countries. There has to be a political struggle, hard political work done at all levels.

WANG XIAOQIANG:  Yes, I completely agree. Housing in Hong Kong is a good example. The media love to compare Hong Kong and Singapore: they're both major port cities, both former British colonies, similar per capita GDP, similar land area by population, and housing prices are fairly similar. But they never compare the average size of apartments. In 2000, the average amount of living space each Hong Kong resident had was 14 square metres; in Singapore, it was 25 square metres back in 1997. The point of 'one country, two systems' was to let Hong Kong continue with its capitalist economy, while China remained communist. Today, Beijing's housing has been privatized, while a third of Hong Kong residents still live in public housing, with just 11 square metres per head! In terms of per capita GDP, Hong Kong's is $45,000 – the seventh highest in the world. It has overtaken the UK and Sweden. This is one of the richest modern economies in the world.[81] But if you look at quality of life in terms of living space, they don't even compare with Beijing's middle class. And the fundamental difference is on the supply side. It doesn't matter how large the GDP is, how big the cake gets. Hong Kong's 'modern' institutions will always work in favour of the few.[82] Who in Hong Kong wouldn't prefer to have more space? But it is not happening. No one dares go near it.

DENG YINGTAO:  That's right, and as the oil runs out, I believe that the competition and the fighting over resources will get more intense. Internationally, I think everyone has recognized this.[83] The Club of Rome churns out reports left and right on this, saying how many more years of oil and gas we have left. In this book in 1991, I used estimates published by *Scientific American* in 1989. The estimates then said that with existing technology and proved reserves, oil would be gone in another 35 years. That's 2024! It is very close now. Of course, as our oil extraction technology has become more advanced, we are finding more reserves, and as prices rise, oil that used to be too expensive to recover is suddenly becoming interesting. But oil consumption is growing quicker still. Developed countries are feeling the pressure, and they are doing everything they can to develop new energy resources. And just at this historical moment, China has managed to escape absolute poverty, but has not yet fully modernized. And now we want to try to get a share of some resources; fine, we can't go to the Middle East, but can we go to Africa? Can we go to places where you've found no oil? No. Because Western modernization is always dependent on oil. Oil flows in its veins. Wherever oil may be found, whatever distant corner of the planet it is in, the West sees it as strategic reserves for its own modern society. The USA has built 800 military bases around the world. It is not doing that to be a good Samaritan.[84] The only option for us is to find oil within our own borders, and even then we have to be strong enough to stop the Western powers invading or sectioning off part of our territory.

Just recently a French critic examined America's strategy for the twenty-first century, examining why the USA has been sponsoring colour revolutions in regions with significant oil reserves, and why it has been so willing to take military action against Afghanistan, Iraq, Syria and Libya. It is because America wants to split the twenty-first century world into two zones: a stable core, led by America, and a chaotic 'other' region:

> The role of the Pentagon will be to ensure the civilised world gets access to the necessary natural resources located in the periphery, which is inept to make use of them… the world [is divided] into two zones – stable and chaotic – where the second only serves as the reservoir of natural resources for the first…[85]

230  *Afterword*

In other words, when there is not much oil left, you either maintain a tight grip on it, as with America carefully propping up ancient emirates; or you foment independence in an attempt to reach some 'mutually beneficial' understanding. Either you democratize, or we'll come and take you out, and keep your resources for ourselves. Most of the borders of developing nations were drawn by imperialist colonizers working on the principle of 'divide and rule'. All of these countries have major divisions between different races, ethnicities, religions, tribes, rich and poor, etc. There are long-standing historical grievances, deep-seated enmities that make unity very hard to achieve. You wave the flag of democracy, fund an opposition, enforce a no-fly zone, and if all else fails you send in the army to remove a strongman government. Then you march home in triumph, oil reserves safely in your pocket.

WANG XIAOQIANG: This is the backdrop against which China is conducting its 'reform and opening up'. Some of the people have become rich first – China now has more millionaires than America. Leveraging our 1.3 billion people, a small minority have been able to use the pre-existing Western model to modernize. That's not so difficult. What's really hard is modernization for the many. Xi Jinping wrote recently that 'Living standards for the Chinese people have made a historic shift up from the level of subsistence...we will stick resolutely to the path of prosperity for all.'[86] It is very exciting to see this direction and this level of determination. Very gratifying! And this brings us back to the question of *Remaking China*: modernization for a billion plus Chinese people. Where is the energy for prosperity for all going to come from? Of course, with oil and gas, we just have to work with what we can get through peaceful means. But there is no way that's going to be enough, and sooner or later it is going to run out, so we must think about new models of development. We must think about (1) *diverting rivers and* (2) *planting grass*. International competition for resources is only going to get more intense. We need a 'new energy revolution and shift in development model' if the Chinese people are to get their day in the sun. The problem is that the few who got rich first are now extremely comfortable. They don't see any problem with the Western model. Now you come along and say you want to divert rivers, plant grasses and do a lot of stuff that has nothing to do with conventional lifestyles and economic models. Of course some people are going to be against it. Of course there are going to be doubts. The reason is very simple: this is a road that no one has taken before. If no one has gone this way before, how do you know there's a road to take? It makes me think of what Lu Xun said about roads.[87]

DENG YINGTAO: Huh, so the conventional model is the way to go, is it? Germany and Japan were late to the party, had to fight for energy in the markets, and it caused not just one world war, but two, plus the detonation of atomic bombs! It wasn't so very long ago, you know.[88] This is not just a question of hurt feelings or preferences. There is not much oil and gas left, and just at this critical moment, China has moved beyond subsistence, moved out of poverty, and is just kicking for modernity. We are now the biggest car market in the world, the biggest oil importer in the world, taking our oil wherever we can get it – Africa, Central Asia….We're just a few years away from real modernization now – Beijing turned into a parking lot before you could say 'peaceful rise'. And there's a billion or more people who are also itching to consume oil just like they do in the West. At this point, the West is thinking, if we don't put a lid on this, we're going to get squeezed out here![89] Just lately there was the book *Oil Wars*,[90] which explains how we're seeing more and more talk of 'containing China'. It has become an acceptable cause for action in some circles. It is no longer just a question of clamping down whenever China tries to reach beyond its borders. There's tension in the East China Sea and the South China Sea. They've brought it to our own doorstep. There is no precedent in history for a country under this kind of pressure 'sticking resolutely to the path of prosperity for all' and trying to effect universal modernization. We're in new territory here. We have to be bold, and we have to aim high, aim for a full new energy revolution, to decisively shift the way we grow. We will do our thing within our own borders; try to create new energy resources. Surely it's fine if this elephant wants to eat grass, right? If you won't even accept that, then we've got trouble. If you are going to come in here trying to carve off Tibet and its water, Xinjiang and its plains; if you're going to come and cut off this elephant's legs; if you're going to break us up into little pieces so that the Chinese people can't support themselves, can't eke out a space for themselves in this world…well then, we'll have to fight!

WANG XIAOQIANG: I'm very worried about the situation now as well. The 'gambler's economy' is now a runaway train. It is rolling on and on, to the point now where no one dares make the RMB convertible, even though we have billions of dollars in foreign currency reserves. The core problem now is that if some area of the world can't be found to donate vast sums to the USA, the American economy will just collapse and never recover.[91] The financial crisis has been going on for several years now, and we're already into the third round of quantitative easing. Geithner knows perfectly well that the bad debts he's paying interest on today are even worse than Lehman Brothers back in 2008. Even so, the Federal Reserve can't just give free money to the governments and banks of Iceland, Greece and Spain! But their bad debts are all interconnected with the bad debts of US financial institutions.

America's manufacturing sector is now just 17 per cent of its economy, and most of that is high tech manufacturing, which can't be transferred overseas for legal reasons. So long as there are still restrictions on selling weapons, it doesn't matter how high the stock markets go, you're still stuck with unemployment. Even if you bring back all of the manufacturing that you've outsourced overseas, start making TVs, fridges, washing machines and bicycles in America again, even if you force the RMB to appreciate, you're still not going to be competitive with 'Made in China'. 'Made in the USA' is good for high tech and military stuff. For example, in 2010 they sold the Saudis some weapons that they were phasing out for $60 billion.[92]

232  *Afterword*

The media loves to talk about increasing levels of understanding between the US and China. But there's really nothing more to know about our respective industrial mixes and relative advantages. It is as clear as daylight for anyone who wants to see. All the US needs to do is carve up the last major communist state into seven or eight little chunks, split it up into lots of separate countries like the Arab countries, then each country will busy itself with buying high-tech Western weapons to maintain their super-modernized elites. And the USA can sell its arms, like it does to Taiwan now, then come to each Chinese state and play referee; maintain order among us. All of these seven or eight little wannabe Chinas will keep on running their sweatshops and exporting cheap plastic tat to maintain American lifestyles. And they'll follow in the footsteps of Taiwan, jostling in the name of 'regional stability' to buy up whatever weaponry the USA discards as it upgrades. GDPs will continue to rise quickly throughout East Asia, the US' trade deficit and unemployment problems will be solved, and credit ratings for dollar bonds will rise to quadruple A, five-A, eight-A, whatever.[93]

The mix of markets, reciprocity and bureaucracy that we choose is a result of the choices we make as we compete with each other. Unfortunately, the voice of so-called international experience is much louder than that of Deng Yingtao in his hospital bed. And the conventional wisdom out there is that we should make markets and bureaucracies our principal mechanisms.

DENG YINGTAO: That might be the way the options fall out in the end. They might think up some plot to overthrow the Communist Party and carve up the Chinese state. But it is not going to happen! There are a lot of reciprocity arrangements where you'd never imagine finding them. Ostrom listed many in her books. Imagine we cover up the answer with a piece of cloth and pose the question this way: we have free riders and ambiguous property rights, how can we solve these problems? Then those such as Wu Jinglian would answer without hesitation: markets and shareholding.... But when we whip away the cloth and show what's underneath, well, isn't that interesting? It is extraordinary, the systems that have persisted for hundreds and thousands of years are the reciprocity systems. They have highly developed incentives and penalties, and they are amazingly efficient.[94] So Ostrom didn't receive the Nobel Prize for inventing some new principle. She received it for doing strong empirical work on something that already exists out there, for researching what real life looks like. And in the same spirit, there are five of Mao Zedong's political concepts, which I'm sure will stand the test of time.

The first is, 'The world belongs to us, everybody pitch in.'[95] That was Mao's view of ownership. Based on this view of ownership, we get the second concept: If everyone cuts firewood, the flames burn high. That was Mao's take on efficiency. Third: From many people, great men will emerge. Of course, when he talks about great men, he's not just saying we should wait passively for a king, a Yao or a Shun. 'Great men' includes Lin Yishan, our modern day Yu the Great; Shi Guangyin and Niu Yuqin, the worker ants

*Afterword* 233

who held back the sand; Wang Wei, who knocked an American spy plane out of the sky; Yang Liwei, our first man in space.... Some people claim that China breeds nothing so well as traitors, but I don't think that's true. If you look through our history, there are thousands of heroes who have sacrificed themselves for their country: Liu Hulan, Dong Cunrui, Huang Jiguang, Mao Anying, Lei Feng, Wang Jie....[96] 'Six hundred million in this land all equal Yao and Shun.'[97] Which gives us the fourth concept: the masses are the real heroes.

The fifth concept is: imperialism and all reactionaries are paper tigers. Mao Zedong said, tigers can kill, so how can they be paper? You hear a lot of talk now about how many troops the KMT poured into fighting the Japanese. Those soldiers weren't just frightened to death by paper tigers. They died on their feet, fighting in bloody battles. So why did the KMT get beaten so badly? Twenty or 30,000 troops from the Japanese Kwantung Army took on hundreds of thousands of Chinese troops from the northeast, and it was a rout. The Imperial Japanese Army had better equipment, didn't they? And a lot of the aeroplanes they later used to bomb north China were captured from Zhang Xueliang. This tiger was only tamed to a paper tiger by the sheer scale of the people's war. Given the first four ideas there, it doesn't matter how strong an enemy is; arm the people, and the enemy will be defeated. So given these five concepts, their strategy was just wishful thinking. They were crazy to think they could win.

WANG XIAOQIANG: Of course, I agree with you, but today, the first truth is privatization. Farmers and agricultural workers – including Shi Guangyin and Niu Yuqin – are now a disadvantaged group, both in theory and in practice. And because of their weakness, the paper tigers have turned back into real tigers.

DENG YINGTAO: We do have to face up to that reality, you're right. We can't dodge it. But I always say 'you can't ignore reality'. The facts on the ground will always play out, no matter how you try to stop them. Zeng Guofan said that human achievement comes about in two ways: passion and necessity. And necessity occupies much the greater part. People get creative when their backs are against the wall. Modernization that allows the few to lord it over the rest of us cannot be a lasting situation for us in China. China has a deeply ingrained tradition of meritocracy, so no minority can seize permanent power. Last time I was talking to you about a French book – I'm still looking for it – which says that today, everyone can read and write....

WANG XIAOQIANG: Don't worry about the reference – I know what you mean. There's a famine right now in Africa, with who knows how many people starving to death every day, and we watch it on our colour TVs interspersed with adverts for canned pet food, slimming pills and liposuction. 'In the years when even the dogs and swine eat as well as people, you don't think to lay in stores; when people are starving to death, you don't think to distribute from the storehouses.' *One world; one dream.* You might have given everyone a mobile phone, but I'm still starving to death here! And don't you realize that

234 *Afterword*

there might be just a few who start to get ideas, a few bull-headed ones, a few who aren't ready to settle for what comes their way, and are willing to put up a bit of a struggle. Sometimes it gets to the point where people say, yeah, I might not make it, but I'm taking someone down with me. That's what happened to King Jie; it ended the Xia Dynasty.[98] So you'd got these hotheaded individuals, and in their state of hunger and confusion, they are not really going to distinguish who is wearing what uniform, are they? I find it extraordinary – every day on TV we see reports that these Muslim suicide bombers are getting themselves to heaven to get 72 virgins. Have they never worried, if they're running a company where a dozen people in a row just throw themselves off buildings, that none of them might think, seeing as I'm going to die anyway.... If poor Chinese factory workers ever sat down with some of these suicide bombers, things might start to get a lot louder than they are today.

DENG YINGTAO: That's what I mean when I say you can't ignore reality. If you don't provide for the majority, if you only allow a small elite to modernize, then you're never going to have security. Markets, bureaucracies, reciprocity – at the end of the day, these are all about smoothing the relationship between the many and the few. That's especially true of reciprocity. For example, to maximize the efficiency of a company, every employee has to be involved. But there is a constraint, which is that leaders and government officials have to lead by example, even though they get more than everyone else. For example, in Mondragon, the ratio of executives' wages to ordinary workers' wages used to be 3:1. This meant that senior managers got relatively low pay. The ratio later grew to 5:1 because competition for managers increased, and they found that headhunters kept stealing their key workers.[99] So what is it that produces the greatest efficiency through the golden rule? There is law called the folk theorem, which says, suppose you're the leader of an organization, and that in strict terms, your marginal return on your contribution to the organization should be ten, with the rest to be divided among the other members. But perhaps this allocation of profits will upset the balance of compensation across the organization, and that will impact negatively on the incentives that the group offers. In that situation, what every organization needs is someone who is willing to voluntarily take only nine, to give up his tenth share and allow everyone else to share it out. That way the organizational incentives can be maintained.[100]

WANG XIAOQIANG: You mean that for any organization, be it a company, a state or society, if they use the Golden Rule to maximize their efficiency, this places certain demands on the managers within that organization. To each according to his work – those who make a greater contribution can receive a greater share, but it has to be constrained, because there is a threshold value; a measure which cannot be exceeded. If you go beyond this measure, then your x-efficiency is going to suffer.

DENG YINGTAO: Right, and it doesn't matter whether the incentives we are talking about are positive or negative. Positive incentives are bonuses; negative incentives are penalties, right? The folk theorem proves that this is true. So then

I was thinking, they always say that everyone is rational, and no one would be willing to accept lower compensation. But that's not right, many people would. That's exactly how the Yuejia Army was. In Chinese, we like to talk a lot about men of virtue. There's another famous line from the Mencius, which says: 'Having a steady heart when you have no steady livelihood – only the noble can do this.' What's clever here is that Mencius is saying two things. First, those with steady livelihoods have steady hearts, and those without steady livelihoods may not be faithful in their hearts. That's the first part, but think of the second:[101] in any group of a few dozen people, there is bound to be a Lei Feng. More than one, most likely. So this is a precondition for reciprocity to work, which in economic theory cannot be satisfied, but in reality often occurs. Leaders who are willing to sacrifice a little of their own personal interest for the benefit of the group do exist, and in fact can be found everywhere.

WANG XIAOQIANG: So given that, the question is what methods, mechanisms or arrangements will make these leaders willing to serve the many? Within a family, a group, a region or a nation, what makes leaders willing to do their best for the majority, and what puts those who are willing into positions of authority?

DENG YINGTAO: This is the underlying question that will determine whether our red government can maintain its grip on power. I think back to Mao, and three major advances that I believe he wanted to achieve: the first is industrialization, and it is complete. This provides the physical, material foundation for modernization for the Chinese people. It was also the foundation for what we've achieved during the reform and opening up: fast economic growth and our transition from subsistence to no poverty. Mao and his generation overturned all of the old ideologies that gripped this country; they built real independence for the Chinese people; they took over all of the old capitalist and bureaucratic enterprises, and took on 156 new objectives as well. Within an unbelievably short time, they built a complete mix of mostly state-owned industries; and they developed atomic weaponry, guided missiles and satellite technology. Second, they ended the cycle of dynastic rulers fighting and replacing one another. Third, they created rule by the many. This last political advance is not yet complete.

WANG XIAOQIANG: I think the last two can be combined into a single item. In order to truly end the cycle of political fighting and displacement and produce a lasting order, it has to be rule by the many. Right now corruption is getting worse and worse. It is very serious in a lot of places. People don't work 'for the people', everything is 'for the dollar'. That's why you've been grinding away at this for getting on 30 years now. Even when people hear what you're working on – the river diversion, the biofuel grasses – and they realize how important it is, they won't actually work on it themselves, because there's no way to get it done. Develop the West! There's plenty of sloganeering about it. Workers from Xinjiang go down to the factories in Guangdong, and then there's fighting and things get ugly. Just today, I was reading a paragraph from this book that you wrote 20 years ago.

236  *Afterword*

Currently China, squeezed as it is between the dual pressures of limited natural resources and consumer demand, faces a fundamental choice. There are three scenarios for modernization: (1) To forever teeter at the threshold of success. (2) To adopt short-sighted and passive strategies. (This means following in the footsteps of developed countries – and will inevitably require China to perform a volte-face in the not-too-distant future, for which the country will pay a heavy price.) (3) To be prepared henceforth to make gradual, far-sighted adjustments in the development model it adopts.

'Is China capable of implementing the third choice successfully?'[102]

## The political revolution

WANG XIAOQIANG: There are many examples of successful operations based on reciprocity: Nanjie, Huaxi, or a few years back there was Dazhai.[103] But the folk theorem tells us what Mencius said: 'only the noble can do this'. You have to have a strong, motivated leader. So succession becomes a problem. If we look at it on a national scale, North Korea has had three generations of Kims. In Cuba the presidency has passed from one Castro brother to the other. It doesn't matter what the structure of your polity is; it doesn't matter whether you have elections or not. You have to have a strong leader to take the reins of power.

The Party has made some serious mistakes on this issue, on the question of finding successors. The wave of democratization that we see sweeping across the world has brought disastrous instability to many countries, just as it did to China in the past, and it brings with it the danger of national division and the break up of the state. The clearest example is Yugoslavia, a country that used to enjoy living standards close to those of developed countries. But democratization is nothing more or less than a subset of westernization, and it is a clear example of why you need checks and balances and mutual oversight. Corrupt officials are like weeds. They are springing up in every unattended corner, more grasping than ever, and that is driving a surge in public opinion and in the media toward democratization. We will need reforms in the government in order to successfully effect modernization for the many in this country. And it is going to be hard. Again, there is no precedent for this, so the CPC will have to overturn existing ideologies just like it did back at the time of the revolution. It will have to align and mobilize huge numbers of people if there is to be any chance of success.

DENG YINGTAO: My views on political reform can be summed up in five phrases: *Names matter; Party members first; limited terms; checks and balances; Party and people.*

WANG XIAOQIANG: I see. Mao Zedong wrote about this. He asked why Song Dynasty historians chose to start *The Comprehensive Mirror to Aid in Government* (Sima 1084), their comprehensive history of China, with the partition of the state of Jin. Of course, sometimes titles can be misleading – there are always going to be people who lie about who they are to make a quick buck – but titles matter. The minute you allow any leeway with titles, you open yourself up to all sorts of fraud. Everyone is going to claim some kind of title, and you end up with a country that is little more than a chessboard for the destructive games of warlords.

DENG YINGTAO: That is one common way of thinking about it. What I mean by the first part, 'names matter', is that we must proudly fight to keep the red flag in place forever. The Communist Party of China (CPC) has been in power for 60 years now, and it has done amazing things. Of course there have also been major oversights; it has made terrible errors, and the people have paid an enormous price. You can talk about conforming to international standards, but calls for a multi-party system have been around since 1957. People then said, let's allow other parties to take a turn at government. Why should the CPC just go on and on in power? We didn't agree to it then, and you know why not? Some people said that the Party's power was just fallout from the Japanese invasion; that it was illegal because it had not been confirmed through a democratic election. Twenty-eight years of war, and all of the Liu Hulans, the Dong Cunruis, Huang Jiguangs, Mao Anyings…. all the thousands of heroes who gave their lives – ordinary farmers wheeling their wheelbarrows to bring supplies to our fighters, carrying stretchers and caring for the wounded. Don't these count for as much as a vote? Don't they show what the will of the people is?

WANG XIAOQIANG: Yang Songlin put this the right way, I think. The Communist Party must lead the country, because only the Communist Party has the hammer and sickle on its flag. Every Party member must swear when they join the Party that they will serve the people.[104] If there is any party today that is calling for modernization for the masses, that is seeking equality for all, and that has the hammer and sickle on its flag, then sure! They can take a turn in government. But wouldn't that just be the Communist Party? What I mean is, the purpose of any political reforms must be to see who will serve the people best.

After the break up of the Soviet Union and the changes in Eastern Europe, everyone was naturally worried that a 'colour revolution' could happen here. They were looking for a way to maintain order, stop things from turning chaotic. But now, 30 years after the beginning of the reforms and opening up, we have built a market economy. Some people are now rich. And every interest group, every class is trying to promote its own political agenda, to change the social superstructure through whatever means it can. With all of the interacting forces from the international situation and the domestic situation, it is hard to stop and take stock. Changes happen without anyone really driving them. We are working to achieve shared prosperity, but we are fighting against the tide, and we're actually moving backwards at the moment. We can't solve this problem through negativity, passivity, compromise and defensiveness. We can't just patch it up. We have to get with the times, be proactive and ambitious about our political reforms.

238  *Afterword*

DENG YINGTAO: The promotion of democracy should start with and be based around Party members. There is a very clear logic to this. The CPC represents the base and the power of the Chinese leadership. If you can't reform your own base, then how can you ever get started? The only alternative, surely, would be to allow the CPC to be pushed aside and allow some other minority to seize power. Reforming the CPC, our name matters: our prime directive to serve the people remains unchanged. With all the changes of the last 30 years, the introduction of a market economy, reforms to align with international convention, it is no surprise that there have been shifts in our lifestyles and in the way our economy works. Corruption was inevitable in some ways. The key problem is that we lack the mechanisms to make big moral choices for our country: choosing our development model, our path to the future, our fundamental political principles. How do we ensure that we are fighting for the modernization of the many? If we want to hold to this principle, we have to explore ways of building stronger political systems, with mature sets of interweaving institutions that can monitor, check and balance each other.

So, given that modernization for the many is our guiding principle, the natural path for political reform is increasing levels of democratic involvement among Party members. There is no other way to boost the Party's political legitimacy. This is the second part: 'Party members first.' That article that I photocopied for you is about 'How political parties in other countries keep party members at the centre.' This is a new move among political parties all over the world, including bourgeois parties.[105] When you develop your market economy, and you are engaging with money and capitalists all the time, corruption is bound to occur. But you should be able to see that Mammon can corrode a few officials with power to trade; but it can't corrode away 80 million Party members. No one has that much money! And if all 80 million Party members were lured by filthy lucre, well then, we'd be well on the way to our objective of sharing the wealth equally throughout society, wouldn't we?

Or to look at it another way: it is 20 years since the collapse of the socialist polity. The crisis in belief in the socialist ethic is very serious. If China has indeed been totally corrupted, if it is just a nation of rent-seekers, then the Communist Party is finished anyway. The reason that the red flag is still flying today is because in every industry and every place of work, Party members are there, at the coalface, with the people. They are still fighting for their beliefs, in whatever way they can. Just after the evening news on CCTV every evening, they have a programme that tells you about a Party member and how they are carrying on the fight. I'm sure most of these stories are absolutely true. In our surveys of what's happening on the front lines of economic development, we have found dedicated Party members everywhere. They are the people that Lu Xun saw: the unrecognized hard workers, the battlers, the unresting advocates, the endless seekers after something better. These are the backbone of China.[106]

Intra-Party democracy is a democracy that gives voice to these people, a democracy for the backbone of China. We want to give these people the right to speak, the right to hold institutions accountable, and the right to participate in policy decisions. Some will say, why should we give these kinds of political privileges to Party members? The reason is simple: because each one of them has sworn an oath to the hammer and sickle. If you swear that you will give yourself – up to and including giving your life – for the modernization of the many, then you can be granted the privileges of a 'member-owner' of the Party. The Party congresses that are held every five years should be turned into democratic parliament sessions for Party members who have sworn the oath. At an appropriate pace, Party representatives in each area would gradually increase participation in decision-making by local Party members; the number of policy issues resolved by commands coming down from the Central Committee would be reduced. For major questions of principle or policy direction, modern communications technology will enable us to skip the local Party meetings process. We can organize open ballots, and all Party members will be able to vote for the policies they support. *It is a new era now.* The penetration of television, mobile phones and the internet goes far beyond what anyone ever imagined before. A Party that represents a modern economy should move with the times.

The last 30 years have seen enormous advances in our economy and in our political system. One important example is my third point, 'limited terms': we have shifted away from giving politicians authority for life, and moved to a system of limited terms. The most senior members of the leadership do not stay in office any longer than two terms, and officials have defined retirement ages. These institutional arrangements are still far from perfect, of course. One issue is what to do with retired officials. Now that life expectancies are so much longer than they used to be, there is a large pool of officials who have had to retire at the legally mandated age. How can we ensure that this group continues to be actively involved in decision-making, policy discussions and operational feedback? One idea is to continue to use the old consultative committee system. This could actually be a great opportunity for growth for the Party. Developing and focusing the functions of the NPC (National People's Congress) and CPPCC (Chinese People's Political Consultative Conference) is something that the Party should very much be thinking about. We don't want to roll back what we've already achieved. We should keep the limited terms, but we need to legislate and develop better systems for broader policy consultation, broader participation in political decision-making and broader institutional oversight of the executive government.

Third, 'checks and balances' means that we should look to the experience of Japan's LDP (Liberal Democratic Party). They are a single party that has held power for decades, and the party maintains balance through internal factions, which restrain each other. There is a book called *A History of the LDP's Civil Wars*, which is very much worth reading. The party president,

240    *Afterword*

director of executive affairs and director of policy research split the power between them, each of them leading one of the three main factions. They are selected through internal elections and factional deals.[107] Mao Zedong said, 'Wherever you have a group of people together, they will split into left, right and centre.'[108] 'A party without factions would be bizarre.'[109] Even though everyone takes the same oath to serve the masses, and our basic orientation is the same, on many issues there are going to be some who are a little more radical, some who are a little more conservative, and some who take a centrist position. The LDP president serves as prime minister, and is responsible for the party's overall political stance. The director of executive affairs is responsible for party internal affairs. The director of policy research is responsible for research and consistency in policy lines. One of each of these three key positions is held by a leader of the party's left, right and centre factions. Once you have the principle of limited terms and factions within the party, then you get an effective system of checks and balances. Each faction can have a turn in power, so any extreme policies are corrected on an ongoing basis. You create an interactive, regulated, balanced structure, which maintains stability through alternation of power.[110]

Given that modernization for the majority is an area in which we have to explore, experiment and test a wide range of new practices, as we go through this historical process, we will need a way to generate multiple policies and multiple approaches. During the war, the extreme pressure of our external environment meant that intra-Party struggle was often extremely vicious. A lot of people who were good, dedicated Party members were hurt. During peacetime, particularly now, when the whole world is demonizing the Communist Party, we have to find ways to learn the painful lessons of the past. We have to get out of the knee-jerk habit of labelling anything we disagree with as 'anti-Party'. We have to properly allow and listen to different opinions. We have to accept that people will form groups, and fully recognize the reality that factions exist. Then we have to conduct normal Partyinternal debate, regulated by proper Party rules.

Fourth, 'Party and people'. As Party-internal democracy develops and turns into an effective, open system, it will inevitably change the way the Party relates to the public and to other political parties. The NPC and the CPPCC will certainly start to actually exercise the authority that they nominally hold. And given the reality of a highly polarized society in which industrial and agricultural workers are highly disadvantaged, the next priority is ensuring the rights of workers by reforming and building unions and agricultural cooperatives. *They should be organizations in which workers and farmers have a real voice, modern collectives. Alliances of workers and farmers under the guidance of the Party.* These political processes will be very complex, and their consequences far-reaching. Party-internal democracy is interwoven with democracy for the whole country, and questions of political unity – one country and two systems for Hong Kong, unification with Taiwan – will be raised as well. With care and sensitivity we must

Afterword 241

explore and press on with these challenges. They are a part of the new social systems that we must build along the way to modernization for the many.

WANG XIAOQIANG: No wonder, then, that you read Nan Huai-chin's *Selections from the Analects* eight times, and then condensed it to a quarter of its length as your *Reader for Chinese Traditional Culture*.[111] The way you imagine political concepts makes me think immediately of the TCM principle of preventing illness in the first place: better to improve your health first than try to deal with health problems as they arise. So you have a flexible preventative system that considers the season and your environment, that balances and checks yin with yang and yang with yin, because these two elements produce each other and restrain each other.

DENG YINGTAO: It is not just Chinese culture. In the West, control theory has produced a lot of work, which shows very clearly that in a system with only positive feedback, you get reports delivered to the bosses full of whatever the bosses want to hear; bosses become more and more convinced of their own abilities; and ultimately problems build up in the system until it collapses!

Ultimately, what I believe is that if we want to live up to our name and keep the red flag flying over China, then we have to advance. *We have to have a national resurgence in which each person and organization plays the role they are supposed to play.* We have to bring modernization to the many. That will be China's great contribution to what socialism can and should be. Party internal democracy, affirming the principle of democracy and building it into our society: 'names matter; Party members first; limited terms; checks and balances; Party and people'. All of these principles overlap and feed into each other. This is how I see political reform in this country: at the heart of it is reform of the CPC. If we want to modernize the many, if we want to keep the red flag flying, we have to make bold, dramatic political reforms. Of course there are great risks in this strategy. But we should be bold. The key principles are 'names matter' and 'Party members first'. The deciding factor in the success or failure of any reform is trust in the people and using the power of the people. If we make bold use of the power of the whole Party membership, reaffirm the Party's role in the service of the people, then these reforms will work just as previous reforms have, because they have a firm foundation. Leveraging the 80 million Party members will be the institutional guarantee that the CPC can continue to successfully lead China's 1.3 billion people.

WANG XIAOQIANG: The TV show *Liu Luoguo* had a song with some lyrics that capture it well: 'This world is a balance scale, and the counterweight is the people.' The CPC serves the people. Eighty million members who have sworn loyalty to the hammer and sickle are the counterweight. On issues of fundamental political orientation like modernization for the many versus the few, issues of fundamental moral urgency, it would be worth conducting a ballot among Party members, so that they can be directly involved: become the counterweight.

DENG YINGTAO: We have to be very clear that we are not reforming just for the sake of reform. Nor are we pursuing some ideal of universal equality. This is

242  *Afterword*

not a simple question of principle; it is an extremely practical, extremely real – and therefore extremely difficult – choice. Ostrom says that 'institutional economists assume that the efficiency of institutional arrangements depends on the specific type of problem that they exist to solve'.[112] *There is no historical precedent for modernization for the many.* Making more than a billion Chinese people rich will more than exhaust all of the world's oil reserves. So, (1) the international economy, politics and strategy; (2) development model; and (3) a country's economic model, political systems and even the polity, the country itself, are all completely bound up with one another. We have to look at them all in terms of the most basic things: water resources and the allocation of land. We need *The New Energy Revolution and Shift in Development Model,* with innovation in our theoretical understanding and in our organizations. We need to factor in productivity, economic relationships, our economic infrastructure and the social superstructure that arise upon them. 'Around the world, more than one and a half billion people – roughly one-quarter of the world – lack access to electricity or fossil fuels.'[113] If the CPC successfully leads China on a pathway of modernization for the many, if it can find a better way forward than the Western model, then we won't need another world war to achieve modernization for the developing nations – for all of the seven billion people on the planet, or even for the ten billion that there will be in 2050. With basis of distributed, renewable energy, tailored to make best use of local resources, we can achieve a measure of co-existence and compatibility with nature. Resources can be used sustainably, and the economy can grow sustainably. That's what we should be working for.

WANG XIAOQIANG: 'Listening to you, master, is better than reading ten thousand books', so the story says. For the first time, I think I know what that line means! There's no such thing as a free lunch. You proposed the 'three-body problem' in the early 1980s. At that time, in 1980, the USA was consuming 11 tons of coal equivalent; Japan 6 tons, and China 0.6 tons. By 2005, it was 1.7 tons.[114] Just looking at these numbers and doing the calculations, it doesn't matter how many books we read, how far we go, how much we talk about it, in 30 years' time, we're going to hit a dead end. We are fans of Sweden's democratic socialism, aren't we? Their Social Democratic Party also follows Engels. If we use your three-ingredient 'recipe' as our guide, Sweden's proportion of reciprocity is much higher than the Hong Kong government's – despite the claims of Hong Kong to be run 'for the people'. And what's really worth us paying attention to is that *the Swedish government has announced that they will be a zero-oil country by 2020!* Buses and government vehicles in the capital are now all running off biofuel or methane.[115] In 2007, the European Renewable Energy Council and Greenpeace projected that in 2050, *half of all the world's energy demand could be met using renewable energy sources.*[116] Since the outbreak of the US financial crisis, the Party has repeatedly called for a faster shift in our development model. If I may be so bold, I'm going to make a prediction: if China starts to do these

*Afterword* 243

resource calculations in earnest;[117] if we divert water and plant grass for biomass; if we make a commitment to use only domestic oil by the year 2050, and take real action to achieve that goal, or at least to get our oil imports trending downwards; then there is real hope. Hope for the peaceful rise of China, hope for achieving modernization and hope for the resurgence of the Chinese people!

The old development and industrial models were based on non-renewable energy sources, built up drop by drop over millennia. They exploit and weaken the slow churn of material and energy in our biosphere. This is a route to development and modernity for the few only. For the vast majority of people, that kind of development is a dead end. The new model for development and industry is one that benefits by enhancing the biosphere's natural processes. It is based on distributed, renewable energy. It is the way in which China and the majority of the world's inhabitants are going to achieve modernization. Of course, there are centuries of work to be done yet. 'Every 500 years, a true king arises', Mencius said. Let's hope that's true.[118]

## Notes

1 Philip Hand studied Chinese and linguistics at Cambridge, interpreting at Shanghai International Studies University and translating at Birmingham. He specializes in translating social science research. He lives in Xiamen, southeastern China, with his wife and children.
2 Deng Yingtao, Wang Xaoqiang, Cui Heming and Yangshuang, *Remaking China*, (*zai zao zhongguo*), Shanghai, Wenhui chubanshe, 1999, and Deng Yingtao, Wang Xiaoqiang and Cui Heming, *Strategies for the Development of the West*, (*xibu da kaifa*) Wenhui chubanshe Shanghai, 2001.
3 p. 187.
4 CITIC Press, 1991. Reissue with additional material and English translation published by Strong Wind Press.
5 See 鄧英淘:《新能源革命與發展方式躍遷》217~221頁, 彭小蒙:〈后记〉。 (PENG Xiaomeng, 'Afterword', in DENG Yingtao, *The New Energy Revolution and Shift in Development Model*, 2011, pp. 217–21).
6 王小强:《 "摸著石頭過河": 中國改革之路—對薩克斯和科爾奈的批評》。 (WANG Xiaoqiang, *China's Price and Enterprise Reform*, 1998).
7 'What I have called the "three-body problem" – the combination of the external environment, China's internal structure, and its goals and the direction in which it evolves – directly determines the way in which China modernizes, and the degree of success it achieves.' See the introduction to this volume.
8 The first Chinese studies of development models date to the end of 1984. It was clear at that time that China could not, and should not, go the same way as the developed world and adopt the 'classic' development model. There was also a growing awareness that the development model then current in China, which had as its chief aim to satisfy people's basic needs, had drawbacks. See p. 4.
9 'Since World War II, the major industrialized powers – the United States, Japan, and the Western European countries – have jointly consumed the lion's share of the global energy supply…. As recently as 1990, China accounted for a mere 8 percent of global energy consumption while the United States was absorbing 24 percent of the available supply and the Western European nations 20 percent.' (Michael Klare, *Rising Powers, Shrinking Planet*, 2009).

244 *Afterword*

10 In 2002, Frank Gaffney, a former US Assistant Secretary of Defense, made the following impassioned argument at a Congress hearing on 'oil diplomacy'

> if the Chinese economy achieves per capita energy consumption levels comparable to those of Japan…China alone would require some 70 percent of the world's current oil production. Should, on the other hand, the Chinese reach contemporary American consumption levels…the People's Republic alone would require more than the entire global production of oil. This is obviously a formula for a conflict with China... they are working assiduously to develop relationships with oil suppliers, most of them being what we call 'rogue states'…They are trading oil for advanced weaponry, in some cases weapons of mass destruction-relevant technology
>
> (Toby Shelley, *Oil: Politics, Poverty and the Planet*, 2006 pp. 177–8)

11 On 14 April 2010, Obama said in an interview on Australian radio:

> Well you know I think China has an enormous interest in solving this problem. You know if you talk to Chinese leaders I think they will acknowledge immediately that if over a billion Chinese citizens have the same living patterns as Australians and Americans do right now then all of us are in for a very miserable time, the planet just can't sustain it, so they understand that they've got to make a decision about a new model that is more sustainable that allows them to pursue the economic growth that they're pursuing while at the same time dealing with these environmental consequences.
>
> (*Face to Face with Obama*, Australian Broadcasting Corporation, http://www.abc. net.au/7.30/content/2010/s2872726.htm)

12 The idea I laid out in that paper was that simply copying the Western economic structures and regulatory mechanisms wouldn't resolve the structural challenges that China's developing industries face. I introduced the concepts of 'short-term constraints on resources', and 'a new developmental stage', and I proposed for the first time that the situation China faces is so different from the West that they can't really be mentioned in the same breath. (鄧英陶、羅小朋:〈論總量分析和總量政策在我國經濟理論與實踐中的局限性 —— 兼析我國經濟運行中的某些基本特徵〉,《經濟研究》1987 年 6 月號;《鄧英淘集》129~153 頁) (DENG Yingtao, LUO Xiaopeng: "The limitations of numerical limit-based policy in China's economic theory and practice, with an examination of some fundamental features of China's economy," *Economic Research Journal*, June 1987; *Deng Yingtao Collected Works*, 1989, pp. 129–53).

13 鄧英陶:〈在雙重壓力下選擇長期發展方式〉, 國家體改委中國經濟體制改革研究所編:《中國:發展與改革》1988 年 1 月號;《鄧英淘集》251~268頁; 國務院農研中心發展研究所:《走向現代化的抉擇》三章〈制約: 在雙重壓力下選擇長期發展方式〉41~57頁。(DENG Yingtao 'Selecting a development model while under dual pressure' in CESRRI ed., *China: Development and Reform*, January 1988; *Deng Yingtao Collected Works*, 1989, p. 251–68; 'Constraints: selecting a long term development model under dual pressure', Chapter. 3 of Research Centre for Rural Development ed. *Choices on the Road to Modernization*, pp. 41–57).

14 For example, in 1982 and 1983, China exported 20 million tons of crude and refined oil, and oil made up 23.8 and 21.0 per cent of our exports. (*China Statistical Yearbook 1984*, pp. 381, 389).

15 Michael Klare, *Rising Powers, Shrinking Planet*.

16 In 2005, China National Petroleum Corporation bid successfully for shares in Syria's Al Furat Petroleum Company (Michael Klare, *Rising Powers, Shrinking Planet*).

17 China's African initiative first got under way in the mid-1990s in Sudan, when China National Petroleum Corporation acquired a controlling share in the Greater

Nile Petroleum Operating Company (GNPOC), Sudan's leading oil producer. Since then, CNPC has expanded its presence, obtaining a substantial interest in pipelines, a refinery in Khartoum, and other energy assets... Although Chinese leaders have gone to great lengths to protect their extensive investments in Sudan – even to the point of risking international approbation for their close association with Khartoum – it is not apparent that these assets can be safeguarded forever... [Given the gravity of the situation in Darfur,] It is entirely possible, then, that China's Sudanese investments may not prove as durable or attractive as they once appeared.

(Michael Klare, *Rising Powers, Shrinking Planet*)

18  For example, Kuwait did not allow the formation of political parties until it was rescued by George Bush Sr in the first Gulf War. Qatar is home to a US 'Central Command' base; the hereditary monarch has produced a constitution. The Jordanian monarchy has produced a constitution, which concentrates power in the hands of the Hashemite royal house. The king has the right to approve and promulgate laws, appoint a prime minister, call and dismiss parliament, and command the army. Oman is a monarchy with no constitution and no parliament, and political parties are banned. Saudi Arabia is a monarchy with no constitution. Political parties are banned. (See 王小強:《"文明衝突"的背後》(WANG Xiaoqiang, *Behind the 'Clash of Civilizations'*, 2004)).

19  'Nevertheless, some American policymakers regularly portray China's energy endeavors on the continent as a significant threat to U.S. interests, requiring a forceful riposte.' In 2005, the chairman of the House of Congress Subcommittee on Africa (part of the Foreign Affairs Committee) said:

> ...the Chinese intend to aid and abet African dictators, gain a stranglehold on precious African natural resources, and undo much of the progress that has been made on democracy and governance in the last 15 years in African nations. This is an extremely worrying situation.

In 2006, The report to Congress by the US-China Economic and Security Review Commission said:

> China's strategy of securing ownership and control of oil and natural gas assets abroad could substantially affect U.S. energy security—reducing the ability of the global petroleum market to ameliorate temporary and limited petroleum supply disruptions in the United States and elsewhere... China's energy policies, taken as a whole, are not consistent with the economic or geopolitical behavior of a responsible stakeholder; they distort markets and destabilize volatile regions.

(Michael Klare, *Rising Powers, Shrinking Planet*).

20  For details, please see the Strong Wind Press website: www.hkstrongwind.com(accessed 6 December 2013).
21  See: 鄧英淘、何維凌:《動態經濟系統的調節與演化》,《鄧英淘集》, 鄧英淘、姚鋼、徐笑波、薛玉煒:《中國預算外資金分析》, 陳吉元、鄧英淘、薛玉煒、劉建進:《中國農村的變革與發展》,姚鋼、鄧英淘、薛玉煒、徐笑波:《發展·變革·反思》,徐笑波、鄧英淘、薛玉煒、劉建進、胡斌:《中國農村金融的變革與發展》, 農村經濟年度分析課題組:《經濟綠皮書: 中國農村經濟發展年度報告》1992~1994 年, 中國社科院經濟文化研究中心:《三網合一》、《家電世界》(DENG Yingtao, HE Weiling, *Regulation and Evolution of Dynamic Economic Systems, 1985*; DENG Yingtao *et al.*, *Deng Yingtao Collected Works*; DENG Yingtao, YAO Gang, XU Xiaobo, XUE Yuwei, *Analysis of China's Extra-Budgetary Funds*, 1990; CHEN Jiyuan, DENG Yingtao, XUE Yuwei, LIU Jianjin, *Rural Reforms and Development in China*, 1992; YAO Gang, DENG Yingtao, XUE Yuwei, XU Xiaobo, *Development, Reform, Reflections*, 1992; XU Xiaobo, DENG

246 *Afterword*

Yingtao, XUE Yuwei, LIU Jianjin, HU Bin, *Changes and Development in Rural Finance in China*, 1994; Rural Development Institute, *Economy Green Paper: Annual Report on the Development of China's Rural Economy 1992–94*; CASS Centre for Economic and Cultural Research, *Integrating Three Networks*; *Domestic Appliances*, 2000) etc.

22 Research Centre for Rural Development ed., *Development Research Report 4*, September 1988.

23 李周等：《全國百家鄉鎮企業經濟典型調查——西安生態養殖場》：另見董建勤：〈旅遊到豬場〉，《人民日報》2000 年 6 月 16 日 9 版。(LI Zhou *et al.*, *Survey of the Best 100 Village Enterprises – The Xi'an Eco-Animal Breeding Farm*, 1998. See also DONG Jianqin, "Holiday on a pig farm," in *People's Daily*, September 16, 2000, p.9, http://www.people.com.cn /BIG5/channel1/13/20000616/105878.html).

24 'Deng Yingtao of the Rural Development Institute made some important suggestions for improvements to the research plan and to this book. He visited the site twice, and edited the entire book.' 李周等：《全國百家鄉鎮企業經濟典型調查 — 西安生態養殖場》第 216 頁。(LI Zhou *et al.*, *Survey of the Best 100 Village Enterprises - The Xi'an Eco-Animal Breeding Farm*, p. 216).

25 Former premier and, at the time of the trip, general-secretary of the Communist Party of China. *Trans.*

26 Influential economist and government advisor. *Trans.*

27 Headwaters of the Brahmaputra. *Trans.*

28 《再造一個中國——溯天運河簡介及其意義淺析》. The research group had not yet been set up, so this report was published under the name of the International Issues Group, Centre for Economic and Cultural Research (http://lib.cnki.net/cjfd/ ZGSW812.009.html, accessed 6 December 2013). See also 鄧英淘：《再造中國，走向未來，1~14頁。(DENG Yingtao, *Remaking China, Moving Forward*, pp. 1–14). Shuoma is curve of the Yarlung-Tsangpo River in Tibet; Tianjin is on the eastern coast of China. *Trans.*

29 See the introduction by Nan Huai-chin to *Remaking China* (http://www.hkstrongwind. com/ product/780531649x.aspx, accessed 6 December 2013).

30 Headwaters of the Salween. *Trans.*

31 Headwaters of the Mekong. *Trans.*

32 盧躍剛：《長江三峽: 半個世紀的論證》。(Lu Yuegang, *Three Gorges: Fifty Years of Evidence*, 1993).

33 楊世華：《林一山治水文選》編者的話。(YANG Shihua, "Editor's note" in *Hydrological Writings of Lin Yishan*, 1992 ). See also 楊世華：《葛洲壩工程的決策》，長江水利委員會宣傳新聞中心：《林一山與長江人》，盧躍剛：《長江三峽》 (YANG Shihua, *Decision-making for the Gezhouba Dam*, 1995; Yangtze Hydrological Committee, *Lin Yishan and the People of the Yangtze*, 2001; Lu Yuegang, *The Yangtze Three Gorges: Fifty Years of Evidence*).

34 Mythical king who first controlled the waters of the Yellow River to ease the dangers of flooding in northern China. *Trans.*

35 *In the dry northwest of China, the water and sand of the Yellow River are not flood threats, as they are in the lower reaches, but precious resources. It is an enormous waste to allow them to flow into the ocean.*

The greatest error in the approaches to Yellow River control has been to see the Yellow River as a problem. Its waters and silt have been seen as something to defend against, to channel directly to the ocean. Hydrologists have failed to see this water and silt as an agricultural resource to be exploited and maximized. The high silt content of the Yellow River is a complex phenomenon. It won't be changed simply by conserving the topsoil in the wetlands of its headwaters. Conservation of topsoil is a rather primitive concept. We should more properly think of the best way to use topsoil and wetlands.

So Lin Yishan always advocated using the water of the Yellow River above the Sanmenxia Dam, and providing water to the eastern areas around the lower Yellow River through a water diversion scheme bringing water north from the Yangtze. (See 林一山：〈治理黃河應立足于把黃河水沙喝光吃淨〉，《當代治黃論壇》6~16 頁；《林一山治水文選》〈黃河水沙資源利用問題〉；林一山：〈河流辯證法與沖積平原河流治理〉第五章〈"兩論"與黃河流域的治理開發〉；《林一山縱論治水興國》第十章〈治黃大方略〉、第 19 章〈再談治黃大方略〉；鄧英淘；《再造中國，走向未來》53.〈治理黃河的關鍵 ─ 在中游吃淨水沙資源〉、54.〈再談治理黃河的關鍵 ─ 在中游吃淨水沙資源〉。(LIN Yishan, 'Managing the Yellow River should involve making full use of its water and silt', in *Contemporary Yellow River Management Forum*, pp. 6–16; 'On the exploitation of Yellow River water and silt', in *Selected Hydrological Writings of Lin Yishan*, 1995; '5. Two philosophies and their relevance to controlling the Yellow River', in *River Dialectics and Flood Control for River Plains*, 2007; '10. Strategies for controlling the Yellow River' and '19. Strategies for controlling the Yellow River revisited', in CASS, *Lin Yishan on Flood Control for National Development*, 2007; DENG Yingtao, '53. Key to controlling the Yellow River: full exploitation of mid-reach water and silt' and '54. Further thoughts on the key to controlling the Yellow River: full exploitation of mid-reach water and silt', in *Remaking China, Moving Forward*).)

36 See 林一山：《中國西部南水北調工程》；《林一山縱論治水興國》第一章〈關於西線調水〉，第二章〈大西線調水與西部大開發〉，第三章〈西部調水工程的經濟可行性〉，第四章〈林一山與西部南水北調工程〉。(LIN Yishan, *The South–North Water Transfer Project in Western China*, 2001; '1. The western channels for water diversion', '2. Water diversion through the western channel and the development of western China' and '3. Economic feasibility of water diversion in western China' in CASS, *Lin Yishan on Flood Control for National Development*).

37 鄧英淘：〈附錄I(第二章的附錄)對R與S間反比關係的一點認識〉，〈附錄II(第三章的附錄)對水流運動中分力與合力的幾點認識〉，林一山：《河流辯證法與沖積平原河流治理》178~186頁。(DENG Yingtao, 'Appendix I (Chapter 2) A point on the inverse relationship between R and S' and 'Appendix II (Chapter 3) Some points on the combination and decomposition of forces in water flow', in LIN Yishan, *River Dialectics and Flood Control for River Plains*, pp. 178–86).

38 Twentieth century historian who famously dictated his books after going blind, while his wife served as amanuensis. *Trans.*

39 See 鄧英淘：《再造中國 走向未來》49.〈什麼是"大西線"〉，50.〈再談林陳鄧大西線方案〉，51.〈風電對大西線調水的意義〉。(DENG Yingtao, '49. What is the 'western channel'?', '50. Further remarks on the Lin-Chen-Deng "western channel"', '51. Wind power and water diversion through the western channel', in *Remaking China, Moving Forward*).

40 See 鄧英淘：《新能源革命與發展方式躍遷》9.〈風能資源的利用與開發〉 (DENG Yingtao, '9. Use and development of wind energy resources', in *The New Energy Revolution and Shift in Development Model*).

41 Shortly before the time of the interview, there was a well-publicized brawl in a factory in Guangdong between a group of ethnically Chinese workers and a group of ethically Uighur workers. *Trans.*

42 The westernmost channel or 'western route' of the South–North Water Transfer Project. *Trans.*

43 See 鄧英淘：《再造中國，走向未來》19.〈三江並流貫通調水方案〉，49.〈什麼是"大西線"〉，50.〈再談林陳鄧大西線方案〉。(DENG Yingtao, '19. Connection and diversion at Three Parallel Rivers', '49. What is the "western channel"', '50. Further remarks on the Lin-Chen-Deng 'western channel', *Remaking China, Moving Forward*).

44 鄧英淘、王小強、崔鶴鳴、楊雙：《再造中國》。(DENG Yingtao, WANG Xiaoqiang, CUI Heming, YANG Shuang, *Remaking China*).

248 *Afterword*

45 See 鄧英淘:《再造中國 走向未來》20. 〈陜北生態建設考察報告〉 楊瑩:〈一戶治沙 11 萬畝 ── 靖邊縣農民牛玉琴訪談紀要〉,〈聯合190戶貧困戶治沙 20 萬畝 ── 定邊縣農民石光銀訪談紀要〉; 鄧英淘等:《西部大開發調研實錄》 351~361 頁。〉 (DENG Yingtao, '20. Report on the natural environment in northern Shaanxi', in *Remaking China, Moving Forward*; YANG Ying, 'One household stops desertification on 110,000 *mu*! An interview with Niu Yuqin, Jianbian County farmer'; '190 poor farming families cooperate to stop desertification on 200,000 *mu* – An interview with Shi Guangyin, Dingbian County farmer' in DENG Yingtao, *Notes from Surveys of Development in the West*, 2001, pp. 351–61).

46 See 鄧英淘:《再造中國, 走向未來》12. 〈西部調水, 事關全域, 大有可為 ── 甘、、寧二省水土資源問題考察報告〉 (DENG Yingtao, '12. Water diversion: the key to everything, and feasible - report on water and soil resources in Gansu and Ningxia', in *Remaking China, Moving Forward*).

47 See 鄧英淘:《新能源革命與發展方式躍遷》5. 〈太陽能資源的開發利用〉。(DENG Yingtao, '5. Use and development of solar energy resources', in *The New Energy Revolution and Shift in Development Model*).

48 See 鄧英淘:《新能源革命與發展方式躍遷》4. 〈礦物燃料與交通用能〉, 6. 〈汽車燃料甲烷化〉。 (DENG Yingtao, '4. Fossil fuels and transport energy', '6. Converting vehicles to methane', in *The New Energy Revolution and Shift in Development Model*).

49 See 鄧英淘:《新能源革命與發展方式躍遷》代序: 〈三重大變局〉。(DENG Yingtao, 'Introduction: Three important changes' in *The New Energy Revolution and Shift in Development Model*).

50 See 鄧英淘:《新能源革命與發展方式躍遷》8. 〈生物質能的開發與利用〉。(DENG Yingtao, '8. Use and development of biomass energy' in *The New Energy Revolution and Shift in Development Model*).

51 See 鄧英淘:《新能源革命與發展方式躍遷》10. 〈塔里木盆地光热水土資源綜合利用構想〉 (DENG Yingtao, '10. A vision of integrated use of the solar, mineral, water and land resources of the Tarim Basin', in *The New Energy Revolution and Shift in Development Model*).

52 《史記‧貨殖列傳》 ('Biographies of the merchants', *Records of the Grand Historian*). Nan Huai-chin comments: 南懷瑾:《老子他說續集》,〈小國寡民就是地方自治〉 469~472頁。(NAN Huai-chin, 'Small countries means local autonomy' in *More What Laozi Said*, 2009, pp. 469–72).

> As I see it, Laozi's argument is not significantly different from the Confucian idea of Great Unity. But Laozi approaches it by describing the ideal state, while the Confucian text, the 'Great Unity' chapter in the *Classic of Rites*, explains the underlying principles. The two are both expressions of the same ancient Chinese traditions, and it would be a great pity to declare them two separate 'schools' just because of some textual differences.... So the ideal of 'never in their lives do they engage with the people of another state' would be hard to achieve unless the whole world – all of humanity – was in a state of wealth and happiness. That would be the only way to realize this perfect world.
> (南懷瑾:《孟子旁通》229~230頁 (NAN Huai-chin, *A Book of Mencius*, 1991, pp. 229–30))

53     According to the Department of Energy, the 440 civilian power reactors now in operation around the world require between 165 and 185 million pounds of uranium per year. At these rates of consumption, the available supply – mostly concentrated in mines and stock-piles in Australia, Canada, Namibia, Niger, South Africa, the United States and the former Soviet Union – is considered adequate for another 40 years.

> (Michael Klare, *Rising Powers, Shrinking Planet*)

*Afterword* 249

54 'The sage king soothes our material wants, so he ends strife in this world.' (曾國藩: 〈《王船山遺書》序〉, 塗小馬、崔泳准:《曾國藩文選》49 頁 (Zeng Guofan, 'Introduction', in *Bequeathed Writings of Wang Fuzhi*, reprinted in TU Xiaoma, CUI Yonghuai, ed, *Zeng Guofan Selected Works*, 2001, p. 49).

55     For a company, the Golden Rule means that the company operates almost entirely for the benefit of its employees. The Golden Rule strategy is a cooperative strategy. The other extreme is individual maximization, or cost minimization. At this extreme, the company attempts to minimize the amenities (including wages) that it provides to its employees, and at the same time to maximize what it obtains from the employees. This strategy is one of complete antagonism.... For the employees, the Golden Rule strategy means that they work as though they are the owners of the company. That is to say, they work for the interests of the company. They treat their work in the same way as they hope the company will treat them. The employees' Golden Rule strategy is a cooperative strategy. At the other end of the scale, they will do what they can to minimize their 'input' while still receiving the same pay. This strategy is one of complete antagonism.
Roger Frantz, *X-efficiency: Theory, Evidence and Applications*, (throughout, quotations have been back-translated. *Trans*.).

In general, '*The Golden Rule seems to be a universal phenomenon in human society… The Golden Rule was universally recognized in early societies.*' It is 'do not do to others what you would not have done to yourself' (Ken Binmore, 'The Golden Rule' in *Natural Justice*, 2010.

56 'No stick is commonly flourished. What happens most of the time is that the carrot is withdrawn a tiny bit. Shoulders are turned slightly away. Greetings are imperceptibly gruffer. Eyes wander elsewhere...' (Ken Binmore, *Natural Justice)*.

     Making the family the unit of contractual governance has the advantage of limiting opportunistic behaviour and reducing transaction costs and information asymmetries.... The guilt created by disloyalty limits opportunistic behaviour between family members. And the emotional bonds between group members also show that the punishments for members who break the rules are not dependent on the intervention of public officials; and are the more powerful for it.
     (Ostrom *et al.*, *Institutional Incentives and Sustainable Development*, 2000)

57 Roger Frantz, *X-efficiency: Theory, Evidence and Applications*, 1993.

58     For some reason, efficiency has been changed into allocative efficiency only.... Economics was defined as the logic of the allocation of scarce resources to alternative uses. Markets were then studied from the viewpoint that they allocated society's economic resources efficiently to alternative uses. What got lost in this progression of economics was the businessman's idea and the engineer's idea of efficiency'

so, 'x represents the non-allocative (lack of) efficiency which was previously unexplained.... X-efficiency attempts to more generally research the psychological bases for individual work (effort) choices, and how individuals are affected by their group'. (Roger Frantz, *X-efficiency: Theory, Evidence and Applications*).

59 Corporations compete to survive. 'Neoclassical choice theory (among others) analyzes the impact of external factors on corporate performance. That is because they believe that they believe these factors to be relatively easy to measure and analyze.' But in reality, 'But given equal technology, the organization of employees is perhaps the most important factor deciding productivity levels - that is the power of the ability to assign positions.' (Roger Frantz, *X-efficiency: Theory, Evidence and Applications*).

250  *Afterword*

60 'In every hierarchy, employees tend to rise to their level of incompetence.... In time, every post tends to be occupied by an employee who is incompetent to carry out its duties.... Work is accomplished by those employees who have not yet reached their level of incompetence.' (Peter and Hull, *The Peter Principle*, 2007 pp. 22–4).

61 A private army which supported the Southern Song Dynasty after northern China had been occupied by the invading Jurchens. *Trans.*

62 See Chapter 3, 'Breakdown of natural resources'.

63 There is disagreement among scientists about the date of peak oil, but none of the predictions place it any later than 2020. There is consensus that we are very close to entering a period of oil scarcity.' (浩君:《石油到底出了什麼問題》181頁 (HAU Jun, *What's the Problem with Oil*, 2005, p. 181)).

> *Many experts believe that when it comes to petroleum, this process of exhaustion is already well under way....* While oil accounted for approximately 40 percent of world energy use in 2006 (natural gas, the number two fuel, supplied only 25 percent) and is expected to remain number one in 2030, *it is the energy source most likely to dwindle in the decades ahead...* the oil giant BP has used the best information available to estimate that the world currently possesses 6.405 trillion cubic feet of conventional gas reserves – enough to satisfy world demand for sixty-four years at the current rate of consumption, or forty years at the higher rates projected by the DoE for 2010 and beyond (emphasis added).
>
> (Michael Klare, *Rising Powers, Shrinking Planet*)

64 See 鄧英淘:《再造中國, 走向未來》20. 〈陝北生態建設考察報告〉 (DENG Yingtao, '20. Report on the natural environment in northern Shaanxi' in *Remaking China, Moving Forward*).

65     Today, systems analysis depends on very rough categorisation, labelling systems either as public or private, that is, either as part of the state or part of the market. This has led to a simplistic diagnosis for market failures and for state failures: either they require government intervention, or they require privatization.... Just as the old analysis overly simplified the choice between state and market, the assumption that one has to choose either centralisation or decentralisation is also too simplistic.... *Privatisation is not a panacea.*

> (Ostrom *et al.*, *Institutional Incentives and Sustainable Development*)

66 'No market can exist for long without underlying public institutions to support it. In field settings, public and private institutions frequently are intermeshed and depend on one another, rather than existing in isolated worlds.' (Ostrom, *Governing the Commons*, 2000, p. 15).

67 See Ostrom *et al.*, *Institutional Incentives and Sustainable Development*, especially Chapter 9, 'Polycentric institutional arrangements'.

68     My 'organism' is a type of human situation. I call this situation a CPR [common-pool resource] situation.... Because the individuals involved gain a major part of their economic return from CPRs, they are strongly motivated to try to solve common problems to enhance their own productivity over time.

> (Ostrom, *Governing the Commons*, p. 26)

69 In the USA, 'the Midwest townships are based upon land survey units... the result is that nearly 55% of townships serve less than 1000 residents. In 1982, only 1019 townships had over 1000 residents'. Municipalities (cities, villages and incorporated towns). 'More than 141 million people reside within the boundaries of a municipality' (Vincent Ostrom, Robert L. Bish, Elinor Ostrom, *Local Government in the United States*, 2004, pp. 5–7).

# Afterword    251

70 Incentives go beyond just financial rewards and penalties. They are the positive and negative changes that people can feel in their outcomes. These feelings may be produced by specific actions taken within a certain system, against the backdrop of a certain entity and social climate. Other types of motivation include: (1) opportunities for promotion, increase in prestige or obtaining personal authority; (2) improvements in the quality of the physical environment, including tidier, quieter surroundings or a private office; (3) pride in one's own work, the service one provides to one's family or other people, or patriotism or religious feeling; (4) comfort and satisfaction in one's social relations; (5) consistency with familiar practice and attitudes; (6) a sense of participation in something important. Incentives arise from a wide range of causes, and individual values or the values of a shared institutional culture can be strong motivators.

> (Ostrom *et al.*, *Institutional Incentives and Sustainable Development*)

71 It is interesting that Elinor Ostrom, who did receive a Nobel Prize, believed the same as Vincent Ostrom. *In the writing for which she was cited, she refers to her husband's books with the very highest praise*:

> As Vincent Ostrom has so well demonstrated (1986a, 1987, 1989), when the 'theory of the state' is used as the theory underlying a concept of democratic self-governance, basic contradictions exist. As long as a single center has a monopoly on the use of coercion, one has a state rather than a self-governed society.
>
> (Ostrom, *Governing the Commons*, p. 222)

72 鄧英淘、崔之元、苗壯:《南街村》。(DENG Yingtao, CUI Zhiyuan, MIAO Zhuang, *Nanjie Village*, 1996).

73 By the late 1970s, Mondragon had a modern cooperative technical education system and '70 cooperative factories with a workforce of over 15,000 cooperative members, and had a credit cooperative bank with 93 branches and 300,000 accounts'. (Thomas and Logan, *Mondragon: An Economic Analysis*, 1991, p. 1).

74 Using mathematical formulae and diagrams, Olson gives a powerful argument that because of the danger of free riders, '*If the members of a large group rationally seek to maximize their personal welfare, they will not act to advance their common or group objectives....*' Olson reaches the strong conclusion that,

> *Just as it was not rational for a particular producer to restrict his output in order that there might be a higher price for the product of his industry, so it would not be rational for him to sacrifice his time and money to support a lobbying organization to obtain government assistance for the industry. In neither case would it be in the interest of the individual producer to assume any of the costs himself. A lobbying organization, or indeed a labor union or any other organization, working in the interest of a large group of firms or workers in some industry, would get no assistance from the rational, self-interested individuals in that industry.*
>
> (Mancur Olson, *The Logic of Collective Action*, 1995, pp. 2, 11, emphasis in the original)

> On the basis of these conclusions, Olson went on to write *The Rise and Decline of Nations and Power and Prosperity*, stressing that the source of a nation's prosperity is the government's strong and consistent protection of free market competition.

75 (汪甯、蔡書凱:〈國家理論:一個經濟學的分析角度〉,《國外理論動態》2010 年 4 期 83~85 頁。(WANG Ning and CAI Shukai, 'Theory of the state: an economic perspective', *Foreign Theoretical Trends* 4, 2010, pp. 83–5)). This paper is a digest of Yoram Barzel, *A Theory of the State: Economic Rights, Legal Rights, and the Scope of the State*, 2006.

252 *Afterword*

76 Since Garrett Hardin's challenging article in *Science* (1968), the expression 'the tragedy of the commons' has come to symbolize the degradation of the environment to be expected whenever many individuals use a scarce resource in common.... The tragedy of the commons, the prisoner's dilemma, and the logic of collective action are closely related concepts in the models.... At the heart of each of these models is the free-rider problem.

(Ostrom, *Governing the Commons*, pp. 2, 6)

77 Ostrom *et al.*, *Rules, Games, and Common-Pool Resources*, 2011.
78 《毛澤東選集》四卷 1131頁。(MAO Zedong *Selected Works of Mao Zedong*, 1991, vol. 4, p. 1131).
79 An American named Locke

has opened a factory half way up the side of Mount Fuji called the Mt Fuji Canned Fresh Air Factory. They use extremely cheap and attractive packaging to make boxes of cans, fill them with clean fresh air from Mt Fuji, and stamp on a picture of the mountain. When this product was marketed, it had a certain appeal to people who have lived for years in polluted big cities. This type of can is very cheap, and sales are enormous. Mt Fuji Canned Fresh Air took Japan by storm. Locke is also preparing to export it. He is looking at the USA, Europe and tropical countries. Locke has appointed an assistant to run the fresh air factory, and has sent other assistants to develop new products – lake air, ancient forest air, mountain peak air, and air from the Alps.

(《經營謀略全書》(*The Book of Business Strategies*), http://www.lantianyu.net/pdf30/ts057019_8.htm).

80 〈"空氣罐頭"成張家界旅遊最新特產〉 '"Fresh air in a can" the next big idea for Zhangjiajie's tourism industry' (http://www.citure.net/info/2010726/2010726101952.shtml).
81 The U.S. magazine Global Finance published a survey of GDP in 182 countries and territories in 2010. The top ten were: Qatar, Luxembourg, Norway, Singapore, Brunei, USA, Hong Kong, Switzerland, the Netherlands and Australia. Hong Kong's per capita GDP is listed as $44,840, in seventh position. (http://www.stockfans.net/viewthread.php? tid=17947).
82 See 中信泰富政治暨經濟研究部：《加快轉變經濟發展方式》 (CITIC Pacific Political/Economic Research, *Faster Changes in China's Growth Model*, 2009).

83 we can expect the struggle over energy to override all other considerations, national leaders to go to extreme lengths to ensure energy sufficiency for their countries, and state authority over domestic and foreign energy affairs to expand. Oil will cease to be primarily a trade commodity, to be exchanged on the international market, becoming instead the pre-eminent strategic resource on the planet, whose acquisition, production, and distribution will increasingly absorb the time, effort, and focus of senior government and military officials.

(Michael Klare, *Rising Powers, Shrinking Planet*)

84 'Africa now provides about 20 percent of America's imported oil, and its share is expected to rise to 25% by 2015, as new offshore fields in Angola and Nigeria come online. In 2007, the US President established the Africa Command (AFRICOM), America's first foreign command to be established since President Carter created the nucleus of the Central Command – with responsibility for protecting the Persian Gulf oil flow – in 1980. And while oil is only one of the concerns that figured in the Bush administration's decision to establish AFRICOM, its belief that 'African oil is of strategic national interest to us' was indubitably a key factor.

(Michael Klare, *Rising Powers, Shrinking Planet*)

*Afterword* 253

85 〈改造世界 — 美國21世紀的超級計畫〉,《參考消息》 2011 年 4 月 21 日 10 版。 ('Libya and the new US strategic doctrine', extracts published in *Reference News*, April 21, 2011, p. 10, under the title 'Changing the world: America's grand plan for the 21st century').

> Many of the themes that have since dominated public discussion of US energy policy were raised at a 2005 Congress hearing: that oil and natural gas resources are finite and possibly inadequate to satisfy both rising American and international needs; that China was emerging as America's most significant rival in the struggle to secure the world's untapped oil and gas reserves; and that this struggle could someday lead to violent conflict. 'In a world in which [energy] resources are certainly finite, and possibly contracting,' Pentagon consultant Frank J. Gaffney Jr. testified, 'we will inevitably find ourselves on a collision course with Communist China, particularly if world-wide demand for oil approaches anything like the projected 60 percent growth over the next two decades'
>
> (Michael Klare, *Rising Powers, Shrinking Planet*)

86 習近平: 〈致亞洲政黨 "發展與社會共用" 專題會議的賀信〉, 《人民日報》 2011 年 9 月 5 日 (XI Jinping, 'Address to the International Conference of Asian Political Parties special conference on "Development and People's Access"' in *People's Daily* 5 September 2011) (http://paper.people.com.cn/rmrb/html/2011-09/05/nw.D110000 renmrb_20110905_1-03.htm?div=-1, accessed 6 December 2013).

87 '這正如地上的路: 其實地上本沒有路, 走的人多了, 也便成了路。' (It is just the same as roads on the ground. To begin with, there were no roads; where many people walked, roads appeared). *Trans.*

88 In 1932, 55% of the oil imported by the puppet state Manchukuo came from American oil companies. After the Marco Polo Bridge incident in 1937, 'during the first three years of the Japanese invasion of China, 70% of the 40 million tons of petrol used by the invading army was supplied by American oil companies including Mobil and Texaco.... From the 1931 Mukden incident, Japan's pretext for invading China, up until the early 1940s, the USA was Japan's largest supplier of oil. Japan used on average 5 million tons of oil per year, and 90% of it had to be imported from the USA'. (江紅: 《為石油而戰》140~141頁 (JIANG Hong, *Oil Wars*, pp. 140–1)). In 1940, when Japan signed up to the Axis powers with Germany and Italy, the USA was forced to ban the sale of oil to them, 'and that lit the fuse to the war'. (王豐等:《石油資源戰》72頁 (WANG Feng *et al.*, *Oil Resource Wars*, 2003, p. 72)).

89 'China has one fifth of the world's population, but it has less than 2% of the world's oil reserves.' (Paul Roberts, *The End of Oil, 2005*) Since 1990, in China,

> Nationally, total production is growing at less than 2 percent a year, while demand for oil is growing by 7 percent.... China offers a dramatic and disturbing hint of the size and shape of the emerging energy economy, and the tensions that will keep that economy in a constant state of flux. Already, our energy system is straining to produce adequate energy supplies. Oil is becoming physically and politically harder to find.
>
> (Ibid., pp. 145, 160)

90 JIANG Hong, *Oil Wars*.

91 See 王小強:《投機賭博新經濟》五章〈迫近中國的金融危機〉和中信泰富政治暨經濟研究部:《加快轉變經濟發展方式》。(WANG Xiaoqiang, "The financial crisis presses on China," in *Gambler's Economy*, 2007; and CITIC Pacific Political/ Economic Research, *Faster Changes in China's Growth Model*).

92 〈賣沙特六百億軍火, 美國想幹什麼?〉,《人民日報》2010 年 9 月 1 6 日 ('What is the USA doing selling $60bn of arms to Saudi Arabia?' *People's Daily*, 16 September 2010, http://news.xinhuanet.com/world/2010-09/16/c_12573964.htm, accessed 6 December 2013).

## 254  *Afterword*

93 See 王小強:《史無前例的挑戰》附錄:〈哀莫大於分裂〉 (WANG Xiaoqiang, *Challenges Unprecedented in History* 2006, particularly 'Appendix: No fate worse than disunion'). According to figures published by the US Department of Commerce on 11 February 2011, the USA's trade deficit with China in 2010 was \$273.07bn. (〈2010 年中美貿易情況〉 (China–US trade in 2010), http://mds.mofcom.gov.cn/aarticle/date/201102/20110207409467.html?723069832=39327266, accessed 6 December 2013). 'The United States Arms Control and Disarmament Agency estimates that the Middle East accounted for 43% of all arms imports in 1992–1994, and 70% of the region's imports were in the eight Gulf states.' (安維華、錢雪梅:《海灣石油新論》401 頁, (AN Weihua, QIAN Xuemei, *A New Theory of Gulf Oil*, 2000, p. 401).

94 The youngest set of institutions to be analyzed in this chapter is already more than 100 years old. The history of the oldest system exceeds 1,000 years. The institutions discussed in this chapter have survived droughts, floods, wars, pestilence, and major economic and political changes.... The Swiss and Japanese mountain commons have been sustained, if not enhanced, over the centuries while being used intensively. Ecological sustainability in a fragile world of avalanches, unpredictable precipitation, and economic growth is quite an accomplishment for any group of appropriators working over many centuries. Keeping order and maintaining large-scale irrigation works in the difficult terrain of Spain or the Philippine Islands have been similarly remarkable achievements... Generations of Swiss and Japanese villagers have learned the relative benefits and costs of private-property and communal-property institutions related to various types of land and uses of land. The villagers in both settings have chosen to retain the institution of communal property as the foundation for land use and similar important aspects of village economies.

(Ostrom, *Governing the Commons*, pp. 58–61)

95 A banner that Mao wrote when working as a young teacher at the primary school attached to Hunan No. 1 Teachers College (http://www.ysyfx.com.introduce).

96 Celebrated war heroes and representatives of the communist spirit. *Trans.*

97 A line from Mao Zedong's poem *Farewell to the God of the Plague*. Yao and Shun were mythical great kings of early China, the originators of much of Chinese culture. *Trans.*

98 NAN Huai-Chin, *Mencius*, King Hui of Liang, Part I.

99 See Thomas and Logan, *Mondragon: An Economic Analysis*, Chapter 6.

100 It has been proved in game theory that rational altruism produces fair reciprocal systems. '...nobody knew to whom the idea should be attributed. It is therefore called the folk theorem... the folk theorem tells us that many efficient equilibria are available as possible social contracts'. (Ken Binmore, *Natural Justice*, pp. 10, 14; see also Chapter 1 'Moral science' and Chapter 5 'Reciprocity').

101 NAN Huai-chin, *Mencius*, 'King Hui of Liang' and 'Teng Wen Gong'.

102 See p. 24–25.

103 Villages which did not privatize their economies in the 1980s, but kept everything collective, and subsequently achieved great wealth. *Trans.*

104 楊松林:〈重建歷史文化觀, 重溫新民主主義〉中"共產黨執政合法性來自哪裡"一節,《香港傳真》 (YANG Songlin, 'Rebuilding our understanding of history and culture, reviving the new democracy movement', *HK Fax*, particularly the section 'Where does the legitimacy of the Communist Party's rule come from').

105 代金平、唐海軍:〈國外政黨是如何維護黨員主體地位的〉,《北京日報》2010 年 7 月 5 日 (DAI Jinping, TANG Haijun, "How political parties in other countries keep party members at the centre," *Beijing Daily*, 5 July 2010).

106 We have always had them: the unrecognized hard workers, the battlers, the unresting advocates, the endless seekers after something better.... Even in the 'official histories',

which sometimes seem to be little more than family albums for the great and the good, you can still catch glimpses of their vigour. They are the marrow of China. (魯迅:《且介亭雜文》94 頁 (LU Xun, *Essays from a Room on the International Battlements*, 1973, p. 94)).

107 'The president, director of executive affairs and director of policy research are known as the LDP's "three powers". The system of allocating these three roles to the three LDP factions is called the 'three power split.' (伊藤昌哉:《自民党戰國史》4 頁 (ITO Masaya, *A History of the LDP's Civil Wars*, 1984, p.4))

108 'Except in the desert, wherever you have a group of people together, they will split into left, right and centre; and this will still be true 10,000 years from now.' 《毛澤東選集》四卷428頁。(MAO Zedong, *Selected Works of Mao Zedong*, vol. 4, p. 428).

109 Our party is not in a single party system. There are other political parties; and there are factions within the Party. That's how it has always been. It's normal. In the past we criticised the KMT for not allowing other political parties, and for having no internal factions. We said, 'A single party system is nothing but royalism. A party without factions is bizarre.' It's the same for the Communist Party. You think it has no factions? Of course it does. For example, there are two factions when it comes to the issue of mass movements, though one faction has considerably more support than the other.
(毛澤東:《在中共八屆 11 中全會閉幕會上的講話》1966 年 8 月 12 日, 中共中央檔刊印 (Mao Zedong, 'Remarks at the closing of the 11th plenary of the 8th general committee', 12/8/1966, *CPC Documents*)).

110 Anyone who wishes to become president of the party and prime minister must first become a faction leader.... The president is selected through one of two processes: one is a party ballot, as in the party's constitution; the other is through a deal. But both processes require the acceptance of the majority of party members.... The president of the party becomes prime minister after a vote in the Diet (the candidate approved by the lower house becomes prime minister), and then wields full governmental authority. That's why in Japan the president of the party and the prime minister are the same concept. When political problems start to accumulate (economic troubles, sensitive diplomatic issues, failure to get legislation passed by the Diet, etc.), the newspapers, TV and magazines will start to criticise the cabinet. Within a year, public opinion will turn against them. Then the factions within the party will start to play their appointed role of restraining each other's excesses. This is similar to the adversarial role played by an opposition party, and soon enough a political crisis is forced. When a cabinet is faced by this sort of opposition, its authority is rapidly weakened. The term for president of the party is two years. At the end of each term, the president must once again demonstrate that he has the support of the majority of the party, and this process determines whether he can continue in office, or must resign. When there is a handover of power, it is generally a leader of another faction who takes over.
(伊藤昌哉:《自民党戰國史》5-6頁 (ITO Masaya, *A History of the LDP's Civil Wars*, pp. 5–6)).

111 See 鄧英淘改編(南懷瑾原著):《中國傳統文化導讀》 (DENG Yingtao, ed., *Reader for Chinese Traditional Culture* in NAN Huai-chin, *Selections from the Analects*, 1990).

112 Ostrom *et al.*, *Institutional Incentives and Sustainable Development*.

113 2.5 billion people still rely on wood, dried animal manure, or other so-called biomass for nearly every calorie of energy used for cooking, heating and lighting... In all some 3 billion people – almost a third of the world's population – rely on

256  *Afterword*

energy systems that fail to meet even the most basic human needs. As developing nations have the fastest population growth, energy poverty – the slow-motion failure of energy security – is sure to be one of the most serious problems of the next several decades.

(Paul Roberts, *The End of Oil*, pp. 8, 241)

114  See p. 20, Table 1.2, and 鄧英淘:《新能源革命與發展方式躍遷》7 頁。 (DENG Yingtao *The New Energy Revolution and Shift in Development Model*, p. 7).

115  In the first half of 2007, over 20,000 alternative fuel vehicles were sold in Sweden, 15% of all new cars sold.

Over the past 5–10 years, Sweden has started to promote the bioethanol industry. Today, bioethanol-fuelled cars are everywhere in Sweden…. EU figures show that renewables now make up 28% of Sweden's energy mix, four times more than the European average. Only 32% of the country's power now comes from oil, a big decrease from the peak of 77% in 1970… The Swedish Energy Agency funds 400–500 research projects each year, disbursing about 1.5bn krona. Energy research projects are sprouting up all over the country. For example, in the polar town of Örnsköldsvik, nearly 10bn has been invested in a plan to produce vehicle fuel from sawdust within ten years…. About 5% of Sweden's energy comes from biomass today, and by 2020, that will increase to 20%.

(趙華:〈瑞典邁向"無油國家"底氣何在〉,《中國石化雜誌》2010 年六期 (ZHAO Hua, 'Sweden's confidence as it marches towards being an "oil-free country"', *Sinopec News* 6, 2010. Available online at http://monthly.sinopecnews.com.cn/shzz/ content/2010-07/23/content_840441.htm, accessed 6 December 2013)).

116  鄧英淘:《新能源革命與發展方式躍遷》11頁。 (DENG Yingtao, *The New Energy Revolution and Shift in Development Model*, p. 11).

117  See  鄧英淘:《新能源革命與發展方式躍遷》12.〈中國能源經濟的未來〉。(DENG Yingtao, '12. The future for China's resource economy', in *The New Energy Revolution and Shift in Development Model*).

118  鄧英淘:《新能源革命與發展方式躍遷》215~216頁。 (DENG Yingtao, *The New Energy Revolution and Shift in Development Model*, pp. 215–16).

# References

AN Weihua and QIAN Xuemei, eds, *A New Theory of Gulf Oil*, Shehui Kexue Chubanshe Publishers, 2000. 安維華、錢雪梅主編：《海灣石油新論》，社會科學文獻出版社 2000.

Apostol, G. P., ed., *Contemporary Capitalism*, Sanlianshudian Publishers, 1979. 罗〕格.普.阿波斯托尔主编：《当代资本主义》，三联书店 1979 年。

Asimov, I., *Asimov's Guide to Science*, Basic Books Inc., New York, 1972. I.阿西摩夫：《宇宙、地球和大氣》，科學出版社 1979 年。(*The Universe, the Earth and the Atmosphere*, Kexue Chubanshe Publishers, 1979).

Barzel, Y., *A Theory of the State: Economic Rights, Legal Rights, and the Scope of the State*, Chinese edition published by Shanghai Caijing Daxue Chubanshe Publishers, 2006.

Binmore, K., *Natural Justice*, Chinese edition published by Shanghai Caijing Daxue Chubanshe Publishers, 2010.

Brown, Lester R., *Building a Sustainable Society*, W. W. Norton & Co, New York, 1982. 莱斯特·R.布朗：《建設一個持續發展的社會》科技文獻出版社 1984 年，第 207 頁.

Brown, Lester R., *The Twenty Ninth Day*, W. W. Norton & Co, New York, 1978. L. R. 布朗：《第 29 天》科技文獻出版社，1986 年，108 頁。(Kejiwenxian Chubanshe Publishers, 1986, page 108).

Brown, Lester R., ed., *State of the World 1985: A Worldwatch Institute Report on Progress Toward a Sustainable Society*, W. W. Norton, New York, 1985. 莱斯特·R.布朗等：《經濟社會科技 — 1985 年世界形勢述評》科技文獻出版社 1986 年，第 329頁 (Kejiwenxian Chubanshe Publishers, 1986, page 329).

Brown, Lester R., ed., *State of the World 1988: A Worldwatch Institute Report on Progress Toward a Sustainable Society*, W. W. Norton, New York, 1988. 莱斯特·R.布朗等：《經濟社會科技 — 1988 年世界形勢述評》，科技文獻出版社 1989 年，第 248 頁。(Kejiwenxian Chubanshe Publishers, 1989, page 248).

CASS Centre for Economic and Cultural Research, ed., *Lin Yishan on Flood Control for National Development*, Changjiang Chubanshe, 2007. 中國社會科學院經濟文化研究中心主編：《林一山縱論治水興國》，長江出版社 2007.

CASS Centre for Economic and Cultural Research, *Domestic Appliances Studies in the Development of China's Appliance Industry*, Zhongguo Shenji Chubanshe Publishers, 2000. 中國社科院經濟文化研究中心：《家電世界: 中國家電產業發展戰略研究》，中國審計出版社 2000.

CASS Centre for Economic and Cultural Research, *Integrating Three Networks: Studies in the Development of China's Power Industry*, Zhongguo Shenji Chubanshe Publishers, 2000. 中國社科院經濟文化研究中心：《三網合一: 中國電訊產業發展戰略研究》，中國審計出版社 2000.

## 258   References

CHEN Bing, '240 million illiterates – awaiting urgent attention' in *Economics Daily* newspaper, 12 April 1989. 陳冰:〈2.4億文盲: 亟待高度重視〉,《經濟日報》1989 年 4 月 12日.

CHEN Jiyuan, DENG Yingtao, XUE Yuwei and LIU Jianjin, *Rural Reforms and Development in China,* Guangdong Gaodeng Jiaoyu Chubanshe Publishers, 1992. 陳吉元、鄧英淘、薛玉煒、劉建進:《中國農村的變革與發展》, 廣東高等教育出版社 1992.

CH'IEN Mu, *Speaking Blindly of Things Learned Late in Life*, Guangxi Shifan Daxue Chubanshe Publishers, 2004. 錢穆:《晚學盲言》,廣西師範大學出版社 2004.

China Statistics Bureau, *Digest of China Statistics 1989*, Zhongguotongji Chubanshe Publishers, 1989. 中國統計局編:《中國統計摘要(1989)》,中國統計出版社 1989 年.

CHUN Mei, 'Sun city' in *New Perspectives*, 1985, issue 13, page 15. 春梅:〈太陽城〉,《新觀察》1985 年第 13 期, 第 15 頁.

CITIC Pacific Political/Economic Research, *Faster Changes in China's Growth Model*, Strong Wind Press, Hong Kong: 2009. 中信泰富政治暨經濟研究部:《加快轉變經濟發展方式》, (香港)大風出版社 2009.

Clark, C.W., *Mathematical Bioeconomics: The Optimal Management of Renewable Resources*, J. Wiley & Sons, New York, 1976. C. W.克拉克:《數學生物經濟學: 更新資源的最優管理》农业出版社, 1984 第 4 頁 (Nongye Chubanshe Publishers, 1984, page 4).

DENG Yingtao and H. E. Weiling, *Regulation and Evolution of Dynamic Economic Systems,* Sichuan Renmin Chubanshe Publishers, 1985. 鄧英淘、何維淩:《動態經濟系統的調節與演化》, 四川人民出版社 1985.

DENG Yingtao *et al.*, *Deng Yingtao Collected Works: Seeking Truth, Development*, Heilongjiang Jiaoyu Chubanshe Publishers, 1989. 鄧英淘集 — 求實 · 發展》, 黑龍江教育出版社 1989.

DENG Yingtao, *A New Development Model and China's Future*, CITIC Press, 1991. 鄧英淘:《新發展方式與中國的未來》, 中信出版社 1991.

DENG Yingtao, CUI Zhiyuan and MIAO Zhuang, *Nanjie Village*, Dangdai Zhongguo Chubanshe Publishers, 1996. 鄧英淘、崔之元、苗壯:《南街村》, 當代中國出版社 1996.

DENG Yingtao, ed., *Reader for Chinese Traditional Culture* (selections from Nan Huaichin), Nanhai Chubanshe Publishers, 2000. 鄧英淘改編 (南懷瑾原著):《中國傳統文化導讀》, 南海出版公司 1999.

DENG Yingtao, *Remaking China, Moving Forward*, Strong Wind Press, Hong Kong, 2010. 鄧英淘:《再造中國, 走向未來》, (香港) 大風出版社 2010.

DENG Yingtao, *The New Energy Revolution and Shift in Development Model*, Strong Wind Press, Hong Kong, 2011. 鄧英淘:《新能源革命與發展方式躍遷》, (香港)大風出版社 2011.

DENG Yingtao, WANG Xiaoqiang and CUI Heming and YANG Shuang, *Remaking China*, Wenhui Chubanshe Publishers, 1999. 鄧英淘、王小強、崔鶴鳴、楊雙:《再造中國》, 文匯出版社 1999.

DENG Yingtao, WANG Xiaoqiang and CUI Heming, eds, *Notes from Surveys of Development in the West: Three Essays on Remaking China,* Zhongyang Bianyiju Chubanshe Publishers, 2001. 鄧英淘、王小強、崔鶴鳴編著:《西部大開發調研實錄 — 再造中國三編》, 中央編譯局出版社 2001.

DENG Yingtao, WANG Xiaoqiang and CUI Heming, *Strategies for the Development of the West: Remaking China Continued,* Wenhui Chubanshe Publishers, 2001. 鄧英淘、王小強、崔鶴鳴:《西部大開發方略 — 再造中國續編》, 文匯出版社 2001.

DENG Yingtao, WANG Xiaoqiang and CUI Heming, eds, *Notes from Surveys of Development in the West II: Four Essays on Remaking China*, self-published, 2002. 鄧英淘、王小強、崔鶴鳴編著:《西部大開發調研實錄之二 — 再造中國四編》, 自印 2002.

DENG Yingtao, YAO Gang, XU Xiaobo, XUE Yuwei, *Analysis of China's Extra-budgetary Funds*, Zhongguo Renmin Daxue Chubanshe Publishers, 1990. 鄧英淘、姚鋼、徐笑波、薛玉煒:《中國預算外資金分析》, 中國人民大學出版社 1990.

Duvigneaud, P., *La Synthese Ecologique: Populations, Communautes, Ecosystemes, Biosphere, Noosphere*, Doin, Paris, 1974. P.迪維諾:《生態學概論》科學出版社, 1987 年, 227-228頁. (Kexue Chubanshe Publishers, 1987, pages 227–8).

Emsley J., 'Planting trees for the chemicals industry' in *World Science*, 1988, issue 10, page 15. 〈為化學工業植樹〉,《世界科學》1988 年第 10 期，第 15 頁.

Frantz, R., *X-efficiency: Theory, Evidence and Applications*, Chinese edition published by Shanghai Yiwen Chubanshe Publishers, 1993.

GAN Daochu, 'Ceramics – the new star' in *Science Daily*, 4 March 1990. 甘道初:〈陶瓷新秀〉,《科技日報》1990 年 3 月 4 日.

Goble, Frank G., *Third Force: The Psychology of Abraham Maslow*, Grossman Publishers, New York, 1970. 弗蘭克·戈布爾:《第三思潮》上海譯文出版社, 1987 (Shanghaiwenyi Chubanshe publishers, 1987).

GU Jian, 'Keeping fresh eggs without the need for cold storage or electricity', *Farmers Daily* newspaper, 22 February, 1990. 顧健:〈不用冷庫不耗電, 照樣可以貯鮮蛋〉,《農民日報》1990 年 2 月 22 日.

GUO Peizhang *et al.*, 'An important task in increasing production and practicing economy' in *Economic Reference*, 18 February 1987. 郭培章等人:〈增產節約中的一個重要課題〉,《經濟參考》1987 年 2 月 18 日.

Hall, Robert E. and John B. Taylor, *Macroeconomics: Theory Performance and Policy*, W. W. Norton & Co, New York, 1986. 羅伯特·E.霍爾等:《宏觀經濟學 — 理論、運行和政策》中國經濟出版社, 1988.

Hardy, R. N., *Temperature and Animal Life*, Edward Arnold, London, 1979. R. N.哈迪:《溫度與動物生活》, 科學出版社, 1984 年, 29 頁, Kexue Chubanshe Publishers, 1984, page 29.

HAU Jun, *What's the Problem with Oil*, Haige Wenhua Chubanshe Publishers, Taiwan, 2005. 浩君:《石油到底出了什麼問題》, 臺灣 海鴿文化出版圖書有限公司 2005.

Hawken, P., *The Next Economy*, Henry Holt and Co., New York, 1983. 保爾·霍肯:《未來的經濟》1985 年，科技文獻出版社, 第 92 頁。(Kejiwenxian Chubanshe publishers, 1985, page 92).

HUANG Yuyao, 'The ecological route to making resources from waste water' in *An Encyclopedia of Knowledge*, 1989, issue 8. 黃玉瑤:〈污水資源化的生態學途徑〉,《百科知識》1989 年第 8 期.

HUANG Zhiguang, 'Astonishing high temperature metal phase change energy storage technology' in *Science Daily* newspaper, 12 December 1989. 志光:〈令人矚目的高溫金屬相變貯能技術〉,《科技日報》1989 年 12 月 12 日.

ITO Masaya, *A History of the LDP's Civil Wars: Studies in Power*, Chinese edition published by Shijie Zhishi Chubanshe Publishers, 1984. （日）伊藤昌哉:《自民党戰國史 — 權力的研究》, 世界知識出版社 1984.

JIA Xiaohui and ZHANG Fengsha, 'Correct food structure and nutrition guarantees improved physique in the entire population' in *Science Daily* newspaper, 11 May 1989. 賈曉慧、張風莎:〈正確的食物結構與營養 — 提高全民身體素質的保證〉,《科技日報》1989 年 5 月 11 日.

260 *References*

JIANG Hong, *Oil Wars: A Historical Review of America's Oil Hegemony*, Dongfang Chubanshe Publishers, 2002. 江紅:《為石油而戰 — 美國石油霸權的歷史透視》, 東方出版社 2002.

KEN-ICHI Kimura, *Solar House*, Xinshidai Chubanshe publishers, 1986, page iii. 木村建一:《太陽房》譯序, 新時代出版社 1986 年, 第 iii 頁.

Klare, M., *Rising Powers, Shrinking Planet*, Chinese edition published by Hainan Chubanshe Publishers, 2009.

Lepage, Henri, *Demain le Capitalisme* ('Capitalism Tomorrow'), Le Livre de Poche, Paris, 1978 亨利·勒帕日:《美國新自由主義經濟學》第 239 頁.

Lepage, Henri, *American Neo–liberal Economics*. Possibly Henri Lepage, *Demain le liberalisme*, Librairie Generale Francaise, 1980 亨利·勒帕日:《美國新自由主義經濟學》, 北京大學出版社 1985 年, 第 217 頁 (Beijingdaxue Chubanshe Publishers, 1985, page 217).

Lepatte (or Lepeter?), Christine, 'The social price paid for economic growth' in *Economics in Translation*, 1987, issue 3. 克里斯汀·雷帕特:〈經濟增長的社會代價〉,《經濟學譯叢》1987 年第 3 期.

LI Zhou, LI Yiqing, ZHANG Yuhuan and YIN Xiaoqing, 'The Xi'an eco-animal breeding farm', in *Survey of the Best 100 Village Enterprises*, ed. CHEN Jiyuan, DENG Yingtao and TANG Hejian, Dangdai Zhongguo Chubanshe Publishers, 1998. 李周、李誼青、張玉環、尹曉青:《西安生態養殖場》; 陳吉元主編, 鄧英海、唐合儉副主編:《全國百家鄉鎮企業經濟典型調查》, 當代中國出版社 1998 年.

LIANG Houfu, 'Comparitive study of lifestyles in different countries' in *World Economy, Science and Technology*, 8 January 1985. 梁厚甫:〈各國「生活模式」的比較研究〉,《世界經濟科技》1985 年 1 月 8 日.

LIANG Yibin, 'Xie Xingjian and development of energy' in *Economics Daily* newspaper, 8 May 1989.

LIN Yishan, *River Dialectics and Flood Control for River Plains*, Changjiang Chubanshe Publishers, 2007. 林一山:《河流辯證法與沖積平原河流治理》, 長江出版社 2007.

LIN Yishan, *The South–North Water Transfer Project in Western China*, Zhongguo Shuili Shuidian Chubanshe Publishers, 2001. 林一山:《中國西部南水北調工程》, 中國水利水電出版社 2001.

LING Zhengjun, 'Solar-powered household appliances' in *China Youth Daily*, 8 December 1989. 凌征均:〈太陽能家用電器〉,《中國青年報》1989 年 12 月 8 日.

Link, A. and W. Catton, *American Epoch: A History of the United States since 1900*, Chinese edition published by Zhongguo Shehui Kexue Chubanshe, 1983.

LIU Xin, 'Ten years of the widening gap between rich and poor', *Renminribao* newspaper, 2 February 1990. 劉昕:〈南北貧富差距擴大的十年〉,《人民日報》1990 年 2 月 2 日.

LIU Yi, 'Technological progress is necessary to reduce energy levels' in *Science Daily*, 21 September 1989. 劉怡:〈節能降耗必須靠技術進步〉,《科技日報》1989 年 9 月 21日.

LU Xun, *Essays from a Room on the International Battlement*, Renmin Wenxue Chubanshe Publishers, 1973. 魯迅:《且介亭雜文》, 人民文學出版社 1973.

LU Yuegang, *Three Gorges: Fifty Years of Evidence*, Zhongguo Shehui Kexue Chubanshe, 1993. 盧躍剛:《長江三峽: 半個世紀的論證》, 中國社會科學出版社 1993.

MA Hong and SUN Shangqing *et al.*, *A Study of China's Economic Structure*, Remin Chubanshe Publishers, 1983, page 293. 馬洪、孫尚清等:《中國經濟結構問題研究》, 人民出版社 1983 年, 第 293 頁.

MAO Zedong, *Selected Works of Mao Zedong*, Renmin Chubanshe Publishers, 1991. 《毛澤東選集》, 人民出版社 1991.

Meadows, Donella H., Dennis L. Meadows, Jørgen Randers and William W. Behrens III, *The Limits of Growth*, the Club of Rome, 1972. (米多斯等:《增長的極限》, 商務印書館 1984 年 (Shangwuyinshuguan Publishers, 1984).

NAN Huai-chin, *A Book of Mencius*, Guoji Wenhua Chuban Gongsi Publishers, 1991. 南懷瑾:《孟子旁通》, 國際文化出版公司 1991.

NAN Huai-chin, *More What Laozi Said*, Laogu Wenhua Shiye Publishers, 2009. 南懷瑾:《老子他說續集》, 老古文化事業股份有限公司 2009.

NAN Huai-chin, *Selections from the Analects,* Fudan Daxue Chubanshe Publishers, 1990. 南懷瑾:《論語別裁》, 復旦大學出版社 1990.

National Bureau of Statistics of China, ed., *China Statistical Yearbook 1984*, Zhongguo Tongji Chubanshe Publishers, 1984. 國家統計局編:《中國統計年鑒1984》, 中國統計出版社 1984.

Nebel, B. J. and T. T. Wright, *Environmental Science: The Way the World Works*, Kexue Chubanshe Publishers, 1987, pages. 110–11. 內貝爾:《環境科學: 世界存在與發展的途徑》年, 頁, 科学出版社.

Nomura Research Institute (NRI) 'Shinjidai no sentan sangyō: asu o hiraku seichō sangyō o tenbōsuru', Nomura Sōgō Kenkyū Jōhō Kaihatsubu, Tokyo, 1987, page 149. 〔日〕野村綜合研究所:《新時代的尖端產業》, 科技文獻出版社 1987 年, 第 149 頁.

Olson, M., *The Logic of Collective Action*, Chinese edition published by Sanlianshudian Publishers, 1995.

Olson, M., *Power and Prosperity*, Chinese edition published by Shanghai Renmin Chubanshe Publishers, 2005.

Olson, M., *The Rise and Decline of Nations: Economic Growth, Stagflation, and Social Rigidities*, Chinese edition published by Sanlianshudian Publishers, 2007.

Ostrom, E., *Governing the Commons*, Chinese edition published by Sanlianshudian Publishers, 2000.

Ostrom, E., R. Gardner and J. Walker, *Rules, Games, and Common-pool Resources*, Chinese edition published by Shanxi Renmin Chubanshe Publishers, 2011.

Ostrom, E., L. Schroeder and S. Wynne, *Institutional Incentives and Sustainable Development: Infrastructure Policies in Perspective*, Chinese edition published by Sanlianshudian Publishers, 2000.

Ostrom, V., *The Intellectual Crisis in American Public Administration*, Chinese edition published by Sanlianshudian Publishers, 1999.

Ostrom, V., *The Political Theory of a Compound Republic*, Chinese edition published by Sanlianshudian Publishers, 1999.

Ostrom, V., R. Bish and E. Ostrom, *Local Government in the United States*, Chinese edition published by Beijing Daxue Chubanshe Publishers, 2004.

Patrick, H. and H. Rosovsky, eds, *Asia's New Giant: How the Japanese Economy Works*, Brookings Institute, Washington, DC, 1976. 休·帕特里克等人:《亞洲新鉅人 — 日本經濟是怎樣運行的》上海譯文出版社, 1982 (Shanghaiyiwen Chubanshe Publishers, 1982).

Patrick, H. and H. Rosovsky, eds, 'Pacific Rim countries and region – a great global economic power' in *World Economy, Science and Technology*, 5 April 1988. 〈太平洋沿岸國家和地區 — 全球的重大經濟力量〉,《世界經濟科技》1988 年 4 月 5 日.

Peter, L. and R. Hull, *The Peter Principle*, Chinese edition published by Jixie Gongye Chubanshe Publishers, 2007.

Randall, Alan, *Resource Economics: An Economic Approach to Natural Resource and Environmental Policy*, 1981. 阿蘭 蘭德爾:《資源經濟學: 從經濟角度對自然資源和環境政策的探討》, 1989 年, 商務印書館, 第 193 頁。(Shangwuyinshuguan Publishers, 1989, page 193).

## 262  References

Repetto, Robert, W. Magrath, M. Wells, C. Beer and F. Rossini, *Wasting Assets: Natural Resources in the National Income Accounts*, World Resources Institute, Washington, DC, 1989. 《科技日報》1989 年 5 月 24 日 [*Science and Technology Daily* newspaper, 24 May, 1989.).

Research Centre for Rural Development, *Choices on the Road to Modernization: Report on Issues for China's Long-term Development,* Jingji Kexue Chubanshe Publishers, 1987. 國務院農研中心發展研究所:《走向現代化的抉擇 — 關於中國長期發展問題的報告》, 經濟科學出版社 1987.

Rifkin, Jeremy and Ted Howard, *Entropy: A New World View*, The Viking Press, New York, 1980. 杰里米 里夫金等《熵: 一種新的世界觀》, 年, 第頁, 上海译文出版社 (Shanghaiyiwen Chubanshe Publishers, 1987, page 227).

Roberts, P. *The End of Oil*, Chinese edition published by CITIC Press, 2005.

Rural Development Institute, *Economy Green Paper: Annual Report on the Development of China's Rural Economy 1992*, Zhongguo Shehui Kexue Chubanshe, 1993. 農村經濟年度分析課題組:《經濟綠皮書: 1992 年中國農村經濟發展年度報告》, 中國社會科學出版社 1993.

Rural Development Institute, *Economy Green Paper: Annual Report on the Development of China's Rural Economy 1993*, Zhongguo Shehui Kexue Chubanshe, 1994. 農村經濟年度分析課題組: 《經濟綠皮書: 1993 年中國農村經濟發展年度報告》, 中國社會科學出版社 1994.

Rural Development Institute, *Economy Green Paper: Annual Report on the Development of China's Rural Economy 1994*, Zhongguo Shehui Kexue Chubanshe, 1995. 農村經濟年度分析課題組:《經濟綠皮書: 1994 年中國農村經濟發展年度報告》, 中國社會科學出版社 1995.

SAKAIYA Taichi, *The Knowledge-value Revolution, or A History of the Future*, Kodansha International, Tokyo, 1985. 堺屋太一:《知識價值革命》, 東方出版社 1986 年, 第 205頁。

Sasson, Albert, 'Biotechnologies: challenges and promises', Unesco, Paris, 1984. 阿爾貝薩松:《生物技術—挑戰與希望》科技文獻出版社, 1986 年第 267 頁。(Kejiwenxian Chubanshe Publishers, 1986, page 267).

Shelley, T., *Oil: Politics, Poverty and the Planet*, Chinese edition published by Chenxing Chuban Youxian Gongsi Publishers, Taiwan, 2006.

SIMA Guang, *Comprehensive Mirror to Aid in Government*, 1084. 司马光: 资治通鉴: 1084. www.guoxue.com/shibu/zztj/zztjml.htm (accessed 29 January 2014).

Staats, John and Carl Eicher, 'A historical investigation into agricultural development' in *Translations of Economics Documents*, 1987, issue 11, page 42. 約翰·斯塔兹、卡爾·艾切爾:〈農業發展觀的歷史考察〉,《經濟學譯叢》年第 11 期, 第頁。

State Council Technology and Economics Research Centre, China, Year 2000, Research Report 1: 'China's natural resources in the year 2000', 1984.

SU Zhen, 'Rich country, strong people – outline of Japan's educational reform' in *An Encyclopedia of Knowledge*, 1984, issue 11. 蘇真:〈富國強民之道 — 日本教育改革簡述〉,《百科知識》1984 年第 11 期。

The Year 2000 Research Group, *China in the Year 2000*, published by Kexuejishuwenxian Chubanshe Publishers, 1984.

Thomas, H. and C. Logan, *Mondragon: An Economic Analysis*, Chinese edition published by Sanlianshudian Publishers, 1991.

TIAN Yi, extracts, '"American disease" needs an Eastern remedy', in *Contemporary Thought*, 1986, issue 6. 田一摘編:〈「美國病」需東方藥〉,《當代思潮》1986 年, 第 6 期。

Toynbee, A. J. 'Who will inherit the West's position of world dominance?' in *Translated Extracts from Philosophy, History and Economics*, Shanghai Renmin Chubanshe publishers, 1974, issue 4. 湯因比：〈誰將繼承西方在世界的主導地位〉，《外國哲學歷史經濟摘譯》，上海人民出版社 1975 年，第 4 期。

TSUCHIDA, Atsushi, 'Water, life forms, humanity and entropy' in *World Science*, 1986, issue 9. 槌田敦等：〈水、生物、人類與熵的理論〉，《世界科學》1986 年第 9 期。

TU Xiaoma and CUI Yongzhun, eds, *Zeng Guofan Selected Works*, Hangzhou Daxue Chubanshe Publishers, 2001. 塗小馬、崔泳准選注：《曾國藩文選》，蘇州大學出版社 2001.

Volkenstein, M. V., *An Introduction to Physics and Biology*, Academic Press, New York, 1985, pages 104–5. M. V.伏爾更斯坦：《現代物理學與生物學概論》，復旦大學出版社 1985 年，第 104, 105 頁。(Fudandaxue Chubanshe Publishers, 1985, pages 104–5 ).

Wade, Charles G., *Contemporary Chemistry: Science, Energy, and Environmental Change*, Macmillan, New York, 1976. G.韋德：《能源與環境變化》科學出版社：1983, 第 255頁。(Kexue Chubanshe Publishers, 1983, page 255).

WANG Feng, LIU Hongyi and LI Jianhua, *Oil Resource Wars*, Zhongguo Wuzi Chubanshe Publishers, 2003. 王豐、劉洪義、李建華：《石油資源戰》，中國物資出版社 2003.

WANG Xiaoqiang, *Behind the 'Clash of Civilization: An Interpretation of the Resurgence of Islamic Fundamentalism,* Strong Wind Press, Hong Kong, 2004. 王小強：《"文明衝突"的背後 — 解讀伊斯蘭原教旨主義復興》，(香港) 大風出版社 2004.

WANG Xiaoqiang, *Challenges Unprecedented in History: Reading Recent American Writing on Strategy*, Strong Wind Press, Hong Kong, 2006. 王小強：《史無前例的挑戰 — 讀美國近來戰略研究》，(香港) 大風出版社 2006.

WANG Xiaoqiang, *China's Price and Enterprise Reform*, Macmillan Press, London, 1998.

WANG Xiaoqiang, *Gambler's Economy*, Strong Wind Press, Hong Kong, 2007. 王小強：《投機賭博新經濟》，(香港) 大風出版社 2007.

WANG Xiaoqiang, *Only Socialism Can Save China*, 2010–2011. 有社会主义才能救中国，No. 2011-7, 9, No. 2010-37, No. 2011-44.  www.hkstrongwind/default.aspx (accessed 29 January 2014).

WANG Yucheng, 'Social ecology and social development' in *Social Sciences Outside China*, 1988 issue 1, page 18. 王興成：〈社會生態學與社會發展問題〉，《國外社會科學》1888 年第 1 期，第 18 頁。

XIA Weisheng, *An Exploration of Human Ecology*, Gansu Renmin Chubanshe Publishers, 1984. 夏伟生：《人类生态学初探》甘肅人民出版社.

XU Xiaobo, DENG Yingtao, XUE Yuwei, LIU Jianjin and HU Bin, *Changes and Development in Rural Finance in China*, Dangdai Zhongguo Chubanshe Publishers, 1994. 徐笑波、鄧英淘、薛玉煒、劉建進、胡斌：《中國農村金融的變革與發展》，當代中國出版社 1994.

YAN Lixian, 'On dependency theory', in *Foreign Social Sciences*, 1988 issue 4 page13, 1998. 嚴立賢：〈依附理論述評〉，《國外社會科學》，年第期 第頁.

YANG Donghua, *Analysis of Exergy and Energy Levels*, Kexue Chubanshe Publishers, 1986, number 4, page 5. 楊東華：《火用分析和能級分析》，科學出版社 1986年，第 4 5 頁.

YANG Jihe, *et al.*, *The Mathematics of Biology*, Kexue Chubanshe Publishers, 1982, translated from Batschelet, Edward, *Introduction to Mathematics for Life Scientists*, 1979: 96. 楊紀坷等：《生物數學概論》，科學出版社 1982 年 9 月，第 70 頁.

YANG Shihua, ed., *Selected Hydrological Writings of Lin Yishan*, Xinhua Chubanshe Publishers, 1992. 楊世華主編：《林一山治水文選》，新華出版社 1992.

YANG Shihua, ed., *Decision-making for the Gezhouba Dam: Selected Hydrological Writings of Lin Yishan Volume II*, Hubei Kexue Jishu Chubanshe Publishers, 1995. 楊世華主編：《葛洲壩工程的決策 — 林一山治水文集之二》，湖北科學技術出版社1995.

Yangtze Hydrological Committee, ed., *Lin Yishan and the People of the Yangtze*, Wuhan Chubanshe Publishers, 2001. 長江水利委員會宣傳新聞中心編：《林一山與長江人》，武漢出版社2001.

264    *References*

Yangtze River Committee, ed., *Contemporary Yellow River Management Forum*, Kexue Chubanshe Publishers, 1990. 黃河水利委員會《當代治黃論壇》編輯組編:《當代治黃論壇》, 科學出版社  1990.

YAO Gang, DENG Yingtao, XUE Yuwei and XU Xiaobo, *Development, Reform, Reflections: Studies on the Directions and Progress of China's Reforms*, Zhongguo Renmin Daxue Chubanshe Publishers, 1992. 姚鋼、鄧英淘、薛玉煒、徐笑波:《發展·變革·反思 — 中國體制改革的進程和趨向研究》, 中國人民大學出版社  1992.

YU Yonglong, 'Food structure is a national policy issue', in *People's Daily* newspaper, 2 March 1988. 余永龍:〈食物結構問題是個國策問題〉,《人民日報》1988 年  3 月  2 日.

YU Quanyu and LI Xiaogang, 'An analysis of $300 per capita GNP', *Renminribao* newspaper, 22 January 1990. 喻權域、李曉崗:〈析人均國民生產總值三百美元〉,《人民日報》年月日.

ZHENG Zhuyuan, *Economic Development on Both Sides of the Taiwan Straits*, Taibeishilianchuban Shiyegongsi Publishers, 1983. p.181.  鄭竹園:《臺灣海峽兩岸的經濟發展》, 臺北市聯經出版事業公司年, 第頁.

ZHOU Meiying, trans, 'Hydrogen – fuel of the future' in *World Science*, 1988, issue 11. 周美瑛譯:〈氫氣 — 未來的燃料〉,《世界科學》1988 年第  11 期.

# Index

AAEC (average abundance of the Earth's crust) 32–3

abundance theories of resource exploitation 31–2, 33, 35–6

accumulated external diseconomy 63, 64, *64*

accumulated externality *65*

agricultural production **21**, 23, 161, 208; and farm products 40–1, 70, 195–6

air-conditioning, use of 149, 210

algae cultivation 163

arable resources 57–9 *see also* deserts of northwest China; forests; grassland management

*Art of War, The* 138, 218

ASHA index, the 5–6

Asian Tiger exporting countries 12–13, 168, 174

atmosphere of Earth, the 97

Atsushi Tsuchida 97

attenuated property rights 50

basic needs model of development 11, 13

basic resources industry recession in 1980s 130

beef consumption 70, 126, 147

Beijing and pollution xiv

bicycles as transport 144, **145**, 159, 166, xix, xxviii; under new development model 166, 173, 182

'big bang' theory 91

biological cycle, the 97–8

BMR (basal metabolic rate) 111–12

Boltzmann, Ludwig 81, 87

bureaucracies and market resource allocation 216–18, 221–2

calorific intake 28

canned air 228, 252n79

capitalism and x-effiency 224–5

carbon dioxide emissions 67, xxv, **xxvi**, xxvi–xxvii, **xxx**

car market, the 69, 73, 74, 166, xxi, xxiv; in the United States 29, **145**, 146, 183, 185

Carnot's 1824 theorem 81

Carson, Rachel xvii, xxviii

cell biopolymers 92

child illiteracy 167–8

Chinese civilization 105, 107, 108, 205, 209, 218

Chinese development: after meeting of basic needs 185–7; knowledge resources and education 151–2; and the protection rule 135–40, *136*, *139*

Chinese modernization and reform xv–xix

circulating fluidized bed boiler technology 164

city, the, as open system *84*

classical model of development 1–2, 16, 100–1; basis of 70, 104, 105, 106; dependence on categories of natural resources 39, 96; differences with new development model 177–9, xv; and the path for China 4–5, 172, 177, xv–xviii; and use of stocks resources 27–31, 36–7, 66–9, 74, 135–6, *136*, 211 *see also* new development models

Class III resources *see* non-recyclable, non-renewable resources

Class II resources *see* recyclable non-renewable resources

Clausius, Rudolf 81

climate change and global warming 63–4, 65–6, 67

closed systems 82, *83*, 88

clothing expenditure 157–8

coal and energy consumption 207, 242, xxv, xxvi

## 266  Index

collective-ownership disasters 53–4
common ownership of resources 54
communism and resource allocation 224–7
compensation for losses and GNP accounting 102
conditional entropy 92–3
congestion and user competition for resources 43–4, *44*
conservation of energy, law of 81, 111
consumer choice and rationality 113–14, 122, 130–1
consumer needs and desires 141; develop demand for eco-friendly products 182
consumption and human well-being xvii
copper mining 32, 33, 98
'correlation' 51
CPC (Communist Party of China), the 222, 237, 238–9, 240, 242
cultural activities and human development 133–4

Daly, Herman 101
deficit spending and national debt 18, 100–1, 103
Deng Yingtao: on agricultural production 209–10; on bureaucracies 216–18; on Chinese modernization 191–3, 207–8, 227–8, 230–6, 241–3, xiv–xviii; on communism and resource allocation 222–3, 224–7; on development of northwest China 206–7; on energy resources and industrial infrastructure 208–9, 211–13; on need for real-world examples to follow 195–6; on political reform 236–41; on reciprocity and resource allocation 213–16, 218–22, 228–30, 232, 234; on sustainability and hydro power 196–205, 210; on the US 229–30, 231–2
depreciation of natural resources 72
deserts of northwest China 206–7, 211
developing countries 13–16, 103, 228, xxviii; aid to 2, 3, 6; cultural differences with developed world 106; gap with developed world 2–4, 5, 7, 69, 109, 160; path of development 1–2, 4, 27, 174, xxvii; technologies suited to 152
differential pricing 188
dissipative structure theory and open systems 83–5, 89, 90
drug-trafficking and abuse 123

Earth, the 95–6, 97–8; resources of 32–5, 40
eco-industrial revolution xviii
ecological threshold, the 62
ecology of Earth, the 97–8
economic constraints and consumer choice 122, 125–6
economic growth 6–7, 15, 71, 78; and Engel's Law 110; future scenarios of 18, xxvi; historical Chinese rates 11, 167, 169, 173; measurement of 101, 102–3 *see also* GNP
economics-environment accounting system 102
ecosystems and dry matter productivity 92
ecosystems and self-regulation 62, 135
education as social investment 151–2, 167–8, 170, xvii
efficiency and energy use 73
egg preservation 164
electricity generation 164, 208–9, xxiv–xxv; and energy use 146, 210
energy, conversion of 81–2
energy consumption 31, 164, 181, 183, 192–3, xxiv; for China's development xvi, xviii, xx–xxi; of coal 207, 242, xxv, xxvi; future projections 23–5, **25**, xxvi, **xxvi**
energy efficiency standard of urban buildings 182, xxiii
energy intensity of transportation modes in the USA 144, **145**
energy-matching rule, the 146
energy resources and production 23, 32–4, 207
energy-saving measures 144–6, **145**, **147**, 147–8, 182–3
Engel's Law 110, *111*, 112–14, *113*, 116–17, *117*; evidence for 129–30, 131–2, *132*; and generalized income 126–8, *128*, 132–3; and income elasticity 115–16
'entropy,' concept of xxxn1, xv
entropy, law of 80–1, 91–6, 99; *Entropy: A World View* (book) 73, 74, 77–80; and evolution 85–90, *86*, *87*, **90**; reduced by circulation of water and air 97–8 *see also* thermodynamics
environment, the 149–50; and development 177, 179, 206–7, xvi–xvii, xviii
equilibrium structure and exchange of matter and energy 84–5
equipartition theorem of GDP 211

## Index 267

equivalence principle and material consumption, the 131–2, *132*, 146–8, **147**, 152

evolution and entropy 85–90, *86*, *87*, **90**

exclusivity and rights to resources and goods 45–7, 58, 61

exports 14, xx, xxi

externality and group interests 48–52, 219; accumulated external diseconomy 63, 64, *64*, *65*

extraction costs of resources 32–4, 41, 60–2, 211, 229

family planning and population growth xxii

farm products, production of 40–1, 70, 195–6

FDI (foreign direct investment) xxi

FDR (Federal Republic of Germany), the 102–3, 165

feed grain for beef production 70, 147

fertilizer output 19–23, **21**

flea and the elephant metaphor, the 12–13, 196

flow rate of consumption, the 146

flow resources and flow technology 104, 106, 140, 178, 184; new sources of 108, 137–8, 152, 153, 165, 171 *see also* solar energy

FMS (flexible manufacturing systems) 166

folk theorem, the 234

food consumption 28–9, 30, 122–3, 155–6, 173; of beef 70, 126, 147 *see also* farm products, production of

food production 27–8, xvii–xviii *see also* nutritional needs of humans

forests: benefits of 56–7, 65, 162–3, 195, 209, 219; exploitation of 64–5, 73, 171, xviii

formation of resources 95

fossil fuel 30, 31, 36, 40 *see also* non-renewable resources; oil and gas consumption

free markets and efficient use of resources 56

fuel efficiency standards 119

fusion energy 95, 99, 137

gap between developing and developed countries 2–4, 5, 7

GDP 15, 160, 211, xxii, xxiii, xxvi *see also* GNP

generalized income and Engel's Law 126–8

global business system, the xxi

global consumption 80, 96

global military spending 124

global rationality constraint on humans 123–4

GNP 11, 18, 19, 71, 80, 96, 100–3; Chinese growth rate in 167, 169, 173; per capita measures and living standards 23–5, **25**, 184, 186–7

Golden Rule and reciprocal systems, the 214, 216, 249n55

Gordon's Rule for open-access resources 55, 56, 58, 59, 67, 235

Grant, Kenneth 58

grassland management 209–10, 211–12

gravitational force **90**, 90–1

grazing rights on public land 53–4

GT (group technology) 166

Han Dynasty, the 205, 209

Hawken, Paul 173

healthcare 159–60, 173; in the United States 30–1, 160

heat and power technologies 164

heat death of the universe 90, 91

Hong Kong and Singapore housing 228–9

horizontal efficiency extraction of resources 61

Hotelling's Rule 54–5, 56, 57, 58, 60, 67

housing 158, 228–9, xxii–xxiii

human beings 100; and lack of rationality 113–14, 118, 122, 130–1; material needs of 120–6, 129, 132–3; needs for existence 39, 155–9

human development 103–4; and the ecosystem 62–6, *63*, *64*, 67

human resources and knowledge resources 150, 167

hydro technologies in China 197–8

illusions about 'classic' development 100

income elasticity 114–15

indicators for material and energy consumption 181–2

individualism in the West 105–6, 107, 109

Indonesian consumption of resources 71, 72

industrialization 104

Industrial Revolution, the 105, 216

information technology and Chinese development xviii

Inkeles, Alex 169

268 *Index*

insurance rule and the future use of resources, the *139*, 139–40
intellectual property rights 220
internal combustion engine, the 185
internalization and property rights 50
internal structure and the 'three-body' problem 1–2
international economy in the 1980s, the 130
international environment and Chinese modernization xx–xxi
International Institute for Applied Systems Analysis 67
'invisible hand,' of the free market, the 53, 69
irreversibility *see* reversibility and irreversibility
isolated systems 82, *82*, 86, 88, 89, 94, 95–6
Italian tertiary industry 166–7

Jacobs, Jane xix
Japan and educational reform 151, 152
Japanese model of development, the 24, 192, 215–16

knowledge resources and human resources 150, 151–2

LDP (Liberal Democratic Party) of Japan, the 239–40, 255n110
leisure time, increase in 149
Lepatte, Christine 100–1, 102
life and the sun's energy 78
life expectancy 5, *128*, 160, 169, 181, xxii, **xxix**; and modern medicine 30, 31
'limits to growth' theorists 33, 34–5
limits to the supply of natural resources 31–4, 72, 79, 96, 135–6, *136*; through the market mechanism 68, 69
literacy levels 151, 167–8, 170
living standards 184–5, xxii–xxiii, xxiv, xxviii
local government in the US 223–4, 250n69
localization of energy industry and production 209
long-term development model 11–12
low-entropy society, the 79
low-grade ore and 'limitless' deposits 33

machinery industry in China 166
macroscopic entropy 92, 93

Mao Zedong 198, 199, 222, 232, 233, 236, 240
market allocation mechanisms 69, 222
market interest rates and resource exploitation 59–62
market mechanism limitations to resource exploitation 68, 69
material constraints on humans 121–2
material consumption 132–3
matter, motion of 85
meat production and the environment 28–9, 147, 156–7, xvii *see also* food consumption
membrane separation technology 171
methane 208–9, 212
methylcellulose as raw material 171
militaries as bureaucracies 218
mineral resources 32–7, **37**, 59–61; US consumption of 31–2, 36–7
minimum rule, the 140–1, 152, 180
MITI (Ministry of International Trade and Industry) of Japan 165
modernization, scenarios for 24–5, 155, 161–9; indicators for a modernized society 169–74, 181; means of achieving 181–2 *see also* new development models
modern medicine and life expectancy 30, 31
modern stocks technology 137, 138, 140
MSY (maximum sustainable yield) 54, 55, 59, 135, 137, 179
multinationals in developing countries 14

national accounting and GNP 101–2
national income calculation system, the 73
natural constraints on humans' needs 120–1
natural resources: exploitation of 32–7, **37**; types of 40
nature and man xvii
new development models xv, xix, xx, xxviii; for China 107–9, 133, 152–4, 172–4, 179–81, 183, 187; choosing of 4–8, 177, 180; differences with classical model 177–9, 243n7; scenarios for Chinese modernization 24–5, 155, 161–9 *see also* classical model of development
*Next Economy, The* 126
non-attenuated property rights 48, 54–5, 189–90
non-discriminatory pricing 188
non-exclusive resources 46, 118

Index  269

non-material needs of humans 123
non-recyclable, non-renewable resources
141, 143–4, 146, 152
non-renewable resources 40, 59–62, 211,
212, xxv; future use of 74, 96, 180;
limits to and the classic development
model 66, 70, 104, 178 *see also* oil and
gas consumption; 'stocks' resources
'non-scarce' resources 44, 45
non-separable, non-exclusive resources
48, 56, 57, 66
non-separable exclusive resources 48
non-separable resources 41–2, *42*, 43, 45,
119
northwest China, development of 206–7
nuclear power 212
nutritional improvements 70, xxii
nutritional needs of humans 124, 155–6,
161, xv; American food consumption
27–8

Obama, Barack 244n11
Occam's razor 186
oil and gas consumption 185, 193, 207,
xx–xxi; exhaustion of 220, 222, 228,
229, 250n63
open-access resources 55–6, 67–8
Opening-up (Open Door) Policy 19
open systems 82–3, *84*, 88–9
optical fibres and the communications
industry 166
optimum efficiency of resource
extraction 61
order and disorder and structure 85
Ostrom, Elinor 223, 225, 226, 232, 242,
251n71
Ostrom, Vincent 224, 251n71
over-exploitation of non-renewable
resources 66–7, 68
over-use of renewable resources 41
ownership of resources 189

Pareto efficiency 43, 47–8, 50, 51–2, 55,
188–9, 222
pathological illness and hospital care 159
per capita national incomes 6–7, 18, 19,
23, 80, 131, 169; comparison between
China and the US 186; comparisons
between 1960 and 1970 19–24,
**20–2, 25**
per capita spending 160
Peter Principle, the 217, 218, 250n60
petroleum-based civilization 98–9
photosynthesis 98

physical constraints to development 18
pig farming 194–5
planned economies of socialist
countries 7
plant product diet of China 156–7
plasma cosmology theory 91
pollution 65, 98, 100, 131, 135, 137; from
cars 29, 30, 182; as entropy 78, 99; as
externality 48, 49, 50, 51 *see also*
wastage from resource exploitation
polymer materials 171
polymetallic nodule resources 165
population growth 80, 96, xxii, xxvii
Prigogine, Ilya 84, 89
primary industry and Chinese
modernization 161–3, 169
priority rule and educational investment,
the 150–2
private-ownership disaster 54–5
private ownership of resources 57, 58,
61, 189
product design and technological
innovation 141, 143
production and consumption costs and
GNP 102
production processes and waste 182
production rates and energy use 73–4
progress, definition of 70–1, 73, 74, xv
property rights over resources 45–7, 48,
50–1, 179, 189–90
protection rule and the optimal use of
resources, the 135–40
public ownership and responsibility 225
purchasing power in developing
countries 15

Randall Proposition, the 219
rational economic actor, the 220–1, 226
raw material consumption 23–4
reciprocity and resource allocation
213–16, 218–19, 220, 228–30,
234, 242; and bureaucracies 216–18,
221–2; and communism 222–3,
232, 236
recyclable non-renewable resources 42–3,
140–3
recycling 35–6, **142**, 142–3, 171, 173, 184,
xix–xx
refrigerator production **22**, 23
regulations to protect resource
development 56, 57, 180
renewable resources 40–2, *42*, *44*, 58,
107–8, 135; and development xvi,
xix–xx

270  *Index*

resource consumption 72, 79, 96, 107–8, 124–5, 181; in Indonesia 71, 72; restrictions on 153, 173–4, 178, 187
resource economics 54–5, 180
resource reserves and GNP accounting 101–2
resources and limits of capacity 44–5
resources in China 16–17, **17**
restrictions to the second law of thermodynamics 93–4
re-usable non-renewable resources 62
reversibility and irreversibility 85–7, *86*, *87*, 89
road deaths from cars 29

safety rule and optimal use of renewable resources, the 135–8, 152, 180
S-curve and Engel's Law, the 112, *113*, 115, 120, 126
SDA (specific dynamic action) 111–12
seabed mineral exploration 34
sealed systems *83*
secondary industry and Chinese modernization 163–6, 208
separability and the use of resources 41–2, 61
separable exclusive resources 47, 58
separable non-exclusive resources 47
service-maintenance economy, the 143
Shannon information measure formula, the 92
silicon-based ceramics as energy fuel 164, 178
size of China, the, as impediment to development 16
Smith, Adam 73
social discount rates and resource exploitation 61–2
social intervention, need for 118–19 *see also* global rationality constraint on humans
socialism in capitalist countries 226–8
social welfare, meaning of 149
socio-economic systems 89; and the second law of thermodynamics 91
solar energy 108–9, 207–8, 211–12
solar heaters 172, xxiv
solar-powered hydrogen technology 165
solar system, the, and entropy increase 94–5
South Korea 168, 174
South-South Cooperation 3
Soviet housing 158
steel output 19, **20**

stocks resources 40, 95, 107, 138–9, 184; use of in classical model 135–6, *136 see also* non-renewable resources
structural transformation since 1990s 171, xxi–xxii
structure of human activities, the *128*
substitution of natural resources 35, 95
sun, the 93, 94, 96
supersonic flight 70
supply and demand relationships 68, 174; need to regulate 181–2
sustainability at the micro-level 196–7
Sweden and energy consumption 242, 256n115
synthetic and artificial foods 27–8
synthetic products 13, 15; synthetic fibres 23, **25**, 35, 157

Taklamakan Desert, the 211–12
technology and energy 78, 80
temperature differences and equilibrium 90
tertiary industry and Chinese modernization 166–9, 170
tertiary sector in the US 129–30
thermal entropy 99
thermal pollution 99
thermodynamics 74, 82, 84–5, 89; and concept of entropy 81–2, 85, 87–9, 90; first law of 81, 82, 85, 111; second law of 40, 77, 85–7, 89–91, 93–7, 143
Thomson, William 81
'three-bodies' problem, the 1–2, *2*, 4, 243n7
Three Gorges hydro project, the 203–4
time and the individual's income 126–8, *128*
tobacco consumption 117
top-soil as an asset 58
Toynbee, Arnold J. 105
trade relations, need to adjust 15
transport and development 158–9, 166, 173, 185, xix, xxiv
truck-based freight xxiv
tunnel and aqueduct contruction 202–3

uncertainty about the future and risk *139*, 139–40
underground contamination 98
uranium 212, 248n53
urban and rural populations **b170**, xxii, xxviii, **xxix**
urban development 29–30, 171–2, 173, 185, 208, xix–xx, xxiv
Uruguay Round table negotiations 7

US, the: car market 29, **145**, 146, 183, 185; food consumption 28, 147, 156; health care in 30–1, 160; industrial development 79, 105; local government in 223–4, 250n69; mineral resource consumption 31–2, 36–7; resource consumption 31–2, 36–7, 69, 96, 173, 192; strategy for the twenty-first century 229–30, 252n83–4, 253n85; and transport energy efficiency 144, **145**
US economy and the financial crisis, the 231
US Energy Policy and Conservation Act, 1975 183
US Environmental Protection Agency 142
user competition for resources and congestion 43
US per capita spending 160
US-Sino relations 232, 244n10–11, 245n19

vertical non-separability 44

wastage from resource exploitation 70–1, 72–3, 141–2, 164–5, 182
waste disposal from mineral resource exploitation 34

waste heat 99
*Wasting Assets: Natural Resources in the National Income Accounts* 71
water cycle, the 97, 98
water hyacinths 194
water resources in China 17–18, 163, 165, 197–205, 246n35
water resources in Montana 65
West, the, and individualism 105–6, 107, 109
Western theory of modernization 3–4
wheat prices 58
wind generation technologies 200–2, 203
Wolf, Edward C. 118
World Bank, the 13–14
World Resources Institute, the 71–2
worldwide trade and developing countries in the 1980s 14–15
Wu Jinglian 222, 223, 224, 232

x-efficiency 215, 224, 234, 249n58

zero-cost reversible choice 139
Zhang Baomin xiv